Transforming
Power

Energy and Environmental Policy Series

Technology and Energy Choice, Volume 1
John Byrne and Daniel Rich

Energy and Cities, Volume 2
John Byrne and Daniel Rich

Politics of Energy R & D, Volume 3
John Byrne and Daniel Rich

Planning for Changing Energy Conditions, Volume 4
John Byrne and Daniel Rich

Energy, Land and Public Policy, Volume 5
J. Barry Cullingworth

Energy and Environment: The Policy Challenge, Volume 6
John Byrne and Daniel Rich

Governing the Atom: The Politics of Risk, Volume 7
John Byrne and Steven M. Hoffman

Environmental Justice: International Discourses in Political Economy, Volume 8
John Byrne, Leigh Glover, and Cecilia Martinez

Transforming Power: Energy, Environment, and Society in Conflict, Volume 9
John Byrne, Noah Toly, and Leigh Glover

Transforming Power

Energy, Environment, and Society in Conflict

John Byrne, Noah Toly, and Leigh Glover
editors

Energy and Environmental Policy: 9

Transaction Publishers
New Brunswick (U.S.A.) and London (U.K.)

Second Printing 2007
Copyright © 2006 by Transaction Publishers, New Brunswick, New Jersey.

This book is printed on acid-free paper that meets the American National Standard for Permanence of Paper for Printed Library Materials.

Library of Congress Catalog Number: 2006040408
ISBN: 978-1-4128-0514-8
Printed in the United States of America

Library of Congress Cataloging-in-Publication Data

Transforming power : energy, environment, and society in conflict / John Byrne,
    Leigh Glover, and Noah Toly, editors.
        p. cm. — (Energy and environmental policy series ; v. 9)
    Includes bibliographical references and index.
    ISBN 1-4128-0514-7 (alk. paper)
        1. Energy industries—Social aspects. 2. Energy industries—Environmental aspects. 3. Energy policy. I. Byrne, John, 1949- II. Glover, Leigh.
    III. Toly, Noah. IV. Series.
HD9502.A2T697 2006
333.79—dc22   2006040408

Contents

Energy and Environment

Introduction:
Modern Energy and Modern Society

John Byrne, Noah Toly, and Young-Doo Wang

Spiking prices, cartel decisions to limit production, regional conflicts to control ever scarcer reserves, periodic accidents, spills, and explosions, all are assured to bring attention to the operations of the global energy system. Rising in importance are headlines that associate modern energy with modern environmental problems ranging from climate change to public health advisories that urban air is, on occasion, unfit for human consumption. Shuttling from background to foreground (and back) are hopeful projections of technological solutions to energy problems. Policy discussions focus on efforts to improve technology and subject the sector to increasing doses of market curatives.

Rarely are modern energy's politics and political economy discussed in a sustained manner. When spiking oil prices and cartel-ordered production reductions send skyward the profits of the megacorporate rulers of the sector, politics and political economy questions surface. When ecosystems are harmed or threatened by energy operations, and when national security advisors become anxious about their capacity to control the system, politics and political economy questions gain importance. But when energy headlines fade, inquiry into the sector returns to a state of hibernation (except for 'breaking news' about innovations to revolutionize and lower the cost and, often these days, the environmental impact, of energy use).

The attention-neglect cycle of inquiry into the energy sector belies its social importance. The modern energy regime is to be credited with creating an integrating quantitative and transcendent logic which catalyzed the economic and technological forces underpinning industrial and, now, post-industrial societies. Long ago, Lewis Mumford captured this social role of the modern energy regime and its synergy with other elements of modernity (1961: 570):

> Quantitative production has become, for our mass-minded contemporaries, the only imperative goal: they value quantification without qualification. In physical energy, in industrial productivity, in invention, in knowledge, in population the same vacuous expansions and explosions prevail.

The coevolution of modern energy and modern economies has resulted in "'synergistic development'—a process of reinforcing growth between [energy] and...economy" (Byrne et al., 2004: 495)[1] and this synergism is now embedded in both.

The modern energy-economy synergy was propelled neither by energy scarcity nor by a sudden technological breakthrough. As to the former, low-entropy energy from the sun was (and is) available in virtually unlimited quantities and has been socially appropriated for millennia by various means. Indeed, until the industrial revolution, energy technics[2] were generally focused upon the conversion of biomass into carbohydrates to energize work by humans and animals. These deliver ample energy flows but at lower intensities than modern economic growth demands and were largely abandoned by the Global North early in the twentieth century. It is important to note, however, that movement from a carbohydrate to a hydrocarbon economy could not have been driven by considerations of energy intensity since the modern economy was barely evident when the hydrocarbon substitution was underway. As Mumford (1934) has documented, the transformation of energy systems and economies was coincident, not successive.

On the question of technological breakthroughs, the technology to mine and burn mineral energy had been available at least since the seventeenth century (see Mumford's 1934 discussion of the eotechnic phase of technology-environment-society relations), but was not deployed until the nineteenth and early twentieth centuries when the institutional framework—the "pentagon of power" (Mumford, 1970)—that could systematize a quantitative and ecologically transcendent political economy was established. Hydrocarbon fuels—oil, coal, and natural gas—that powered the industrial revolution are the result of captured energy in the form of fossilized plant matter from the carboniferous period of the paleozoic era. The rate of exploitation of these fuels is limited by the rate and incremental cost at which they can be extracted and combusted, a chiefly technological and economic, rather than ecological or social, function. In this way, fossil fuels held the promise of transcending the natural rate at which solar energy reaches the surface of the earth and is stored in various forms appropriate to both endosomatic and exosomatic uses.[3] As well, fossil fuels enabled a transcendence of social rhythms that had dictated the pace at which energy might be exploited, contributing to the replacement of a largely subsistence-based economy with the modern surplus economy.

The irony of modernity's successful quantification and ecological transcendence is now obvious. Combustion of fossil fuels has led to rapid exhaustion of mineral energy, with oil reserves, for example, expected to peak and decline early in this century (Deffeyes, 2001; Goodstein, 2004; Roberts, 2004). Modern societies have consumed 12 million years of decayed biomass in 300 years (Dukes, 2003) and now have no natural feasible replacement.

But an additional legacy of modern energy's attempted transcendence is increasing atmospheric concentrations of greenhouse gases, which cause global warming and are traceable to our overactive appetite for "buried sunshine" (Dukes, 2003). Both the industrial and post-industrial eras—despite the latter's purported dematerialization—have descended into this continual state of fossil fuel scarcity and global ecological risk in no small measure because of the carbonization of their energy systems.

In *Technics and Civilization*, Mumford describes (1934: 151 - 211) the rise of "carboniferous capitalism" in the "paleotechnic phase" of technology-environment-society relations. During this phase, "an alliance of science, capitalism, and carbon power" reorganizes social order for the purposes of fulfilling an underlying imperative of ceaseless growth (Byrne et al., 2002: 267). The accompanying concentration of political and economic power has a specific ecological manifestation: energy pollution as "a functional element of human progress" (Byrne et al., 2002: 267).

While ecological degradation is the focus of much criticism regarding the effects of carboniferous capitalism, Mumford also stressed the social relations engendered by the conventional energy system. Indeed, despite many important advances, human life and livelihoods have been risked under the modern energy regime. Since the emergence of carbon-mediated social relations, an ever present social crisis can be observed, but has been largely ignored (Mumford, 1934: 161): "What paleotect dared to ask himself whether labor-saving, money-grabbing, power-acquiring, space annihilating, thing producing devices were in fact producing an equivalent expansion and enrichment of life." Contemporarily, the intersecting social and environmental consequences of modernized energy can be described as follows (Byrne et al., 2002: 268):

> Environmental costs of production and wealth creation were considered, when considered at all, in the aggregate and not the particular. Accordingly, pollution became a "social cost," implying that the burdens were collective, as were the benefits. Nothing could be more misleading; the costs and benefits of pollution were sharply and equivocally divided within society and between societies from the onset of industrialization to the present day.

Energy systems have underpinned and constructed deeply unequal social relations, as well as imbalanced nature-society relations, since the dawn of the fossil fuel era.

The synergies of industrialization and conventional energy are now everywhere evident. Just as industrialization has been largely co-evolutionary with the conventional energy regime (see Norgaard, 1994), their coevolved social project is predictably similar: environmental conditions constructed by the combustion of fossil fuels mediate social relations in much the same way as described by Mumford, concentrating the capacity to valorize and distribute privilege among wealthy communities and their preferred ecologies, while concentrating environmental and social harm among the marginalized and vulnerable. The confluence of the forces of fossil energy, market power, and engineered social existence has produced a global order that is "beyond nature," operating on the shared, quantity-based logic of modern technology and economics (i.e., more, faster, and bigger are better).

This volume of the *Energy and Environmental Policy Series* examines conflicts evident in the current energy regime and latent in emerging proposals to correct them. After an initial chapter assessing the scope and depth of the contemporary discourse on energy-society relations, the volume addresses four theaters of conflict. Chapters 2 and 3 examine modern energy's role in alternately deepening and alleviating poverty. Chapters 4 and 5 take up the security implications of the sector's operations and vulnerabilities. In Chapters 6 and 7, neoliberalism's agenda of economic globalization is analyzed in the context of energy system development. Finally, chapters 8 and 9 investigate the environmental reform strategies of modern energy, questioning the nature and extent of 'green' energy promises.

Chapter 1 explores the social project of modern energy, characterizing the origins and implications of conventional and sustainable strategies. John Byrne and Noah Toly reveal the discursive continuities between conventional and sustainable proposals to further modernize the modern energy regime, finding both preoccupied with technical and economic criteria. Their chapter concludes that neither strategy furnishes a serious inquiry into the governance and political economy of energy.

Chapter 2, by Joan Martinez Alier, explores the modern relationship between energy, the environment, and poverty. A history of the discourse is offered that reveals the preponderance of economic and physical concerns about energy transitions. Martinez-Alier organizes a critique of this tendency, engaging the ecological and social relations mediated by energy regimes. He concludes with a discussion of agendas for integrating concerns for ecological integrity and social equity.

Margaret Skutsch and Joy Clancy examine the relationship between energy, gender, and poverty in chapter 3. The authors give special attention to the gender dimension of energy poverty, exploring the personal and social effects of sustained biomass use as well as the promises and perils of transitions to other fuels. Skutsch and Clancy explain the lack of attention to poverty and, more significantly, gender, in the debate regarding energy transitions.

Michael Klare analyzes the security dimensions of the conventional energy program, focusing on military conflict as a social implication of continued dependence upon oil. Building on his recent books addressing *Resource Wars* and the relationship between *Blood and Oil*, chapter 4 discusses the globalization of the U.S. Carter Doctrine and its implications for continued military deployments in the face of increasing oil demand and decreasing supplies.

Kenneth Bergeron and Andrew Zimmerman train a critical eye on the resurgent nuclear power lobby in the face of global terrorism, finding that, in spite of its past social failures and present risks of terrorist attack, the commitment to atomic fission as a solution to the problems of the fossil energy regime remains strong. Chapter 5 explains why neither a record of catastrophe nor vulnerability to terrorism are likely to derail embedded political support for nuclear power.

Navroz Dubash and James Williams explore the underexamined social dimensions of electricity liberalization in chapter 6. The authors analyze many of the aims of electricity reform as part of a broad policy critique of economic globalization. Their chapter identifies shortcomings in the reform strategy concerning matters of governance, equity, and environmental protection, and concludes with observations on the future of liberalization.

Chapter 7 inquires into the origins and implications of the World Bank's commitment to financing large hydroelectric projects. While some regard large-dam hydroelectricity as potentially sustainable, its poor social and environmental record argue against such a characterization, according to Peter Bosshard. Despite past failures, the World Bank continues to support projects, which Bosshard explains is a result of the politics of developmentalism as embraced by multilateral organizations and, often, their nation-state partners which serve global economic interests at the expense of livelihood needs.

In chapter 8, the most abundant conventional fuel—coal—is critically analyzed. Proposals to address its environmental deficiencies through geosequestration are considered as a means of saving the coal industry. Many have proposed geosequestration of carbon dioxide from coal combustion as part of a "clean coal" initiative that would abate this fuel's contribution to climate destablilizing greenhouse gas emissions. Mark Diesendorf, however, finds that the discourse has lacked serious consideration of coal's multiple environmental and social problems, and the risks attendant to geosequestration itself.

Leigh Glover closes the volume with an analysis of the increasing corporate support for renewable energy. Chapter 9 examines the transition of renewable energy enthusiasts from counter culture to mainstream and the corresponding movement of renewable technologies from the domain of small-distributed generation to large-scale applications suitable only to the centralized mode of energy distribution that has been the hallmark of modern energy. Glover finds that this evolution undermines renewable energy's potential to spark ecological improvement or, more generally, social transformation.

Notes

1. While Byrne et al. (2004) deploy the concept of synergistic development to analyze the modern electricity sector, it can be applied to the whole of industrial and postindustrial energy.
2. Mumford (2000: 15) coined this term, which, in a series of lectures at Columbia University, he defined as "that part of human activity wherein, by an energetic organization of the process at work, man controls and directs the forces of nature for his own purposes."
3. In Chapter 2 of this volume, Joan Martinez-Alier (2006) describes these two uses. Endosomatic use of energy is as food and exosomatic uses include "fuel for cooking and heating, and as power for the artefacts and machines produced by human culture."

References

Byrne, J., Glover, L., Lee, H., Wang, Y.-D., and Yu, J.-M. (2004). Electricity Reform at a Crossroads: Problems in South Korea's Power Liberalization Strategy. *Pacific Affairs, 77*(3), 493 - 516.

Byrne, J., Glover, L., and Martinez, C. (2002). The Production of Unequal Nature. In J. Byrne, L. Glover and C. Martinez (Eds.), *Environmental Justice: Discourses in International Political Economy* (Vol. 8, pp. 230 - 256). New Brunswick, NJ and London: Transaction Publishers.

Deffeyes, K. (2001). *Hubbert's Peak: The Impending World Oil Shortage.* Princeton, NJ: Princeton University Press.

Dukes, J. S. (2003). Burning Buried Sunshine: Human Consumption of Ancient Solar Energy. *Climatic Change*(61), 31 - 44.

Goodstein, D. (2004). *Out of Gas.* New York: W. W. Norton and Company.

Martinez-Alier, Joan. (2006). Energy, Economy, and Poverty: The Past and Present Debate. In J. Byrne, N. Toly and L. Glover (Eds.), *Transforming Power: Energy, Environment, and Society in Conflict.* New Brunswick, NJ and London: Transaction Publishers.

Mumford, L. (1934). *Technics and Civilization.* New York: Harcourt Brace & Company.

Mumford, L. (1961). *The City in History: Its Origins, Its Transformations, and Its Prospects.* New York: Harcourt Brace Jovanovich, Inc.

Mumford, L. (1970). *The Pentagon of Power: The Myth of the Machine, Volume Two.* New York: Harcourt Brace Jovanovich, Inc.

Mumford, L. (2000). *Art and Technics.* New York: Columbia University Press.

Norgaard, R. B. (1994). *Development Betrayed: The End of Progress and a Coevolutionary Revisioning of the Future.* New York: Routledge.

Roberts, P. (2004). *The End of Oil.* Boston, MA: Houghton Mifflin Company.

1

Energy as a Social Project:
Recovering a Discourse

John Byrne and Noah Toly[1]

From climate change to acid rain, contaminated landscapes, mercury pollution, and biodiversity loss,[2] the origins of many of our least tractable environmental problems can be traced to the operations of the modern energy
system. A scan of nightfall across the planet reveals a social dilemma that also
accompanies this system's operations: invented over a century ago, electric
light remains an experience only for the socially privileged. Two billion
human beings—almost one-third of the planet's population—experience
evening light by candle, oil lamp, or open fire, reminding us that energy
modernization has left intact—and sometimes exacerbated—social inequalities that its architects promised would be banished (Smil, 2003: 370 - 373).
And there is the disturbing link between modern energy and war.[3] Whether as
a mineral whose control is fought over by the powerful (for a recent history of
conflict over oil, see Klare, 2002b, 2004, 2006), or as the enablement of an
atomic war of extinction, modern energy makes modern life possible *and*
threatens its future.

With environmental crisis, social inequality, and military conflict among
the significant problems of contemporary energy-society relations, the importance of a social analysis of the modern energy system appears easy to
establish. One might, therefore, expect a lively and fulsome debate of the
sector's performance, including critical inquiries into the politics, sociology,
and political economy of modern energy. Yet, contemporary discourse on the
subject is disappointing: instead of a social analysis of energy regimes, the
field seems to be a captive of euphoric technological visions and associated
studies of "energy futures" that imagine the pleasing consequences of new
energy sources and devices.[4]

One stream of euphoria has sprung from advocates of conventional energy, perhaps best represented by the unflappable optimists of nuclear power

1

who, early on, promised to invent a "magical fire" (Weinberg, 1972) capable of meeting any level of energy demand inexhaustibly in a manner "too cheap to meter" (Lewis Strauss, cited in the *New York Times* 1954, 1955). In reply to those who fear catastrophic accidents from the "magical fire" or the proliferation of nuclear weapons, a new promise is made to realize "inherently safe reactors" (Weinberg, 1985) that risk neither serious accident nor intentionally harmful use of high-energy physics. Less grandiose, but no less optimistic, forecasts can be heard from fossil fuel enthusiasts who, likewise, project more energy, at lower cost, and with little ecological harm (see, e.g., Yergin and Stoppard, 2003).

Skeptics of conventional energy, eschewing involvement with dangerously scaled technologies and their ecological consequences, find solace in "sustainable energy alternatives" that constitute a second euphoric stream. Preferring to redirect attention to smaller, and supposedly more democratic, options, "green" energy advocates conceive devices and systems that prefigure a revival of human scale development, local self-determination, and a commitment to ecological balance. Among supporters are those who believe that greening the energy system embodies universal social ideals and, as a result, can overcome current conflicts between energy "haves" and "have-nots."[5] In a recent contribution to this perspective, Vaitheeswaran suggests (2003: 327, 291), "today's nascent energy revolution will truly deliver power to the people" as "micropower meets village power." Hermann Scheer echoes the idea of an alternative energy-led social transformation: the shift to a "solar global economy... can satisfy the material needs of all mankind and grant us the freedom to guarantee truly universal and equal human rights and to safeguard the world's cultural diversity" (Scheer, 2002: 34).[6]

The euphoria of contemporary energy studies is noteworthy for its historical consistency with a nearly unbroken social narrative of wonderment extending from the advent of steam power through the spread of electricity (Nye, 1999). The modern energy regime that now powers nuclear weaponry and risks disruption of the planet's climate is a product of promises pursued without sustained public examination of the political, social, economic, and ecological record of the regime's operations. However, the discursive landscape has occasionally included thoughtful exploration of the broader contours of energy-environment-society relations.

As early as 1934, Lewis Mumford (see also his two-volume *Myth of the Machine*, 1966; 1970) critiqued the industrial energy system for being a key source of social and ecological alienation (1934: 196):

> The changes that were manifested in every department of Technics rested for the most part on one central fact: the increase of energy. Size, speed, quantity, the multiplication of machines, were all reflections of the new means of utilizing fuel and the enlargement of the available stock of fuel itself. Power was dissociated from its natural human and geographic limitations: from the caprices of the weather, from the irregularities that definitely restrict the output of men and animals.

By 1961, Mumford despaired that modernity had retrogressed into a life-harming dead end (1961: 263, 248):

> ...an orgy of uncontrolled production and equally uncontrolled reproduction: machine fodder and cannon fodder: surplus values and surplus populations...
>
> The dirty crowded houses, the dank airless courts and alleys, the bleak pavements, the sulphurous atmosphere, the over-routinized and dehumanized factory, the drill schools, the second-hand experiences, the starvation of the senses, the remoteness from nature and animal activity—here are the enemies. The living organism demands a life-sustaining environment.

Modernity's formula for two centuries had been to increase energy in order to produce overwhelming economic growth. While diagnosing the inevitable failures of this logic, Mumford nevertheless warned that modernity's supporters would seek to derail present-tense[7] evaluations of the era's social and ecological performance with forecasts of a bountiful future in which, finally, the perennial social conflicts over resources would end. Contrary to traditional notions of democratic governance, Mumford observed that the modern ideal actually issues from a pseudomorph that he named the "democratic-authoritarian bargain" (1964: 6) in which the modern energy regime and capitalist political economy join in a promise to produce "every material advantage, every intellectual and emotional stimulus [one] may desire, in quantities hardly available hitherto even for a restricted minority" on the condition that society demands only what the regime is capable and willing to offer. An authoritarian energy order thereby constructs an aspirational democracy while facilitating the abstraction of production and consumption from non-economic social values.

The premises of the current energy paradigms are in need of critical study in the manner of Mumford's work if a world measurably different from the present order is to be organized. Interrogating modern energy assumptions, this chapter examines the social projects of both conventional and sustainable energy as a beginning effort in this direction. The critique explores the neglected issue of the political economy of energy, underscores the pattern of democratic failure in the evolution of modern energy, and considers the discursive continuities between the premises of conventional and sustainable energy futures.

The Abundant Energy Machine[8]

Proposals by its stakeholders to fix the modern energy system abound. Advocates envision bigger, more expensive, and more complex machines to spur and sate an endlessly increasing world energy demand. From clean coal to a revived nuclear energy strategy, such developments promise a worldwide movement to a cleaner and more socially benign energy regime that retains its modern ambitions of bigger, more, and better. Proponents even suggest that we might have our cake and eat it too, promoting patterns of energy production, distribution, and consumption consistent with an unconstrained ideology of quantification while also banishing environmental threats and taming social risks that energy critics cite in their challenges to the mainstream. Consistent with a program of ecological modernization, the conventional energy regime's architects are now exploring new technologies and strategies that offer what are regarded as permanent solutions to our energy troubles without harming our ecological future or disturbing the goal of endless economic growth and its attendant social relations.

Greening Fossil Fuels

Among the most prominent techno-fixes for modern energy are those seeking to "green" the fossil fuels (see, e.g., Jaccard, 2005). The substitution of natural gas for other hydrocarbons, the emergence of "clean coal," the "ecologically sustainable" mining of what are supposed to be vast, untapped oil reserves in heretofore unfriendly terrains,[9] and the geological sequestration of climate-destabilizing CO_2 emissions are among the most favored in this category. Each represents an effort to legitimate the conventional energy regime without displacing fossil fuel's powerful role in rationalizing centralized energy production and distribution.

Natural gas is said to provide efficiencies equal to, or exceeding, the other fossil fuels while generating far fewer environmentally harmful consequences; as a replacement for oil and coal, it would result in decreased acid rain, smog, and mercury pollution. Natural gas emits fewer pollutants—among them greenhouse gases such as carbon dioxide. In this regard, it is advocated as an effective means by which to mitigate global warming. Low emissions of sulfur dioxide and particulate matter are also benefits of natural gas. Furthermore, the extraction, processing, and consumption of the fuel is said to produce very little solid waste and to have minimal impacts on water quality, unlike coal and oil (Cassedy and Grossman, 1998: 111 – 114).

But while its environmental effects may merit consideration of natural gas as a transitional fuel, the social hazards of bringing this energy source to market are very real. Michael Klare has written of potential armed conflicts to control natural gas reserves and the attendant transportation infrastructure (Klare, 2002b). Bringing natural gas to market will inevitably involve expensive liquefaction of the gas—by cooling it to -259 degrees Fahrenheit (-162 degrees Celsius)—and transportation on potentially vulnerable supertanker ships. And concerns have risen regarding the safety of natural gas receiving terminals in an age of global terrorism (Testa, 2004). A recent study by researchers at Sandia National Laboratories examined the catastrophic potential of explosions, fires, and fireballs caused by ramming, triggered explosion, hijacking, or external terrorist actions such as attack by missile or plane (Hightower et al., 2004). Damage risked by potential explosion, either at a terminal or on a ship, is immense. There are currently five natural gas receiving terminals in the continental United States—one in the highly populated Boston metropolitan area. Forty more are proposed for North American coasts, with nineteen having already received regulatory approval despite the risks of terrorist attack (Federal Energy Regulatory Commission (U.S.), 2005).

Coal, on the other hand, is not nearly as combustible as natural gas. Unlike oil and natural gas, many of the world's largest national energy consumers have significant domestic supplies. It remains plentiful and cheaply extracted, making global conflict over the resource unlikely. For these reasons, coal is enjoying resurgent interest on a scale not seen since the oil embargo of the 1970s. But while the potential for terrorist exploitation and international conflict over coal are low, other social consequences of its extraction and consumption are significant. The polluting effects of coal mining and combustion perpetuate its reputation as a "dirty fuel" contributing to public health problems and significant social inequities.

Truly greening coal would require a great deal of effort from mine to smokestack and beyond. Clean coal proponents advocate use of types of coal lower in sulfur content, gasification of the mineral, and sequestration of its carbon dioxide emissions. While these steps, if successful, would address some of coal's most pernicious effects—air pollution and increased GHG emissions—they leave many other consequences unattended. The environmental and social effects of mining and washing coal are not addressed by most proposals. Neither are its other social consequences: continued vulnerable centralized production, diversion of water from other purposes, land degradation, and extensive hazards to labor (Diesendorf, 2006).

Proposals for oil differ from those for coal and natural gas. Here, attention is mainly focused on cleaning up its transport and processing and making end-use technology more efficient. Today, enormous vessels move petroleum supplies across oceans in stunning volumes: the amount of oil alone annually carried in cargo holds roughly equals the combined amount consumed annually by the United States, the European Union, and China (Department of the Interior (U.S.), 2002). Interestingly, more than one billion gallons per year fail to reach a market, but nevertheless come ashore (Department of the Interior (U.S.), 2002). The 1989 Exxon Valdez oil spill illustrates the phenomenon. On March 23, the Exxon Valdez oil tanker hit a reef in the Alaskan Prince William Sound and spilled nearly 10 million gallons of crude, causing well-documented ecological harm.[10] While the spill's social implications received less attention, they were no less significant. Gill and Picou note that the compromise, and even extinction, of local cultures can accompany oil transport accidents (1996: 167):

Of all the groups negatively impacted by the *Exxon Valdez* oil spill, in many ways Alaska Natives were the most devastated. The oil spill destroyed more than economic resources, it shook the core cultural foundation of Native life. Alaska Native subsistence culture is based on an intimate relationship with the environment. Not only does the environment have sacred qualities for Alaska Natives, but their survival depends on the well-being of the ecosystem and the maintenance of cultural norms of subsistence. The spill directly threatened the well-being of the environment, disrupted subsistence behavior, and severely disturbed the sociocultural milieu of Alaska Natives.

Of the spill's impact, Chief Walter Meganack (cited in Gill and Picou, 1996: 167) commented: "the excitement of the season had just begun, and then, we heard the news, oil in the water, lots of oil killing lots of water. It is too shocking to understand. Never in the millennium of our tradition have we thought it possible for the water to die, but it is true." What for some was an example of the environmental implications of the "normal accident" (Perrow, 1984) associated with the modern energy regime was, in fact, a threat to the very way of life of some Alaskan Natives.

Following such a high profile failure as the grounding of the Exxon Valdez (in fact, only the fifty-third largest oil spill in modern times—*Oil Spill Intelligence Report*, 2001), one might think that advocates of the conventional energy regime would practice a measure of modesty in their planning for the future. On the contrary, such failures seem only to stimulate even more grandiose ideas. No doubt future ships will come equipped with improved navigation technology to reduce accidents. Yet, one accident with a new vessel could trigger environmental catastrophe well beyond the Exxon Valdez episode. In this regard, it seems that a commitment to "green" fossil fuels can, nevertheless, result in an escalation of "brown" consequences and heightened risks, a phenomenon observed by Ulrich Beck (1992).

Ecological and cultural threats of the magnitude of the Exxon Valdez incident have much to do with the scale principles of the fossil fuel regime. Without unending energy demand, the system's risks in production and transportation are unnecessary. And without large ships, large ports, and large energy demand, the economics of fossil fuels falls apart. Such synergies drive the development of conventional techno-fixes.

Importantly, the higher and higher financial costs of propping up the fossil fuel regime never seem to doom such thinking.[11] Why is it that a commitment to fossil energy enlarges as the crises it causes deepen? In a recent book, Huber and Mills (2005: 165, emphasis added) suggest that "energy is the key to survival *and* prosperity" and that the only solution to today's energy problems is increased consumption aided by tomorrow's technical developments. They argue that (2005: xxiii, xxvi) "energy begets more energy; tomorrow's supply is determined by today's consumption. The more energy we seize and use, the more adept we become at finding and seizing still more....Energy isn't the problem. Energy is the solution." Huber and Mills also highlight the synergistic relationship between modern energy, modern technology, and the pursuit of "more" (2005: 155, emphasis added): "We will never stop wanting more logic, more memory, more vision, more range—all of which depend upon high grade energy—because we are built to want more of these things, *an unlimited more*."

Describing the ideal energy regime as a "perpetual motion machine" (2005: 4), Huber and Mills suggest that energy consumption spurs technical developments that permit the extraction and consumption of even greater quantities of energy in more usable forms despite, or even because of, increased waste. Emerging technologies, suggest Huber and Mills, are (2005: 43):

> ...as revolutionary as Watt's steam regulator was in 1763, as Otto's spark-ignited petroleum in 1876, as Edison's electrically-heated filament in 1879, as de Laval's hot-gas turbine in 1882. And they too will redefine, yet again, how much energy we want and how much we can get. We will want more—much more. And we will get it, easily. Unless, somehow, our optimism, drive, courage, and will give way to lethargy and fear.

Such sanguinity names its source—modernist confidence in science, technology, and business. The alliance of these three institutions, through a common language of quantity (Mumford, 1934; see also Kumar, 1978, 1988, 2005; Nye, 1999) built the world order in which our daily lives now transpire. Hesitation in the support of this alliance is tantamount to a civilization losing courage, surrendering to lethargy and fear. For conventional energy's enthusiasts, we have nothing to fear—neither climate change nor conflict over energy resources—but fear, itself. In this respect, our future cannot spring from anywhere other than a "bottomless well" (Huber and Mills, 2005) of energy and optimism.

Remaining modern, however, also demands an increasing commitment to override what lags behind from a modernist point of view. The bottomless wells to which Huber and Mills refer are increasingly found among the most vulnerable ecologies and communities, and their sacrifice to deliver more energy also involves the geological scale refinement of physical formations, biological scale modification of evolution, and historical scale alteration of social relations. A recent advertisement by Occidental Petroleum blends modernist ideology with the hubris of modern management as "Oxy brings energy to energy solutions" (Occidental Petroleum Corporation, 2005):

> Oxy is on the cutting edge in using advanced techniques to maximize the recovery of oil and natural gas worldwide. Energy is the lifeblood of the sustainable development process that is critical to overcoming poverty and raising living standards. And we're working hard to meet the world's ever growing demand for reliable energy supplies.

While the company imagines energy as the lifeblood of progress, the U'wa people in Colombia, on whose lands the oil envied by Occidental Petroleum resides, describe it as the lifeblood of "Mother Earth." Oil extraction would represent the slow death of both ecology and culture for the U'wa (J. T. Roberts and Thanos, 2003; Lee, forthcoming).

In addition to a disregard for cultural continuity in traditional and indigenous communities, extending the capacity to exploit fossil fuels through modernization of the conventional energy regime carries an additional requirement. As Michael Klare (2004, 2006) indicates, continued dependence upon oil, coupled with diminishing supplies and increasing demand, is likely to mean increased global conflict. The same can be said of natural gas (Klare, 2002b: 81 - 108). An industrialized world moored to the conventional energy regime will, in all likelihood, force further needs to militarize its operations.

Giant Power Revivalism

Life extension projects for the conventional energy regime are not limited to technological "greening" of fossil fuels. Plans also include a revival of "Giant Power" strategies, which had happened upon hard times by the 1980s. Gifford Pinchot, a two-term governor of Pennsylvania (1922-1926 and 1930-1934) is credited with coining the term in a speech, proclaiming:

> Steam brought about the centralization of industry, a decline in country life, the decay of many small communities, and the weakening of family ties. Giant Power may bring about the decentralization of industry, the restoration of country life, and the upbuilding of small communities and the family. [T]he coming electrical development will form the basis of a civilization happier, freer, and fuller of opportunity than the world has ever known.

The first proposals for Giant Power involved the mega-dams of the early and middle twentieth century. The U.S. pioneered this option with its construction of the Hoover, Grand Coulee, and Glen Canyon Dams, among others (Worster, 1992; Reisner, 1993). Undertaken by the U.S. Bureau of Reclamation, these projects were intended to "reclaim" the energy and water development potential from the rivers of the western United States. These were truly mammoth enterprises resulting in integrated water and energy resource development on scales previously unknown. Construction of the Glen Canyon Dam was authorized by the U.S. Congress under the Colorado River Storage Project. Built from 1957 to 1964, it was originally planned to generate 1,000 MW. Over the next few decades two additional generators were added to the dam, allowing the dam to produce 1,296 MW. In 1991 Interim Operating Criteria were adopted to protect downstream resources, which limited the dam releases to 20,000 cubic feet of water and the power output to 767 MW. The dam currently generates power for roughly 1.5 million users in five states (Bureau of Reclamation (U.S.), 2005a).

Mega-dams, such as the Glen Canyon, lost social support in the United States in the 1970s as ecological impacts and financial risks slowed interest. But many countries have shown a resurgent interest in large dams as an energy strategy. Canada has committed to building what will be one of the largest dams in the world—Syncrude Tailings—which will have the largest water impoundment volume in the world at 540 million cubic meters (Bureau of Reclamation (U.S.), 2005b). And China, with more than 20,000 dams of more than fifteen meters in height is constructing what will be the largest hydroelectric facility in the world on Earth's third largest river. The Three Gorges Dam, on the Yangtze, at a "mere" 575 feet tall—sixty-first tallest in the world—will have a generating capacity of more than 18,000 MW, roughly equivalent to 10 percent of China's electricity demand. This will require twenty-six hydro turbines, purchased from ABB, Alstom, GE, Kvaerner, Siemens, and Voith, highlighting the synergies between global corporatism and Giant Power (Power Technology, 2005).

Large-scale hydropower represents an attempt at a techno-fix of the democratic-authoritarian variety. Without disrupting the conventional energy regime's paradigm of centralized generation and distribution, large dams purport to deliver environmentally benign and socially beneficial electricity in amounts that reinforce the giant character of the existing dams. In fact, both ecologically and socially disruptive, large dams represent continued commitment to the promises, prospects, and perils of the conventional energy regime and its social project (McCully, 2001: 265; Hoffman, 2002; Totten, Pandya, and Janson-Smith, 2003; Agbemabiese and Byrne, 2005; Bosshard, 2006).

A second mega-energy idea has been advanced since the 1950s—the nuclear energy project. Born at a time in U.S. history when there were no pressing supply problems, nuclear power's advocates promised an inexhaustible source of Giant Power. Along with hydropower, nuclear energy has been conceived as a non-fossil technical fix for the conventional energy regime.

But nuclear energy has proven to be among the most potent examples of technological authoritarianism (Byrne and Hoffman, 1988, 1992, 1996) inherent in the techno-fixes of the conventional energy regime. On April 26, 1986, nuclear dreams were interrupted by a hard dose of reality—the accident at Chernobyl's No. 4 Reactor, with a radioactive release more than ten times that of the atomic bomb dropped on Hiroshima (Medvedev, 1992). Both human and non-human impacts of this greatest of technological disasters have been well-documented (Medvedev, 1992). The Chernobyl explosion and numerous near-accidents, other technical failures, and extraordinary cost-overruns caused interest in nuclear energy to wane during the 1980s and 1990s.

Notwithstanding a crippling past, the nuclear lobby has engineered a resurgence of interest through a raft of technological fixes that purport to prevent future calamitous failures while capitalizing on the supposed environmentally sound qualities of nuclear power. Huber and Mills, for example, title one of their chapters "Saving the Planet with Coal and Uranium" (2005: 156 - 171). A spokesperson for the Electric Power Research Institute has recently suggested that new pebble-bed modular reactors are "walk-away safe—if something goes wrong, the operators can go out for coffee while they figure out what to do" (quoted in Silberman, 2001). Such claims are eerily reminiscent of pre-Chernobyl comparisons between the safety of nuclear power plants and that of chocolate factories (*The Economist*, 1986). Huber and Mills go even further, claiming nuclear power will exceed the original source of solar power—the sun (2005: 180): "Our two-century march from coal to steam engine to electricity to laser will...culminate in a nuclear furnace that burns the same fuel, and shines as bright as the sun itself. And then we will invent something else that burns even brighter."

Critics, however, note that even if such technical advances can provide for accident-free generation of electricity, there are significant remaining social implications of nuclear power, including its potential for terrorist exploitation and the troubling history of connections between military and civilian uses of the technology (Bergeron, 2002; Bergeron and Zimmerman, 2006). As well, the life-cycle of nuclear energy development produces risks that continuously challenge its social viability. To realize a nuclear energy-based future, massive amounts of uranium must be extracted. This effort would ineluctably jeopardize vulnerable communities since a considerable amount of uranium is found on indigenous lands. For example, Australia has large seams of uranium, producing nearly one-quarter of the world's supply, with many mines located on Aboriginal lands (Uranium Information Center, 2005).[12] Even after the uranium is secured and electricity is generated, the project's adverse social impacts continue. Wastes with half-lives of lethal threat to any form of life in the range of 100,000 to 200,000 years have to be buried and completely mistake-free management regimes need to be operated for this length of time—longer than human existence, itself. Epochal imagination of this kind may be regarded by technologists as reasonable, but the sanity of such a proposal on social grounds is surely suspect (Byrne and Hoffman, 1996).

Immaterial techniques

Repair of the existing regime is not limited to efforts to secure increasing conventional supplies. Also popular are immaterial techniques emerging from the field of economics and elsewhere that offer policy reforms as the means to overcome current problems. Electricity liberalization exemplifies this approach. Here, inefficiencies in the generation and distribution of electricity in the conventional energy regime are targeted for remedy by the substitution of market dynamics for regulatory logic. Purported inefficiencies are identi-fied, in large part, as the result of regulations that have distorted market prices either by subsidizing unjustifiable investments or by guaranteeing rates of return for compliant energy companies. Proponents of liberalization promise greater and more reliable energy supplies with the removal of regulation-induced market distortions (Pollitt, 1995; World Bank, 1993, 2003, 2004a).

Environmental concerns with the prevailing energy order can also be used to support liberalized market strategies. For example, while Huber and Mills (2005: 157) suggest that increased use of hydrocarbons is actually the pre-ferred solution to the problem of climate change, arguing that, "for the fore-seeable future, the best (and only practical) policy for limiting the buildup of carbon dioxide in the air is to burn more hydrocarbons—not fewer,"[13] others suggest the superiority of immaterial techniques such as the commercializa-tion of the atmospheric commons. Thus, David Victor (2005) attributes the collapse of the Kyoto Protocol to a failure to embrace the economic superior-ity of emissions trading and other market-oriented mechanisms and calls for conventional energy's collision with climate to be addressed by a healthy dose of competitive marketing of carbon-reducing options. The outcome of a trading regime to reduce carbon will almost certainly be life-extensions for the fossil fuels and nuclear energy since it would 'offset' the carbon problems of the former and embrace the idea of the cost-effectiveness of the latter to avoid carbon emissions.[14]

Such solutions also attempt to mediate the increasing risk that accompa-nies techno-fixes of the conventional energy regime. The current phase of industrialization is replete with efforts to harmonize market and technologi-cal logics in a way that leaves the large-scale centralized energy system intact despite its tendencies to breed significant potential social and environmental crises (Byrne et al, 2002: 287; see also Beck, 1992).

> Progress [has] necessitated commitments to advancing knowledge and its applica-tion, along with the distinctive threats that only modernity could augur. Societies are obliged to place their faith in experts, technocratic systems, and management institu-tions, in the expectation that these offer social and environmental protection. At the same time, catastrophe-scale mistakes are inevitable....Those least equipped to 'model' their problems become the 'lab mice' as human intelligence works out management schemes....

Conventional techno-fixes to increase energy supplies cannot remove risks, nor can market economics, but together they seek to convince society that abandonment of the modern energy project is nonetheless unwarranted.

The search for harmonized market-style policies to strengthen the energy status quo in the face of its mounting challenges reflects the growing politi-cal power of energy neoliberalism in an era of economic globalization (Dubash, 2002; Dubash and Williams, 2006). The two processes build a complimentary, if circular, politics in support of conventional energy: the logic is that global economic development requires energy use, which can only be properly planned if international capitalist institutions can be assured that the lubricant of globalization, namely, the unfettered power of markets, is established by enforceable policy (Byrne et al., 2004). Correspondingly, resulting carbon emissions can only eventually be abated if economic globalization is protected so that international capitalist institutions find it profitable to begin to lower carbon emissions and/or sequester them.[15] Consumers and producers, rather than citizens, are judged to be the proper signatories to the social contract because these participants, without the stain of politics, can find rational answers to our problems.

In sum, conventionalists counsel against preconceiving the social and environmental requirements for an energy transition, preferring a continuation of the existing energy regime that promises to deliver a "reasonable," "practical" future consistent with its past. Scheer (2002: 137) describes the erroneous assumption in such reasoning: "The need for fossil energy is a practical constraint that society must respect, for better or worse; whereas proposals for a swift and immediate reorientation...are denounced as irresponsible." An orderly transition is thus forecast from the current energy status quo of fossil fuel and nuclear energy dominance to a new energy status quo with possibly less carbon, but surely with giant-sized fossil and nuclear energy systems in wide use.

The Sustainable Energy Quest

The problems of the conventional energy order have led some to regard reinforcement of the status quo as folly and to instead champion sustainable energy strategies based upon non-conventional sources and a more intelligent ideology of managed relations between energy, environment, and society consonant with environmental integrity. This regime challenger seeks to evolve in the social context that produced the conventional energy regime, yet proposes to fundamentally change its relationship to the environment (at least, this is the hope). Technologies such as wind and photovoltaic electricity are purported to offer building blocks for a transition to a future in which ills plaguing modernity and unsolved by the conventional energy regime can be overcome (Lovins, 1979; Hawken et al., 2000; Scheer, 2002; Rifkin, 2003; World Bank, 2004b).

While technical developments always include social, material, ecological, intellectual, and moral infrastructures (Winner, 1977: 54 - 58; Toly, 2005), and may, therefore, be key to promoting fundamentally different development pathways, it is also possible that technologies, even environmentally benign ones, will be appropriated by social forces that predate them and, thereby, can be thwarted in the fulfillment of social promises attached to the strategy. Indeed, if unaccompanied by reflection upon the social conditions in which the current energy regime thrives, the transition to a renewable energy regime may usher in very few social benefits and little, if any, political and economic transformation. This is the concern that guides our analysis (below) of the sustainable energy movement.

At least since the 1970s when Amory Lovins (1979) famously posed the choice between "hard" and "soft" energy paths, sustainable energy strategies have been offered to challenge the prevailing regime. Sometimes the promise was of no more than "alternative" and "least cost" energy (Energy Policy Project of the Ford Foundation, 1974a, 1974b; O'Toole, 1978; Sant, 1979), but adjectives such as "appropriate," "natural," "renewable," "equitable," and even "democratic" have also been envisioned (Institute for Local Self-Reliance, 2005; Scheer, 2002: 34).[16] The need to depart from the past, especially in light of the oil crises of the 1970s and the energy-rooted threat of climate change that has beset policy debate since the late 1980s, united disparate efforts to recast and reconceive our energy future.

Partly, early criticisms of the mainstream were reflective of a broader social agenda that drew upon, among other things, the anti-war and anti-corporate politics of the 1960s. It was easy, for example, to connect the modern energy regime to military conflicts of the period and to superpower politics; and it was even easier to ally the mainstream's promotion of nuclear power to the objectives of the Nuclear Club. With evidence of profiteering by the oil majors in the wake of the 1973-1974 OPEC embargo, connecting the energy regime with the expanding power of multinational capital was, likewise, not difficult. Early sustainable energy strategies opposed these alliances, offering promises of significant political, as well as technological, change.

However, in the thirty years that the sustainable energy movement has aspired to change the conventional regime, its social commitments and politics have become muddled. A telling sign of this circumstance is the shifted focus from energy politics to economics. To illustrate, in the celebrated work of one of the movement's early architects, subtitles to volumes included "breaking the nuclear link" (Amory Lovins' *Energy/War*, 1981) and "toward a durable peace" (Lovins' *Soft Energy Paths*, 1979). These publications offered poignant challenges to the modern order and energy's role in maintaining that order.

Today, however, the bestsellers of the movement chart a course toward "natural capitalism" (Hawken et al., 2000), a strategy that anticipates synergies between soft path technologies and market governance of energy-environment-society relations. Indeed, a major sustainable energy think tank has reached the conclusion that "small is profitable" (Lovins et al., 2002) in energy matters and argues that the soft path is consistent with "economic rationalism." Understandably, a movement that sought basic change for a third of a century has found the need to adapt its arguments and strategies to the realities of political and economic power. Without adaptation, the conventional energy regime could have ignored soft path policy interventions like demand-side management, integrated resource planning, public benefits charges, and renewable energy portfolio standards (see Lovins and Gadgil, 1991; Sawin, 2004), all of which have caused an undeniable degree of decentralization in energy-society relations. In this vein, it is clear that sustainability proponents must find ways to speak the language and communicate in the logic of economic rationalism if they are to avoid being dismissed. We do not fault the sustainable energy camp for being strategic. Rather, the concern is whether victories in the everyday of incremental politics have been balanced by attention to the broader agenda of systemic change and the ideas needed to define new directions.

A measure of the sustainable energy initiative's strategic success is the growing acceptance of its vision by past adversaries. Thus, *Small is Profitable* was named 'Book of the Year' in 2002 by *The Economist*, an award unlikely to have been bestowed upon any of Lovins' earlier works. As acceptance has been won, it is clear that sustainable energy advocates remain suspicious of the oil majors, coal interests, and the Nuclear Club. But an earlier grounding of these suspicions in anti-war and anti-corporate politics appears to have been superseded by one that believes the global economy can serve a sustainability interest if the 'raison de market' wins the energy policy debate. Thus, it has been suggested that society can turn "more profit with less carbon," by "harnessing corporate power to heal the planet" (Lovins, 2005; L. H. Lovins and A. B. Lovins, 2000). Similarly, Hermann Scheer (2002: 323) avers: "The fundamental problem with today's global economy is not globalization per se, but that this globalization is not based on the sun—the only global force that is equally available to all and whose bounty is so great that it need never be fully tapped." However, it is not obvious that market economics and globalization can be counted upon to deliver the soft path (see, e.g. Nakajima and Vandenberg, 2005). More problematic, as discussed below, the emerging soft path may fall well short of a socially or ecologically transforming event if strategic victories and rhetorics that celebrate them overshadow systemic critiques of energy-society relations and the corresponding need to align the sustainable energy initiative with social movements to address a comprehensive agenda of change.

Catching the Wind

To date, the greatest success in 'real' green energy development is the spread of wind power. From a miniscule 1,930 MW in 1990 to more than 47,317 MW in 2005, wind power has come of age. Especially noteworthy is the rapid growth of wind power in Denmark (35 percent per year since 1997), Spain (30 percent per year since 1997), and Germany (an astonishing 68 percent per year since 2000), where policies have caused this source to threaten the hegemony of fossil fuels and nuclear energy. Wind now generates more than 20 percent of Denmark's electricity and the country is the world leader in turbine manufacture. And as the Danes have demonstrated, offshore wind has the potential to skirt some of the land-use conflicts that have sometimes beset renewable energy alternatives. Indeed, some claim that offshore wind alone might produce all of Europe's residential electricity (Brown, 2004). National energy strategists and environmental movements in and beyond Europe have recognized the achievements of the Danes, Spaniards, and Germans with initiatives designed to imitate their success.

What are the characteristics of this success? One envied feature is the remarkable decline in the price of wind-generated electricity, from $0.46 per kWh in 1980 to $0.03 to $0.07 per kWh today (Sawin, 2004), very close to conventionally-fueled utility generating costs in many countries, even before environmental impacts are included. Jubilant over wind's winning market performance, advocates of sustainable energy foresee a new era that is ecologically much greener and, yet, in which electricity remains (comparatively) cheap. Lester Brown (2003: 159) notes that wind satisfies seemingly equally weighted criteria of environmental benefit, social gain, and economic efficiency:

> Wind is...clean. Wind energy does not produce sulfur dioxide emissions or nitrous oxides to cause acid rain. Nor are there any emissions of health-threatening mercury that come from coal-fired power plants. No mountains are leveled, no streams are polluted, and there are no deaths from black lung disease. Wind does not disrupt the earth's climate...[I]t is inexhaustible...[and] cheap.

This would certainly satisfy the canon of economic rationalism.

It is also consistent with the ideology of modern consumerism. Its politics bestow sovereignty on consumers not unlike the formula of Pareto optimality, a situation in which additional consumption of a good or service is warranted until it cannot improve the circumstance of one person (or group) without decreasing the welfare of another person (or group).[17] How would one know "better off" from "worse off" in the wind-rich sustainable energy era? Interestingly, proponents seem to apply a logic that leaves valuation of "better" and "worse" devoid of explicit content. In a manner reminiscent of modern economic thinking, cheap-and-green enthusiasts appear willing to set wind to the task of making "whatever"—whether that is the manufacture of low-cost teeth whitening toothpaste or lower cost SUVs. In economic accounting, all of these applications potentially make some in society "better off" (if one accepts that economic growth and higher incomes are signs of improvement). Possible detrimental side effects or externalities (an economic term for potential harm) could be rehabilitated by the possession of more purchasing power, which could enable society to invent environmentally friendly toothpaste and make affordable, energy-efficient SUVs. Sustainable energy in this construct cooperates in the abstraction of consumption and production. Consumption-of-what, -by-whom, and -for-what-purpose, and, relatedly, production-of-what, -by-whom, and -for-what-purpose are not issues. The construct altogether ignores the possibility that "more-is-better" consumption-production relations may actually reinforce middle class ideology and capitalist political economy, as well as contribute to environmental crises such as climate change. In the celebration of its coming market victory, the cheap-and-green wind version of sustainable energy development may not readily distinguish the economic/class underpinnings of its victory from those of the conventional energy regime.

Wind enthusiasts also appear to be largely untroubled by trends toward larger and larger turbines and farms, the necessity of more exotic materials to achieve results, and the advancing complications of catching the wind. There is nothing new about these sorts of trends in the modern period. The trajectory of change in a myriad of human activities follows this pattern. Nor is a critique per se intended in an observation of this trend. Rather, the question we wish to raise is whether another feature in this pattern will likewise be replicated—namely, a "technological mystique" (Bazin, 1986) in which social life finds its inspiration and hope in technical acumen and searches for fulfillment in the ideals of technique (Mumford, 1934; Ellul, 1964; Marcuse, 1964; Winner, 1977, 1986; Vanderburg, 2005).

This prospect is not a distant one, as a popular magazine recently illustrated. In a special section devoted to thinking "After Oil," *National Geographic* approvingly compared the latest wind technology to a well-known monument, the Statue of Liberty, and noted that the new machines tower more than 400 feet above this symbol (Parfit, 2005: 15 - 16). It was not hard to extrapolate from the story the message of Big Wind's liberatory potential. *Popular Science* also commended new wind systems as technological marvels, repeating the theme that, with its elevation in height and complexity lending the technology greater status, wind can now be taken seriously by scientists and engineers (Tompkins, 2005). A recent issue of *The Economist* (2005) included an article on the wonder of electricity generated by an artificial tornado in which wind is technologically spun to high velocities in a building equipped with a giant turbine to convert the energy into electricity. Indeed, wind is being contemplated as a rival able to serve society by the sheer technical prowess that has often been a defining characteristic of modern energy systems.

Obviously, wind energy has a long way to go before it can claim to have dethroned conventional energy's "technological cathedrals" (Weinberg, 1985). But its mission seems largely to supplant other spectacular methods of generating electricity with its own. The politics supporting its rapid rise express no qualms about endorsing the inevitability of its victories on technical grounds. In fact, Big Wind appears to seek monumental status in the psyche of ecologically modern society. A recent alliance of the American Wind Energy Association and the U.S. electric utility industry to champion national (subsidized) investment in higher voltage transmission lines (to deliver green-and-cheap electricity), illustrates the desire of Big Wind to plug into Giant Power's hardware and, correspondingly, its ideology (see American Wind Energy Association, 2005, supporting "Transmission Infrastructure Modernization"). The transformative features of such a politics are unclear. Indeed, wind power—if it can continue to be harvested by ever-larger machines—may penetrate the conventional energy order so successfully that it will diffuse, without perceptible disruption, to the regime. The air will be cleaner but the source of this achievement will be duly noted: science will have triumphed still again in wresting from stingy nature the resources that a wealthy life has grown to expect. Social transformation to achieve sustainability may actually be unnecessary by this political view of things, as middle-class existence is assured via clean, low-cost and easy-to-plug-in wind power.

Small-is-Beautiful Solar[18]

The second fastest growing renewable energy option—solar electric power—is proving more difficult to plug in. Despite steady declines in the cost per kWh of energy generated by photovoltaic (PV) cells, this alternative remains a pricey solution by conventional standards. Moreover, the technology does not appear to have significant scale economies, partly because the efficiency of PV cannot be improved by increasing the size of the device or its application. That is, unit energy costs of large installations of many PV arrays do not deviate appreciably from those for small installations comprised of fewer arrays. Instead, the technology seems to follow a modular economic logic in which unit costs neither grow nor decline with scale. Some have praised this attribute, suggesting that PV's modularity means there are no technical or economic reasons for scaling its application to iconic levels that conventional power plants now represent, potentiating a more robust system of distributed generation and delivering clean energy to previously marginalized populations (Martinot and Reiche, 2000; Martinot et al., 2002).

Small-Is-Beautiful Solar is attributed with social empowerment potential by Vaitheeswaran (2003: 314) who notes that PV (and other small scale electricity generation technologies) can overcome social barriers through a "collision of clean energy, microfinance, and community empowerment," three properties that may lift the burden of poverty and promote democratic social relations. "Micropower," he argues (2003: 314), "is beginning to join forces with village power." Thus, it would seem that a Solar Society might depend upon a different politics than Big Wind in displacing a fossil and nuclear energy driven world economy.

Perhaps because PV has, so far, found wider social usage in rural contexts where poverty (as modernly conceived) persists, discussions, in fact, crop up about solar's social project. For example, arguments have formed around the gender interests of PV, at least as it has been diffused in rural life to date (see, for example, Allerdice and Rogers, 2000). And criticism has surfaced about PV's 'capture' by the state as a tool to quiet, if not mollify, the rural poor (Okubo, 2005: 49 - 58). There has even been a charge that PV and other renewables are being used by multilateral organizations such as the World Bank to stall Southern development. By imposing a fragmented patchwork of tiny, expensive solar generators on, for example, the African rural landscape, instead of accumulating capital in an industrial energy infrastructure, the World Bank and other actors are accused of being unresponsive to the rapid growth needs of the South (Davidson and Sokona, 2002; Karekezi and Kithyoma, 2002). A related challenge of PV's class interests has raised questions about the technology's multinational corporate owners and offered doubts about successful indigenization of solar cell manufacturing (Able-Thomas, 1995; Guru, 2002: 27; Bio-Energy Association of Sri Lanka, 2004: 20). Regardless of one's position on these debates, it is refreshing to at least see solar energy's possible political and economic interests considered.

But PV's advocates have not embraced the opportunities created by its rural examiners to seriously investigate the political economy of solar energy. The bulk of solar research addresses engineering problems, with a modest social inquiry focused on issues of technological transition in which solar electricity applications are to find their way into use with as little social resistance or challenge as possible. A green politics that is largely unscarred by conflict is, and for a long time has been, anticipated to characterize an emergent Solar Society (Henderson, 1988; Ikeda and Henderson, 2004). Likewise, solar economics is thought to be consensual as non-renewable options become too expensive and PV cells, by comparison, too cheap to be refused their logical role (see, for example, Henderson, 1995, 1996; Rifkin, 2003). It seems that a solarized social order is inevitable for its proponents, with technological breakthrough and economic cost the principal determinants of when it will arrive.

In this regard, ironically, Small-is-Beautiful Solar shares with Big Wind the aspiration to re-order the energy regime without changing society. Despite modern society's technological, economic, and political addiction to large-scale, cheap energy systems that solar energy cannot mimic, most PV proponents hope to revolutionize the technological foundation of modernity, without disturbing its social base. A new professional cadre of solar architects and engineers are exhorted to find innovative ways of embedding PV technology in the skin of buildings (Strong, 1999; Benemann, Chehab, and Schaar-Gabriel, 2001), while transportation engineers and urban planners are to coordinate in launching "smart growth" communities where vehicles are powered by hydrogen derived from PV-powered electrolysis to move about in communities optimized for "location efficiency" (Ogden, 1999; Holtzclaw et al., 2002). The wildly oversized ecological footprint of urban societies (Rees and Wackernagel, 1996) is unquestioned as PV decorates its structure.

These tools for erecting a Solar Society intend to halt anthropogenic changes to the chemistry of the atmosphere, rain, and soil mantle while enabling unlimited economic growth. In the Solar Society of tomorrow, we will make what we want, in the amounts we desire, without worry, because all of its energy is derived from the benign, renewable radiation supplied by our galaxy's sun. Compared to Big Wind, PV may cost more but it promises to deliver an equivalent social result (minus the avian and landscape threats of the former) and, just possibly, with a technical elegance that surpasses the clunky mechanicalness of turbines propelled by wind. In this respect, Solar Society makes its peace with modernity by leaving undisturbed the latter's cornucopian dreams[19] and, likewise, poses no serious challenge to the social and political structures of the modern era.

At this precise point, inequality and conflict can only be conceived in Solar Society as the results of willful meanness and greed. While the solar variety of technological politics guiding society may be relatively minimalist—no towering new monuments or spectacular devices are planned—it would be no less committed to the ideals of technique in shaping social experience and its self-assessment. Similarly, its economics would warmly embrace a form of consumptive capitalism, although with cleaner inputs (and possibly throughputs) than before.

While the discussion here of sustainable energy advocacy has concentrated on its wind- and solar-animated versions, we believe that strategies anticipating significant roles for geothermal, biomass, micro-hydro, and hydrogen harvested from factories fueled by renewables anticipate variants of the social narratives depicted for the two currently most prominent renewable energy options. The aim of producing more with advancing ecological efficiency in order to consume more with equally advancing consumerist satisfaction underpins the sustainable energy future in a way that would seamlessly tie it to the modernization project.[20]

Democratic Authoritarian Impulses and Uncritical Capitalist Assumptions

When measured in social and political-economic terms, the current energy discourse appears impoverished. Many of its leading voices proclaim great things will issue from the adoption of their strategies (conventional or sustainable), yet inquiry into the social and political-economic interests that power promises of greatness by either camp is mostly absent. In reply, some participants may petition for a progressive middle ground, acknowledging that energy regimes are only part of larger institutional formations that organize political and economic power. It is true that the political economy of energy is only a component of systemic power in the modern order, but it hardly follows that pragmatism toward energy policy and politics is the reasonable social response. Advocates of energy strategies associate their contributions with distinct pathways of social development and define the choice of energy strategy as central to the types of future(s) that can unfold. Therefore, acceptance of appeals for pragmatist assessments of energy proposals, that hardly envision incremental consequences, would indulge a form of self-deception rather than represent a serious discursive position.

An extensive social analysis of energy regimes of the type that Mumford (1934; 1966; 1970), Nye (1999), and others have envisioned is overdue. The preceding examinations of the two strategies potentiate conclusions about both the governance ideology and the political economy of modernist energy transitions that, by design, leave modernism undisturbed (except, perhaps, for its environmental performance).

The Technique of Modern Energy Governance

While moderns usually declare strong preferences for democratic governance, their preoccupation with technique and efficiency may preclude the achievement of such ambitions, or require changes in the meaning of democracy that are so extensive as to raise doubts about its coherence. A veneration of technical monuments typifies both conventional and sustainable energy strategies and reflects a shared belief in technological advance as commensurate with, and even a cause of, contemporary social progress. The modern proclivity to search for human destiny in the march of scientific discovery has led some to warn of a technological politics (Ellul, 1997a, 1997b, 1997c; Winner, 1977, 1986) in which social values are sublimated by the objective norms of technical success (e.g., the celebration of efficiency in all things). In this politics, technology and its use become the end of society and members have the responsibility, as rational beings, to learn from the technical milieu what should be valorized. An encroaching *autonomy of technique* (Ellul, 1964: 133 – 146) replaces critical thinking about modern life with an awed sense and acceptance of its inevitable reality.

From dreams of endless energy provided by Green Fossil Fuels and Giant Power, to the utopian promises of Big Wind and Small-Is-Beautiful Solar, technical excellence powers modernist energy transitions. Refinement of technical accomplishments and/or technological revolutions are conceived to drive social transformation, despite the unending inequality that has accompanied two centuries of modern energy's social project. As one observer has noted (Roszak, 1972: 479), the "great paradox of the technological mystique

[is] its remarkable ability to grow strong by chronic failure. While the treachery of our technology may provide many occasions for disenchantment, the sum total of failures has the effect of increasing dependence on technical expertise." Even the vanguard of a sustainable energy transition seems swayed by the magnetism of technical acumen, leading to the result that enthusiast and critic alike embrace a strain of technological politics.

Necessarily, the elevation of technique in both strategies to authoritative status vests political power in experts most familiar with energy technologies and systems. Such a governance structure derives from the democratic-authoritarian bargain described by Mumford (1964). Governance "by the people" consists of authorizing qualified experts to assist political leaders in finding the efficient, modern solution. In the narratives of both conventional and sustainable energy, citizens are empowered to consume the products of the energy regime while largely divesting themselves of authority to govern its operations.

Indeed, systems of the sort envisioned by advocates of conventional and sustainable strategies are not governable in a democratic manner. Mumford suggests (1964: 1) that the classical idea of democracy includes "a group of related ideas and practices... [including] communal self-government... unimpeded access to the common store of knowledge, protection against arbitrary external controls, and a sense of moral responsibility for behavior that affects the whole community." Modern conventional and sustainable energy strategies invest in external controls, authorize abstract, depersonalized interactions of suppliers and demanders, and celebrate economic growth and technical excellence without end. Their social consequences are relegated in both paradigms to the status of problems-to-be-solved, rather than being recognized as the emblems of modernist politics. As a result, modernist democratic practice becomes imbued with an authoritarian quality, which "deliberately eliminates the whole human personality, ignores the historic process, [and] overplays the role of abstract intelligence, and makes control over physical nature, ultimately control over man himself, the chief purpose of existence" (Mumford, 1964: 5). Meaningful democratic governance is willingly sacrificed for an energy transition that is regarded as scientifically and technologically unassailable.

Triumphant Energy Capitalism

Where the power to govern is not vested in experts, it is given over to market forces in both the conventional and sustainable energy programs. Just as the transitions envisioned in the two paradigms are alike in their technical preoccupations and governance ideologies, they are also alike in their political-economic commitments. Specifically, modernist energy transitions operate in, and evolve from, a capitalist political economy. Huber and Mills (2005) are convinced that conventional techno-fixes will expand productivity and increase prosperity to levels that will erase the current distortions of inequality. Expectably, conventional energy's aspirations present little threat to the current energy political economy; indeed, the aim is to reinforce and deepen the current infrastructure in order to minimize costs and sustain economic growth. The existing alliance of government and business interests is judged to have produced social success and, with a few environmental correctives that amount to the modernization of ecosystem performance, the conventional energy project fervently anticipates an intact energy capitalism that willingly invests in its own perpetuation.

While advocates of sustainable energy openly doubt the viability of the conventional program and emphasize its social and environmental failings, there is little indication that capitalist organization of the energy system is faulted or would be significantly changed with the ascendance of a renewables-based regime. The modern cornucopia will be powered by the profits of a redirected market economy that diffuses technologies whose energy sources are available to all and are found everywhere. The sustainable energy project, according to its architects, aims to harness nature's 'services' with technologies and distributed generation designs that can sustain the same impulses of growth and consumption that underpin the social project of conventional energy. Neither its corporate character, nor the class interests that propel capitalism's advance, are seriously questioned. The only glaring difference with the conventional energy regime is the effort to modernize social relations with nature.

In sum, conventional and sustainable energy strategies are mostly quiet about matters of concentration of wealth and privilege that are the legacy of energy capitalism, although both are vocal about support for changes consistent with middle class values and lifestyles. We are left to wonder why such steadfast reluctance exists to engaging problems of political economy. Does it stem from a lack of understanding? Is it reflective of a measure of satisfaction with the existing order? Or is there a fear that critical inquiry might jeopardize strategic victories or diminish the central role of 'energy' in the movement's quest?

Transition without Change: A Failing Discourse

After more than thirty years of contested discourse, the major 'energy futures' under consideration appear committed to the prevailing systems of governance and political economy that animate late modernity. The new technologies—conventional or sustainable—that will govern the energy sector and accumulate capital might be described as *centaurian technics*[21] in which the crude efficiency of the fossil energy era is bestowed a new sheen by high technologies and modernized ecosystems: capitalism without smoky cities, contaminated industrial landscapes, or an excessively carbonized atmosphere. Emerging energy solutions are poised to realize a postmodern transition (Roosevelt, 2002), but their shared commitment to capitalist political economy and the democratic-authoritarian bargain lend credence to Jameson's assessment (1991) of postmodernism as the "cultural logic of late capitalism."

Differences in ecological commitments between conventional and sustainable energy strategies still demarcate a battleground that, we agree, is important—even fundamental. But so also are the common aspirations of the two camps. Each sublimates social considerations in favor of a politics of more-is-better, and each regards the advance of energy capitalism with a sense of inevitability and triumph. Conventional and sustainable energy visions equally presume that a social order governed by a 'democratic' ideal of cornucopia, marked by economic plenty, and delivered by technological marvels will eventually lance the wounds of poverty and inequality and start the healing process. Consequently, silence on questions of governance and social justice is studiously observed by both proposals. Likewise, both agree to, or demur on, the question of capitalism's sustainability.[22] Nothing is said on these questions because, apparently, nothing needs to be.

If the above assessment of the contemporary energy discourse is correct, then the enterprise is not at a crossroad; rather, it has reached a point of acquiescence to things as they are. Building an inquiry into energy as a social project will require the recovery of a critical voice that can interrogate, rather than concede, the discourse's current moorings in technological politics and capitalist political economy. A fertile direction in this regard is to investigate an energy-society order in which energy systems evolve in response to social values and goals, and not simply according to the dictates of technique, prices, or capital. Initial interest in renewable energy by the sustainability camp no doubt emanated, at least in part, from the fact that its fuel price is non-existent and that capitalization of systems to collect renewable sources need not involve the extravagant, convoluted corporate forms that manage the conventional energy regime. But forgotten, or misunderstood, in the attraction of renewable energy have been the *social* origins of such emergent possibilities. Communities exist today who address energy needs outside the global marketplace: they are often rural in character and organize energy services that are immune to oil price spikes and do not require water heated to between 550º and 900º Fahrenheit (300º and 500º Celsius) (the typical temperatures in nuclear reactors). No energy bills are sent or paid and governance of the serving infrastructure is based on local (rather than distantly developed professional) knowledge. Needless to say, sustainability is embodied in the lifeworld of these communities, unlike the modern strategy that hopes to design sustainability into its technology and economics so as *not* to seriously change its otherwise unsustainable way of life.

Predictably, modern society will underscore its wealth and technical acumen as evidence of its superiority over alternatives. But smugness cannot overcome the fact that energy-society relations are evident in which the bribe of democratic-authoritarianism and the unsustainability of energy capitalism are successfully declined. In 1928, Mahatma Gandhi (cited in Gandhi, 1965: 52) explained why the democratic-authoritarian bargain and Western capitalism should be rejected:

> God forbid that India should ever take to industrialization after the manner of the West. The economic imperialism of a single tiny island kingdom (England) is today keeping the world in chains. If an entire nation of 300 million took to similar economic exploitation, it would strip the world bare like locusts. Unless the capitalists of India help to avert that tragedy by becoming trustees of the welfare of the masses and by devoting their talents not to amassing wealth for themselves but to the service of the masses in an altruistic spirit, they will end either by destroying the masses or being destroyed by them.

As Gandhi's remark reveals, social inequality resides not in access to electric light and other accoutrements of modernity, but in a world order that places efficiency and wealth above life-affirming ways of life. This is our social problem, our energy problem, our ecological problem, and, generally, our political-economic problem.

The challenge of a social inquiry into energy-society relations awaits.

Notes

1. The authors wish to thank four dear colleagues for their counsel in the preparation of this chapter: Young-Doo Wang, Cecilia Martinez, Leigh Glover, and Kristen Hughes.
2. Climate change is caused by increasing atmospheric concentrations of greenhouse gases due primarily to the combustion of fossil fuels. Climate change is also among the leading causes of biodiversity loss, causing extinction at latitudinal and elevational extremes (Chapin et al., 2000).
3. For a discussion of the role of energy in the Iraq and Darfur conflicts, see Klare (2002a) and Gidley (2005).
4. The modest literature vowing to examine the relationship between energy and society mostly amounts to a project of technological literacy (see, e.g., Cassedy and Grossman, 1998; Schobert, 2001; Tester et al., 2005). Technological literacy is certainly important to the engagement of energy-society relations, but a social analysis limited to the literacy project is insufficient. A departure from the literacy objective is the collaboration of Jose Goldemberg, Thomas B. Johansson, Amulya K. N. Reddy, and Robert H. Williams (1987; see also Johansson and Goldemberg, 2002; Goldemberg, 2003), who organized a volume replete with social analyses of energy systems (although a substantial part of the book also intends to improve its readers' understanding of the scientific and technical features of energy systems). Interestingly, this volume, *Energy for a Sustainable World*, focused on energy needs and conflicts in developing countries and, thereby, was able to direct attention toward the social dimensions of energy production, distribution, and use. A

minority of scholars and activists has pursued this approach; some have contributed to this volume.

5. See, e.g., Amory Lovins' promise of a "natural capitalism" energized by the wind and sun, and his forecast of a "negawatt" revolution caused by investment in energy efficiency (Lovins and Gadgil, 1991; Lovins, 1996; Hawken, Lovins, and Lovins, 2000: 279).

6. On the one hand, Scheer (2002) is confident about the prospects of a market- and technology-led transition to a socially equitable, sustainable energy future, displaying optimism that techno-economic fixes are sufficient to solve social problems. In this instance, he does not offer a *social* analysis of sustainable energy development. On the other hand, he has written an in-depth, insightful *social* critique of the fossil fuel-based energy regime that, interestingly, challenges the premises of economic and technological optimism cited by its supporters.

7. In his 1983 article, "Present Tense Technology: Technology's Politics," David Noble evaluated the social capacity for a critical perspective on technology given the futurist orientation of technological politics.

8. Taken from the title of their 1986 argument, Byrne and Rich offer an analysis of the conventional energy regime's uninterrupted belief in the prospects for energy abundance.

9. Consider, for example, the proposal to mine oil in the Arctic National Wildlife Refuge (see www.anwr.org).

10. The oil spread to five National Wildlife Refuges and three National Parks, covering an area of 900 square miles and washing hundreds of miles of shoreline with a black tide. The estimate of bird kills was 100,000, including 150 bald eagles. Approximately 1,000 sea otters were also lost. Debris from the clean up of the oil spill was in excess of 50,000 tons (Byrne et al., 2002).

11. However, architects of the fossil fuel regime are quick to point out the unreasonably high cost of solar energy systems (see, for example, Huber and Mills, 2005).

12. Similarly, much of the uranium in the U.S. is mined on Native American lands (Martinez and Poupart, 2002: 138 – 139; Byrne and Hoffman, 2002: 105).

13. Huber and Mills (2005: 157) suggest that renewable energy deployment for emissions abatement requires so much land set aside for sufficiently large amounts of wind and solar energy to be collected that this would preempt floral carbon sequestration, resulting in little or no net carbon reduction. Further, they argue that floral carbon sequestration is more efficient than renewable energy-based carbon mitigation.

14. Researchers long ago showed the error in thinking that nuclear power is a cost-effective method of reducing carbon emissions (Keepin and Kats, 1988).

15. The U.S. Energy Policy Act of 2005 exhibits the logic of policy harmonization, calling for massive incentives to the energy majors in order for them to find additional supplies of fossil fuels needed to secure American economic growth for the foreseeable future. The carbon problem is left to sort itself out. Recent efforts in the European Union to incentivize carbon reductions *and* secure energy supply is another example (European Union, 2005). While different and consequential in many respects, both rely heavily on the ideas and tools of energy neoliberalism.

16. The Institute for Local Self-Reliance, a Minnesota non-profit organization, suggests that "technological innovations are making it increasingly possible to think about a more decentralized and environmentally benign energy system. Democratic energy means an energy system where the consumer can become a producer, where power plants are located near where the energy is consumed, and where the decisions about the structure of the energy system is made in large part by those who will feel the impact of those decisions" (www.newrules.org/de).

17. Vilfredo Pareto's (1906: 261, emphasis in original) definition is interesting: "We will say that the members of a collectivity enjoy *maximium ophelimity* in a certain position when it is impossible to find a way of moving from that position very slightly in such a manner that the ophelimity enjoyed by each of the individuals of that collectivity increases or decreases. That is to say, any small displacement in departing from that position necessarily has the effect of increasing the ophelimity which certain individuals enjoy, and decreasing that which others enjoy, of being agreeable to some, and disagreeable to others."

18. E. F. Schumacher (1973) argued for the superiority of human-scale industry and economics, opposing blind commitment to economies of scale and suggesting that small can be beautiful.

19. See Byrne and Yun (1999) and Byrne and Glover (2005) for a general discussion of this neoliberal dream state.

20. Albeit, the sustainable energy strategy (compared to its conventional energy competitor) embraces the task of modernizing ecology-society relations in a manner not achievable by fossil fuels and nuclear power.

21. For this insight we are indebted to Albert Borgmann (1992: 86), who writes of recent developments in information technologies: "To prosper, instrumental hyperreality must retain the shape of a centaur. The refined part must remain attached to the crude part."

22. See O'Connor (1994) for an analysis of capitalism's (un)sustainability.

References

Able-Thomas, U. (1995). Technology Transfer of Photovoltaic Systems to Developing Countries (pp. 14).

Agbemabiese, L., and Byrne, J. (2005). Commodification of Ghana's Volta River: An Example of Ellul's Autonomy of Technique. *Bulletin of Science, Technology, and Society, 25*(1), 17 - 25.

Allerdice, A., and Rogers, J. H. (2000). *Renewable Energy for Microenterprise*. Boulder, CO: National Renewable Energy Laboratory.

American Wind Energy Association. (2005, August 9). Energy Policy Act Signed by President Improves Market Access for Wind Power. Retrieved on October, 14 2005. Available at www.awea.org.

Bazin, M. (1986). The Technological Mystique and Third World Options. *Monthly Review, July/August*, 98 - 109.

Beck, U. (1992). From Industrial Society to the Risk Society: Questions of Survival, Social Structure, and Ecological Enlightenment. *Theory, Culture, and Society, 9*(1), 97 - 123.

Benemann, J., Chehab, O., and Schaar-Gabriel, E. (2001, March). Building-integrated PV Modules. *Solar Energy Materials and Solar Cells*, 345 - 355.

Bergeron, K. D. (2002). *Tritium on Ice: The Dangerous Alliance of Nuclear Weapons and Nuclear Power*. Cambridge, MA: MIT Press.

Bergeron, K. D., and Zimmerman, A. D. (2006). Nuclear Power in an Age of Global Terrorism. In J. Byrne, L. N. Toly, and L. Glover (Eds.), *Transforming Power: Energy, Environment, and Society in Conflict*. New Brunswick, NJ and London: Transaction Publishers.

Bio-Energy Association of Sri Lanka. (2004). *The Dendro Option for Future Energy Security of Sri Lanka*. Colombo: Bio-Energy Association of Sri Lanka.

Borgmann, A. (1992). *Crossing the Postmodern Divide*. Chicago, Il: University of Chicago Press.

Bosshard, P. (2006). The World Bank's Support for Large Dams: A Case of Institutional Amnesia? In J. Byrne, N. Toly, and L. Glover (Eds.), *Transforming Power: Energy, Environment, and Society in Conflict*. New Brunswick, NJ and London: Transaction Publishers.

Brown, L. (2004). *Europe Leading World into Age of Wind Energy*. Retrieved October 10, 2005. Available at www.earth-policy.org/Updates/Update37.htm.

Brown, L. (2003). *Plan B: Rescuing a Planet Under Stress and a Civilization in Trouble*. New York: W. W. Norton and Company.

Bureau of Reclamation. (2005a). *Glen Canyon Powerplant*. Retrieved October 10, 2005. Available at www.usbr.gov.

Bureau of Reclamation. (2005b). World's Largest Dam by Volume. Retrieved October 13, 2005. Available at www.usbr.gov.

Byrne, J., and Glover, L. (2005). Ellul and the Weather. *Bulletin of Science, Technology, and Society, 25*(1): 4 – 16.

Byrne, J., Glover, L., Lee, H., Wang, Y.-D., and Yu, J.-M. (2004). Electricity Reform at a Crossroads: Problems in South Korea's Power Liberalization Strategy. *Pacific Affairs, 77*(3), 493 - 516.

Byrne, J., Glover, L., and Martinez, C. (2002). The Production of Unequal Nature. In J. Byrne, L. Glover and C. Martinez (Eds.), *Environmental Justice: Discourses in International Political Economy* (Vol. 8, pp. 230 - 256). New Brunswick, NJ and London: Transaction Publishers.

Byrne, J., and Hoffman, S. (2002). A 'Necessary Sacrifice:' Industrialization and American Indian Lands. In J. Byrne, L. Glover and C. Martinez (Eds.), *Environmental Justice: Discourses in International Political Economy* (pp. 97 - 118). New Brunswick, NJ and London: Transaction Publishers.

Byrne, J., and Hoffman, S. (1996). The Ideology of Progress and the Globalization of Nuclear Power. In J. Byrne and S. Hoffman (Eds.), *Governing the Atom: The Politics of Risk* (Vol. 7, pp. 11 – 46). New Brunswick, NJ and London: Transaction Publishers.

Byrne, J., and Hoffman, S. (1992). Nuclear Optimism and the Technological Imperative: A Study of the Pacific Northwest Electric Network. *Bulletin of Science, Technology, and Society 11*, 63 – 77.

Byrne, J., and Hoffman, S. (1988). Nuclear Power and Technological Authoritarianism. *Bulletin of Science, Technology, and Society 7*, 658 – 671.

Byrne, J., and Rich, D. (1986). In Search of the Abundant Energy Machine. In J. Byrne and D. Rich (Eds.), *The Politics of Energy Research and Development* (Vol. 3, pp. 141 – 160). New Brunswick, NJ and London: Transaction Publishers.

Byrne, J., and Yun, S.-J. (1999). Efficient Global Warming: Contradictions in Liberal Democratic Responses to Global Environmental Problems. *Bulletin of Science, Technology, and Society, 19*(6), 493 - 500.

Chapin III, F. S., Zavaleta, E. S., Eviner, V. T., Naylor, R. L., Vitousek, P. M., Reynolds, H. L., et al. (2000). Consequences of Changing Biodiversity. *Nature, 405*(11 May 2000), 234 - 242.

Cassedy, E. S., and Grossman, P. Z. (1998). *Introduction to Energy: Resources, Technology, and Society*. Cambridge: Cambridge University Press.

Davidson, O., and Sokona, Y. (2002). *Think Bigger, Act Faster: A New Sustainable Energy Path for African Development*. Cape Town: EDRC.

Department of the Interior (U.S.). (2002). OCS Oil Spill Facts. Washington, DC: Department of the Interior Minerals Management Service.

Diesendorf, M. (2006). Can geosequestration save the coal industry? In J. Byrne, N. Toly, and L. Glover (Eds.), *Transforming Power: Energy, Environment, and Society in Conflict*. New Brunswick, NJ and London: Transaction Publishers.

Dubash, N. (2002). *Power Politics: Equity and Environment in Electricity Reform.* Washington, DC: World Resources Institute.

Dubash, N., and Williams, J. (2006). The Political Economy of Electricity Liberalization. In J. Byrne, N. Toly, and L. Glover (Eds.), *Tranforming Power: Energy, Environment, and Society in Conflict.* New Brunswick, NJ and London: Transaction Publishers.

Ellul, J. (1997a). Chronicle of the Problems of Civilization: I. By Way of a Brief Preface (M. Dawn, Trans.). In M. Dawn (Ed.), *Sources and Trajectories: Eight Early Articles by Jacques Ellul That Set the Stage* (pp. 10 - 28). Grand Rapids, MI: Wm. B. Eerdmans Publishing Co.

Ellul, J. (1997b). Needed: A New Karl Marx! (Problems of Civilization II) (M. Dawn, Trans.). In M. Dawn (Ed.), *Sources and Trajectories: Eight Early Articles by Jacques Ellul that Set the Stage* (pp. 29 - 48). Grand Rapids, MI: Wm. B. Eerdmans Publishing Co.

Ellul, J. (1997c). Political Realism (Problems of Civilization III) (M. Dawn, Trans.). In M. Dawn (Ed.), *Sources and Trajectories: Eight Early Articles by Jacques Ellul that Set the Stage* (pp. 49 - 91). Grand Rapids, MI: Wm. B. Eerdmans Publishing Co.

Ellul, J. (1964). *The Technological Society* (J. Wilkinson, Trans.). New York: Vintage Books.

Energy Policy Project of the Ford Foundation. (1974a). *Exploring Energy Choices.* Washington, DC: Ford Foundation.

Energy Policy Project of the Ford Foundation. (1974b). *A Time to Choose.* Washington, DC: Ford Foundation.

European Union. (2005). The Energy Dimension of Climate Change. Retrieved on October 14, 2005. http://europa.eu.int/pol/ener/index_en.htm.

Federal Energy Regulatory Commission (U.S.). (2005). Existing and Proposed North American LNG Terminals. Washington, DC: Federal Energy Regulatory Commission.

Gandhi, M. K. (1965). *My Picture of Free India.* Bombay: Pearl Publications.

Gidley, R. (2005, June 17). Oil Discovery Adds New Twist to Darfur Tragedy. *Reuters.*

Gill, D. A., and Picou, J. S. (1996). The Day the Water Died: Cultural Impacts of the Exxon Valdez Oil Spill. In J. S. Picou (Ed.), *The Exxon Valdez Disaster: Readings on a Modern Social Problem* (pp. 167 - 187). Dubuque, Iowa: Kendall/Hunt Publishing Company.

Goldemberg, Jose. (2003). Energy and Sustainable Development. In J. G. Speth (Ed.), *Worlds Apart: Globalization and the Environment* (pp. 53 – 65). Washington, DC: Island Press.

Goldemberg, J., Johansson, T. B., Reddy, A. K. N., and Williams, Robert H. (1987). *Energy for a Sustainable World.* Washington, DC: World Resources Institute.

Guru, S. (2002). *Renewable Energy Sources in India: Is It Viable?* New Delhi: Julian Simon Center for Policy Research.

Hawken, P., Lovins, A. B., and Lovins, L. H. (2000). *Natural Capitalism: Creating the Next Industrial Revolution.* Boston, MA: Back Bay Books.

Henderson, H. (1996). *Building a Win-Win World: Life Beyond Global Economic Warfare.* San Francisco, CA: Berrett-Koehler Publishers.

Henderson, H. (1995). *Paradigms in Progress: Life Beyond Economics.* San Francisco, CA: Berrett-Koehler Publishers.

Henderson, H. (1988). *The Politics of the Solar Age.* Indianapolis, Indiana: Knowledge Systems.

Hightower, M., Gritzo, L., Luketa-Hamlin, A., Covan, J., Tieszen, S., Wellman, G., et al. (2004). *Guidance on Risk Analysis and Safety Implications of a Large Liquefied*

Natural Gas (LNG) Spill Over Water. Albuquerque, New Mexico and Berkeley, CA: Sandia National Laboratories.

Hoffman, S. (2002). Powering Injustice: Hydroelectric Development in Northern Manitoba. In J. Byrne, L. Glover and C. Martinez (Eds.), *Environmental Justice: Discourses in International Political Economy* (pp. 147 - 170). New Brunswick, NJ and London: Transaction Publishers.

Holtzclaw, J., Clear, R., Dittmar, H., Goldstein, D., and Haas, P. (2002). Location Efficiency: Neighborhood and Socio-Economic Characteristics Determine Auto Ownership and Use - Studies in Chicago, Los Angeles, and San Francisco. *Transportation Planning and Technology, 25*(1), 1 - 27.

Huber, P. W., and Mills, M. P. (2005). *The Bottomless Well: The Twilight of Fuel, The Virtue of Waste, and Why We Will Never Run Out of Energy*. New York: Basic Books.

Ikeda, D., and Henderson, H. (2004). *Planetary Citizenship: Your Values, Beliefs, and Actions Can Shape a Sustainable World*. Santa Monica, CA: Middleway Press.

Institute for Local Self-Reliance. (2005). Democratic Energy. Retrieved on October 19, 2005. Available at www.newrules.org/de.

Jaccard, M. (2005) *Sustainable Fossil Fuels: The Unusual Suspect in the Quest for Clean and Enduring Energy*. Cambridge: Cambridge University Press.

Jameson, F. (1991). *Postmodernism: Or the Cultural Logic of Late Capitalism*. Raleigh, NC: Duke University Press.

Johansson, T. B., and Goldemberg, J. (2002). *Energy for Sustainable Development: A Policy Agenda*. New York: United Nations Environment Program.

Karekezi, S., and Kithyoma, W. (2002). Renewable Energy Strategies for Rural Africa: Is a PV-Led Renewable Energy Strategy the Right Approach for Providing Modern Energy to the Rural Poor of sub-Saharan Africa. *Energy Policy*(30), 1071-1086.

Keepin, B., and Kats, G. (1988). Greenhouse Warming: Comparative Analysis of Nuclear and Efficiency Abatement Strategies. *Energy Policy 16*(6), 538 – 561.

Klare, M. T. (2006). The Globalization of the Carter Doctrine. In J. Byrne , N. Toly, and L. Glover (Eds.), *Transforming Power: Energy, Environment, and Society in Conflict*. New Brunswick, NJ and London: Transaction Publishers.

Klare, M. T. (2004). *Blood and Oil: The Dangers and Consequences of America's Growing Dependency on Imported Petroleum*. New York: Metropolitan Books.

Klare, M. T. (2002a, October 7). Oiling the Wheels of War. *The Nation*.

Klare, M. T. (2002b). *Resource Wars: The New Landscape of Global Conflict*. New York: Owl Books.

Kumar, K. (2005). *From Post-Industrial to Post-Modern Society: New Themes of the Contemporary World*. Malden, MA: Blackwell.

Kumar, K. (1988). *The Rise of Modern Society: Aspects of the Social and Political Development of the West*. Oxford: Blackwell.

Kumar, K. (1978). *Prophecy and Progress: The Sociology of Industrial and Post-Industrial Society*. New York: Penguin Books.

Lee, T. (Forthcoming). The Clash Between Globalization and Indigenous Livelihoods: The Case of the U'wa in Colombia. *Bulletin of Science, Technology, and Society*.

Lovins, A. B. (2005, September). More Profit with Less Carbon. *Scientific American*, 74 - 83.

Lovins, A. B. (1996). Negawatts: Twelve Transitions, Eight Improvements, and One Distraction. *Energy Policy, 24*(4), 331 - 343.

Lovins, A. B. (1981). *Energy/War: Breaking the Nuclear Link: A Prescription for Non-Proliferation*. New York: Harper Collins Publishers.

Lovins, A. B. (1979). *Soft Energy Paths: Toward a Durable Peace*. San Francisco, CA: Harper Collins Publishers.

Lovins, A. B., Datta, E. K., Feiler, T., Rabago, K. R., Swisher, J. N., Lehmann, A., et al. (2002). *Small is Profitable: The Hidden Economic Benefits of Making Electrical Resources the Right Size*. Snowmass, CO: Rocky Mountain Institute.

Lovins, A. B., and Gadgil, A. (1991). *The Negawatt Revolution: Electric Efficiency and Asian Development*. Snowmass, CO: Rocky Mountain Institute.

Lovins, L. H., and Lovins, A. B. (2000). Harnessing Corporate Power to Heal the Planet. In *The World and I*. Washington, DC: Washington Times Corporation.

Marcuse, H. (1964). *One-Dimensional Man: Studies in the Ideology of Advanced Industrial Society*. Boston, MA: Beacon Press.

Martinez, C., and Poupart, J. (2002). The Circle of Life: Preserving American Indian Traditions and Facing the Nuclear Challenge. In J. Byrne, L. Glover and C. Martinez (Eds.), *Environmental Justice: Discourses in International Political Economy* (pp. 119 - 146). New Brunswick, NJ and London: Transaction Publishers.

Martinot, E., A. Chaurey, D. Lew, J. R. Moreira, and N. Wamukonya. (2002). Renewable energy markets in developing countries. *Annual Review of Energy and the Environment* 27, 309 - 348.

Martinot, E., and K. Reiche. (2000). Regulatory approaches to rural electrification and renewable energy: case studies from six developing countries. Washington, DC: World Bank.

McCully, P. (2001). *Silenced Rivers: The Ecology and Politics of Large Dams*. New York: Zed Books.

Medvedev, Z. (1992). *The Legacy of Chernobyl*. New York: W. W. Norton and Company.

Mumford, L. (1970). *The Pentagon of Power: The Myth of the Machine, Volume Two*. New York: Harcourt Brace Jovanovich, Inc.

Mumford, L. (1966). *Technics and Human Development: The Myth of the Machine, Volume One*. New York: Harcourt Brace Jovanovich, Inc.

Mumford, L. (1964). Authoritarian and Democratic Technics. In *Technology and Culture* (Vol. 5, pp. 1 - 8). Chicago, IL: University of Chicago Press.

Mumford, L. (1961). *The City in History: Its Origins, Its Transformations, and Its Prospects*. New York: Harcourt Brace Jovanovich, Inc.

Mumford, L. (1934). *Technics and Civilization*. New York: Harcourt Brace & Company. *New York Times*. (1955, August 7).

Nahajima, W. andVandenburg, W.H. (2005) A Failing Grade for the German End-of-Life Vehicles Take-Back System. Bulletin of Science, Technology and Society, 2512), 170-186.

New York Times. (1954, September 17).

Noble, D. F. (1983). Present Tense Technology: Technology's Politics. *Democracy*, 3(2), 8 - 24.

Nye, D. E. (1999). *Consuming Power: A Social History of American Energies*. Cambridge, MA: MIT Press.

Occidental Petroleum Corporation. (2005, April 4). Bringing New Energy to Energy Solutions. *Wall Street Journal*, R13.

O'Connor, M. (1994) *On the Misadventures of Capitalist Nature*. In M. O'Connor (Ed.), *Is Capitalism Sustainable?* (pp. 125-151) New Yrok: Guliand Press.

Ogden, J. M. (1999). Prospects for Building a Hydrogen Energy Infrastructure. *Annual Review of Energy and Environment*, 24: 227 – 279.

Oil Spill Intelligence Report. (2001). Oil Spills more than 10 Million Gallons.

Okubo, N. (2005). *PV-based Electrification for Sustainable Rural Livelihoods: A Case Study of Implementation Strategies in the Dominican Republic*. Unpublished Thesis. Newark, DE: Center for Energy and Environmental Policy, University of Delaware.

O'Toole, J. (1978). *Energy and Social Change*. Cambridge, MA: MIT Press.

Parfit, M. (2005, August). Future Power: Where Will the World Get its Next Energy Fix? *National Geographic, 208,* 2 - 31.

Perrow, C. (1984). *Normal Accidents: Living with High Risk Technologies*. New York: Basic Books.

Pollitt, Michael G. (1995). Ownership and Performance in Electric Utilities : The International Evidence on Privatization and Efficiency. Oxford, Oxford University Press.

Power Technology. (2005). Three Gorges Dam Hydroelectric Power Plant, China. Retrieved on October 13, 2005. Available at www.power-technology.com.

Rees, W., and Wackernagel, M. (1996). Urban Ecological Footprints: Why Cities Cannot be Sustainable – And Why They are a Key to Sustainability. *Environmental Impact Assessment Review, 16*: 223-248.

Reisner, M. (1993). *Cadillac Desert: The American West and Its Disappearing Water*. New York: Penguin.

Rifkin, J. (2003). *The Hydrogen Economy*. New York: Tarcher.

Roberts, J. T., and Thanos, N. D. (2003). Indigenous Peoples, Development Megaprojects, and Internet Resistance. In *Trouble in Paradise: Globalization and Environmental Crises in Latin America* (pp. 165 - 191). New York: Routledge.

Roosevelt, M. (2002, August 26). The Winds of Change. *Time.*

Roszak, T. (1972). *Where the Wasteland Ends: Politics and Transcendence in Postindustrial Society*. Garden City: Doubleday.

Sant, R. W. (1979). *The Least-Cost Energy Strategy*. Pittsburgh, PA: Carnegie Mellon University Press.

Sawin, J. (2004). *Mainstreaming Renewable Energy in the 21st Century*. Washington, DC: Worldwatch Institute.

Scheer, H. (2002). *The Solar Economy: Renewable Energy for a Sustainable Future*. London: Earthscan.

Schobert, H. H. (2001). *Energy and Society: An Introduction.* New York: Taylor and Francis Group.

Schumacher, E. F. (1973). *Small Is Beautiful: Economics as if People Mattered*. New York: Harper and Row.

Silberman, S. (2001, July). The Energy Web. *Wired, 9.07.*

Smil, V. (2003). *Energy at the Crossroads: Global Perspectives and Uncertainties*. Cambridge, MA: MIT Press.

Strong, S. (1999). New Photovoltaic Products Are Integrated into the Building Skin. *Architectural Record, 187*(12), 229.

Testa, K. (2004, February 16). Are Natural Gas Ships 'Boat Bombs' for Terror? *Associated Press.*

Tester, J. W., Drake, E. M., Golay, M. W., Driscoll, M. J., and Peters, W. A. (2005). *Sustainable Energy: Choosing Among Options*. Cambridge, MA: MIT Press.

The Economist. (2005, September 29). The Power of Spin. *The Economist.*

The Economist. (1986, March 29). The Charm of Nuclear Power. *The Economist.*

Toly, N. J. (2005). A Tale of Two Regimes: Instrumentality and Commons Access. *Bulletin of Science, Technology, and Society, 25*(1), 26 – 36.

Tompkins, J. (2005, October 1). Wind Power Reconsidered. *Popular Science.*

Totten, M., Pandya, S. I., and Janson-Smith, T. (2003). Biodiversity, Climate, and the Kyoto Protocol: Risks and Opportunities. *Frontiers in Ecology and the Environment, 1*(5), 262 - 270.

Uranium Information Center. (2005). Australia's Uranium. Retrieved October 14, 2005. Available at www.uic.com.au.

Vaitheeswaran, V. (2003). *Power to the People: How the Coming Energy Revolution Will Transform an Industry, Change Our Lives, and Maybe Even Save the Planet.* New York: Farrar, Straus and Giroux.

Vanderburg, W. H. (2005). *Living in the Labyrinth of Technology.* Toronto: University of Toronto Press.

Victor, D. G. (2005). *The Collapse of the Kyoto Protocol and the Struggle to Slow Global Warming.* Princeton, NJ: Princeton University Press.

Weinberg, A. (1985). *The Second Nuclear Era: A New Start for Nuclear Power.* New York: Praeger.

Weinberg, A. (1972). Social Institutions and Nuclear Energy. *Science, 177*: 27 – 34.

Winner, L. (1986). *The Whale and the Reactor.* Chicago, IL: University of Chicago Press.

Winner, L. (1977). *Autonomous Technology: Technics Out-of-Control as a Theme in Political Thought.* Cambridge, MA: The MIT Press.

World Bank (2004a). Power's Promise: Electricity Reforms in Eastern Europe and Central Asia. Washington, DC: World Bank.

World Bank (2004b). *Sustainable Energy: Less Poverty, More Profits.* Washington, DC: World Bank.

World Bank (2003). *Private Sector Development in the Electric Power Sector.* Washington, DC: Operations Evaluation Department, World Bank.

World Bank (1993). *The World Bank's Role in the Electric Power Sector : Policies for Effective Institutional, Regulatory, and Financial Reform.* Washington, DC, World Bank.

Worster, D. (1992). *Rivers of Empire: Water, Aridity, and the Growth of the American West.* Oxford: Oxford University Press.

Yergin, D., and Stoppard, M. (2003). The Next Prize. *Foreign Affairs, 82*(6): 110 – 121.

Energy and Poverty

2

Energy, Economy, and Poverty: The Past and Present Debate

Joan Martinez-Alier

Human Uses of Energy

One fundamental notion of human ecology and ecological economics is the distinction—first noted by A. J. Lotka (1911)—between the endosomatic use of energy (as food) and the exosomatic use of energy as fuel for cooking and heating and as power for the artefacts and machines produced by human culture. While the differences in the direct use of food energy are small, the differences among humans in the exosomatic use of energy may be on the order of one to one hundred. All humans are biologically programmed to eat a certain amount of food per day that has been expressed in kilocalories since around 1,860. One person may eat the equivalent of between 1,500 and 2,500 kcal per day. Since one calorie is equal to 4.18 joules, a daily food intake of 2,400 kcal is equal to 10 MJ (megajoules), a convenient round number. A person five or ten times richer than the average of his/her society is not for this reason going to consume five or ten times the food energy. This is not a matter of taste or inscrutable preference. Simply, human metabolism does not allow such energy intake. Indirectly, however, if the diet becomes based on meat products, the food chains are longer and more energy is consumed. But even then, the human stomach has limited capacity. In some cultures, being some-what fat is still a desirable social attribute, as poor people have difficulties in getting the minimum amount of food energy; indeed, some starve for lack of calories or malnutrition. In affluent societies almost nobody starves, and indeed poor people are (as in the United States) fatter on average than rich people—probably the first time this has happened in human history. How-ever, neither rich nor poor can consume more food energy per day than their bio-metabolism allows as the resulting obesity would lead to illness. Econo-mists have long noticed that the proportion of total expenditure going to food decreases with income—an observation codified in Engel's law. In other words, the income-elasticity of demand for food is low, and quickly becomes zero, although for some particular types of food (and drink) it might be quite high. For some foods (potatoes, bread, manioc), income-elasticity of demand quickly becomes negative.

Regarding the exosomatic use of energy, there is no biological limit. Over the course of history, humans have developed many artefacts and machines that use energy for production or amusement. This energy usually comes from the sun. Biomass accumulated by photosynthesis is used as food energy and in large amounts for exosomatic use as cooking fuels (fuelwood, charcoal); it is transformed by animals into dung used for fertilizers or for domestic fuel; sugar cane is used as bagasso fuel in sugar mills or as ethanol for cars; wood is used for building and carpentry or for paper. Exosomatic energy may also derive from other sources: coal, oil or gas represent the fossil fuels while windmills and waterfalls represent renewable sources. Atomic fission in nuclear power stations and geothermal generation represent still more sources. Since the Industrial Revolution, the fossil fuels have dominated energy statistics in affluent countries, and now represent the most significant source of energy in the world at large.

However, contrary to widespread belief, during the twentieth century there has not been a substitution of oil and gas, nuclear power and hydroelectricity, for biomass and coal at the world level. Such substitution took place in the United States, Western Europe and the United Kingdom after 1960, but in the world in general all energy sources have increased in the twentieth century. New sources add to the supply of energy, they do not substitute for the old sources. About six times more mineral coal was extracted in 2000 than in 1900 (McNeill, 2000). The human population grew by a factor of four in the twentieth century and biomass must have increased by a similar factor, given that less fuelwood and charcoal is used in some parts of the world but also that diets have become more meat-based in the rich countries and that many more people are cooking with wood, charcoal or dung in 2005 than in 1900 because of population growth. There are about twice as many poor peasants and rural laborers in the world today as one hundred years ago, though the number will substantially decrease in the twenty-first century if the Chinese and Indian economic growth rates (fuelled by coal, oil and gas) continue. Even so, some urban inhabitants are also still cooking with wood or charcoal, thus maintaining significant biomass use. Such uses will be discussed in detail in a later section.

While the endosomatic energy consumption of one well-fed person is 10 MJ per day and therefore 3.65 GJ per year, the exosomatic use of energy varies very much. Poor people use some energy for cooking (perhaps more than for eating, if they cook in open fires), some energy to feed domestic animals (one or two cows per family), and some for making clothes and repairing habitations. They might have a pump for the well, if they are better off—if not, they will use human work to get water, such work being a transformation of the food energy intake. They will also do some travel in overcrowded buses or trains. Altogether, perhaps another 5 or 6 GJ of energy per person/year will be used exosomatically. (We are not counting here the warmth provided directly by the sun and indeed the other environmental services, such as the rain and the carbon cycle, driven by solar energy.) In order to increase their standard of living, poor people must increase their exosomatic energy use—even in rich countries some poor people cannot warm themselves enough in winter due to so-called 'fuel-poverty.'

Consider now a citizen of a rich suburb, going to work every day by car, driving 50 km (25 each way) and using at least 3 liters of petrol (30,000 kcal). For this travel to work, alone—not counting Sunday outings or holidays and leaving aside all the energy used for other purposes or spent in the manufacture of commodities purchased—the expenditure of energy is over ten times more than the direct food energy intake of a well fed person.

In poor countries, food energy is a substantial part of the total use of energy—on the order of one-half or one-third. In other words, the exosomatic/endosomatic energy ratio (Giampietro, 2003) is two or three to one. In the wealthiest countries of the European Union, the energy use per person per year is of the order of 200 GJ; it is higher in the United States where the exosomatic/endosomatic ratio can exceed 100.

The unequal exosomatic use of energy largely explains the differences in per capita emissions of carbon dioxide, and therefore explains the international conflict over the property rights to carbon sinks (oceans, soils, new vegetation) and the atmosphere as a temporary reservoir. This conflict has been interpreted as a contested "carbon debt" from rich to poor on the assumption that all humans have the same rights to the oceans and to the atmosphere (Agarwal and Narain, 1991).

Social Metabolism: A Brief Intellectual History

There has been a historic divorce between the economists' approach to energy as just one sector of the economy, and a "socio-metabolic" view of the economy in terms of the study of the flow of energy and materials. Both the Marxist perspective and the neoclassical perspective will be considered here.

In the 1970s, a physical point of view, emphasizing the flows of materials and energy, emerged among coherent research groups studying human society and economy. Some authors wrote histories of the use of energy in the economy (Cipolla,1974; Sieferle, 1982; Debeir, Deléage, Hémery, 1986; Hall, Cleveland, Kaufman, 1986; McNeill, 2000). The notion of energy return on energy input (EROI) was applied to the economy by Charles Hall and other ecologists. Now, authors working on "industrial metabolism" (Ayres, 1989) or "social metabolism" (Fischer-Kowalski, 1998) look at the economy in terms of flows of energy and materials. At a macro level, such studies have shown that economic growth follows a parallel path to the use of energy in the economy (counting the energy as "physical work output as distinguished from energy (exergy)") (R. U. Ayres and Warr, 2002).

Earlier approaches also accounted for this relationship. A recent rediscovery of Marx's social metabolism has highlighted his contribution (Foster, 2000). We know that Marx introduced after 1857-1858 and in *Capital* (1867) the notion of "metabolism" between humans and nature. Alfred Schmidt (1978) explained the role of the concept of *Stoffwechsel* (metabolism) in Marx's work on the development of capitalism, noting Moleschott's and Liebig's influence (Schmidt, 1978: 86-9; Martinez-Alier with Shlüpmann, 1987: 220-6).[1] Liebig was one of the founders of agricultural chemistry and was associated with a future leading sector of the economy, the fertilizer industry. He may also be associated with an ecological vision as he is recognized as one of the founders of ecology, before the name itself was invented (Kormondy, 1965). Politically he developed an argument against latifundist agriculture and agricultural exports because the plant nutrients would not return to the soil. Instead, he favored small-scale agriculture and dispersed settlements. Marx quoted this opinion favorably on several occasions. Marx wrote to Engels on 13 February 1866 stating that Liebig's agricultural chemistry was more important for the discussion on decreasing returns than all economic arguments taken together. However, Marx dismissed the notion of decreasing returns in agriculture, pointing out in the context of his praise for Liebig's agricultural chemistry and its promise of artificial fertilizers that it did not make sense to assume that the agricultural produce of Britain would increase in a diminishing ratio to the increase of the laborers' employed, because in practice there was at the time both an increase in production and an absolute decrease in the number of laborers (*Capital*, I, chapter 13). Clearly, Marx was not worried about crises of subsistence.

The link between material metabolism (*Stoffwechsel*, exchanges of materials) and the flow of energy at the level of cells and organisms was made in the 1840s. It was then also understood that agriculture could be represented in terms of changes in the flow of energy and not only as an intervention in the cycling of plant nutrients (Mayer, 1845, used *Stoffwechsel* for energy flow). Metabolism was therefore used not only for materials, but also for energy (Haberl, 2001). Of course, while materials could be recycled, energy could not. The theory of the direction of the flow of energy was developed after 1850 and the establishment of the Second Law of Thermodynamics. Marx and Engels were interested in energy. For instance, Engels wrote to Marx on 14 July 1858 commenting on Joule's work on the conservation of energy (of 1840) as something well known to them. Marx was interested in new sources of energy: Hydrogen had already been discussed as a source of energy and Marx wrote to Engels on 2 April 1866 that a certain M. Rebour had found the means of separating the oxygen from hydrogen in water for very little expense.

At a more general level, one interesting point arises from Engels' unwillingness to understand how the First and Second Laws could apply at the same time: the "dialectics of nature" failed him there. Engels became aware of Clausius' concept of entropy and wrote to Marx (21 March 1869): "In Germany the conversion of the natural forces, for instance, heat into mechanical energy, etc. has given rise to a very absurd theory—that the world is becoming steadily colder...and that, in the end, a moment will come when all life will be impossible...I am simply waiting for the moment when the clerics seize upon this theory." Indeed, both the clerics and W. Thomson (Lord Kelvin) brandished the Second Law, the latter in religious tirades about "heat death," although he could have had no inkling of nuclear fusion as the sun's source of energy. Josef Popper-Lynkeus (1838-1921), who with Ernst Mach became one of the sources of inspiration for the anti-metaphysical philosophy of the Vienna Circle, complained in 1876 about W. Thomson's "theological handling of Carnot's law" (Martinez-Alier with Schlüpmann, 1887: 197). However, Engels' dislike of the Second Law was not only motivated by its religious use, or abuse. He believed it would be transcended as ways would be found to re-use the heat irradiated into space.

Another interesting point is Engels' 1882 reaction (in letters to Marx) to Podolinsky's work (Marx and Engels, 1976). Podolinsky had studied, we might say, the entropy law and the economic process, and he tried unsuccessfully to convince Marx that their relationship could be brought into Marxist analysis. Politically he was not a Marxist, he was a Ukrainian federalist narodnik. He had critiziced Marx's overpowering behavior at the Congress of the International of 1872, praising instead the anarchist James Guillaume. However, he himself saw his work on the energetics of agriculture as a contribution to Marxism. Writing to Marx on 8 April 1880, he said: "With particular impatience I wait for your opinion on my attempt to bring surplus labour and the current physical theories into harmony." In his article (published in long versions in Russian in 1880 and in German in 1883, and in short French and Italian versions in 1880 and 1881, respectively)[2] Podolinsky started by explaining the laws of energetics, quoting from Clausius that although the energy of the Universe was a constant, there was a tendency toward the dissipation of energy or, in Clausius' terminology, there was a tendency for entropy to reach a maximum. Podolinsky did not discuss explicitly the difference in thermodynamics between open, closed and isolated systems, although he stated explicitly, as the starting point of his analysis, that at the present time the Earth was receiving enormous quantities of energy from the sun, and would do so for a very long time. All physical and biological phenomena were expressions of the transformations of energy. He did not enter into the controversies regarding the creation of the Universe and its "heat-death," nor did he discuss the relations on Earth between thermodynamics and the theory of evolution. He certainly realized that the availability of energy was a crucial consideration for the increase (or decrease) of population. However, he thought that the distribution of production was explained by the relations between social classes: "in the countries where capitalism triumphs, a great part of work goes toward the production of luxury goods, that is to say, toward a gratuitous dissipation of energy instead of toward increasing the availability of energy." Podolinsky knew that the energy available for humankind came mainly from the sun, giving figures for the solar constant. He explained how coal and oil, wind energy and water power were transformations of solar energy, mentioning tides as another possible source of energy. He then started his analysis of the energetics of agriculture, remarking that only a very small proportion of solar energy was assimilated by plants.

He explained that plants assimilated energy, and animals fed on plants and degraded energy. This formed the *Kreislauf des Lebens*: "We have in front of us two parallel processes which together form the so-called circle of life. Plants have the property of accumulating solar energy, but the animals, when they feed on vegetable substances, transform a part of this saved energy and dissipate this energy into space. If the quantity of energy accumulated by plants is greater than that dispersed by animals, then stocks of energy appear, for instance in the period when mineral coal was formed, during which vegetable life was preponderant over animal life. If, on the contrary, animal life were preponderant, the provision of energy would be quickly dispersed and animal life would have to go back to the limits determined by vegetable wealth. So, a certain equilibrium would have to be built between the accumulation and the dissipation of energy." Human labor also had the virtue of retarding the dissipation of energy, achieving this primarily by agriculture, although the work of a tailor, a shoemaker or a builder would also qualify, in Podolinsky's view, as productive work, affording "protection against the dissipation of energy into space."

Through agricultural activity, human work and the work of animals driven by humans were able to increase the availability of energy. This he showed by comparing the productivity of different types of land use taking statistics from France (he was living at the time in Montpellier). Table 2.1 summarizes his data (see Martinez-Alier with Schlüpmann, 1987: 48, for information on sources). Podolinsky compared wheat agriculture, sown pastures, forest and natural pastures, concluding that production was higher when there was an input of human and animal work. Thus, comparing wheat agriculture to natural pastures, each kcal put in contributed to an increase of 22 kcal of production. If forests were taken as the terms of comparison, the energy productivity of human and domestic animals work was even higher. Notice that Podolinsky was counting human and animal work, that is, not the food intake but the work done. He did not include solar radiation in the input of energy, because he was writing as an ecological economist and solar radiation is indeed a free gift of nature (moreover without an owner so that there is no payment of rent). Podolinsky concluded that work could increase the "accumulation of energy on earth."

Table 2.1

Annual Production, and Energy Input (Only Work by Humans and Domestic Animals) Per Hectare, Averages for France in 1870, According to Podolinsky

	Production (kg)	Production (kcal)	Energy input (kcal)
Forest	900 (dried wood)	2,295,000	Nil
Natural pastures	2,500 (hay)	6,375,000	Nil
Sown pastures	3,100 (hay, excluding seed)	7,905,000	37,450 (50 horse-hours and 80 man-hours)
Wheat	800 (wheat) and 2,000 (straw) (excluding seed)	8,100,000	77,500 (100 horse-hours and 200 man-hours)

Energy values of wood, hay and straw, 2,550 kcal/kg, of wheat 3,750 kcal/kg. Hours of work converted into kcal: 645 kcal/hour of horse-work, 65 kcal/hour of man-work.

Although Podolinsky mentioned guano, and although he must have been keenly aware of the war then raging for Peruvian or Chilean saltpeter (one early bulk commodity), he did not subtract from the output, or include in the input, the energy contents and cost of fertilizer. Nor did he consider the energy spent by steam engines for use in threshing. His methodology is nevertheless basically the same as that used later for establishing the energy balance of particular crops, or for small-scale societies, or for the entire agricultural sector of particular countries (Rappaport, 1967; H.T. Odum, 1971; D. Pimentel and M. Pimentel, et al. 1973; 1979; Leach, 1975; Fluck and Baird, 1980).

Podolinsky then went on to explain the capacity of the human organism to do work, apart from which "it would be difficult to explain the accumulation of energy on the surface of the earth under the influence of labour." Quoting from Hirn and Helmholtz, he concluded correctly that "man has the capacity to transform one-fifth of the energy gained from food into muscular work," remarking that man was a more efficient transformer of energy than a steam engine. He then used a steam-engine metaphor to put across a general theoretical principle on the minimum natural conditions of human existence, from an energy point of view. He wrote that humanity was a "perfect machine" in Sadi Carnot's sense: "humanity is a machine that not only turns heat and other physical forces into work, but succeeds also in carrying out the inverse cycle, that is, it turns work into heat and other physical forces which are necessary to satisfy our needs, and, so to speak, with its own work turned into heat is able to heat its own boiler."

Now, for humanity to ensure its minimum conditions of existence (its endosomatic requirement, we would say today), each calorie of human work must then have a productivity of five calories. Taking into account that some (children and the elderly, for example) may not be able to work and that there are other energy needs apart from food energy, the necessary minimum productivity would be closer to ten or more. If that minimum is not achieved, then "scarcity appears and, many times, a reduction of population." Podolinsky then established the basis for a view of the economy in terms of energy social metabolism, looking at the energy return to energy input in a framework of reproduction of the social system. He thought that he had reconciled the physiocrats with the labor theory of value, although the physiocrats (in the eighteenth century) could not have seen the economy in terms of energy flow.

Podolinsky also emphasized the difference between using the flow of solar energy and the stock of energy in coal. The task of labor was to increase the accumulation of solar energy on earth, rather than the simple transformation into work of energy already accumulated on earth, more so since work done with coal was inevitably accompanied by a great dissipation of heat-energy into space. The energy productivity of a coalminer was much larger than that a primitive farmer could obtain, but this energy surplus from coal was transitory, and moreover (Podolinsky added in a footnote) there was a theory which linked climatic changes to concentrations of carbon dioxide in the atmosphere, as Sterry Hunt had explained at a meeting of the British Society for the Advancement of Science in the autumn of 1878. Podolinsky was not, however, at all pessimistic about the prospects for the economy, and he was hopeful for the direct use of solar energy for industrial purposes, referring to the "solar engine of M. Mouchot" (Mouchot, 1879). One could envisage that one day solar energy would be used directly to make chemical syntheses of nutritive substances, bypassing agriculture. Thus, a proper discussion of the demographic question had to account for "the relations between the general quantity of energy on earth and the quantity of humans who live on it." This was a more relevant consideration, in his explicit view, than the Malthusian prognosis. He was also hoping (as he had written to Marx on 30 March 1880, sending his work to him) to develop applications of his energy accounts to different forms or modes of production.

Podolinsky's work is relevant not only in the Marxist context. He had a short life but he left a trace in Ukrainian federalist politics (as a friend of

Drahomanov) and also in the Narodnik movement against the Russian autocracy. He was trained as a medical doctor and physiologist and his work on energy and the economy received Vernadsky's approval. In a section of *La Geochimie*, Vernadsky wrote about several authors (among them Felix Auerbach, with his notion of *Ektropismus*, and John Joly) who had explained that life was a process that reversed or slowed down the dissipation of energy. He then wrote a memorable phrase assessing Podolinsky's contribution: "Podolinsky had studied the energetics of life and tried to apply his findings to the study of the economy" (Vernadsky, 1924: 334-5).

The link between the use of energy and human culture, in the form of "social energetics" (without historical statistical work) became well established and debated in Europe around 1900. Some Marxist authors (e.g., Bogdanov, 1873-1928; Bukharin, 1888-1938) adopted this outlook, and their work has been seen (Susiluoto, 1982) as an anticipation of Bertalanffy's systems theory which grew out of the links between thermodynamics and biology. But, to repeat, there is no line of ecological Marxist history based on quantitative studies of material and energy social metabolism. Moreover, Lenin wrote a diatribe against Ostwald's social energetics in the context of his polemics against Bogdanov and against Mach's "empiriocriticism" (Martinez-Alier with Schlüpmann, 1987: 225-8). This was before the October Revolution of 1917. Afterward, Lenin's ill-considered remarks became sacred to the faithful. Thus, on the occasion of the publication of Engels' *Dialectics of Nature* in 1925 (out of drafts and notes he had left behind) on the thirtieth anniversary of his death, Otto Jenssen printed once again Engels' critical letters to Marx on Podolinsky (first published in 1919), and explained that Engels had anticipated a critique of Ostwald's social energetics even before Ostwald himself appeared on the scene (Jenssen, 1925: 13). Marxism, therefore, has had a historically ambivalent relationship with the study of energy-society relations.

Otto Neurath's Naturalrechnung

In my view, an important contribution to the biophysical approach to the economy was made later, in the first half of the twentieth century, by Otto Neurath (1882-1945). A famous logical empiricist philosopher of the Vienna Circle, he was also an economist or economic historian, and a Marxist in at least two senses. First, he defended a democratically planned economy based on physical accounting in energy and material (*Naturalrechnung*); in this he was influenced by Popper-Lynkeus' and Ballod-Atlanticus' quantitative, realistic "utopias." In the so-called Socialist Calculation debate of 1919 and following years, Neurath introduced the idea of incommensurable values in the economy (hence the recent interest in his work taken by ecological economists—see, for example, Martinez-Alier with Schlüpmann, 1987; O'Neill,

1993; Martinez-Alier, Munda and O'Neill, 1998; O'Neill, 2002). Second, in the context of the Vienna Circle's project of the Encyclopedia of Unified Science of the 1930s and 1940s, he defended a dialectical view of history (although he did not like the word "dialectics") as putting together the findings of the different sciences regarding concrete processes or events. The findings of one science, collected in the Encyclopedia, with regard to one particular process or event, should not be contradicted by the findings or assumptions of another science also present in the Encyclopedia. An attempt at reconciliation or removal of the contradiction should be attempted. "Consilience" (to use today's Edward Wilson's word) should be the rule of the Encyclopedia.

Neurath's preoccupation was the object of critique by market liberals. Hayek's especially strong criticism against "social engineering" (1952) was directed, as John O'Neill has put it, "at the whole tradition which attempts to understand the ways in which economic institutions and relations are embedded within the physical world and have real physical preconditions, and which is consequently critical of economic choices founded upon purely monetary valuation." Hayek implicitly criticized the view of the economy in terms of "social metabolism." While Patrick Geddes, Wilhelm Ostwald, Frederick Soddy and Lewis Mumford were all rudely dismissed by Hayek, it is the work of Otto Neurath that was the primary target of Hayek's criticism.

Hayek was not alone, as Max Weber had also reserved great criticism for Neurath in *Economy and Society* (1909). More significant, however, were Weber's polemics against Wilhelm Ostwald in 1909. Ostwald (who was a well known chemist) was trying to interpret human history in terms of energy use. He proposed two simple laws, which are not untrue, and which might act in opposite directions. First, the growth of the economy implied the use of more energy, and the substitution of new forms of energy for human energy. Second, this came together with a trend toward higher efficiency in the transformation of energy. Weber (1909) wrote a famous, ironic review—much praised by Hayek in the 1940s—of Ostwald's position, insisting on a separation between the sciences; chemists, he thought, should not write on economic history. Max Weber's basic point (Martinez-Alier with Schlüpmann, 1987, chapter 12) was that economic decisions by entrepreneurs on new industrial processes or new products were based on monetary costs and prices. It could so happen that a production process was less efficient in energy terms and nevertheless it would be adopted because it was cheaper. Thus, energy accounting was irrelevant to economics. It must be said that Weber did not question energy prices as we would today in accounting for inter-generational allocation of exhaustible resources and local or global externalities.

Ostwald influenced many authors, among them Henry Adams (1838-1918) who proposed a "law of acceleration" of the use of (final) energy: "the coal output of the world, speaking roughly, doubled every ten years between 1840 and 1900, in the form of utilized power, for the ton of coal yielded three or four times as much power in 1900 as in 1840." It is worthwhile pointing out that from the liberal camp, Karl Popper, in his polemic against Marxist laws of history, *The Poverty of Historicism*, thought it worthwhile to attack also Adams in a footnote, without even mentioning the word "energy," because Adams had dared to propose a historical law. Adams, though, was certainly not a Marxist; he was a Bostonian aristocrat who thought the world would probably come to a bad end socially and technologically.

Ostwald's influence extended to anthropologist Leslie White (1943, 1959), who, also inspired by evolutionary anthropologists Morgan and Taylor, wrote on energy and the evolution of culture. He highlighted the evolution of capacities for harnessing energy in increasing magnitudes and in various forms, in a dialectical framework between the technological (defined by the availability and the efficiency in the transformation of energy), the social (in terms of Marxist "relations of production"), and the cultural-symbolic systems.

In analyses of the relationship between energy and economy, Marx's doubts on the benefits of economic growth, clearly expressed in his ecological critique of capitalist agriculture, were not forgotten, although the technological optimists, who believed in the development of the productive forces, predominated. One of most influential Marxist technological optimists of the twentieth century was the historian of science J.D. Bernal. In the 1950s, he was totally in favor of the "civil" use of nuclear energy, of which Lewis Mumford was a notable critic (Thomas, et al. 1956: 1147). Mumford, described by Ramachandra Guha as the "forgotten American environmentalist" ("forgotten" in comparison to G.P. Marsh, John Muir, Gifford Pinchot, Aldo Leopold, and Rachel Carson), was intellectual an heir to Patrick Geddes, William Morris and John Ruskin—he was not of the Marxist tradition.

Patrick Geddes and Ecologically Unequal Exchange

Lewis Mumford's mentor, Patrick Geddes (1854-1932), a biologist and urban planner, early on attacked the arguments of neoclassical economists such as Walras because they did not account for flows of energy, materials and waste (Martinez-Alier with Schlüpmann, 1987, chapter 6); but he did not discuss Marx. Geddes (1885) proposed the construction of a sort of input-output table inspired by the *Tableau Economique* of the Physiocrat François Quesnay. The first column would contain the sources of energy as well as the sources of materials that are used, not for their potential energy, but for their other properties. Energy and materials were transformed into products through four stages: extraction, manufacture, transport and exchange. Estimates were needed of the losses (dissipation and disintegration) required at each stage. The quantity of the final product (or "net" product, in physiocratic terms) might seem surprisingly small in proportion to the gross quantity of potential product. However, the losses at each stage were not accounted for in economic terms. The final product was not added value at all. It was the value remaining from the energy and materials available at the beginning once they had been through all stages.

Geddes' scheme is relevant to the attempt by several authors today to develop a theory of ecologically unequal exchange between the metropolitan centers and the world peripheries. In neoclassical economics, provided that markets are competitive and ruled by supply and demand, there cannot be unequal exchange. This could only arise from monopoly or monopsony conditions, non-internalized externalities, or excessive discounting of the future. In an ecological economic theory of unequal exchange, one could say that the greater the portion of original exergy (available energy or "productive potential" in the exported raw materials) that has been dissipated in producing the final products or services (in the metropolis), the higher the prices of these products or services (Hornborg, 1998; Naredo and Valero, 1999). This was indeed implied by Geddes with different words. Thus, Hornborg concludes, "market prices are the means by which world system centres extract exergy from the peripheries," sometimes helped, one must say, by military power.

At the beginning of European colonization, the goods imported were what Immanuel Wallerstein called "preciosities," such as gold, silver and pepper. The means of transport at the time were such that other more bulky trade was not possible. Indeed, such goods, diamonds for instance, of high economic value per kilogram, are still very much sought after. Their ecological and social rucksacks are enormous: their effects on the social metabolism and the human livelihood of the exporting countries might be terrible, but the goods themselves are marginal for the direct social metabolism of the importing countries. Some "preciosities," such as sugar, later became bulk commodities significant to the social metabolism of importing countries. Sidney Mintz showed the role of sugar in providing cheap calories for feeding the English working class (Mintz, 1985). Other bulk commodities—guano and Chilean saltpeter between 1840 and 1914, iron ore, copper and other metals, and certainly oil and gas today—also became essential for the social metabolism of importing countries. In this sense, Europe has never been so colonialist as today. Gasoline stations on German motorways should have signs reading "Kolonialwaren."

The metropolitan centers import far more materials (in tons) than they export. The United States now imports more than half the oil it consumes, on the order of 10 mbd of oil—about 500 million tons per year or 2 tons per person/year of oil imports. In fact, a large part of the exported/imported materials are the so-called "energy carriers" (oil, coal, gas). In the nineteenth and early twentieth centuries, the countries of today's European Union largely depended on their own coal and biomass as a source of energy; now the

European Union is a large net importer of fossil fuels. Taking all materials together (energy carriers, minerals, metals, biomass), the European Union is importing about four times more material than it is exporting. Meanwhile, Latin America appears to be exporting six times more than it imports (Giljum and Eisenmenger, 2004). Pérez Rincon (2004) calculated that Colombia's exports per year are about 70 million tons, of which a substantial part is coal and oil, while imports are 10 million tons. So, in Latin America, there is a need for a new "ecological Prebisch"[3] who would theorize the economic policies appropriate to such a situation in terms of "natural capital depletion taxes" and claims for the repayment of the "ecological debt" because of "ecologically unequal trade" since prices do not take into account exhaustion of resources, negative externalities, or the accumulation of a "carbon debt." Of course, this might be applied to other regions, as well. But countries of high population density in Asia whose economies are rapidly growing, are probably becoming large net importers of oil, gas and other bulk commodities. Ecologically unequal exchange would be relevant among regions inside China and India, but perhaps no longer externally.

Fuel Poverty as a Cause of Deforestation

There are people so poor around the world that they have difficulty in getting enough food to eat; and they may be so poor, that even when they have food, they lack the fuel to cook it. This is energy poverty, a condition with significant social and environmental implications. In principle, compared to using fossil fuels, using biomass for cooking is a good idea because the biomass grows again capturing carbon dioxide, while the fossil fuels release by combustion the carbon that was safely trapped under the earth in biomass produced a very long time ago.

In the trajectory from biomass to hydrocarbons, there seems to be a 'natural' and universal hierarchy in the use of domestic fuel (Foley, 1985). As income increases, wood, charcoal and dung are replaced by kerosene and butane gas or LPG (in bottles), which are in turn replaced by piped gas or electricity. Pricing policies may accelerate this process or slow it down.[4] In my view, appropriate pricing policies favoring the distribution of LPG are important measures to take in meeting the needs of the poor and the environment. The World Bank is against subsidizing LPG and in favor of social reforestation programs. However, it would be scandalous if a deforestation crisis were to occur in a dry region of an oil exporting country such as Mexico, Ecuador or Nigeria because rural families were too poor to buy LPG.

Such deforestation is not always caused by poverty, nor is it always caused by cooking needs. In Central America, deforestation was very fast in the 1960s and 1970s, the main reason was land clearance for cattle ranching, encouraged by easy access to subsidized credit and the protected U.S. meat market. In Brazil today, one main cause of deforestation is the expansion of the soybean frontier. In South-East Asia, rapid deforestation has been caused by exporters of tropical hardwoods. In many coastal tropical countries, mangrove forests disappear because of the shrimp export industry. However, in some arid regions of Asia, Africa and Latin America, one reason for deforestation remains the use of firewood or charcoal as fuel by the poor.

Demand for such fuel destroys forests near villages and towns in many countries, and the loss of trees leads to increasing erosion. Where dried dung is used instead of firewood, soil fertility is lost and harvests are reduced. This is less common in Latin America than in Asia or Africa, partly because the contribution of dung and firewood to total energy consumption is lower, and partly because the depletion of forest resources that would leave the population without firewood is not as great a problem in the humid tropical regions. In Latin America the main threat to forests is "colonization." Forests are being cut down faster than they can regenerate, and the valuable wood is burnt on the spot or left to rot. Other enemies of the forests are cattle ranching and logging (only species such as mahogany are extracted, but at the cost of widespread devastation), and the building of roads into forests for the purposes of oil extraction or mining, prime examples of export pressure on resources. Exacerbating the destruction, new settlers then use such roads to access and colonize the forest.

The resulting lack of firewood is a problem in only a few regions of Latin America, basically in arid or semi-arid regions like the Andes, the coastal regions of Peru, the *sertôes* in Brazil, and parts of Central America. The Peruvian and Bolivian mountains suffer a high risk of becoming deserts with an acute shortage of firewood (Harrison, 1984: 30). In some areas of the Andes, trees like *Polylepis* and *Buddleia* were almost wiped out and the last resort was the collection of dung for fuel. The use of dung for fuel is common in Asia, the Middle East, and Africa, where an estimated 400 million tons of dung are burnt per year, each ton implying the loss of 50 kg of cereal yield (Dourojeanni, 1982: 340). Poverty fosters the further destruction of tree cover, in turn affecting the water cycle and leading to soil erosion, while the use of dung as an alternative fuel for cooking or heating promotes the loss of soil fertility. Herdsman and peasants living in the mountains of Peru and Bolivia have not yet been able to afford LPG and must use dung for fuel (Godoy, 1984; Winterhalder et al. 1974). In this case, the economy is closed to external energy flow due to the lack of hard cash to pay for it.

Estimated consumption of firewood may be about 750 kg per person per year (Foley, 1985: 256). Since the energy of the firewood consumed per person is twice the energy consumed as food, this may lead to great pressures on resources in densely populated areas. Like most medium-income regions, there is a long term tendency in Central America toward the replacement of firewood by kerosene or bottled gas, which was temporarily halted by the rise in oil prices after 1973 and 1979 (Leonard, 1987: 62). In Costa Rica, a rainy and mountainous country, cooking with hydroelectricity is common and deforestation is not caused by the collection of firewood for cooking. The causes of deforestation in Costa Rica have been quite different.

In some countries or regions, domestic demand for firewood or dung cannot be satisfied without reducing food production. A higher price for firewood may increase the territory for growing trees, almost in the same way that a higher price for oil may stimulate exploration for new reserves. However, as there is the Hubbert curve for oil, also the availability of land for forestry cannot be increased beyond a certain limit. Despite successful social forestry and biogas programs in many countries (including India), the pressure remains. If firewood, charcoal and dung were replaced by LPG, the surplus demand would be easily manageable. The quantity of LPG necessary is much less than that of the energy equivalent of firewood or dung substituted, because stoves that use LPG are more efficient. In this particular case, increasing incomes lead to a decrease in exosomatic energy use, as large quantities of firewood can be replaced by small quantities of fossil fuel.

Social preference for LPG as domestic fuel is undeniable, and is due to cleanliness, time and effort saved in collecting wood and in cooking, and lower amounts of indoor pollution than those caused by burning firewood, charcoal or dung. Assuming that the annual use is about 500 kg of firewood per person, with an energy content equivalent to 0.35 tons of oil per ton of firewood, and if we take into account the greater efficiency of stoves that use LPG (compared to modern firewood stoves with an efficiency of 15 percent or less, LPG stoves have an efficiency of 40 to 50 percent), we conclude that LPG cooking for three billion poor people in the world, would amount to about 200 million tons of oil (4 mbd). This is about five times Spain's annual consumption of oil, or one-fifth of U.S. consumption. Oil is cheap enough for rich people—it is taxed after it is imported (heavily taxed in Europe and Japan), and even then it is used in large quantities in rich countries—but it is too expensive to be used a domestic fuel by the poor.

Perhaps oil and gas should be taxed not after they are imported into rich countries but at the point of extraction ("natural capital depletion taxes" and taxes to compensate for local and global externalities). Such taxes (collected perhaps by a UN agency) should be recycled toward environmental and social purposes (renewable energies and the struggle against "fuel poverty" and other forms of poverty).

It is not in the interests of the rich countries for the poor countries to attain comparable levels of per capita consumption—not only in the kitchen but in all spheres of life, including private transport in cars. Using present technologies, this would lead to a dramatic increase in the rate of depletion of oil and gas, and would greatly increase local and global pollution problems. But here we are discussing a different problem. Poverty causes deforestation because the poor are not able to ascend the hierarchy of domestic fuel use. However, the impact on world oil demand if firewood (and dung) were replaced by oil products would be manageably small.

Urban Lifelines

Such transitions, however, carry other social implications. Ascending the energy ladder often includes increasing commercialization of energy supplies. And in a context of increasing liberalization, there is a worldwide claim against increased water and electricity prices that urban poor people cannot afford, after such services are privatized. Environmental groups in Latin America have developed the idea of a *piso de dignidad*: a dignity floor or a dignity line equal to minimum livelihood requirements. Poor people have a right to increase consumption up to this "dignity line," while rich people should diminish their consumption in order not to exceed their fair environmental space. This is a concept of environmental justice that goes beyond a concern with the disproportionate social distribution of environmental damage. It adopts the perspective of environmental human rights in the sense that all must have access to such livelihood resources.

In South Africa, a demand for a free "lifeline" of 50 liters of water per person/day, plus 1 kwh per household/day, was put forward by social movements in Soweto and other townships in Johannesburg (Bond, 2002) which at the same time complained against the energy and minerals export strategy of the government and also its water policy of cheap prices for large industries and rich consumers. Therefore, a preoccupation with the satisfaction of human needs spills over into interrogation of the market economy from an environmental point of view. This concern motivated the march from the township of Alexandra to Sandton in Johannesburg in August 2002 during the WSSD, trying to awaken the official UN conference, so dominated by international corporations, to livelihood issues.

Consorting with activists is a great source of knowledge regarding such issues. In September 2003, a year after marching from Alexandra to Sandton, I had the chance to attend a three-day meeting on Environmental Rights and Human Rights in Cartagena, Colombia, in advance of the general assembly of Friends of the Earth. One of the speakers was Duduzile Mphenyeke, an activist from Soweto where, as in the impoverished barrios of Cartagena called Nelson Mandela, El Pozón, Olaya Herrera and La Boquilla, people go on the street to complain against the cutting off of electricity to poor homes. In Cartagena, the electricity company is now the Spanish Unión Fenosa (known throughout Latin America by a derogatory epithet, Unión Penosa). In South Africa it is the public company Exkom. On the same day when Duduzile Mphenyeke recounted her Soweto "lifeline" stories to the Friends of the Earth, in the barrios outside the historic walls of Cartagena there had been by coincidence a night of street demonstrations against the electricity company. Leaflets distributed by activists from Nelson Mandela explained that this barrio of 55,000 people had been born from those displaced by rural violence. Its main problems, in addition to Colombia's ubiquitous political violence, were electricity cuts and proximity to a waste dumping ground. Its local leader Libardo Hernandez had been killed in May 2003.

The South African activist's views were based on her experience in the Johannesburg townships. She proposed that impoverished communities and households have a right to certain free amounts of water and electricity—livelihood was more important than money. She struck a cord in Cartagena inside and outside the Friends of the Earth's assembly, also criticizing African export policies based on subsidized electricity and water for industries such as aluminium. Colombian journalists and others noticed the South-South parallels (*El Tiempo* (Caribe), 18 Sept. 2003).

Lessons from India

Such South-South parallels provide occasion for cooperation in addressing the various challenges of energy-society relations. However, in some countries, such as India and China, current economic growth and its effects on poverty dominate all other considerations. The economic boom goes together with a boom in energy consumption and in material inputs that start from very low per capita levels and will probably grow at the same rate of growth of the economy. But the social implications of such growth are significant. Witness the growth of the mining sector in both countries, and the many accidents in coal mining in China. Is economic growth and "trickle down" the only practical way to diminish poverty? And what will be the environmental effects of the present path of economic growth? I shall focus on India, the case with which I am most familiar.

One would like to be able to argue, with Indira Gandhi, that less poverty implies a better environment. In today's language, we would always be in a win-win, downward Environmental Kuznets Curve in which income growth is accompanied by better environmental quality. However, energy use, water consumption, the flow of materials, and many environmental and health risks (such as those from the nuclear industry and motorized transport) will increase in India with economic growth. In my visits to India, I cannot avoid a feeling of excitement when I notice the present high rate of economic growth. I remember the poverty of Spain in the 1940s and 1950s and I am so glad it no longer exists—though I know how much the Spanish economy depends on imported fossil fuels. In Spain the economy and the material inputs have grown in parallel. Imports have grown (measured in tons) far more than exports (Carpintero, 2002). Would it be possible for all countries in the world replicate such trajectory? Would it be wise?

Because of remittances from abroad and increasing exports, the Indian economy suffers no bottleneck of foreign reserves to pay for imports. If currents rates of economic growth are maintained over ten or twenty years, then this will likely make a very significant contribution alleviating the poignant poverty of the country. Redistribution, both national and international (including payments to India on account of the "carbon debt"), is an ecologically more sustainable though politically more difficult method of poverty reduction than growth. However, if "trickle down" based on growth founded on fossil fuels is what is politically available, let us have it—anything, but the existing cruel poverty. Nevertheless, sentiments must be tempered by reason. Over the next decades, as the Indian economy locks itself into a pattern of carbon dioxide emissions similar to the European per capita level, then India—with a population of 1.3 billion people—by herself would increase by 40 or 50 per cent the total of today's world emissions, while what is required is 60 or 70 per cent decrease from today's global emissions levels.

Furthermore, the relations between poverty and environment are multifaceted (Jodha, 1998; Nadkarni, 2000). The Brundtland report of 1987 saw poverty as the main enemy of the environment. However, against the Brundtland report and against Indira Gandhi's statement in Stockholm in 1972 that "poverty is the worst form of pollution," two main points have been made. First, wealth implies a larger consumption of energy and resources than poverty; second, the poor, because of their direct reliance on natural resources outside the market (perhaps in the form of common property resources), are often careful environmental managers. The rich, although they might feel that they live outside nature, or that nature is only for holidays and the weekends, in fact use more resources and sinks per capita than the poor, and therefore are more (and not less) dependent on nature than the poor. However, the rural poor have more direct knowledge and are better managers of nature than the urban rich—simply compare the ethno-botanical knowledge of various groups of people.

Notice also that economic accounting distorts the importance of the environment for human welfare. In India, there are figures showing that common property resources (CPR) contribute a larger amount of money per year than foreign assistance from the World Bank and other institutions. Of course, the results of any such analysis are to some extent dependent upon the methods of economic valuation of the services provided by such CPR. However, economic valuation is irrelevant in order to assess the *livelihood value* of resources such as water, firewood, soil fertility, and pastures that are essential for people who have no money to buy substitutes for them. In India, one liter of bottled water costs twelve rupees (2004), about one-fourth of a daily rural wage. In fact, a part of income growth goes simply to compensate for the loss of free resources no longer available because of environmental degradation and population growth. Conventional economics does not account for losses of so-called "natural capital" and "environmental services."

Poverty leads sometimes to environmental degradation but the relation between poverty and environmental degradation adopts many other forms (Nadkarni, 2000). One type of economic growth might increase both poverty and environmental degradation, for instance the expropriation of tribal people to the benefit of open cast mining. Another might allow rural people to move up the domestic energy "ladder." Use of firewood and dung for domestic fuel might decrease in India over the next years as LPG becomes more affordable (in 2003 a 14 kg cylinder of LPG cost about 270 rupees, while the rural daily wage was in many regions below fifty rupees, i.e.; below one euro). Securing a domestic LPG 'lifeline' would be good for the environment. However, economic growth will lead to the abandonment of practices that avoid environmental degradation, such as high rates of recycling of materials among the poor, the use of rural labor for water harvesting, the customary periods of rest by traditional fishermen during the monsoon, and the preservation of "sacred groves," among others.

Many of India's besetting environmental crises are caused by increased social and environmental vulnerabilities attendant to globalization. Because of Bhopal, Indian NGOs have led the international debate on the lack of corporate accountability, highlighting environmental liabilities of foreign companies as items of ecological debt (as shown by the Chevron-Texaco case in Ecuador). Despite the Enron controversy in Dabhol (Maharashtra) and other cases, transnational corporations are relatively absent from Indian politics compared to Latin America or Africa; nevertheless, the international guidelines proposed by Greenpeace for the behavior of companies bear the name of Bhopal. Despite such a high profile, India lacks strong debate on the North-South "ecological debt," or on one aspect of it, the "carbon debt." Official India is a silent partner in the international meetings on climate change. Actually, the fact that India will quickly increase its consumption of fossil fuels (supplied not only by domestic extraction but also by imports) will also make it more unlikely that India takes a leading role in the "carbon debt" discussion. India's official spheres have anyway been reluctant to take this role. Indeed, Anil Agarwal's position (Agarwal and Narain, 1991) was better known outside India than in India. And there are competent ecological economists in India who nevertheless lack political clout. The debate on ecology and the economy is not strong apart from occasional accidents. The language of economic growth (without ecology) is common to the BJP and the Congress. The lack of debate on an ecological economy is disappointing because Gandhian economics (as expressed in his own words, or as interpreted more systematically in Kumarappa's "economics of permanence") had a worldwide influence in the growth of environmentalism and ecological economics.

The Indian environmental movement has been strong in the last three decades. It has been an inspiration to others since the Chipko movement in the 1970s, led by Gandhians. There are many movements of Gandhian descent in "village India" (e.g., keeping the seeds, making one's own clothes, spreading agricultural innovations, water harvesting, new forms of using solar energy), but there is no general alternative to the current rapid economic growth based on copied technologies. Energy sources for this growth will not be limited to fossil fuels, but will also include large amounts of nuclear energy—including perhaps one or more breeder reactors—in the coming years. Water desalination (for urgent needs or for luxury use) will increase the energy input into the economy. Extant partial critiques of the general model of economic growth do not provide comprehensive guidelines for an alternative path, ensuring blind spots in energy transition movements. For instance, where are the social forces pushing for an alternative electrical energy plan for India that will allow 0.5 kw of power per person, without nuclear power, without increasing carbon dioxide emissions, and without big dams? Sustainable practices are becoming post-modern, ornamental experiments, kindly regarded as harmless by the economic and political powers. You do a little water harvesting while I build a very big dam. You build a breeder reactor while I build some biogas and solar energy capacity in rural areas.

Despite the grave social implications of climate change, greenhouse policies have no place in Indian electoral politics, and her governments have never been willing to play a leadership role on climate change together with the AOSIS countries and Bangladesh. On the contrary, a certain amount of carbon uptake is being "outsourced"—in the form of tree plantations—to southern countries, including India. Now, with the car industry definitively taking over as one main driver of industrialization, the government of India, rather than asserting "equal entitlements" to oceans and the atmosphere, and claiming therefore the "carbon debt," is more likely to attempt to import oil and gas from the Greater Middle East and neighboring countries such as Burma (Myanmar). Indian politicians of both main parties refuse to consider the social implications of energy and environment as one political issue, either internally or internationally. Given the large potential weight of India in the world economy and politics, such trends are of interest not only to Indian citizens.[5]

Conclusion

Economic growth goes together with an increasing availability of energy, and also with an increasing efficiency in the use of energy by given technologies. Technologies change, and new products often imply a larger use of energy. Humans differ little in the food energy they consume, but the socially determined differences in the exosomatic use of energy are today larger than ever. Poor people struggle to get the minimum amounts of energy they need and there cannot be a substantial improvement in their standard of living without an increase in the efficiency and amount of energy they use. Indeed, in order to get out of poverty, humans need a little more energy for endosomatic use and substantially more energy for exosomatic use, to a level of some 50 GJ per person/year.

One mode by which the relationship between energy and society may be analyzed relies upon a "socio-metabolic" view of the economy—studying the flow of energy and materials and the production of waste; this perspective owes its intellectual foundation to some natural scientists who wrote about the economy already in the nineteenth century. Unfortunately, economists—whether of the liberal or Marxist variety—failed to adopt a "socio-meta-bolic" view of the economy. Marx and the Marxist historians or economists did not take the opportunity offered by Podolinsky's work to look at the economy in terms of the flow of energy. For their part, neoclassical econo-mists (despite Jevons' well known interest in the availability of coal) saw the economy as a closed system where prices are formed and into which "exter-nal" effects should be brought only by economic valuation. The scarcity of fossil fuels (which are not produced, only extracted) gave rise to a discussion (Gray, 1914; Hotelling, 1931) on the inter-generational optimal path of ex-traction, which depended upon the interest rate. Only much later, in the sec-ond half of the twentieth century, did a new wave of natural scientists—and also this time some dissident economists such as Georgescu-Roegen, Ken-neth Boulding, Herman Daly—start (again) to see the economy as a sub-system embedded in a physical system that could be described in terms of flows of materials and energy, and the production of waste. New fields of study associated with the emergence of such interests—ecological econom-ics and industrial ecology—developed after 1990.

In ecological economics we look at the economy from a physical point of view in terms of "social metabolism," and from a social point of view in terms of the distribution of resource or sink property rights and the resulting con-flicts. The economy (as described by the system of economic accounts based on prices and quantities transacted in markets) is a subsystem of the wider physical and social systems, nested or embedded in the social and physical environments. Energy is not a "sector" of the economy. On the contrary, the market economy as a whole is only one part of the human ecology that must be characterized in terms of the human influence on the flows of energy and materials and interference in the biogeochemical cycles (for instance, in the carbon cycle, with the enhanced greenhouse effect). There is a clash between economic growth (at the present level of population density and with today's technologies) and the natural environment—a conflict largely related to the extraction, distribution, and consumption of energy and bearing significant so-cial implications. Economic growth, using more materials and energy, is gener-ally based upon a uniform pattern, disseminating similar technologies worldwide and implying the loss of traditional knowledge and biodiversity. The view that this energy-driven growth can continue indefinitely is wrong, and also it is wrong to think that economic growth may take place (with today's technologies which are now reaching China and India) with less use of energy.

And there are limitations on the sources of energy: there are scarcities marked by the Hubbert curve on oil extraction (the peak in world oil extraction will be reached soon); there are limits because of the uncertain perils of nuclear energy technologies; and there is significant opposition to hydroelectric dams. There are also the limits marked by the absorption of carbon dioxide by the oceans, soils and new vegetation. Concentrations of carbon dioxide in the atmosphere are increasing, with increasing conflict between rich and poor regarding the allocation of rights to carbon sinks and the atmosphere as a temporary deposit.

Because of such limits, governance is of utmost importance; a democratic, non-market, deliberation of the use of energy in the world becomes urgent. How much exosomatic energy are we going to use? From which sources will it be extracted? How are we going to share it in the present generation and among generations? These were Otto Neurath's questions. They should include discussion on the use of biomass for ethanol for cars that might compete with food and other domestic uses. In which case, we must also decide how much biomass and territory to leave for other species. Deliberations are required on the path of extraction of coal, oil and gas, and on the local impacts of extraction (for instance, the devastation caused by oil extraction in the Niger Delta or in Amazonia).

Just as there are conflicts over the extraction and transport of energy, there are also conflicts on the distribution of the different forms of pollution caused by some forms of use of energy. International networks born of local conflicts have an important role to play in such deliberations. For example, Oilwatch has raised the profile of social conflicts over energy-related environmental degradation. In 1993 a class action suit was started in the United States by a group of indigenous people and settlers from the northern part of the Amazonian region of Ecuador, claiming that Texaco had contaminated their water, killed their food supply and caused disease. No one can dispute that Texaco, whose official abode was then in White Plains, N.Y., and which later merged with Chevron, through its subsidiary in Ecuador between the early 1970s and the late 1980s polluted the water and the soil. It might be argued that its successor, Petroecuador, has inherited the same practices. That area is still dotted with viscous black pools of water which was extracted with the oil, later deposited into these pools which sometimes overflow, or suddenly catch fire and fill the air with black particles. There are reports of increased cancer rates. Texaco also opened up roads that facilitated the arrival of settlers to the forest, damaging the livelihood of the indigenous Cofanes and other tribes. It also built the trans-Andean pipeline to Esmeraldas, which has had many leaks. The case was submitted under the Alien Torts Claims Act, intended to provide a federal forum in the United States for aliens suing domestic entities for violations of the law of nations. And the *New York Times* (editorial, 19 February 1999) stated that the case should be heard "in the only forum that can provide a fair trial and enforce penalties, an American court." However, the case went back to Ecuador by a decision of the American court and in 2005 is being heard in Ecuador. A final decision on the compensatory and punitive damages to be awarded (if any) is still pending. There are many other similar cases around the world. The logic of economics is here relevant, as it was for the Exxon Valdez case of 1989. Technical questions are: Is contingent valuation acceptable to the courts? Are valuations of externalities from old cases transferable to new cases? In the case of the U'Wa in Colombia against Occidental Petroleum (Oxy) in the late 1990s, a different language was used, that of sacredness. The U'Wa argued also that their land was protected as indigenous territory under the Constitution. While the U'Wa in Colombia expressed the view that both the soil and the subsoil of their territory were sacred, Oxy insisted that in Colombian law the riches of the subsoil belong to the State, and that eventual damages to U'Wa property would be compensated. Clearly, such ecological and social conflicts are often also conflicts on languages of evaluation (Martinez-Alier, 2002).

Oilwatch provides information on such conflicts in fragile tropical areas from its secretariat in Ecuador, and through members in other Southern countries. In Kyoto, in December 1997, at the negotiations on climate change, Oilwatch produced a widely distributed statement linking local damages from oil extraction and global climate change. Despite the repeated assertions by scientists that fossil fuel combustion should decrease in the world because of the increased greenhouse effect, and despite the awareness that burning the available reserves will be already most problematic from this point of view, the oil frontier has kept moving into new—and often more vulnerable—areas at great local cost. And every oil well stopped, every pipeline delayed, was a contribution to the fight against climate change as well as the struggle to maintain the integrity of local environments, argued Oilwatch in Kyoto. What was needed was a program to provide energy to the two billion poorest people for the livelihood needs, not a continuous expansion of oil extraction and consumption.

And while the extraction and transport of fossil fuel energy and the oil refineries produce a multitude of ecological conflicts in the world, they are not alone. The production of hydroelectricity in large dams also produces conflicts. This is why the International Rivers Network arose, and why the World Commission on Dams criticized the World Bank for its policies. Nuclear power continues to be dangerous, and therefore polemical, though it is growing in India and in China. Quite often, poor people oppose the damage done to the environment and to their own livelihoods by big energy projects. Listening to them or to the NGOs that support them could help in developing a new world energy policy based on real needs and could assist in the advancing energy's social project.

Notes

1. Marx became so keen on the concept of metabolism that in a letter to his wife (21 June 1856), he nicely wrote that what made him feel like a man was his love for her, and not his love for Moleschott's metabolism or for the proletariat.
2. A Spanish translation was published in Martinez-Alier ed., 1995. The German version with the title Menschliche Arbeit und Einheit der Kraft, appeared in March-April 1883 in *Die Neue Zeit*, the new journal of the Social Democratic Party (i.e., the Marxist party).
3. Raul Prebisch was the chief economist at the UN Economic Commission for Latin America (CEPAL) in Santiago, Chile, and in the 1950s and 1960s argued together with his colleagues against specialization in the export of primary commodities because of deteriorating terms of trade.
4. Electricity is not a sensible source of energy for cooking when it implies transforming fossil fuels into electricity with a great loss of heat, and then electricity again back into heat.
5. The points made in this section on India are developed at greater length in Martinez-Alier (2005).

References

Agarwal, A., and Narain, S. (1991). *Global warming: a case of environmental colonialism*, Center for Science and Environment, Delhi.

Ayres, R.U., Ayres, L., and Warr, B.. (2002). *Exergy, power and work in the US economy, 1900-1998*, CMER-INSEAD, working paper.

Ayres, R.U. (1989). Industrial metabolism. In J. Ausubel (Ed.), *Technology and Environment* (pp. 23-49).Washington, DC: National Academy Press.

Bond, P. (2002). *Unsustainable South Africa*, Merlin Press.

Carpintero, O. (2002). La economía española: el "dragón europeo" en flujos de energía, materiales y huella ecológica, 1955-1995. *Ecología Política*, 23, 85-125.

Cipolla, C. (1974). *The economic history of world population*, 6th ed. London: Penguin.

Debeir, J.C., Deléage, J. P., and Hémery, D. (1986). *Les servitudes de la puissance. Une histoire de l'energie.* Paris: Flammarion.

Dourojeanni, M. (1982). *Recursos naturales y desarrollo en América latina.* Lima: Universidad de Lima.

Engels, F. (1925), *Dialektik der Natur (Dialectics of Nature), Marx-Engels-Werke*, 20, 307-568. Berlin: Dietz Verlag.

Fischer-Kowalski, M. (1998). Society's metabolism: the intellectual history of materials flow analysis, Part I: 1860-1970, Part II (with W. Huettler): 1970-98. *Journal of Industrial Ecology*, 2(1): 61-78 and 2(4), 107-136.

Fluck, R. C., and Baird, D. C. (1980). *Agricultural energetics*. Westport: Avi Publishing Co..

Foley, G. (1985). Wood fuel and conventional fuel in the developing world. *Ambio* 14(4-5), 253-57.

Foster, J. B. (2000). *Marx's ecology. Materialism and nature.* New York: Monthly Review Press.

Geddes, P. (1885). An analysis of the principles of economics. *Proceedings of the Royal Society of Edinburgh*, 17 March, 7 April, 16 June, 7 July 1884, repr. London: William and Norgate.

Giampietro, M. (2003). *Multi-scale intergrated analysis of agroecosystems.* Boca Raton FL: CRC Press.

Giljum S., and Eisenmenger, N. (2004). North-South Trade and the Distribution of Environmental Goods and Burdens: a Biophysical Perspective. *The Journal of Environment & Development*, *13*(1), 73-100.

Godoy, R. (1984). Ecological degradation and agricultural intensification in the Andean highlands. *Human Ecology*, *12*(3), 359-383.

Gray, L. C. (1914). Rent under the assumption of exhaustibility. *Quarterly Journal of Economics*, 28, 466-489.

Haberl, H. (2001). The energetic metabolism of societies', Parts I and II. *Journal of Industrial Ecology*, *5*(1), 11-33 and *5*(2): 71-88.

Hall, C. H., Cleveland, C. J., and Kaufman, R. (1986). *Energy and resources quality: the ecology of the economic process*. New York: Wiley.

Harrison, P. (1984). *Land, Food and People*. Rome: FAO.

Hayek, F.A. von. (1952). *The Counter-Revolution of Sciece. Studies on the Abuse of Reason*. Glencoe: Free Press.

Hornborg, A. (1998). Toward an ecological theory of unequal exchange: articulating world system theory and ecological economics. *Ecological Economics*, *25*(1), 127-36.

Hotelling, H. (1931). The Economics of Exhaustible Resources. *The Journal of political economy*, *39*(2), 137-175.

Jenssen, O., (Ed.) (1925). *Marxismus und Naturwissenschaft: Gedenschrifts zum 30. Todestage des Naturwissenschaftlers Friedrich Engels, mit Beiträgen von F. Engels, Gustav Eckstein und Friedrich Adler*. Berlin: Verlagges des Allgemeinen Deutschen Gewerkschaftsbundes.

Jodha, N. S. (1998). Poverty and environmental resource degradation. An alternative explanation and possible solutions. *Economic and Political Weekly*, *33*(36-37): 2384-90.

Kormondy, E. J. (1965). *Readings in ecology*. Englewood Cliffs, New Jersey: Prentice-Hall.

Leach, G. (1975). *Energy and food production*. Guildford: IPC Science and Technology Press.

Lotka, A. J. (1911). Die Evolution von Standpunkte der Physik. *Annalen der Naturphilosophie*, 10, 59-74.

Martinez-Alier, J., with Schlüpmann, K. (1987). *Ecological economics: Energy, environment and society*. Oxford: Blackwell.

Martinez-Alier, J., Munda, G., and O'Neill, J. (1998). Weak comparability of values as a foundation for ecological economics. *Ecological Economics*, 26, 277-86.

Martinez-Alier, J. (2002). *The environmentalism of the poor. A study of ecological conflicts and valuation*, Cheltenham: Edward Elgar.

Marx, K., and Engels, F. (1976). *Lettres sur les sciences de la nature et les mathematiques*. Paris: Mercure de France.

Marx, K. (1867-1894). *Das Kapital (Capital)*, vol. I (1867), vol. III (1894). Frankfurt-Vienna-Berlin: Ullstein Verlag.

Mayer. J. R. (1845). *Die organische Bewegung in ihrem Zusammenhang mit dem Stoffweschsel*. Heilbronn, published also in *Die Mechanik der Wärme: gesammelte Schriften*. Stuttgart, 1893, and in W. Ostwald, *Klassiker der exacten Naturwissensschaften*, Akademische Verlag, Leipzig, 1911.

McNeill, J. R. (2000). *Something new under the sun. An environmental history of the tewnetieth-century world*. New York: W. W. Norton.

Mintz, S. (1985). *Sweetness and Power. The place of sugar in modern history*. London: Penguin.

Moleschott, J. (1850). *Lehre der Nahrungsmittel. Für das Volk*. Erlangen: Enke.

Moleschott, J. (1851). *Physiologie des Stoffwechsels in Planzen und Thieren.* Erlangen: Enke.

Moleschott, J. (1852). *Der Kreislauf des Lebens.* Mainz: Von Zabern.

Mouchot, A. (1879). *La chaleur solaire et ses applications industrielles.* Paris: Gauthier-Villars.

Nadkarni, M. V. (2000). Poverty, environment and development: a many patterned nexus. *Economic and Political Weekly, 35*(14), 1184-90.

Naredo, J. M., and Valero, A. (1999). *Desarrollo económico y deterioro ecológico.* Madrid: Argentaria-Visor.

O'Neill, J. (1993). *Ecology, policy and politics.* London: Routledge.

O'Neill, J. (2002). Socialist calculation and environmental valuation: money, markets and ecology. *Science and Society, 66,* 137-151.

Odum, H. T. (1971). *Environment, power and society.* New York: Wiley.

Perez Rincon, M. A. (2004). El comercio exterior colombiano: ¿Una nueva vorágine? Aportación a la teoría del intercambio ecológicamente desigual. *Ecología Política,* 27.

Pimentel, D. and Pimentel, M. (1979). *Food, energy and society.* London: Arnold.

Pimentel, D. et al.. (1973). Food production and the energy crisis. *Science,* 182, 443-9.

Podolinsky, S.A. (1880) Trad cheloveha: ego otnoshenie K raspredeleniiu energii (Human labor and its relations to the distrubution of energy). Slovo, 4 (5) 135-211.

Rappaport, R. (1967). *Pigs for the ancestors: ritual in the ecology of a New Guinea people.* New Haven, CT: Yale University Press.

Schmidt, A. (1978), *Der Begriff der Natur in der Lehre von Marx,* 3rd ed. Frankfurt-Cologne: EVA.

Sieferle, R. P. (1982). *Der unterirdische Wald. Energiekrise und industrielle Revolution.* Munich: Beck (English trans., White Horse Press, Cambridge, U.K., 2001).

Susiluoto, I. (1982). *The origins and development of systems thinking in the Soviet Union: Political and philosophical controversies from Bogdanov and Bukharin to present-day reevaluations.* Helsinki: Suomalainen Tiedeakatemia.

Thomas, W. L., Sauer, C. O., Bates, M., and Mumford, L. (Eds.) (1956). *Man's Role in Changing the Face of the Earth.* Chicago, IL: University of Chicago Press.

Vernadsky, V. (1924). *La Géochimie.* Paris: Alcan.

Weber, M. (1909). Energetische Kulturtheoriene. *Archiv für Sozialwissenschaft und Sozialpolitik,* 29. Repr. in Max Weber, Gessamelte Aufsätze zur Wissenschaslehre, 3rd ed. Tübingen: J.C.B. Mohr.

White, L. (1959). The energy theory of cultural development. In M. H. Fried (Ed.), *Readings in Anthropology* (pp. 139 – 46). New York: Thomas Y. Cromwell.

White, L. (1943). Energy and the evolution of culture. *American Anthropologist, 45*(3), 335 - 356.

Winterhalder, B. P., Larsen, R., and Thomas, Y. B. (1974). Dung as an essential resource in a highland Peruvian community. *Human Ecology,* 2, 89-104.

3

Unraveling Relationships in the Energy-Poverty-Gender Nexus

Margaret Skutsch and Joy Clancy

Introduction

It has long been established that poor people in the developing world mostly use traditional forms of biomass (wood, charcoal, agricultural residues, dung) as their energy carriers[1] and that, in many areas, there is an increasing shortage in the supply of these biomass fuels, which adds to the burden of those whose responsibility it is to collect them. Christened 'the other energy crisis' by the World Resources Institute as early as 1975 (Eckholm, 1975), this situation is still very much part of the daily life of the around two billion people who have no access to modern forms of energy (World Bank, 1996); by and large, these two billion people are also the poorest people on earth. This linkage between energy and poverty is well known—but there has been little attempt to analyze the relationship in depth. The inconvenience of biomass fuel is easy to imagine, but what are its implications for development? Does the use of biomass fuel retard development? Does the availability of modern energy[2] drive development forward? At the national level, growth in the use of fossil fuels correlates highly with increases in GNP.[3] Strong associations between increases in commercial energy consumption and increases in the Human Development Index (HDI) have also been demonstrated (Suarez, 1995). However, very little is known about the impacts of modern energy at the local level on livelihoods or on the pathways it perhaps opens. Causal links between micro-level energy interventions and impacts are difficult to determine empirically (IDS, 2003) due to the large number of intervening factors. Energy as a social project is largely unexplored.

The provision of household biomass energy is primarily the responsibility of women through the gender division of labor. Much of it is used for cooking in devices that are inefficient and the emissions of which pose serious hazards to health. Kirk Smith is often quoted for his calculation that the smoke inhaled by a woman over a traditional *chula* is equivalent to that from smoking ten packs of cigarettes per day (Smith, 1987). Provisioning of fuel for these stoves may involve women walking many kilometers several times a week, carrying loads of up to thirty-five kilograms per trip. It is beyond doubt that the drudgery associated with traditional biomass fuels falls squarely on the shoulders of poor women all over the world. Various projects and programs have attempted to improve this situation by the dissemination of improved cookstoves, but only a few of these initiatives have achieved sustained use. Fewer still have been successful in wide-scale market dissemination.

However, women's needs for, and use of, energy are not limited to cooking. It can be argued that a lack of energy for productive purposes and for income generation limits opportunities for economic advancement, reinforcing poverty and limiting opportunities to make structural changes in economic, social and political senses. The question remains, however: Does increased access to energy alter traditional patterns of gender relations by changing power divisions and emancipating women while at the same time reducing poverty?

This chapter attempts to unravel some of the relationships in the gender, energy and poverty nexus. It starts by explaining that there is an energy dimension to poverty, and considers why energy policy and planning in most developing countries has paid scant attention to this. It then moves on to gender aspects of energy and why gender, too, is not usually considered. There are of course links and overlaps between the failure to address poverty and the failure to address gender issues, but we share the view of Jackson (1998) that the lack of attention to gender cannot wholly be explained as a subset of the more general failure to deal with poverty. There are other factors that explain gender blindness in the energy sector.

Energy Poverty

Energy poverty is a concept that captures the energy dimension of poverty. It has been defined as the absence of sufficient choice in accessing adequate, affordable, reliable, high quality, safe and environmentally benign energy services to support economic and human development (Reddy, 2000).[4] The energy-impoverished generally have no choice but to use unprocessed biomass fuels such as wood, agro-wastes and dung for cooking and heating purposes, candles or simple oil (kerosene) wick lamps for lighting, and have no electricity connection. There can be two reasons for this (Sinha, 2005 forthcoming): either reliable modern energy services are simply not present in the areas where poor people live, or they are available, but are beyond the financial reach of the poor, either because the fuel itself is too expensive or because the necessary appliances are. The fulfillment of either or both of these conditions at the household level qualifies as energy poverty.

A large amount of literature appeared in the 1980s describing the energy problems of the rural poor (see, i.e., Dunkerley, 1979; Munslow et al., 1988; Leach and Mearns, 1988). Many studies suggested that the use of biomass fuels has a number of repercussions for poor people. Biomass fuel quality is low. When burnt it gives off quantities of smoke and particulates that are recognized as having negative effects on health. In rural areas, the several hours a day spent in collecting fuel means this time cannot be used for other livelihood activities (Agarwal, 1986; Tinker, 1984). Although nearly every household in rural areas uses some biomass as an energy carrier, many poor households use it exclusively (Reddy, 2000). Wealthier households are sometimes able to purchase higher quality fuels and the appliances required to use them. These are appropriate for some end-uses, for example, quick meals and tea might be cooked on a kerosene stove. Such households may spend less time foraging for fuel in forests and farmland than poorer families, although a recent study indicates that average consumption of biomass in rural India does not decline with increasing income, as it remains the primary cooking fuel (Pachauri et al., 2004).

While it is difficult to generalize across all developing countries, kerosene is widely available even in remote rural areas and indeed could be considered the main lighting source of the developing world. It is still subsidized in many places. Cheap and relatively efficient kerosene stoves are also available and are used not only in urban areas as an alternative to charcoal braziers but also by better-off households in many rural areas, for quick cooking (convenience) or for serving guests (status). Even in these households, however, biomass provides the fuel for the main cooking activities that require large quantities of energy (cooking grains, beans, and meat). Although the convenience of kerosene as a cooking fuel is known and appreciated, and while some families have sufficient funds to purchase a stove, kerosene is considered either relatively too expensive for most cooking, or in some other way unsuitable (or unsafe). The option of moving the first step up the so-called energy ladder[5] is clearly present for such families, but is not fully utilized. The underlying motivations for an upward transition to more efficient and less polluting fuels, or, indeed, motivations for not moving up this ladder, are not fully understood.

The energy-poverty nexus in urban areas has been less researched than in rural areas although the body of knowledge is now beginning to grow (Barnes, 1995; Doig, 1998; ESMAP, 1999; Dube, 2002; Meikle and Bannister, 2003). Greater reliance, even by poor households, on purchased fuels, (including biomass fuels such as wood and charcoal), characterizes the urban situation. Poorer urban people spend a high proportion of their income, (typically 20 percent), on fuels (Barnes, 1995; ESMAP, 1999), even though they use much less fuel than wealthy families. They pay more for energy services than the wealthy. A case in point is household lighting: many poor families use candles, that are inherently inefficient and very expensive (see table 3.1). A similar paradox can be found in the use of dry cell batteries. Barnett (2000) notes that although they are widely used in radios and tape players, they are a very expensive way of buying electricity (about U.S. $400 per kWh, while in most Northern countries grid electricity sells at about U.S. $ 0.40 per kWh). Survey data from Uganda in 1996 showed 94 percent of rural households not connected to the electricity grid used dry cell batteries and were estimated to be spending about U.S. $6 per household per month on them (Barnett, 2000). Why are they so popular as an energy source at these exorbitant prices? The reason is at least partly because batteries, unlike grid electricity, match the cash flows of people with low incomes—small amounts on an irregular basis.

Table 3.1
Relative Energy Conversion Efficiency of Other Fuels Compared to Electricity
(typical values)

Cooking		Lighting		Appliances	
Energy Source	Efficiency*	Energy Source	Luminous Efficiency	Energy Source	Efficiency*
Electricity	1.00	Electricity	1.00	Grid electricity	1.00
Propane	0.77	Candles	0.02	Dry cell battery	0.90
Fuelwood	0.15	Kerosene	0.01	Car batteries	0.90

*Relative to electricity
Source: Foster 2000 (quoted in IDS, 2003)

People do not make energy decisions on the basis of efficiency; they make them on the basis of unit costs and the money they have in their pocket. Gas is a cheap, efficient and clean fuel for cooking, but the gas cylinder and the stove needed require a lump-sum, which the poor cannot raise, and so they opt for lower first cost options, rather than lower life cycle costs[6] (Reddy and Reddy, 1994). The consequences for the poor are that precious cash resources are used on low quality fuels, which are then used at low efficiency, which, in turn, reduces household ability to accumulate the financial resources necessary for investment in strategies for improving their livelihoods and has negative impacts on their health.

Energy poverty has a number of effects on poor families, that tend to use less energy than wealthier ones in absolute terms. Less water is boiled for drinking and hygiene purposes, increasing the likelihood of water-borne diseases. Illness reduces the ability of poor people to improve livelihoods and increases their vulnerability, not only preventing adults from working effectively but also negatively affecting children's learning. Lack of adequate lighting at home may make studying difficult for poorer children, quite possibly reducing their chances of a successful educational outcome, although the cause and effect between lighting quality in the household and school results has never been adequately tested. Lack of light may also restrict opportunities for extended working hours, and thus reduce the possibilities for extra income generation.

Lack of access to modern energy services means that much of the energy used by the poor is necessarily metabolic (human) energy. Thus water is raised from a well by hand because there is no mechanical or electric pump; cereals are processed by hand because there is no mill; harvested field crops are transported on the head or back instead of by lorry. Hard physical work is tiring, uses time which could otherwise be invested in other activities, and can impair health and even shorten lifespan due to a lack of adequate physical rest and recuperation.

However, access to energy is not just a question of household income. A large number of other factors may create barriers or smooth energy access for poor people. The organization of the delivery system and the modalities of supply are vital. There are a number of schemes for enabling the poor to overcome financial hurdles such as providing credit, subsidies to reduce tariffs, hire purchase, revolving funds and schemes where the up front costs are spread out over a longer period. But banks do not generally have experience in providing loans for energy technology to borrowers requiring small amounts, and tend to be very cautious, not least because of doubts about the ability of such technology to generate sufficient income to repay the loan. Moreover, the levels of lending through development-oriented microcredit programs are usually not sufficient to enable poor people to purchase energy efficient technologies. Very little systematic research has been done on lending and borrowing behavior as regards energy equipment, although there is some interesting data coming from studies of solar energy supply as will be shown below.

Another area of uncertainty is the impact of modern energy on livelihoods. Does the provision of energy help people to move out of poverty? If so, what particular forms of energy? And for what end-uses? Does energy that saves time on particular tasks, result in more time being invested in new, or expanded, productive activities? Does it lessen, or increase, social divisions and inequalities? In the literature, many assumptions are no more than wishful thinking, such as "electric lighting will enable people to study in the evenings." Whether these are the outcomes, and whether they have any influence on their prospects for improved livelihoods, have rarely been studied. The limited empirical data from a World Bank Study in Sri Lanka shows that electric light enabled women to spend more time on household chores, and only a small percentage of them were using it for income-generating activities (Massé and Samaranayaky, 2003). A new research initiative, EASE is, however, directly looking at precisely these types of impact on the basis of case studies of recent energy interventions in the recent past in Tanzania, Vietnam and Bolivia (EASE, 2004). At present, we cannot make conclusive statements, other than to suggest that the relationships between energy and poverty follow the pattern indicated in Box 3.1.

Box 3.1
Linkages Between Energy and Poverty (Source: IDS 2003)

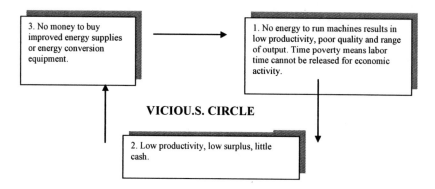

3. No money to buy improved energy supplies or energy conversion equipment.

1. No energy to run machines results in low productivity, poor quality and range of output. Time poverty means labor time cannot be released for economic activity.

VICIOU.S. CIRCLE

2. Low productivity, low surplus, little cash.

The Failure of Energy Planning to Address Energy Poverty

The persistence of energy poverty implies the present structures and processes within the energy sector are not functioning in such a way as to benefit the poor. To understand more clearly why energy planning fails the poor, one has to understand that it involves two quite different sub-sectors: the modern sector, including renewable energy technologies (RETs), and the traditional sector (biomass fuels and metabolic energy). Even a casual examination of national energy planning documents reveals the overwhelming tendency of macro-energy policy to focus on the commercial energy carriers: electricity, coal, gas and petroleum products. Energy planning heavily emphasizes investments necessary to improve supply, while less attention is directed to demand side issues. In some countries there is a growing interest in renewable energies, primarily for electricity generation, and this may be presented as a strategy to provide modern energy for the energy poor. Notably, the traditional sector—even though it supplies 50 percent of total energy in many countries and up to 95 percent in countries such as Ethiopia and Tanzania—receives far less attention.

The Modern Sector: Electricity, Gas, Petroleum Products and RETs

In most developing countries, the electricity grid does not extend to many rural areas because the costs of construction and of supplying scattered communities with relatively small quantities of electricity are perceived as prohibitively high. A total lack of installed supply still dominates the electricity situation in rural Africa. In contrast, in India, the grid extends to a high proportion of villages (around 80 percent), but within the villages, only the richer, more influential, families tend to be connected.[7] This clearly illustrates the two aspects of exclusion from energy supply, which characterize energy poverty. Liquid petroleum products, such as kerosene, are much more widely available, even in Africa; and in many places kerosene for domestic use has at been subsidized by the state, although this practice is on the decline due to market liberalization programs. However supply of these fuels depends on road transport, which may be seasonally unreliable, and the transport costs may increase the fuel cost considerably. Gas (LPG) is particularly vulnerable to supply problems as it requires the efficient distribution of bulky metal cylinders. In many countries, strong government regulation of gas supplies has discouraged private distribution. A shortage of dealers, gas cylinders, and filling stations results. As has been noted, gas equipment also has relatively high up front costs.

New and renewable energy technologies can be considered part of the modern, commercial energy sector and are receiving increasing attention (though still far less than conventional electricity and petroleum products). Most effort has been directed to RETs for decentralized production of electricity (e.g., solar, mini- and micro-hydro, and wind) although biogas has also been taken up, particularly in India, Nepal and China. In general, these technologies were first introduced by research centers or NGOs in experimental, highly subsidized conditions, and their success (particularly as regards reaching the poor) was mixed. Next came a phase in which consumers were expected to cover a large part of the costs; as a consequence, reaching the poor was even more problematic.

The Traditional Energy Sector: Woodfuels and Wastes

Unlike modern fuels, the supply of biomass is still largely unregulated and based in the informal sector. Rural populations generally supply themselves from surrounding forests and from nearby trees, in most cases in quantities that do not exceed sustainability limits. The supply of biomass in urban areas is also uncontrolled and, in most cases, comes from environmentally unsustainable harvesting of wood, either as firewood or for the production of charcoal. The large swathes of deforestation that can be seen expanding around almost all cities in developing countries are the result of this trade, although deforestation in areas far from the cities is usually related not to woodfuel, but to agricultural expansion. The urban trade in firewood and charcoal is informal, but it is commercial and it represents a major economic activity. In some cities a small tax is placed on lorry loads of firewood or charcoal and/or a charge is made for permits to cut the wood, but this is difficult to enforce and in any case is very low. The commercial value of this essentially informal trade is enormous. In the case of Benin, for example, it is believed the value of trade in urban woodfuels is equivalent to that of the electricity sector (Skutsch and van Rijn, 2005). Wood is felled by dealers in state-owned forests, but the trees are not replaced. Past efforts to relieve the resulting firewood shortage by encouraging farmers to grow trees have largely failed because the time and financial costs of these projects far exceed the short-term costs (based on the value of women's time and labor) of gathering fuel from the remaining forests (French, 1986). The Bois de Village program in Burkina Faso in the 1980s and the Village Afforestation Program in Tanzania (Skutsch, 1983) testify to the difficulty of making cultivation of firewood profitable. However, a number of West African countries are beginning to promote projects in which local rural populations are given rights to manage state forest in their vicinity and supply the woodfuel dealers on a sustainable basis, with the support of funding (by the FAO, World Bank RPTES and ESMAP program, Danida, and the Netherlands Development Cooperation, among others) (Dianka, 1999; Foley et al., 1997; Kerkhoff et al., 2001). Such projects are promising in both environmental and social respects.

More common have been attempts to deal with the demand side of the woodfuel problem, with particular emphasis upon cooking. While many such programs have emerged from a public health concern, others have sought reduced fuel use through improved combustion technology. The 1980s saw an outburst of stove programs, many of which failed totally. While improved charcoal stoves have been disseminated quite successfully in Kenya's urban areas, cheap wood burning stoves, that are both efficient and smokeless, appear to be more difficult to design and sell. A variety of reasons has been put forward for the fact that even subsidized wood burning stoves have not been popular: some women prefer flexibility in pot size, the presence of smoke can drives away insects, and fire can be used for both lighting and cooking (Clarke, 1985). Many of these stoves have been shown to hardly reduce fuel consumption outside laboratory conditions (Foley, Moss, and Timberlake, 1984). It would appear, however, that underlying much of the reluctance to adopt such stoves is an economic motive; in the rural areas at least, firewood is still available for free, so why invest money in a device to reduce the amount used? The way that households value the opportunity costs of women's labor has considerable bearing on this. The observation of differences in willingness to pay for stoves in India, where much of women's labor is perceived of as having little cash value, and in China, where women's employment outside the household means time spent gathering fuel has a cash opportunity cost, is instructive (Nathan and Kelkar, 1997). In China, 120 million stoves have been installed in rural areas, compared to 8 million in India (World Bank, 1996).

It is noticeable that there has been very little attention to other woodfuel burning technologies, although their importance is considerable. The production of charcoal, when carried out under traditional conditions, results in considerable inefficiency. There have been some technical developments (for example, the Casamance kiln) but very little uptake not least because the economics of use of such kilns (particularly the returns on labor), are not unfavorable (Skutsch and Sanogo, 2000). Also lacking is a systematic attempt to improve biomass fuel technology in small-scale productive enterprises.

Reasons for the Failure to Address Poor People's Energy Needs

For a number of reasons, mainstream energy policy and planning continue to focus upon commercial energy rather than the biomass problems of the rural poor. Here we note six: the position of commercial energy in the dominant economic development models; political expediency; the influence of donors; current international pressures towards "efficiency" in the energy sector (neo-liberal policy); lack of central authority to govern biomass fuel supply; and finally, lack of understanding of the dynamics between the modern and the traditional energy sectors.

Commercial Energy in the Dominant Economic Paradigm. Modern energy (particularly electricity, but also a reliable supply of petroleum fuels) is viewed by many governments as an, if not *the*, essential element in the development of an industrial economy. At the same time, most governments conceive of development as occurring though a "trickle-down" process, such that wealth has first to be created through industrial expansion before the population as a whole can be moved out of poverty. Modern energy is highly strategic to this enterprise. Reinforcing these notions, the oil crises of the 1970s hit developing countries hardest, disrupting production and bringing many of them to their knees, economically. This lesson has been well-learned, and governments have since pursued the provision of energy infrastructure to curb such vulnerabilities.

Political Expediency. Electricity and petrol supplies have become a major issue in the daily lives of the ruling classes in urban areas, and increasingly in the lives of the urban populace as a whole. These urban populations, because of their physical proximity and visibility to government, wield much more influence than the rural masses. In contrast to the energy concerns of the rural poor, governments are inclined to respond to strikes and demonstrations over shortages in electricity and petrol, by vocal groups for whom modern energy is already economically within reach.

Donor influence. The emphasis on large-scale power generation is also driven by the financing policy of international development agencies that, despite lip service to the energy problems of the rural poor, in most cases promote the simple industrialization model when it comes to energy policy and planning. The interests of the fossil fuel industry and the involvement of large multinationals in the construction of energy plants are significant in this regard. In such a climate, the needs of the biomass-dependent rural poor are ignored.

International Policy Shifts toward Privatization and Commercialization. Privatization and commercialization have major implications for energy access by poor people. Privatization in the energy sector involves the sale of state energy companies, particularly the electricity utilities, to the private sector, as well as the opening up of the market for the private sector to provide other energy services. These trends bring with them wholly new concerns: How will the private sector respond to energy services demand from the rural poor? Will the poor be seen as a mass market needing creative financing programs to facilitate access to energy services, or will they be regarded as too high a risk, providing too low a profit margin? It is, as yet, not clear whether privatization will result in more, or less, access for the rural poor to modern energy forms. Empirical evidence, mainly related to the electricity sector, is only now beginning to emerge (see for example, Reddy, et al., 2002). In some cases, the boundaries of existing services, originally provided with an element of social welfare, are being retracted, as can be seen, for example, in India where previously electrified areas are having services withdrawn based solely on financial criteria (Ministry of Power, 2001). A UNEP (2004) report based on a three continent study suggests that privatization of the electricity sector, in general, appears not to benefit the poor: "when reforms are introduced with the sole intention to improve the performance of utilities, the expected and hoped for social benefits do not necessarily follow."

Petroleum prices have also been affected by deregulation. In many places there have been reductions in subsidies on transport fuels, that have increased the cost of getting to work in urban areas and pushed up prices in general. Clancy (2005) shows that, in Nigeria, the price of all petroleum products has increased since 1990 when the government began to pursue a policy of commercialization prior to privatization. For example, kerosene increased from 0.15 naira/liter in 1990 to 41.25 naira/liter in 2004. These price increases encourage a fuel transition back to wood and charcoal, along with attendant social and environmental implications.

Lack of Central Authority to Govern Biomass Fuel Supply. Contributing to the neglect of poor people's energy needs is that authority over forests and land use planning is not in the hands of the energy ministries, but usually in forestry and environmental ministries. The coordination between these two ministries and the energy ministries is usually rather weak. Energy ministries are chiefly staffed by engineers trained in electrical and chemical engineering at universities in industrialized countries, rather than in the technologies used by most people in their own countries. When national energy plans do make reference to the traditional energy sector, which in some countries contributes more than half of final energy, there are rarely more than a couple of pages devoted to this sub-sector, and investment in it is minimal. In addition, forestry plans are most often more concerned with conservation and timber production than with biomass fuel supply.

Lack of Understanding of the Dynamics between Modern and Traditional Sectors. The lack of cooperation between ministries is characteristic of the failure to understand the linkages between the traditional and the modern energy sectors. Often overlooked are shadow subsidies to biomass fuels. Much biomass—especially that which is traded commercially—is heavily subsidized in the environmental sense and is also taken from nature without paying the replacement cost. If such fuels were to be taxed, and the revenue ploughed back into maintenance of the ecosystems that produce the fuel, not only would the environmental destruction be reduced, but the increased price of the fuel would generate more interest in fuel efficient combustion devices. As has been noted, this has already happened to some extent with charcoal in Africa, the price of which rose rapidly in the 1980s as a result of increasing distances and transport costs. This was met with relatively rapid developments in improved charcoal stoves and their widespread marketing (UNDP, 2001).

It can be argued, based upon the number of people affected, that the central energy policy problem in the world today is the lack of a sensible policy for controlling the supply of firewood and other biomass fuels in developing countries. There is no developing country that has yet systematically introduced a rational policy to deal with both the supply and the demand sides of this problem. While national policymakers have been unresponsive in this regard, there have been a number of promising local projects in several West African countries. As mentioned earlier, in some such projects, city firewood supply and demand have been estimated and parts of the forest have been handed over to rural communities to be managed systematically and sustainably for firewood. The impacts of such initiatives on the price of firewood and on shifts in energy demand still have to be assessed and the overhead costs have to be drastically reduced if such schemes are to be replicated widely. However, it is clear already that this policy is reducing forest degradation in the areas where it has been applied. Moreover, it appears that forest management is an activity in which poor people, particularly women, are heavily involved, providing welcome additional sources of income during the dry season. To systematize such an approach would require changing land tenure rules in many cases, a notoriously difficult and politically sensitive issue and one that involves much more than simply energy.

Targeted Pro-Poor Policies and Programs

Of course not all policies are exclusively focused upon increasing the supply of commercial fuels to the richer parts of the population—both China and South Africa can be cited for their efforts to transcend this fixation. China's on-going program of rural electrification has resulted in the electrification of more than 80 percent of villages; and although not every family in every village is connected, this is generally said to be because of technical and supply failures rather than inability to pay (Wallace, Jingming and Shangbin, 1998). To reach villages off the grid, China has launched a major solar PV program called Brightness. In South Africa, following the end of Apartheid, strong electoral promises were made to increase the number of electricity connections, and enormous strides were taken throughout the 1990s. By the end of 1999, 66 percent of all households had an electricity connection, funded entirely from national resources (SPARKNET, 2004).

Other government efforts to enable access to modern energy sources by low-income groups have mainly deployed subsidies, particularly for kerosene and electricity. The effectiveness of this policy instrument is hotly contested. Most governments, as well as major donors and advisors such as the World Bank, recognize that blanket subsidies have a tendency to benefit rich and urban, rather than poor and rural, populations. This has led to the development of so-called "smart" subsidies for electricity, which are specifically targeted at poorer groups and designed to lower access costs, (e.g., connection fees) rather than operating costs. Such systems generally use cross-subsidization in a deliberate attempt to ensure more equitable access. Due to their lack of support among wealthier segments of the population, they are often only employed to a limited extent (e.g., the Kutir Jyoti program in India). Unfortunately, as has been noted, low domestic tariffs, lifeline tariffs, and kerosene subsidies are increasingly being withdrawn due to external pressure (mostly from the IMF) for energy sector reform. Such reforms, designed to bring about increased efficiency and lower costs though increased private investment and a reduced role of government, are very often presented as pro-poor (Littlechild, 2000). Some proponents claim the poor will be the *primary* beneficiaries of lowered prices resulting from such increased efficiency. However, as has been mentioned, it is questionable whether such privatization of grid energy supply will in fact improve access for low-income groups (Tellam, 2000), since the returns on investment are likely to be low (low potential sales per kilometer of line constructed). Profit maximization would encourage privatized companies to ignore the small and scattered demand of the rural poor.

Decentralized production of electricity is the logical solution to this problem, and there has therefore been considerable interest in new and renewable technologies for this. Experiments by ASTRA in Pura, India, demonstrated that, given good village organization, electricity to serve virtually the entire local population could be generated from communal biogas plants (Reddy, Rajabapaiah, and Somesekhar, 1995). Yet this experiment has yet to be duplicated, let alone spread across India. Initial investment costs have proven to be a significant barrier.

At present, solar energy is the technology considered to have the greatest potential for decentralized generation. But many solar PV programs have faced technical and maintenance problems. And while the earliest programs were carried out on a highly subsidized basis, this is no longer the case, as current programs have developed a concern for financial sustainability; and this has resulted in unit costs that are far too high for the poor majority. For example, researchers in Guatemala found that 50 percent of the population would be unable to afford PV systems at all, between 18 and 25 percent might afford them on a "fee for service" basis, and 15 to 20 percent on a credit system (Allerdice and Rogers, 2000). Only 3 to 5 percent would be ale to pay cash up front (Allerdice and Rogers, 2000).

Notably, most solar applications are for household uses, such as lighting and entertainment appliances, rather than those that might increase income-earning opportunities, though it is true lighting may make it possible for household enterprises to increase productivity by working in the evening hours. For example, Allerdice and Rogers (2000) quote the UNDP ENSIGN program, in which 219 households carrying out small enterprises were supplied with solar energy, and were able to increase their incomes by an average of 53 percent by working at night. However, apart from such entrepreneurial applications the income benefits of electricity are difficult to perceive; and barriers to starting such an enterprise often have nothing to do with energy. Although it is increasingly recognized there are some opportunities for new careers as 'energy entrepreneurs'—commercializing such tasks as battery recharging—such initiatives inevitably require capital and are likely to be seized by those in the community who are already better-off and better trained.

Reformers who recognize the skewed patterns of energy consumption have emphasized issues of equitable electricity supply, and undoubtedly cheap electricity for lighting and small appliances, such as fans, would be highly popular—indeed, one could argue that access for such purposes is a basic need, if not a basic right, in the twenty-first century. Such energy services are not irrelevant—they are crucial for welfare and for a better standard of living. Ideally, they would be available to everyone. As noted, however, success in this regard has been limited to those developing countries in which the public sector has been willing to bear a large part of the costs out of general revenue, and where electricity is regarded as a public service like education or health, not as a consumer good. It might still be argued, though, that this emphasis on electricity for the poor fails to address the chief energy demands of low-income rural households, or their needs for energy for productive enterprises, that usually require process heat or mechanical power. Electricity—grid or solar, subsidized or unsubsidized—is too expensive for such applications.

It seems we are confronted with a further shortcoming of energy planning in this respect. Energy planners—even those who have gone against the mainstream and struggled to consider the needs of poorer populations—have not fully analyzed these needs but instead have focused on supply side issues (how to make cheap electricity or fossil fuels more accessible, how to disseminate certain technologies which appear to be beneficial). Energy has been seen from a sectoral view, rather than as one component of the complex reality in which poor people live. Yet, the sociology of development makes it clear the best way to understand the needs of the poor is holistically, and from the bottom up, rather than through sectoral spectacles. Two new approaches present themselves in this regard, and could be very useful in improving energy planning practice.

The first is the so-called energy services approach, in which the emphasis is not on the fuel or the technology but on the concept of energy *services* (Woroniuk and Schalkwiyk, 1998; IDS, 2003). From such a perspective, an analysis is first made of the purposes for which energy will be used, including the constraints and conditions of such purposes. End-uses are then matched to the most appropriate energy form. This approach, coupled with continuous monitoring, implies a comprehensive analysis of the totality of user needs, rather than a piecemeal, supply driven concern (Anderson et al., 1999).

The second is the sustainable livelihoods approach (SLA), which requires an analysis of how people actually make a living, or survive, in rural areas. The method was developed by the University of Sussex and has been adopted by a number of development agencies, including the UNDP and the UK's Department for International Development (DFID) as the central analytic tool for use in its development programs (DFID, 2002). In the original form of the SLA, energy was not specifically recognized as an important element in people's livelihoods; but Barnett (2001) has shown the necessity of its inclusion and the usefulness of SLA in understanding energy service provision (see also Doig, 1998; Clancy, Skutsch, and Batchelor, 2003; and Clancy, 2005).

Gender Issues in Energy

Despite efforts to address the energy needs of poor populations, the energy-poverty nexus has distinct gender characteristics that are often ignored. Of the approximately 2 billion people living in energy poverty, it is estimated that 70 percent are women, many of whom live in female-headed households in rural areas. It is important to take note of this fact: not only do men and women have different energy needs but they also have different access to resources and decision-making. Women are often limited in their ability to influence processes and resource allocation on many issues including energy. A number of important questions must be considered when attending to the gendered dimensions of the energy-poverty nexus.

Decisions about Energy within the Household and Who Benefits

In households with adult men and women, the gendered division of labor generally allocates the responsibility for household energy provision according to spheres of influence; women are usually responsible for provision of energy for cooking. However, when energy—such as batteries for radios—must be purchased, men enter the decision-making process. In South Africa, high expenditures on batteries are often for the purpose of listening to taped music. In many cases, female members of the household had no access to equipment for these purposes and no control over battery purchase (Makan, 1995). In some households, energy-intensive recreational equipment was purchased before labor-saving devices for domestic chores. One should also consider control of such devices; for example, men may choose to locate a light outside the house for security reasons (such as protecting livestock from theft), while women might prefer to locate the light in the kitchen (for convenience or safety). Many such decisions are made by male members of the household.

Men also influence the acquisition of energy technologies in the kitchen. Although cooking is usually a woman's charge, men will often determine the type of stove technology, if it is to be purchased (Tucker, 1999), and men will often make the decision about when to buy a new stove (Dutta, 1997). Men also make important decisions on other factors—such as material for kitchen walls and roofing—that influence cooking and kitchen comfort (Dutta, 1997).

Men sometimes have reservations regarding the role of women in energy technology use. In Zimbabwe, men are reported to have rejected the use of solar cookers by their wives, since technology and its development are seen traditionally as a male preserve (Nyoni, 1993). Some men have expressed concern about the use their wives would make of the time saved through using new stoves (Wilson and Green, 2000). Others, though, see it as an opportunity for their wives to undertake more productive activities (Wilson and Green, 2000). In such cases, women are keenly aware of the fact that savings in one area of drudgery can result in increased drudgery in another area; McDade and Clancy (2003), for example, show rural electrification can extend the woman's working day and increase the work she is expected to carry out. Jackson's (1997) study of women's involvement in water projects showed some women deliberately adopted a non-participation strategy to avoid increasing their overall workload.

In some cases, however, modern energy services have also been seen to improve gender equality in household tasks: Massé and Samaranayake quote a man who, as a result of electrification, declared "I am now prepared to do ironing and assist my wife in her work: ironing, boiling of water, cooking" (Massé and Samaranayake, 2003). Despite such examples, there can be distinct gender aspects to the distribution of benefits from modern energy carriers. For example, the evaluation of a rural electrification project in Tamil Nadu showed that men benefited more than women as the electricity was used to run irrigation pumps substituting for oxen-drawn water (Rengasamy et al., 2001). Care of the oxen was traditionally a task for men, who gained more free time when the number of draft animals decreased; and they used this time for involvement in politics and improving their agricultural methods, thereby increasing their social and economic capital. However, electricity did not substitute for any of the tasks of women. In other cases, though, women have reported time-savings in a number of chores (see, for example, Masse and Samaranayake, 2003). An evaluation of the distribution of the benefits of a micro-hydro scheme in Sri Lanka found that in connected households, men and women experienced equal (but different) benefits from the energy services provided by electricity (Dhanapala, 1995, cited in Barnett, 2000). Unconnected households experienced an unequal distribution of benefits. These households benefited by access to television in other local households and the possibility of hiring lights for special occasions. Men had greater access to TV because they had greater freedom of movement, particularly at night. However, the contrary is claimed by Allerdice and Rogers (2000) in their study of solar home systems. They found that women and children, who were at home during the day—when solar PV provides the greatest amount of electricity, made greater use of electrical appliances.

Women and men also have different perceptions about the benefits of energy transitions. For example, the above mentioned evaluation of the impact of a micro-hydro scheme in Sri Lanka found that men perceived the benefits of electricity in terms of leisure, quality of life and education for their children; while women saw it as providing a means for reducing personal workload, improving health and reducing expenditure (Dhanapala, 1995, cited in Barnet, 2000). In the study by Massé and Samaranayake, quoted above, 29 percent said they used the extra time for doing additional housework, not for increased leisure; interestingly, less than 5 percent reported using the time for productive activities (Massé and Samaranayake, 2003). A further benefit from electricity is access to appliances such as television, which may be enjoyed by women as well as men. In Nepal, it has been reported that women's empowerment was enhanced when they could see pictures showing that they "don't have to remain as second class citizens" (quoted in Barnett, 2000). The role of TV in women's emancipation is indeed important. A case study in Tunisia showed that watching television enabled women to become more aware of political events and have a greater knowledge of world affairs than their husbands. Through this knowledge, they have apparently gained confidence to speak out and take leadership roles in their communities (Chaieb and Ounalli, 2001).

What one can say about these cases is that they are essentially snapshots, which provide valuable, but anecdotal, insights into particular cases in particular places; some tendencies may certainly be discerned, but they, in some cases, contradict each other. The sometimes contradictory nature of such cases demonstrates a need for local, comprehensive, and bottom-up considerations of energy issues, while highlighting the gender dimension of the energy-poverty nexus.

Implications for Women of Biomass Fuel Use

In biomass-dependent households, fuel collection is generally the burden (physically and metaphorically) of women, including young girls. In rural areas, this can mean spending several hours a day collecting heavy loads of firewood. In urban areas, meeting family fuel needs can entail juggling tight household incomes in order to buy charcoal or kerosene; and increased fuel prices result in less money for food and other essential items, thus increasing household vulnerability. The responsibility for household energy provision affects women's health disproportionately to men's; for example, women experience higher levels of lung and eye disease due to longer hours of exposure to smoke and particulates in kitchens. Fuel collection also reduces the time available to women for contributing to other aspects of livelihood strategies and girls are frequently kept away from school to assist their mothers in such chores.

The full consequences of women continuing to rely on their own energy inputs and biomass fuels are not known. While much excellent research has been conducted into the effect of smoky kitchens on women's and children's health (see e.g., Smith, 1999) other health linkages are not as well-examined. For example, although the amount of time spent by women in collecting and carrying heavy loads of fuel is often noted, the damage these loads cause to women's spines is not well documented.[8] Mechanized transport—even bicycles—would be a great boon to women, not just for hauling fuel, but also for carrying other goods—such as harvested crops—from field to storage and market. Women are also responsible for a number of other survival tasks needed to sustain the household such as water collection, food processing and cooking. Many of these are demanding in terms of both human energy and time. For example, the preparation of many staple root crops and grains takes upwards of an hour of vigorous pounding but the human energy in grain preparation could be simply substituted by a milling machine. Other such energy interventions could also reduce the drudgery involved in these daily household activities.

The whole issue of women's time and effort saving seems not to receive the attention it deserves. This might be attributed to the fact energy planners are not fully aware of the situation regarding women's physical labor. Women's survival tasks are often based on their own metabolic energy inputs and are seldom visible in energy statistics (Cecelski, 1999). As a consequence, the development of labor-saving devices, which could contribute significantly to women's wellbeing, is not high on the agenda of energy planners.

A simple conclusion is clear: the burden of biomass fuel use is a major aspect of most poor women's lives. It absorbs large amounts of time in heavy work, and can have negative effects on health. Despite this recognition of the problem, very little has been done about it.

It would be incorrect however to view women as passive victims of biomass use. Women are also important managers of natural resources and producers of biomass fuels. Women have responded to fuelwood shortages by adopting management strategies to conserve fuel: they shorten cooking times, explore less fuel-intensive cooking and food processing methods, cook fewer meals, serve cold leftovers, change the types of food eaten and purchase other fuels. A great deal can be learned from such coping strategies.

The history of projects that have attempted to introduce improved stoves is instructive. Many such programs have failed, either for economic and technical reasons, or because the technologies have not fit the real needs of the women concerned. Stoves may simply not be used or not replaced when they are broken—often a sign that the technology is unpopular. Where programs have succeeded this has often been because local women have been involved in the design and dissemination of the stoves. In one example, local women were trained as stove masons and marketed these services (Sarin, 1984). Convincing women of the merits of improved and fuel-efficient stoves is considerably easier when their interests are taken into account. And this lesson may certainly be extended to other energy technologies.

While women should play an important role in the choice of such household energy investments, the question remains as to the effects of such technological transitions on women's lives. Does the provision of improved energy services assist in empowering women? Is a lack of energy a key barrier that prevents women from achieving economic, social, and political empowerment? How do women use the time (and money) that may be saved by the transition to more modern fuels?

Again, research proves inconclusive and sometimes contradictory, highlighting the importance of context and diminishing the notion that modern energy services advance the social project of women's empowerment. In a Madagascar stove program, adoption of fuel-efficient stoves is reported to bring an annual savings equivalent to the minimum monthly salary (Bazile, 2002); but the impact on women's lives is not reported. The reality does not always match the rhetoric: as was shown earlier, advocating time-saving energy services to allow for economic activities may instead result in time gained for household chores and child care (Massé and Samaranayake, 2003). It seems, then, that highly differentiated social and cultural mores are more important elements of—or barriers to—empowerment than is technical transition.

The Failure of Energy Planning to Address Gender Issues

The current focus in mainstream energy policies and planning, as noted earlier, is not generally pro-poor, and even pro-poor initiatives have not all been very successful in meeting the real needs of a large part of the population in developing countries. Women, who make up a disproportionate part of the poor, are therefore very much affected by the failure of these policies. And, since women throughout the world are responsible for almost all cooking activities, and in the poorest parts of the world responsible for the supply of fuel for cooking, the total failure of energy policy to engage issues of biomass supply and demand falls most heavily on their shoulders.

As far as cooking is concerned, it is clear that women desperately need either improved biomass burning technology, or the possibility of moving up the energy ladder. As shown earlier, current policies in the modern energy sector militate against any of these options, and pro-poor programs have mainly focused on electricity that, though welcome for other reasons, is usually irrelevant to cooking and most other uses with which women are mainly concerned.

Some have suggested new and renewable technologies as the ideal solutions (see for example, the 2004 International Conference on Renewable Energy Technologies in Bonn: www.renewables2004.de.). Solar cookers seem to be undergoing a period of renewed interest with donors[9] despite the vast majority of past programs having failed miserably. The most serious objections to solar cookers, apart from the cost, are that cooking at midday does not coincide with the time of eating the main family meal in many cultures (Mandhlazi, 1999), and many cooks prefer to cook indoors (Wilson and Green, 2000). The biggest successes in solar cooking have been the very cheapest models that were distributed freely in refugee camps, where there really is no alternative. Micro-hydro is another possibility. It can provide much more power, but is limited to locations with favorable water flow conditions. Wind-generated electricity is likewise geographically handicapped. Further, the cost per kWh is much higher for all these RETs than for grid electricity, which is already considered too high for use in cooking.

Biogas for household cooking and lighting has been somewhat successful—such as in Nepal—but the capital investment required, even where generous subsidies and concessionary loans are provided, means that it may not be a technology for the poorer half of the rural women. In India, the technology is well accepted, but is generally available only to the richer families, since it requires dung from at least four cows and is only really feasible if the cows are stall-fed so that the dung is close at hand to feed the digester. Stall-feeding is essentially an intensive agricultural approach that requires levels of both capital and labor not usually available in poor families. The success of biogas in China, where 5.25m family size plants were operating in 1993 (Keyun, 1995), and where 10m plants are said to be operating today, is interesting not just because of the numbers built, but because an integrated production technique ('4 in 1') has been developed to enable digesters to perform even in areas normally considered too cold. Biogas can also be operated at the community level, as has been demonstrated in both China and India. In all three countries, numerous studies attest to the benefits for women, including the relief from the drudgery of firewood gathering and the ill effects of cooking over wood. The successes of these technologies in this regard are probably attributable in large part to the particular social circumstances of a given community, rather than to the transforming power of any given energy transition.

Where woodfuel is concerned, the promotion of community forest management is perceived to improve the supply of biomass and lead to a sustainable supply. Most of these projects aim to provide sustainable woodfuels for city populations, and in the long run they will inevitably entail higher commercial prices for wood and charcoal, that may affect household budgets with serious implications for urban women. But it may also act as an incentive for the development and marketing of more efficient stoves, that should also have health benefits for women and enable the accumulation of assets (if, for example, the savings shown in Madagascar can be replicated elsewhere—see Bazile, 2002) The rural impact of the commercialization of woodfuel is likely to be felt more gradually. One unexpected outcome is the fact that the rural women involved in forest management are often able to earn a considerable income from this trade, that is not necessarily dominated by men. For example, women in Mali found dry season work on the firewood harvesting system paid better than making local beer, the traditional activity of that season (Skutsch and van Rijn, 2002). Such forest management for woodfuel could be considered as a type of 'energy entrepreneurship,' and while such projects are not yet widespread, they are promising.

Reasons for the Failure of Energy Planning to Address Gender Issues

Current energy policies have been roundly criticised as insensitive to gender (Feenstra, 2002; Annecke, 2003). They tend to reflect men's interests while women's are neglected. Part of the explanation for the neglect of women's use of energy mirrors the failure to look at energy poverty but, even where demand-driven, pro-poor approaches have been adopted, gendered dimensions of energy retain a relatively low profile (Clancy, Skutsch and Batchelor, 2003). Of several important reasons, we will explore two here: the structure of mainstream development theories and the failure of the energy sector to keep abreast of developments in other sectors as regards gender.

Gender in Mainstream Development Theory. Gender issues were until recently totally ignored in mainstream development theories, both of the modernisation and of the Marxist types (Scott, 1995; Moser, 1993). These theories traditionally considered the household to be the basic unit of society, blind to the very different roles and responsibilities of men and women and forgetting women are, as a general rule, an oppressed group. Since the 1970s, though, women's emancipation movements have endeavoured to change attitudes toward gender in the development profession—especially in sectors such as health, nutrition, water and agriculture. This has required a new sensitivity to gender relations, as well as the development of tools to analyze men and women as separate interest groups. It may take a long time, however, before the unconscious, unspoken, unrecognized belief that *energy is gender neutral*, is overcome. Unfortunately, energy is too often perceived as a technical matter: attendant social implications are ignored.

Energy Profession's Failure to Understand the Varied Nature of Women's Needs. For various reasons, the energy profession is widely ignorant of the varied nature of women's needs. An overwhelming emphasis on cooking as the singular gendered dimension of energy is a result of this blindness. Obviously, much of women's energy use involves biomass fuels for cooking. But women have many non-cooking energy needs as well; a number of studies show that many of these are more important than cooking (Mehretu and Mutambira, 1992; Clancy, et al. 2004). Women's metabolic energy is involved in most of these non-cooking dimensions. Women's demand for a flourmill so that they do not have to hand pound grain on a daily basis, is not regarded as an energy need or included in energy plans. But as Cecelski has suggested, it is rather strange that an electric pump is considered to be using energy, but a woman hauling up a bucket on a rope is not (Cecelski, 2003). Regarding gender sensitivity, energy lags behind other sectors. Significantly, there are almost no energy extension workers, while in agriculture and in health such staff are regularly in contact with rural populations and have come to recognize gender issues by exposure to them.

A new sensitivity to such issues could reveal three significant ways in which access to energy services may help women: welfare, opportunity for economic advancement, and emancipation or empowerment. Greater efficiency may promote health while saving time and effort, without fundamentally changing their role or the balance of responsibilities in the family. These are improvements in welfare. Stove projects are typically designed to deliver such welfare benefits, and many non-cooking interventions—such as electric pumps for drawing water—also fall into this category.

Energy may also promote economic advancement for women. Access to, or control over, energy sources, as well as the finances to purchase appliances that make productive use of energy, are important aspects of this advancement. Energy interventions, therefore, may encourage women to become economically stronger, thus benefiting the economy generally and giving them more financial autonomy. Although some agencies (notably the World Bank) consider this to be "empowerment," it is primarily an economic advance and, in most cases, an extension, and improvement, or up-scaling of an existing situation, rather than a radical change in women's position. The provision of energy for women's enterprises is an obvious example, highlighted in particular by a groundbreaking set of case studies by UNDP (2001). Others (see, i.e., Batliwala and Reddy, 1996; Mensah, 2001; and Khan, 2003) have argued that the social position of women could potentially assist their role as energy entrepreneurs: women who live in rural areas know local circumstances and understand local needs; and access to potential female clients is not hindered by social constraints, as it might be in some societies for men from outside the family. But such potential is not realized by providing technology—traditional, conventional, or renewable. It must be promoted by policy changes.

While economically disadvantaged, many women are also socially and politically underprivileged. In many cases, socialization processes have taught them they are inferior or less worthy than men or that certain jobs are not "fitting" for a woman to perform. Empowerment concerns enablement in the face of such challenges, encouraging women to take on new roles. It certainly implies a move toward equality with men in the public sphere and may also suggest changes in gender relations within the household. Few energy services alone, though, can deliver such benefits. Energy may be significant in achieving social and political empowerment it is often not the energy service itself which delivers empowerment benefits so much as the way in which the project is managed and the extent to which women's traditional roles are challenged. Table 3.2 illustrates the translation of general gender goals into energy interventions, and may help to make clear that women's energy needs are not just about cooking.

Conclusion

Energy policy and planning have generally ignored the energy needs of the poor despite a relatively clear link between energy and poverty. Policy gives little heed to the fuel types and combustion technologies used by the majority of the poor, focusing instead upon supply issues in the conventional sector. Electricity has been a significant element of this concern, but there is little chance electricity will reach the majority of the poor in rural areas given the trend towards liberalization. Countries that have experienced a measure of success, despite such challenges, have covered the costs out of general revenue and not treated energy as a consumer good. One can conclude a large level of state subsidy, at least in the infrastructure, is in fact the only way in which the masses can be provided with electricity.[10]

But even if electricity should be supplied to the poor, this would have little impact on the use of traditional energy, as it is a poor substitute for many of the uses for which such energy is required. What is lacking is an energy planning vision that attends to the supply of biomass energy and is cognizant of the dynamic interactions between the modern and the traditional sectors. Without politically sensitive land use interventions there will be no opportunity to promote alternative, efficient, technologies and enable people to slowly start to climb the energy ladder.

Any such policy agenda, though, must also account for the gendered dimensions of energy and poverty. Poor women, as gatherers and users of biomass fuels, suffer the bulk of the problems associated with this sector while their needs are oversimplified by the energy profession. Welfare, economic advancement, emancipation and empowerment are generally regarded as irrelevant to energy transitions. We have shown, however, that energy may play a vital role in these ambitions.

Movement toward a more gender-sensitive approach—strongest in sectors such as health and agriculture—has not yet developed strongly in the energy

Table 3.2
Energy Interventions Meeting Gender Goals

Underlying goal and reason to use the gender analysis	Implication for women	Typical energy interventions
To improve the welfare of women, improve their quality of life and reduce drudgery	Lighten women's work load but without special effort to change their basic role	Improved stoves, power for grinding and husking, powered domestic water supply, electric light in working areas
To improve the production levels of women and their economic opportunities	Create new roles for women that lead to economic growth, this may also lead to the economic independence of the women	Special attention to supplying energy (electrical, mechanical power, or heat) for women's small businesses in the home or outside; usually coupled with credit schemes and technical training
To empower women, help them recognize and break through existing gender relations	Political and decision-making power of women is increased; social norms and opinions about 'appropriate' behavior begin to change. Women's own view of their role and potential begins to change.	Not so much the technology, but *how it is introduced* is crucial. Special attention to including women on organization committees, management training, empowerment consciencisation. Energy itself may be a component in this (e.g., street lighting may facilitate women's meetings in evening and electricity may make internet communication possible, to reducing women's isolation).

field. The lack of gender analysis in energy planning, the tendency to see the household, rather than the people within it, as the unit of consideration, and reluctance to face power and decision-making issues within the household, all militate against the construction of a clearer picture of the gender aspects of energy. These tendencies, in turn, probably relate to the perception of energy as a technical—rather than a social—matter, to the staffing of energy departments dominated by male engineers and to the fact there are few field-level personnel in energy ministries.

A number of basic questions have been suggested: Does the availability of modern energy drive development forward and help to reduce poverty? Can improved access to modern energy help to alter traditional gendered divisions of labor and change the gender balance of power? Can energy empower women? These questions cannot be answered unequivocally; the evidence from scattered case studies is site specific and often contradictory. However, it is evident that energy transitioning and increasing access to services, will not, on their own, ensure the welfare and emancipation of women. If gendered aspects of the energy-poverty nexus are to be adequately engaged, a number of major political transformations have to take place. Women need to be empowered to make choices about energy—both the services and the form of energy to provide that service. Increasing and enabling choice is linked to increased income, sustainable livelihoods and poverty alleviation. Currently favored policies of liberalization need to be reconsidered and governments should contemplate financing both electricity infrastructure and a lifeline of kilowatt-hours out of general revenues. Creative and responsive energy policies should respond to the needs of the poor with a gendered sensitivity currently lacking in planning and administration. Our response to such challenges will determine the future of energy's social project.

Notes

1.   An energy carrier (fossil and biomass fuels, batteries, electricity) is the form in which energy is delivered to the end-user. An energy carrier needs further conversion to useful energy (light, sound, heat, mechanical energy).
2.   Modern energy sources include electricity, coal, oil and its derived products (petrol and diesel) and gas. These energy sources are more convenient (more energy per unit volume, easier to store or distribute) and are more efficient at doing useful work than traditional energy sources while using current commercially available technologies.
3.   For each additional percentage of GNP growth in "all market economies" there is a 0.85 percent growth of primary energy demand (IDS, 2003).
4.   A comprehensive review of definitions of energy poverty and approaches to its measurement may be found in Pachauri et al. (2004).
5.   The energy ladder is a concept used to rank fuels based on consumer preference for efficiency, (with associated cost and time components), and cleanliness. Each rung on the ladder corresponds to the most commonly used fuel by a particular income

group for a specific energy service. For example, for cooking, wood, dung and other biomass fuels are on the bottom rung, with charcoal, coal and kerosene on intermediate rungs, and LPG and electricity on the highest rungs. As one moves up the rungs of the ladder, that is as one switches fuel, the energy released as useful energy increases, while the emission of particulates and other combustion by-products decreases (Reddy, 2000).

6.   Most energy services that have lower costs per unit of received energy on a life cycle costs basis, have higher investment costs.

7.   Metabolic energy is derived from the food we eat. It is rarely measured, despite its significance as part of the energy balance. There are exceptions due to special programs, such as Kutir Jyoti in India, which are targeted at socially and economically weaker sections of the population with specially constructed tariffs, but these are few and far between.

8.   A recent paper by Wickramasinghe (2003) has begun to redress the balance showing the whole biomass fuel cycle has negative consequences for women's health.

9.   For example, a solar cooking workshop was organised in 1999 under the auspices of UNESCO and the European Union.

10. It is worth remembering that the infrastructure for electricity was subsidised by the state in all the industrialized countries on the basis this was a necessary public service.

References

Agarwal, B. (1986). *Cold hearths and barren slopes: the woodfuel crisis in the Third World*. New York: Zed Books.

Allerdice, A., and Rogers, J. H. (2000). *Renewable energy for microenterprise*. Boulder, CO: National Renewable Energy Laboratory.

Anderson, T., Doig, A., Rees, D., and Khennas, S. (1999). *Rural Energy Services*. London: IT Publications Ltd.

Annecke, W. J. (2003). *One man one megawatt, one woman one candle: Women, gender and energy in South Africa, with a focus on research*. PhD dissertation, University of Natal, South Africa.

Barnes, D. (1995). *Consequences of energy policies for the urban poor.* FPD Energy Note No. 7. Washington, DC: The World Bank.

Barnett, A. (2001). Looking at household energy provision in a new way: The Sustainable Livelihoods approach. *Boiling Point*. 46, 30-32. Rugby, U.K: ITDG.

———. (2000). *Energy and the fight against poverty.* Paper given as part of series of Economic Research Seminars at Institute of Social Studies, The Hague, 29th June 2000.

Batliwala, S., and Reddy, A. K. N. (1996). Energy for women and women for energy: A proposal for women's energy entrepreneurship." *ENERGIA News*, 1, 11- 13. Leusden: Energia.

Bazile, D. (2002). Improved cookstoves as a means of poverty alleviation. *Boiling Point*. Number, 48, 20-22, Rugby, UK.

Ceclski, E. (2003). *Enabling equitable access to rural electrification: current thinking on energy, poverty and gender.* Paper prepared for EnPoGen.

———. (1999). *The role of women in sustainable energy development.* Report to the National Renewable Energy Laboratory, Boulder, CO.

Chaieb, S., and Ounalli, A. (2001). Rural Electrification Benefits Women's Health, Income and Status In Tunisia. *ENERGIA News*, 4, 8-20. Leusden: Energia.

Clancy, J.S. (2005). *Urban poor livelihoods: Understanding the role of energy services*. Paper prepared for DFID KaR Project R8348.

Clancy, J. S., Skutsch, M. M., and Bachelor, S. (2003). *The gender-energy-poverty nexus: finding the energy to address gender concerns in development*. Paper prepared for DFID, available at www.energia.org.

Clancy, J. S., Skutsch, M. M., Bachelor, S., Oparaocha, S., and Roehr, U. (2004). *Gender equality and renewable energies*. Thematic background paper prepared for International Conference on Renewables 2004, Bonn, Germany, 1-4 June. Available at www.renewables2004.de.

Clarke, R. (1985). *Wood-stove dissemination*. London: Intermediate Technology Publications.

DFID. (2002). *Energy for the Poor: Underpinning the Millennium Development Goals*. London: Department for International Development. Available at www.dfid.gov.uk.

Dhanapala, K. (1995). *Report on the Gender Related Impact of Micro Hydro technology at the Village Level*. Intermediate Technology Study Report, 2.

Dianka, M. (1999). *Vers une vision Africaine de la gestion surable de la biomasse-energie*. Paper presented at the Symposium La Biomasse Energie pour Developpement et l'Environnement: Quelques Perspectives pour l'Afrique. Abidjan, Cote d'Ivoire, November.

Doig, A. (1998). *Energy Provision to the Urban Poor*. DFID KaR Energy Project R7182, Available at www.dfid-kar-energy.org.uk.

Dube, I. (2002). *Energy Services for the Urban Poor – Part 1*. AFREPREN Working Paper Number 297. Nairobi, Kenya: AFREPREN/FWD. Available at www.afrepren.org.

Dunkerley, J. (1979). Patterns of energy consumption by the rural and urban poor in developing countries. *Natural Resources Forum*. 3.

Dutta, S. (1997). Role of Women in Rural Energy Programs: Issues, Problems and Opportunities. *ENERGIA News*, 4, 11-14. Leusden: Energia.

EASE. (2004). Enabling Access to Sustainable Energy 2004. *Access Newsletter*, 1.

Eckholm, E. (1975). *The Other Energy Crisis: Firewood: Worldwatch Paper Number 1*. Washington, DC: World Watch.

ESMAP. (1999). *Household Energy Strategies for Urban India: The Case of Hyderabad*. Report 214/99. Washington, DC: World Bank.

Feenstra, M. (2002). *Towards a gender-aware energy policy: a case study from South Africa and Uganda*. Masters Thesis, Faculty of Public Administration, University of Twente, Enschede, The Netherlands.

Foley, G., Moss, P., and Timberlake, L. (1984). *Stoves and trees*. London: Earthscan.

Foley, G., Floor, W., Maden, G., Lawali, E. M., Montagne, P., and Tounou., K. (1997). *The Niger Household Energy Project*. Washington, DC: The World Bank.

Foster, V. (2000). Measuring the Impact of Energy Reform—Practical Options. *World Bank Energy and Development Report 2000: Energy Services for the World's Poor*. Washington, DC: The World Bank.

French, D. (1986). Confronting an Unsolvable Problem: Deforestation in Malawi. *World Development*, *14*(4), 531-540.

IDS. (2003). *A Review of the Evidence and Case Studies in Rural China*. A paper prepared for EnPoGen, Asia Alternative Energy Program ASTAE. Washington DC: World Bank.

Jackson, C. (1997). Gender, Irrigation and Environment: Arguing for Agency. *Gender Analysis and Reform of Irrigation Management: Concepts, Cases and Gaps in Knowledge*. Proceedings of the Workshop on Gender and water, 15-19 September 1997. Habarana, Sri Lanka.

Jackson, C. (1998). Rescuing gender from the poverty trap. In Jackson, C. and R. Pearson (Eds.), *Feminist Visions of Development*. London and New York: Routledge.

Kerkhof, P., Madougou, D., and Foley, G. (2001). *A review of the rural firewood market strategy in West Africa*. Report prepared for the World Bank.

Keyun, D. (1995). Renewable Energy Benefits Rural Women in China. In Goldemberg, J. and Johansson, T.B. (Eds). *Energy as an Instrument for Socio- Economic Development*. New York: UNDP.

Khan, J. J. (2003). Case study: Battery operated lamps produced by rural women in Bangladesh. *Energy for Sustainable Development,* 7(3).

Leach, G., and Mearns, R. (1988). *Beyond the Woodfuel Crisis: people, land and trees in Africa*. London: Earthscan.

Littlechild, S. (2000). *Privitisation, Competition and Regulation of the British Electricity Industry with Implications for Developing Countries*. ESMAP Report 226/00, Washington, DC: The World Bank.

Makan, A. (1995). Power for women and men: Towards a gendered approach to domestic policy and planning in South Africa. *Third World Policy Review, 17*(2).

Mandhlazi, W. (1999, June). A reflection on the impact of renewable energy projects on gender. *SAREIN News Flash*.

Massé, R., and Samaranayake, M. R.. (2003). EnPoGen Study in Sri Lanka. *ENERGIA News, 5*(3), 14-16. Leusden: Energia.

McDade, S. and Clancy, J. S. (2003). Gender and Energy. *Energy for Sustainable Development, VII*(3): Special issue on gender and energy.

Mehretu, A., and Mutambira, C. (1992). Gender differences in time and energy costs of distance for regular domestic chores in rural Zimbabwe. *World Development 20*(11), 1675-1683.

Meikle, S., and Bannister, A. (2003). *Energy, Poverty and Sustainable Urban Livelihoods*. DFID KaR R7661. Available at www.difd-kar-energy.org.uk.

Mensah, S. A. (2001). Energy for rural women's enterprises. *Generating Opportunities: Case Studies on Energy and Women*. New York: UNDP.

Ministry of Power. (2001). *Report on Demands of Grants 2001-2002*. Document presented to the Standing Committee on Energy, Thirteenth Lok Sabha, Lok Sabha Secretariat, New Delhi, India, 19 April 2001.

Moser, C. O. (1993). *Gender planning and development: theory, practice and training*. London: Routledge.

Munslow; B., Katerere, Y., Ferf, A., and O'Keefe, P. (1988). *The fuelwood trap: A study of the SADCC region*. London: Earthscan.

Nathan, D., and Kelkar, G. (1997). Wood Energy: The Role of Women's Unvalued Labor. *Gender Technology and Development, 1*(2), 205-224.

Nyoni, S. (1993). *Women and energy: lessons from the Zimbabwe experience*. Working paper 22, Zimbabwe Environment Research Organisation. Harare, Zimbabwe: ZERO.

Pachauri, S., Mueller, A. Kemmler, A., and Spreng, D. (2004). On measuring energy piverty in Indian households. World Development, 32(12), 2083-2104.

Peskin, H., Barnes, D., Domdom, A., and de Gui-Abiad, V. (2000). *New Approaches to Evaluated Rural Electricity Projects*. Power Point Presentation at the World Bank, ESMAP, September, 27.

Ramani, K. V., and Heindemans, E. (2003) *Energy, Poverty, and Gender: A Synthesis*. EnPoGen Report CD Rom. Asian Alternative Energy Program ASTAE. Washington, DC: World Bank.

Reddy, A. K. N. (2000). Energy and Social Issues. *World Energy Assessment*. New York: UNPD.

Reddy, A. K. N., Rajabapariah, P., and Somesekhar, H. I. (1995). Community Biogas Plants Supply Rural Energy and Water – The Pura Village Experience. In Goldemberg, J. and Johansson, T.B. (Eds.), *Energy as an Instrument for Socio-Economic Development*. New York, UNDP.

Reddy, A. K. N., Rajabapariah, P., and Somesekhar, H. I. (2002). Towards a new paradigm for power sector reform in India. *Energy for Sustainable Development*, *VI*(4), 22-29.

Reddy, A. K. N., and Reddy, B. S. (1994). Substitution of Energy Carriers for Cooking in Bangalore. *Energy*. 195, 561-71.

Rengasamy, S. et al.. (2001). *Thaan Vuzha Nilam Tharisu - The Land Without a Farmer Becomes Barren: Policies that Work for Sustainable Agriculture and Rural Livelihoods in Virudhunagar District, Tamilnadu*. London: IIED.

Sarin, M. (1984). *Nada Chula: a Handbook*. Delhi: Voluntary Health Association of India.

Sinha, S. (2005). *Reaching the un-reached: Energy sector reforms in India – will the rural poor benefit?* Working title, PhD Thesis, University of Twente, Enschede, The Netherlands. Forthcoming.

———. (1987). *Biofuels, air pollution and health*. New York: Plenum.

Scott, C. (1995). *Re-thinking modernization and dependency theory*. London: Lynne Rienner.

Skutsch, M. M. (1983). *Why people don't plant trees*. Washington, DC: Resources for the Future.

Skutsch, M. M., and Sanogo, C. (2000). A tale of two women charcoal makers. *ENERGIA News*, *4*(2), 9-10. Leusden: Energia.

Skutsch, M. M., and van Rijn, J. (2005). Gender analysis for energy projects and programs. *Energy for Sustainable Development*.

———. (2002). *Biomass: the Fuel of the Future*. Paper presented to the IXth International Biomass Conference, Amsterdam, June 2002.

Smith, K. (1999). Indoor Air Pollution. *Pollution Management in Focus*. Discussion Note Number 4, August. Washington, DC: World Bank.

SPARKNET. (2004). *South Africa Country Report Synthesis*.

Suarez, C. E. (1995). Energy Needs for Sustainable Human Development. In J. Goldemberg and T. B. Johansson (Eds). *Energy as an Instrument for Socio- Economic Development*. New York: UNDP.

Tellam, I. (2000). *Fuel for change: World Bank Energy Policy-rhetoric vs. reality*. New York/Amsterdam: Zed Books/Both Ends.

Tinker, I. (1984). *The real energy crisis: women's time*. Washington, DC: Equity Policy Center.

Tucker, M. (1999). Can Solar Cooking save Forests? *Ecological Economics*, 31, 77-89.

UNDP. (2001). *Generating opportunities: case studies on energy and women*. New York: United Nations Development Program.

UNEP. (2004). *Disconnected: Electricity reforms impact poor households*. GNESD News, April 2004. Available at http://www.gnesd.org.

Wallace, W.L., Jingming, L., and Shangbin, G. (1998). The use of Photovolatics for Rural Electrification in Northwestern China. Presented at the 2nd World Conference and Exhibition on Photovolatic Solar Energy Conversion, July 6-10.

Wilson, M., and Green, J. M. (2000). The Feasibility of Introducing Solar Ovens to Rural Women in Maphephethe. *Tydskrif vir Gesinsekologie en Verbruikerswetenskappe*, 28, 54-61.

World Bank. (1996). *Rural Energy and Development: Improving Energy Supplies to Two Billion People*. Washington, DC: World Bank.

Woroniuk, B., and Schalkwyk, J. (1998). Energy Policy and Equality between Women and Men. *SIDA Equality Prompt,* 9. Stockholm: Infrastructure Division, SIDA.

Energy and Security

4

Protecting Overseas Oil Supplies: The Globalization of the "Carter Doctrine"

Michael T. Klare

Introduction

The 2003 U.S. invasion of Iraq is certain to be viewed by future historians as one of the pivotal events in modern American history, and much ink will no doubt be consumed in attempting to explain the U.S. decision to remove Saddam Hussein by force. For supporters of the Bush administration, the explanation is obvious: to destroy the weapons of mass destruction (WMD) thought to be possessed by Saddam Hussein and to prevent their transfer to Al Qaeda and other terrorist organizations. But much doubt has been cast on this explanation by the failure of U.S. inspectors to find any WMD in Iraq and the lack of any concrete evidence of ties between the Hussein regime and Osama bin Laden—leaving the question of U.S. motivation for the war largely unresolved. But while debate on this matter is likely to persist for many decades to come, historians would be well advised to begin their search for a convincing explanation by examining the impact of the Carter Doctrine.

The Carter Doctrine was first enunciated on January 23, 1980, when then President Jimmy Carter told Congress that untrammeled access to Persian Gulf oil was essential to the U.S. economy and that any move by a hostile power to block such access would be viewed as an assault on the "vital interests" of the United States and resisted by "any means necessary, including military force." Although promulgated in response to specific events—the Soviet occupation of Afghanistan and the Islamic Revolution in Iran—the doctrine was said to have broad application, extending to any attempt to block the flow of Persian Gulf oil. To implement this policy, Carter established the Rapid Deployment Joint Task Force (RDJTF) and authorized the acquisition of U.S. military facilities in the Gulf area. Every president since 1980 has reaffirmed the basic premises of the Carter doctrine and taken steps to enhance America's capacity to project military force in the greater Gulf area.

Many formative expressions of America's Cold War policy—the Truman Doctrine, the Eisenhower Doctrine and the Nixon Doctrine, among others—have been rendered moot by the end of the U.S.-Soviet rivalry, but the Carter Doctrine remains in full force. The United States continues to rely on Persian Gulf oil for a significant share of its total petroleum supply, and any threat to the delivery of this petroleum would be viewed today—as it was in 1980—as an assault on America's vital interests. With this in mind, American forces still occupy critical positions in the greater Gulf area and the RDJTF—now incorporated into the U.S. Central Command (Centcom)—continues to assume principal responsibility for the safe flow of Persian Gulf oil.

As will be argued, the 2003 U.S. invasion of Iraq can be seen as a natural extension of the Carter Doctrine, as can other U.S. moves in the Persian Gulf. But the logic of the Carter Doctrine is no longer being applied to the Gulf alone: increasingly, access to oil in other producing areas is being viewed as a "vital interest" and thus as something that must be protected by military force when and if necessary. Indeed, the globalization of the Carter Doctrine may prove to be one of the most significant developments of the post-Cold War era.[1]

Origins of the Carter Doctrine

The origins of the Carter Doctrine can be traced back to February 1945, when the United States first established a protectorate over Saudi Arabia and committed itself to the use of military force in protecting Persian Gulf oil. This move was triggered by Washington's concern over the nation's declining output of oil and a desire to ensure the safety of its overseas energy supplies. Until 1945, the United States was largely self-sufficient in petroleum production and (in most years) produced a big enough surplus to satisfy the needs of many foreign consumers as well. But the requirements of wartime consumption, plus intimations of an eventual decline in U.S. output, led President Franklin D. Roosevelt to seek control over major foreign sources of petroleum. By 1943, he had concluded that Saudi Arabia was most likely to assume the role of America's principal foreign supplier, and by 1945 he had determined that the United States must extend some sort of protective umbrella over Saudi Arabia's prolific oil fields. With this in mind, he arranged to meet with King Abdul Aziz ibn Saud, the founder of the modern Saudi dynasty, aboard the *U.S.S. Quincy* while anchored at the entrance to the Nile Canal.[2]

President Roosevelt met with King Abdul Aziz for five and a half hours aboard the *Quincy* on February 14, 1945, discussing a wide range of issues of concern to both leaders. No record was kept of this meeting, but most scholars and policymakers have concluded that Roosevelt and Abdul Aziz agreed to establish a tacit alliance whereby the United States would assume permanent responsibility for protecting the House of Saud against its foreign and domestic enemies in return for exclusive U.S. access to Saudi oil.[3] Certainly, American officials have repeatedly referred to this meeting as the basis for U.S. ties with the kingdom. "We do, of course, have historic ties to governments in the region," then Secretary of Defense Dick Cheney told the Senate Armed Services Committee in September 1990, following the Iraqi invasion of Kuwait. These ties "hark back with respect to Saudi Arabia to 1945, when President Franklin Delano Roosevelt met with King Abdul Aziz on the *U.S.S. Quincy*, toward the end of World War II, and affirmed at that time that the United States has a lasting and a continuing interest in the security of the kingdom"(Senate Committee on Armed Services, 1990: 10).

In line with this arrangement, the United States undertook a variety of measures aimed at providing a defensive shield around Saudi Arabia and its oil fields. These included the establishment of a permanent U.S. military base at Dhahran (beginning in 1946) the supply of advanced U.S. arms to Saudi forces, and the deployment of hundreds (later thousands) of American military instructors and advisers in the kingdom.[4] Initially, however, U.S. officials preferred to rely on Great Britain—for decades the dominant power in the region—to assume primary responsibility for regional security. But when London announced that it could no longer perform this role and would remove its forces from the area by the end of 1971, Washington chose to confer responsibility for regional stability on the Shah of Iran, then America's principal ally in the Gulf.[5] This approach—widely known in Washington as the "surrogate strategy"—prevailed until January 1979, when the Shah was overthrown and replaced by radical Islamic clerics loyal to the Ayatollah Khomeini. The Carter Doctrine, entailing direct U.S. responsibility for Gulf security, was largely adopted in response to this unexpected development.

When first announced, in Carter's State of the Union address of January 23, 1980, the policy was aimed specifically at the oil resources of the greater Gulf region. This area, Carter declared, "contains more than two-third's of the world's exportable oil," and so must not be allowed to fall under the control of hostile forces. "Let our position be absolutely clear: an attempt by any outside force to gain control of the Persian Gulf region will be regarded as an assault on the vital interests of the United States of America, and such an assault will be repelled by any means necessary, including military force" (Carter, 1980: 197). This avowal was directed, in the first instance, toward the Soviet Union, which had occupied Afghanistan just a few weeks earlier, but could also be interpreted as applying to any hostile nation or bloc, such as the extremist Islamic forces then in control of Iran.[6]

To lend credibility to his proclamation, Carter announced a number of moves aimed at beefing up America's capacity to employ force in the Persian Gulf and surrounding areas. The most important of these was the activation of the RDJTF, a new multi-service assault group with responsibility for U.S.

combat operations in the greater Gulf region. Based at MacDill Air Force Base in Tampa, Florida, the RDJTF was given command authority over a wide assortment of air, ground, and naval units.[7] Carter also told Congress on January 23 that "We've increased and strengthened our naval presence in the Indian Ocean, and we are now making arrangements for key naval and air facilities to be used by our forces in the region of northeast Africa and the Persian Gulf" (Carter, 1980: 197–198).

Although critical of President Carter on many issues, President Reagan wholeheartedly endorsed the Carter Doctrine and lent it fresh impetus. On January 1, 1983, he elevated the RDJTF to a full-scale regional headquarters—the U.S. Central Command—granting it equal status to the pre-existing European Command (Eurcom), Pacific Command (Pacom) and Southern Command (Southcom). Reagan also accelerated the acquisition of military bases in the Gulf region and ordered the procurement of additional ships and planes for use by Centcom forces. By the end of his tenure, Centcom had emerged a major military organization with a significant capacity for what the Pentagon calls "power projection" in the Persian Gulf region (Hines, 2002).

Situated, as it is, in the greater Persian Gulf area, Centcom naturally must deal with the threats of terrorism and the proliferation of WMD. From its very inception, however, the command's principal mission has been to protect the flow of Persian Gulf oil in accordance with the Carter Doctrine. This mission is given blunt expression in the testimony given each year by Centcom's top commander to members of Congress. "America's vital interests in the [Gulf] region are long-standing," General J. H. Binford Peay declared in 1997. "With over 65 percent of the world's oil reserves located in the Gulf states of the region—from which the United States imports nearly 20 percent of its needs; Western Europe, 43 percent; and Japan, 68 percent—the international community must have free and unfettered access to the region's resources." All of Peay's successors have reaffirmed this fundamental outlook.

The Carter Doctrine after Carter

The establishment of Centcom was not Reagan's only expression of support for the Carter Doctrine: he also applied this policy to particular developments in the Gulf. When, at the height of the Iran-Iraq War of 1980 to 1988, Iranian forces began to attack Kuwaiti oil tankers while traveling through the Persian Gulf (presumably to discourage Kuwait from providing loans to Iraq for arms procurement) Reagan authorized the "reflagging" of Kuwaiti tankers with the American ensign and their protection by U.S. naval forces. Such action was essential, Reagan declared, to demonstrate the "U.S. commitment to the flow of oil through the Gulf."[8] The involvement of American forces—while described as being neutral with respect to the two belligerents—was actually more beneficial to Iraq than to the Iran and thus contributed to Tehran's decision to abandon the struggle and sue for peace.[9]

The Iran-Iraq war drew to a close in August 1988, with the exhausted and impoverished belligerents agreeing to a cease-fire and peace talks. But peace in the Gulf reigned only briefly. Disappointed with the outcome of the war and facing a mountain of accumulated wartime debt, the Iraqi leader, Saddam Hussein, viewed Kuwait—which was refusing to forgive the debt Baghdad had built up during the war to pay for arms—as the source of his problems. Seizing his small neighbor's rich oil fields looked like a convenient way out of Baghdad's financial predicament. After issuing a series of increasingly threatening (and unheeded) ultimatums to Kuwait, Hussein ordered Iraqi forces into the country on August 2, 1990.

In the months leading up to the invasion, American officials had been struggling to develop a coherent policy on Iraq—with some favoring efforts to placate Saddam Hussein (in the hope of evading a breakdown in relations) and others calling for a tougher approach. But when Iraqi tanks rolled into Kuwait City, the White House instantly concluded that Iraq posed an indisputable threat to America's interests in the Gulf, as encapsulated in the Carter Doctrine. At the first National Security Council meeting convened to discuss the invasion, on the morning of August 2, President George H. W. Bush expressed considerable alarm over the safety of Saudi Arabia and its vital oil supplies. Then, following a meeting at Camp David on August 3, Bush ordered the Department of Defense to begin making plans for military action to defend the Saudi fields, and on August 6—just four days after the Iraqi invasion—authorized Secretary of Defense Dick Cheney to begin deploying American troops in Saudi Arabia.[10]

Oil, and the fate of Saudi Arabia, stood at the center of White House deliberations in the early days of the crisis. In a nationally televised address on August 8, announcing his decision to use military force in the Gulf, Bush cited America's energy needs as his primary impetus. "Our country now imports nearly half the oil it consumes and could face a major threat to its economic independence," he declared. Hence, "the sovereign independence of Saudi Arabia is of vital interest to the United States."[11] Secretary of Defense Cheney sounded the same note, highlighting the threat to oil in his first major statement on the crisis, at a September 11 appearance before the Senate Armed Services Committee. "Once [Saddam] acquired Kuwait and deployed an army as large as the one he possesses," Cheney observed, he would be "in a position to be able to dictate the future of worldwide energy policy, and that [would give] him a stranglehold on our economy" (Senate Committee on Armed Services, 1990: 11). Only later, when American troops were girding for combat with the Iraqis, did administration officials come up with other justifications for war—the need to liberate Kuwait, to destroy Iraqi WMD, to bolster international sanctions against aggression, and so forth. The record makes it clear, though, that the President and his senior associates initially viewed the invasion of Kuwait through the lens of the Carter Doctrine: as a threat to Saudi Arabia and the free flow of oil from the Gulf (Woodward, 1992: 225 – 226, 236 – 237).

The defense of Saudi Arabia against possible Iraqi attack (Operation Desert Shield) eventually gave way to the military campaign to drive the Iraqis out of Kuwait (Operation Desert Storm). Once this had been accomplished, however, Bush Senior balked at invading Iraq itself, fearing a prolonged war and the disintegration of the international Coalition he had so carefully assembled. Instead, Bush initiated—and President Clinton later perpetuated—the "containment" of Saddam, entailing a naval quarantine, the "no fly" zones over northern and southern Iraq and a punishing system of economic sanctions. As noted by Bush Senior and Clinton at the time, containment was intended to achieve "regime change" in Iraq by making conditions so onerous that the population would rise up and overthrow Saddam.

By 2001, however, it had become evident that the strategy was having the opposite effect: instead of turning the masses against the Hussein regime, the sanctions were enhancing Saddam's stature as a vigorous opponent of American imperialism. And despite the terrible drubbing Iraqi forces received during the 1991 Gulf War, Saddam's armies were still seen as a threat to U.S. interests in the Gulf. It is on this basis that the President George W. Bush concluded that an outright invasion of Iraq was the only plausible option for removing the threat posed by the Hussein regime.[12] Whatever the reasons given at the time, the 2003 invasion of Iraq can best be understood as a continuation of the January-February 1991 assault on Iraqi forces in Iraq—an assault that was prompted, in the first instance, by the perceived threat to America's "vital interests" in the Persian Gulf, as articulated by President Carter on January 23, 1980.

Knowing this history helps clarify the debate over whether or not the 2003 Iraq War was prompted by the pursuit of oil. While the administration can claim that it was primarily motivated by concern over the military threat posed by Saddam Hussein, and not by a desire to seize Iraq's oil, the threat that Saddam was said to pose was directed at America's continued control of the Persian Gulf area—and such control has, since Carter's time, been viewed as essential to the uninterrupted flow of Persian Gulf oil. From a geopolitical perspective, then, oil was at the heart of the administration's outlook. Vice President Dick Cheney admitted as much in August 2002, when he told a Veterans of Foreign Wars convention that Saddam had to be removed from office because, once Iraq was equipped with weapons of mass destruction, he "could then be expected to seek domination of the entire Middle East, take control of a great portion of the world's energy supplies, [and] directly threaten America's friends throughout the region."[13]

This interpretation of the invasion is given further credence by the efforts made by American forces to seize Iraqi oil fields in the early days of the fighting and to establish control over other elements of Iraq's far-flung petroleum infrastructure. As has been widely noted, U.S. troops protected the Oil Ministry building in Baghdad while allowing other government buildings and the national art museum to be looted by Iraqi mobs—a decision that, more than any other, might have turned the civilian population against the United States after the fall of Saddam. But even this, and related moves, has not prevented Iraqi insurgents from attacking oil pipelines and refineries on a near-daily basis, thus preventing any increase in Iraqi oil output. Despite heroic efforts by employees of the Halliburton Company and other U.S. oil-service companies, Iraqi petroleum output remains below pre-war levels.[14]

At present, the Pentagon's top priority in Iraq is to defeat the anti-American insurgency now ravaging the country. But, consistent with its historic mission, the U.S. Central Command is also protecting pipelines, refineries, and oil-export facilities throughout Iraq. Although this effort has received far less media attention than the urban warfare in Baghdad and Falluja, it is no less important: With petroleum constituting the nation's only significant source of income, ensuring uninterrupted oil exports is essential for the economic survival of Iraq's U.S.-backed government. However mundane-seeming, these protective operations can be extremely hazardous. On April 24, 2004 two suicide attackers in an explosives-laden boat approached one of the major loading platforms in the Gulf; when a small U.S. Navy vessel interceded, the attacker's boat exploded and three Americans—two from the Navy and one from the Coast Guard—died instantly. Symbolically, this was the first Coast Guard combat fatality since the Vietnam War (Cummins, 2004).

Most of the U.S. oil-protection effort in Iraq is devoted to protection of the country's onshore pipelines and refineries. Heavily-armed Army units patrol the vital pipeline carrying Iraqi petroleum from Kirkuk in the north to the Turkish border, and the equally critical line connecting Kirkuk with Basra in the south. But U.S. Navy and Coast Guard forces also protect the offshore loading platforms that are used to export Iraqi oil by ship through the Persian Gulf. "In the grand scheme of things, there may be no other place where our armed forces are deployed that has a greater strategic importance," Captain Kurt Tidd of the U.S. Fifth Fleet said of this naval mission in July 2004 (cited in Glanz, 2004).

Even if the fighting in Iraq eventually dies down, Centcom will continue to maintain a significant U.S. military presence in the Gulf area and employ force when needed to overcome threats to the free flow of oil. With Saddam Hussein in custody and Iraq under U.S. control, the next most potent threat to American domination is thought to emanate from Iran, now ruled by militant Islamic clerics. American strategists are particularly concerned over the Iranian threat to the Strait of Hormuz—the narrow passageway connecting the Persian Gulf with the Indian Ocean and the world at large. To ensure that Iran will not try to close the Strait by firing on tankers crossing through it—the Iranians have deployed anti-ship missile batteries along the northern shore of the Gulf—Centcom ships and planes patrol the waterway daily and remain poised for an immediate clash with Iranian forces.[15]

Despite the fiasco in Iraq, then, the Carter Doctrine continues to govern U.S. policy in the Persian Gulf area. American forces are likely to remain deployed in the area—and to risk their lives on a daily basis—until the last drop of petroleum is extracted from the region.

The Extended Carter Doctrine

But this is only half of the story. Beginning in the Clinton administration, the Carter Doctrine has been extended to other oil-producing regions of the world, and now covers much of the planet. In addition to protecting the oil of the Gulf, Centcom forces have also assumed responsibility for the protection of energy supplies in Central Asia and the Caspian region. Meanwhile, forces from Eurcom are helping to protect oil pipelines in the Republic of Georgia and oil-rich waters off the coast of Africa; forces from Pacom guard the oil lanes of the South China Sea; and troops from Southcom are helping to protect pipelines in Colombia.

The globalization of the Carter Doctrine began in the mid-1990s, when the Clinton administration determined that the Caspian Sea basin—until 1992 under the effective control of the Soviet Union—could become a major source of oil for the United States and its allies, thereby helping to lessen U.S. dependence on the ever-turbulent Persian Gulf. The newly-independent states of Azerbaijan and Kazakhstan were eager to sell their petroleum wealth to the West, but they lacked an autonomous conduit for exports (at that time, all existing pipelines from the land-locked Caspian passed through Russia) and also faced serious challenges from ethnic minorities and internal opposition movements. To safeguard the future flow of Caspian oil, Clinton agreed to assist in the construction of a new oil pipeline from Baku in Azerbaijan through Georgia to Ceyhan in Turkey (thus bypassing Russia) and to help these states enhance their military capacity. American military aid began flowing to these states by 1997, and at that time U.S. troops began a series of annual joint military exercises with their forces.[16]

Although never formally invoking the Carter Doctrine when announcing these actions, Clinton applied the same "national security" umbrella to Caspian Sea oil during a 1997 White House meeting with Heydar Aliyev, the president (and virtual dictator) of Azerbaijan. "In a world of growing energy demand," Clinton declared, "our nation cannot afford to rely on any single region for our energy supplies." By facilitating Azerbaijan's oil exports, "we not only help Azerbaijan to prosper, we also help diversify our energy supply and strengthen our nation's security."[17]

Clinton also extended this formula to Kazakhstan, another promising source of petroleum, and to Georgia, a major way-station on the proposed

Baku-Tbilisi-Ceyhan (BTC) pipeline from the Caspian to Turkey. In consonance with this outlook, moreover, Clinton authorized military-to-military ties between the Pentagon and these countries' armed forces, and sent U.S. troops on familiarization visits to bases in the region. Although modest in comparison to the military buildup long under way in the Persian Gulf area, these moves established a significant U.S. presence in the Caspian basin. These ties were later utilized by President Bush to facilitate U.S. intervention in Afghanistan following September 11, 2001 but it is important to note that their establishment was originally motivated by a concern over the safety of energy supplies, not the threat posed by terrorism.[18]

It was President Clinton, then, who commenced the globalization of the Carter Doctrine, but it is President Bush who made this a central objective of American foreign policy.

The foreign oil strategy adopted by the Bush administration was a natural consequence of the National Energy Policy (NEP) announced by the White House on May 17, 2001. Widely known as the "Cheney report" after its principal author, Vice President Dick Cheney, the administration plan calls for a substantial increase in U.S. oil imports in order to satisfy soaring demand for basic energy. Much of this imported oil is to come from the Persian Gulf area (which alone possesses sufficient petroleum to met anticipated U.S. requirements in the decades ahead) but, in recognition of the chronic turmoil in the Gulf, the plan also calls for a significant increase in U.S. reliance on emerging producers in other areas of the world (National Energy Policy Development Group, 2001).[19]

The White House did not, of course, emphasize America's growing reliance on imports when releasing the NEP in 2001, suggesting instead that the United States would seek to promote energy "independence" by opening up the Arctic National Wildlife Refuge (ANWR) and other protected wilderness sites to commercial drilling. (I put "independence" in quotation marks because the White House knew full well that its energy plan would entail *increased*, not diminished reliance on imports.) The ensuing debate over the wisdom of drilling in ANWR drowned out any public discussion of other aspects of the administration's plan and, so, most Americans are unaware of its true geopolitical significance.

Before proceeding further in this discussion, it is necessary to say a few words about the global supply of oil and its projected future availability. At present, there is considerable debate in this country as to whether or not the world has arrived at maximum, or "peak," day-to-day oil output. Some experts claim that the current shortages of petroleum (and resulting high prices) are evidence that peak production has already occurred; others argue that these shortages are temporary, and that global output will soon rise again.[20] What is *not* in dispute, however, is that the center of gravity of world oil production is shifting from older fields in the global North, notably in the

USA, Canada, Mexico, and Europe, to less-developed fields in the global South, especially in Africa, Latin America, the Middle East, and the Caspian basin. According to projections released by the U.S. Department of Energy in 2003, the share of total world petroleum output accounted for by the major Northern producers will fall from 27.4 percent in 2002 to 18.3 percent in 2025, while the share held by producers in Africa, Latin America (excluding Mexico) and the Gulf area, will rise from 46.6 to 59.2 percent (Energy Information Administration, 2003: 235). The implications are stark: The more this country comes to rely on petroleum to satisfy a significant share of its energy needs, the deeper will be its reliance on oil from the developing countries.

As previously noted, this reality is not immediately evident from the Cheney report. But careful reading ultimately brings to light the true significance of the Bush-Cheney plan. In chapter 8, "Strengthening Global Alliances," the NEP affirms that because domestic U.S. oil production faces long-term decline, the pursuit of additional foreign supplies must be made "a priority of our trade and foreign policy." In particular, this means obtaining more oil from the Persian Gulf. "Middle East oil production will remain central to world oil security," the report notes and, so, "the Gulf will be a primary focus of U.S. international energy policy." But the NEP also acknowledges the risks entailed in over-reliance on the Gulf and, so, calls for a significant increase in imports from other producing regions. "[The] concentration of world oil production in any one region of the world is a potential contributor to market instability," it states. Accordingly, "greater diversity of oil production...has obvious benefits to all market participants" (National Energy Policy Development Group, 2001: chapter 8, 1 – 6).

The Cheney report identifies many areas as possible sources of non-Gulf oil but, focuses in particular on three key areas: the Andean region of South America (notably Colombia and Venezuela), the west coast of Africa (Angola, Equatorial Guinea, Mali and Nigeria) and the Caspian Sea basin (Azerbaijan and Kazakhstan). "Growing levels of production and exports [from these regions] are important factors that can lessen the impact of a supply disruption [in the Gulf] on the U.S. and world economies," the NEP declares (National Energy Policy Development Group, 2001: Chapter 8, 6 – 7).

So far, so good. But what the report fails to mention is that these areas are no less prone to turbulence and conflict as is the Persian Gulf. Indeed, the current instability in Colombia, Venezuela, Nigeria and other non-Gulf producing areas—combined with the fighting in Iraq—is the primary reason for the current worldwide shortage of petroleum and resulting high gasoline prices. There is, in fact, no real escape from the turmoil associated with oil production.

Why is this so? Part of the answer to this question lies in the fact that these countries, like many of the Gulf producers, bear significant scars from the colonial era. In many cases, their original social structures were severely traumatized by the occupying powers and so the governments erected in the post-colonial era have proved susceptible to corruption, cronyism, and ethnic favoritism. Many of these countries, moreover, encompass ethnic minorities that were incorporated into the original colonial territory at the behest of the imperial powers and thus found themselves in post-independence states with which they have little or nothing in common—often leading to the outbreak of separatist movements or violent drives for regional autonomy. (Examples include the Armenians of Nagorno-Karabakh in Azerbaijan, the Abkhazians and Ossetians of Georgia, the Kurds of northern Iraq, and the occupants of Cabinda in northwest Angola.) At the same time, many groups within these countries continue to harbor strong anti-imperial sentiments and so resent any contemporary intrusion into their societies of Western culture and commerce. (To some degree, this is the source of the fierce anti-Americanism encountered by U.S. forces in Iraq.)

Any or all of this can be said to characterize many of the world's post-colonial societies—oil-producing or not. But the discovery and production of petroleum in such a country almost always leads to further polarization and instability. This is so because the enormous revenues generated by petroleum tend to be monopolized by the clan or clique in control of the government, while the rest of the population receives few, if any, benefits from the nation's natural bounty—thus arousing substantial resentment and internal unrest.[21] And because petro-regimes of this sort often seek to preserve their privileged status by employing the instruments of state security to quash all forms of dissent, the only viable option available to those desiring a change in the status quo is assassination, coup d'etat, or armed revolt.

This picture of instability, division and seething resentments can be found in almost all of the countries on which the United States is coming to rely for its foreign supplies of petroleum. Angola, Azerbaijan, Colombia, Iraq, and Nigeria face internal revolts or potent separatist movements. Saudi Arabia harbors a virulent terrorist movement with hidden offshoots in the other Persian Gulf kingdoms. Venezuela and Iran are wracked by internal political divisions that could erupt in civil disorder and violence at any time. Few of these countries possess mechanisms for the orderly transfer of power from one ruler to another, and, so, recurring succession crises are likely. In all of them, moreover, an increase in oil output is likely to exacerbate the internal social and political pressures, not relieve them.[22]

What this suggests, then, is that increased U.S. reliance on oil from Africa, Latin America, and the Caspian region is certain to entail the same sort of geopolitical risks as have long been evident in the Persian Gulf area. And it is this reality that has driven the Bush administration to globalize the Carter Doctrine and increase the U.S. military presence in these other oil-producing regions.

The Caspian Sea Basin

As noted, this process commenced during the final years of the Clinton administration when military ties were established with the post-Soviet states of the Caucasus and Central Asia. President George W. Bush—who had been highly critical of his predecessor's other foreign policy efforts—was quick to embrace his initiatives in the Caspian basin. Under Bush, U.S. military aid to friendly states in the region was increased and the tempo of military-to-military contacts and joint exercises stepped up. These efforts were all well underway prior to September 11, 2001 but were accelerated significantly in the months that followed. Bush also drew on these ties to gain access to bases in the region to support U.S. military operations in Afghanistan.

Following the defeat of the Taliban, the Bush administration placed fresh emphasis on developing military ties with the states of the Caspian Sea basin. "Our country is now linked with this region in ways we could never have imagined before September 11," Assistant Secretary of State A. Elizabeth Jones told the Senate Foreign Relations Committee in December 2001 (Jones, 2001). In line with this outlook, the administration stepped up visits by senior U.S. military officials to key leaders in the region and significantly increased the flow of military and economic assistance to friendly governments (see, for example, Garamone, 2001). All told, U.S. assistance to the greater Caspian Sea area (including Armenia, Azerbaijan, Georgia, Kazakhstan, Kyrgyzstan, Tajikistan, Turkmenistan, and Uzbekistan) topped $1.5 billion in Fiscal Years 2002-2004, a 50 percent increase over the preceding three-year period (U.S. Department of State, 2003).

In announcing these moves, the White House has repeatedly stated that such action is needed to fight Al Qaeda and to support ongoing U.S. military operations in Afghanistan. But a careful reading of Pentagon and State Department documents suggests that the protection of oil is of paramount concern. Thus, in requesting $51.2 million in economic assistance to Azerbaijan for fiscal year 2005, the administration affirmed that "U.S. national interests in Azerbaijan center on the strong bilateral security and counter-terrorism cooperation [and] the advancement of U.S. energy security." It further noted that "the involvement of U.S. firms in the development and export of Azerbaijani oil is key to our objective of diversifying world oil supplies" (U.S. Department of State, 2003: 322). In line with this reasoning, the Department of Defense is helping Azerbaijan to develop and deploy a small navy in its oil-rich Caspian Sea enclave, whose outer boundaries have been contested by Iran and Turkmenistan (U.S. Department of State, 2003: 323).

The integration of the administration's anti-terrorism and oil-protection policies is also evident in Georgia, the leading recipient of U.S. assistance in the region. According to the Department of State, this aid is intended to help Georgia protect its borders and to safeguard the BTC pipeline (now under construction) against sabotage and insurgent attack. At the heart of this effort is a $64 million "train and equip" program designed to enhance the counterinsurgency capabilities of the Georgian army and its capacity to protect the BTC pipeline route. Some 150 U.S. Special Operations instructors have been deployed in Georgia for this purpose, along with other military specialists.[23] In February 2003, this program was expanded to incorporate an $11 million U.S. effort to train a 400-strong "pipeline protection battalion" for the new Georgian Special Protection Service, an elite unit created by then President Eduard Shevardnadze in early 2003 to guard the Georgian section of the BTC pipeline (Oil and Gas Journal Online, 2003).

When Shevardnadze was ousted by a popular revolt in November 2003, the Bush administration was quick to endorse the new, pro-Western government of Acting President Nino Burdzhanadze. We want "to underscore America's very strong support for stability and security and the territorial integrity here in Georgia," Secretary of Defense Donald Rumsfeld declared after a meeting with Burdzhanadze in Tbilisi on December 5, just two weeks after the revolt. Rumsfeld further indicated that the United States would continue its defense relationship with the Georgian military (U.S. Department of Defense, 2003a; see also Shanker, 2003). This relationship is "strategically important," a high Pentagon official accompanying Rumsfeld explained, both because of its pivotal role in the war on terrorism and also "in terms of energy," as the BTC pipeline passes through that country (U.S. Department of Defense, 2003b). (Burdzhanadze was succeeded by an elected president, Mikhail Saakashvili, on January 25, 2004.)

Meanwhile, in Kazakhstan, the United States is helping to refurbish an old Soviet air base at Atyrau, near the giant offshore Kashagan oil field, which is partly owned by Exxon Mobil, ConocoPhillips, and Royal Dutch/Shell. This base will be used to house a Kazakh "rapid reaction brigade" whose task, according to the Department of State, will be to "enhance Kazakhstan's capability to respond to major terrorist threats to oil platforms or borders" (Nichol, 2002: 3).

The Department of Defense is also building up its capacity for direct military involvement in the region. The temporary bases established at Bishkek in Kyrgyzstan and at Khanabad in Uzbekistan to support American combat in Afghanistan during the war against the Taliban are now being converted into permanent military installations, capable of supporting U.S. operations throughout Central Asia and the Caspian basin (Kaiser, 2002). In addition, senior Pentagon officials have indicated that they are considering the acquisition of additional "forward operating bases" in Azerbaijan and Georgia to support future U.S. troop deployments in the region (Campbell and Ward, 2003: 95 – 103; Jaffe, 2003; Loeb, 2003). The airfield at Atyrau is also being eyed for this purpose: According to the Department of State, the base will house a facility to be used by U.S. and Kazakh troops for "joint training in the area of counter-terrorism"—a possible first-step toward its permanent occupation by American forces (U.S. Department of State, 2003: 348 – 349).

Latin America and Africa

A similar pattern of ever-expanding U.S. military involvement is also evident in the Andean region of South America and the Atlantic states of Africa. Both of these areas are eyed as major sources of imported oil in the future, and both are torn by internal unrest and conflict.

The situation in Colombia is a source of particular concern for American officials. Colombia was once among this country's leading foreign oil suppliers, and has the potential to provide larger volumes in the future. But the civil war that has plagued Colombia over the past few decades has discouraged exploration in new areas and lowered the country's oil output. Contending that the violence in Colombia has produced an atmosphere of lawlessness in which the illegal drug trade can flourish, the United States has long provided arms and other forms of military aid to the country's army and police forces. In 2002, however, the Bush administration announced another key objective for U.S. military assistance: helping the Colombian government to protect the nation's oil pipelines.

Colombia's extensive pipeline network is often attacked by anti-government guerrillas, reducing Colombia's net petroleum exports and depriving the government of a critical source of income. To counter this danger, the White House requested $98 million in 2002 to bolster security along the Caño Limón-Coveñas pipeline—a highly vulnerable 480-mile-long conduit carrying oil from Occidental Petroleum's fields in Colombia's northeast to Coveñas on the Caribbean coast (Grossman, 2002; see also Forero, 2002). These funds—plus another $147 million requested in Fiscal Year 2004—are being used to train and equip elite battalions of the Colombian army to guard the Caño Limón-Coveñas pipeline and to fight rebel forces operating in the vicinity (U.S. Department of State, 2003: 456 – 457; see also Forero, 2002; Wilson, 2003).

Supposedly, the principal objective of this initiative is to boost the Colombian government's export revenues by preventing further attacks on the pipelines. "Lost revenue from guerrilla attacks has severely hampered the GOC's, [Government of Colombia's], ability to meet the country's social, political, and security needs," the State Department reported in 2002. By improving pipeline security, the U.S. will "enhance the GOC's ability to protect a vital part of its energy infrastructure" (U.S. Department of State, 2003: 404). But it is also evident that the White House is also concerned about the recent drop in Colombia's oil exports to the United States—plunging from a peak of 468,000 barrels per day in 1999 to 256,000 in 2002—and the evident reluctance of the major international oil companies to further develop Colombia's untapped reserves (Energy Information Administration, 2003b). By helping to defeat the guerrillas, Washington hopes to make the region safe for oil exploration and thus increase Colombia's future exports to this country (Forero, 2004).

American military involvement in sub-Saharan Africa is at a less advanced stage, but here, too, concern over oil supplies is spurring a major increase in U.S. entanglement. Underlying this effort is growing American reliance on African oil. "Along with Latin America," the Cheney report affirms, "West Africa is expected to be one of the fastest-growing sources of oil and gas for the American market" (National Energy Policy Development Group, 2001: chapter 8, 11). From Washington's perspective, this imbues sub-Saharan Africa with a geopolitical significance it has never previously enjoyed. "African oil is of national strategic interest to us," Assistant Secretary of State Walter Kansteiner declared in 2002, "and it will increase and become more important as we go forward" (cited in Crawley, 2002).

Having been designated as a "national strategic interest" of the United States, African oil is being exposed to the same sort of military initiatives that have long been pursued in the Persian Gulf and, under the extended Carter Doctrine, are now being instituted in the Caspian Sea region and Colombia. As in these other areas, the opening wedge of U.S. involvement in Africa is military assistance and training—an approach that facilitates the establishment of close ties with the region's (often dominant) military elites. The Department of Defense has sharply increased its aid to the two leading African oil producers, Angola and Nigeria, and further increases are likely in the future. Most of this aid—approximately $300 million in fiscal years 2002 to 2004—is being funneled through the Pentagon's Foreign Military Sales (FMS) credit program, the Excess Defense Articles (EDA) surplus-arms giveaway and the International Military Education and Training (IMET) program. Other oil producers in Africa, including Equatorial Guinea, Gabon, and Mali, are also being awarded EDA and IMET assistance (U.S. Department of State, 2003).

But just as U.S. aid to the Caspian states was followed by the insertion of a permanent American military presence in the region, the Department of Defense is slowly expanding its footprint in Africa and beginning to search for permanent bases there. At present, the most visible expression of growing U.S. military involvement is an increased Navy presence along Africa's west coast, the location of its most promising offshore oil fields. In 2003, the head of Eurcom (which exercises control over U.S. forces in sub-Saharan Africa) declared that the aircraft carrier battle groups under his command would shorten their visits to the Mediterranean and "spend half their time going down the west coast of Africa" (cited in Cobb, 2003).

Furthermore, in anticipation that American combat troops will at some point be deployed on the ground in Africa, the Department of Defense is looking for potential basing locations in and around the major oil zones. According to recent media reports, the Pentagon is seeking "bare-bones facilities"—essentially, airstrips with modest logistical capabilities—in Ghana, Kenya, Mali, Senegal and Uganda (Jaffe, 2003; see also Schmitt, 2003). And, while military officials tend to emphasize the threat of terrorism when discussing the need for such facilities, they have told reporters from the *Wall Street Journal* that "a key mission for U.S. forces [in Africa] would be to ensure that Nigeria's oil fields, which in the future could account for as much as 25 percent of U.S. oil imports, are secure" (cited in Jaffe, 2003).

In Africa, then, as in the Gulf area, the Caspian basin and Latin America, the Department of Defense is systematically enhancing its capacity to engage in direct military operations. Typically, these developments are reported piecemeal, as a series of unconnected events, or, at best, as part of a generalized expansion of American military capabilities. But the information provided above suggests something far more intentional and specific—a determined U.S. effort to insert military power into the world's major oil-producing areas and to prepare for future wars over energy. It would appear, moreover, the best way to characterize this process is to see it as the natural expression of the Carter Doctrine's extension from the Persian Gulf to the rest of the developing world.

From this perspective, the 2003 invasion of Iraq should be viewed as not the first—and certainly not the last—of a long series of wars and military interventions over the control of foreign oil. These wars are certain to claim an increasing toll in human life and will impose a severe and growing strain on the federal treasury. For members of the Armed Forces, moreover, they will demand years of dangerous and ignoble work as protectors of pipelines and refineries. No amount of cheap oil can justify a sacrifice this great. It is time to repudiate the Carter Doctrine and the Bush-Cheney energy plan, and begin the necessary transition to a post-petroleum economy based on alternative sources of energy (wind, solar, agricultural, geothermal) high-speed rail and urban/suburban mass transit, and the development of entirely new energy systems (possibly using hydrogen).[24]

Notes

1. The author first advanced this argument in *Blood and Oil: The Dangers and Consequences of America's Growing Petroleum Dependency* (2004: 132-145).
2. For background on these developments, see Painter (1986) and Stoff (1980).
3. For background on this event, see Miller (1980: 128-131).
4. For background on these efforts, see Long (1985).
5. For background and discussion, see Klare (1985: 112-125) and Noyes (1979).
6. For background on the events leading up to this statement, see Palmer (1992: 103-111).
7. For background on the RDJTF and Centcom, see Hines (2002).

8.   From an official announcement delivered by Assistant Secretary of State Richard W. Murphy, as cited in Palmer (1992: 123). For background on these events, see Palmer (1992: 128-149).
9.   For background on these events, see Palmer (1992: 119-149).
10. On the White House reaction to the Iraqi invasion of Kuwait and the decision to respond with military force, see Woodward (1992: 224-273). See also U.S. Department of Defense (1992: 19-20, 32-33).
11. As quoted in *The New York Times*, August 9, 1990.
12. For background and discussion, see Hersh (2002: 34 – 39), Klare (2004: 94 – 99), and Woodward (2002).
13. Address before the annual convention of the Veterans of Foreign Wars, August 25, 2002, as published in *The New York Times*, August 26, 2002.
14. For discussion, see Klare (2004: 99-105).
15. For background and discussion, see Klare (2004: 105 – 110).
16. For background on these developments, see Klare (2001: 1-5, 81-92).
17. "Visit of President Heydar Aliyev of Azerbaijan," statement by the press secretary, the White House, August 1, 1997, electronic document accessed at http://www.whitehouse.gov/ on March 2, 1998.
18. For background, see Klare (2001: 95-97).
19. For summary and discussion, see Klare (2004: 56-73).
20. For background on this debate, see Deffeyes (2001), Goodstein (2004), Heinberg (2003), and Roberts (2004).
21. For discussion of this phenomenon, see Karl (1997).
22. For further development of this argument, see Klare (2004: 120-132).
23. See transcript of a telephone press briefing with Col. Robert Waltemeyer, commander of the Train and Equip program in Georgia, May 30, 2002, electronic document accessed at www.defenselink.mil on May 31, 2002.
24. For a review of such alternatives, see Klare (2004: 193-201).

References

Campbell, K. M., and Ward, C. J. (2003). New Battle Stations? *Foreign Affairs, 82*(5), pp. 95-103.

Carter, President James. State of the Union Address, January 23, 1980, in *Weekly Compilation of Presidential Documents, 16*(4).

Cobb, Jr., C. Larger U.S. Troop Presence May Be Needed in Africa, Says NATO Commander. Posted on allAfrica.com, May 2, 2003, electronic document accessed at www.allafrica.com on May 18, 2003.

Crawley, M. With Mideast Uncertainty, U.S. Turns to Africa for Oil. *Christian Science Monitor*, May 23, 2002.

Cummins, C. As Threats to Oil Facilities Rise, U.S. Military Becomes Protector. *Wall Street Journal*, June 30, 2004.

Deffeyes, K. S. (2001). *Hubbert's Peak: The Impending World Oil Shortage*. Princeton, NJ: Princeton University Press.

Energy Information Administration. (2003). Colombia: Country Analysis Brief. Retrieved on July 14, 2003. Available at www.eia.doe.gov.

Energy Information Administration. (2003). *International Energy Outlook 2003* Washington. DC: Department of Energy.

Forero, J. (2004, October 22). Safeguarding Colombia's Oil. *New York Times*.

Forero, J. (2002, February 6). Administration Shifts Focus on Colombia Aid. *New York Times*.

Forero, J. (2002, October 4). New Role for U.S. in Colombia: Protecting a Vital Pipeline. *New York Times*.

Garamone, J. (2001, December 15). Rumsfeld Meets with Leaders of Caucasus Nations. American Forces Information Service. Retrieved on February 27, 2003. Available at www.defenselink.mil.

Glanz, J. (2004, July 6). 15 Miles Offshore, Safeguarding Iraq's Oil Lifeline. *New York Times*.

Goodstein, D. (2004). *Out of Gas*. New York: W. W. Norton.

Grossman, M. (2002, April 24). U.S. Policy Toward Colombia: Testimony before the Subcommittee for Western Hemisphere Affairs of the Senate Committee on Foreign Relations. Washington, DC. Retrieved on July 1, 2002. Available at www.state.gov.

Heinberg, R. (2003). *The Party's Over*. Gabriola Island, BC: New Society Publishers.

Hersh, S. (2002, March 11). The Debate Within. *The New Yorker*, 34 – 39.

Hines, J. E. (2002). Command History: U.S. Central Command. Retrieved on December 31, 2002. Available at www.centcom.mil.

Noyes, J. H. (1979). *The Clouded Lens*. Stanford, CA: Hoover Institution Press.

Jaffe, G. (2003, June 10). In Massive Shift, U.S. is Planning to Cut Size of Military in Germany. *Wall Street Journal*.

Jones, A. E. (2001, December 13). U.S.-Central Asian Cooperation: Testimony before the Subcommittee on Central Asia and the Caucasus of the Senate Committee on Foreign Relations. Washington, DC. Retreived on July 1, 2002. Available at www.state.gov.

Kaiser, R. G. (2002, August 27). U.S. Plants Footprint in Shaky Central Asia. *Washington Post*.

Karl, T. L.. (1997). *The Paradox of Plenty: Oil Booms and Petro-States*. Berkeley, CA: University of California Press.

Klare, M. T. (2004). *Blood and Oil: The Dangers and Consequences of America's Growing Petroleum Dependency*. New York: Metropolitan Books.

Klare, M. T. (2001). *Resource Wars: The New Landscape of Global Conflict*. New York: Metropolitan Books.

Klare, M. T. (1985). *American Arms Supermarket*. Austin, TX: University of Texas Press.

Loeb, V. (2003). New Bases Reflect Shift in Military. *Washington Post*.

Long, D. E. (1985). *The United States and Saudi Arabia*. Boulder, CO.: Westview Press.

Miller, A. D. (1980). *Search for Security*. Chapel Hill, NC: University of North Carolina Press.

National Energy Policy Development Group. (2001, May 17). *National Energy Policy* Washington, DC: White House.

Nichol, J. (2002, December 11). *Central Asia's New States*. Washington, DC: U.S. Library of Congress, Congressional Research Service.

Oil and Gas Journal Online. (2003, January 23). Azerbaijan, Georgia Address Security Threats to BTC Pipeline. Retrieved on January 24, 2003. Available at www.ogj.pennnet.com.

Painter, D. S. (1986). *Oil and the American Century*. Baltimore, MD: Johns Hopkins University Press.

Palmer, M. A. (1992). *Guardians of the Gulf*. New York: Free Press.

Peterson, S. (2002, March 19). Terror War and Oil Expand U.S. Sphere of Influence. *Christian Science Monitor*.

Roberts, P. (2004). *The End of Oil*. Boston, MA: Houghton Mifflin.

Schmitt, E. (2003, July 5). Pentagon Seeking New Access Pacts for Africa Bases." *New York Times*.

Senate Committee on Armed Services. (1990). *Crisis in the Persian Gulf Region: U.S. Policy Options and Implications*. Hearings, 101st Congress, 2nd Session.

Shanker, T. (2003, December 6). Rumsfeld Visits Georgia to Bind a Partnership with an Ally. *The New York Times*.

Stoff, M. B. (1980). *Oil, War, and American Security*. New Haven, CT: Yale University Press.

U.S. Department of Defense. (2003a, December 5). Background Briefing En Route to Georgia. News Briefing with "Senior defense official." Retrieved on December 8, 2003. Available at www.defenselink.mil.

U.S. Department of Defense. (2003b, December 5). Secretary Rumsfeld Press Conference with Acting Georgian President Burdzhanadze. News Briefing. Retrieved on December 8, 2003. Available at www.defenselink.mil.

U.S. Department of Defense. (1992). *Conduct of the Persian Gulf War: Final Report to Congress*. Washington, DC: U.S. Government Printing Office.

U.S. Department of State. (2003). *Congressional Budget Justification: Foreign Operations, Fiscal Year 2004*. Retrieved on February 27, 2003. Available at www.fas.org.

Wilson, S. (2003, February 6). U.S. Moves Closer to Colombia's War, *Washington Post*.

Woodward, B. (2002). *Bush at War*. New York: Simon and Schuster.

Woodward, B. (1992). *The Commanders*. New York: Simon and Schuster.

5

Nuclear Power in an Age of Global Terrorism: Implications for Energy and National Security

Kenneth D. Bergeron and Andrew D. Zimmerman

Introduction

A computer hacker gains access to a critical computer system monitoring the electricity grid, and plunges 50 million people in the Midwest into darkness. Terrorists crash a Boeing 767 into a nuclear power plant twenty-four miles north of New York City, intent on blowing open the plant's containment structure with the force of the impact and resultant explosion, thereby causing a massive release of radiation. A band of terrorists forcefully takes over a nuclear power plant in southern California, intent on inducing a reactor core meltdown. None of these incidents has actually occurred—at least not yet—but they are all plausible.

What these events have in common is their linkage to America's preoccupation with terrorism, an obvious outgrowth of the terrorist attacks of 9/11. All involve the same basic technological apparatus: electricity-generating plants. And, in at least two of the three scenarios, the technology of nuclear power is featured.

The Need for Assessment

Nuclear energy as a source of electric power was brought into being in the United States (and later the rest of the industrialized world) by a remarkably single-minded effort on the part of the U.S. government and a select group of corporate and academic institutions. This "great nuclear bandwagon" was characterized by an astonishing sanguinity regarding nuclear power's unique problems, such as the potential for nuclear weapons proliferation, the danger of serious nuclear reactor accidents, and the problem of spent fuel disposal.

In the final decades of the twentieth century, critics of the nuclear venture forced these problems increasingly into the light, bringing into question whether nuclear power was capable of fulfilling its implicit social contract. Many of these concerns have been validated by events like the acquisition of nuclear weapons by India and Pakistan, the accidents at Three Mile Island and Chernobyl, and the utter failure of the U.S. Government to construct acceptable disposal facilities for commercial nuclear waste.

In this chapter we explore the dangers and vulnerabilities to terrorist attack facing the 103 commercial nuclear reactors currently operating in the United States. There is no question that these *external* threats are genuine; any realistic appraisal of the vulnerabilities of U.S. national security clearly must account for them. What may not be as clear to a large segment of the American public—or to many government officials, for that matter—are the simultaneous hazards posed by this same fleet of operating reactors, resulting from *internal* risks: conditions with a high potential to inflict damage ranging from extended power outages to reactor meltdowns and major releases of radioactivity. In other words, nuclear power as we know it in the United States (and in much of the rest of the world) simultaneously possesses two types of potential hazards: one internal, in the form of accidents at nuclear plants; the other external, in the form of terrorist attacks of one kind or another. Moreover, as will be discussed, *the internal hazards can be exploited by the external ones.*

We intend to show that commercial nuclear power has done little to enhance U.S. *energy* security, and certainly has done nothing to enhance U.S. *national* security. While this is certainly true of other energy technologies—one need look no further than the current turmoil in the Persian Gulf or other oil and gas-rich regions to see this—no other energy technology is as closely linked with a weapons technology capable of mass destruction. Because of this, after surveying the internal and external hazards we will return to a consideration of their implications for both energy security and national security.

Nuclear Power as a Source of Governing Power

Morone and Woodhouse (1989: 29) noted: "The United States has invested more than $200 billion in an industry that is psychologically unacceptable to a majority of citizens, politically unacceptable to most elected officials, and economically unacceptable to utility companies. Was this inevitable, or did nuclear decision makers commit fundamental errors?" There is a third possibility: that this massive investment in the face of such opposition can best be understood as the imposition of a very determined collective will. But if this collective will was not that of a majority of citizens, most elected officials, or even many utility companies, to whom did it belong?

The answer, we suggest, is that it "belonged" to a loose alliance—a *federation* of sorts—of nuclear reactor manufacturers and their lobby organizations, a dozen or so large nuclear power utilities, a handful of very large engineering and construction firms, at least one major Federal Government regulatory agency, a network of government research laboratories, a collection of academicians, and a cadre of practicing engineers. They were, and are, important not as individuals, or even groups of individuals, but through their participation in *institutions*. In essence, they *govern* key facets of nuclear power production in the United States and beyond. The basis of their governing power is their control over the technology of nuclear power.

'It's the (Political) Economy, *Stupid:' Nuclear Power as an Energy Regime.* In posing the question, "Do artifacts have politics?" Winner (1986: 28-29) helps illuminate the process by which technologies can provide the basis for the creation of institutional power:

> The things we call "technologies" are ways of building order in our world....Consciously or unconsciously, deliberately or inadvertently, societies choose structures for technologies that influence how people are going to work, communicate, travel, consume, and so forth over a very long time....By far the greatest latitude of choice exists the very first time a particular instrument, system, or technique is introduced. Because choices tend to become strongly fixed in material equipment, economic investment, and social habit, the original flexibility vanishes for all practical purposes once the initial commitments are made.

That is to say, such technologies become political institutions in their own right. According to Winner, the key issue is no longer that a given technology "*requires legislation*"—although that may, indeed, be the case—but that it is even more the case that "technology *is legislation*" (1977: 323).

As Byrne and Rich (1986: 154) noted, "The enthusiasm for nuclear power, the institutional resources dedicated to its development, and the resistance to any deviation from the nuclear commitment can only be understood in the context of a ruling ideology of technological optimization."

Viewed in this way, both the physical infrastructure and the "institutional architecture" created during the Manhattan Project of World War II, in which military necessity was wed with academic research and corporate interests, permanently reshaped the social relations associated with invention and innovation, university-based scientific research, and corporate research, design, and development. It embodied powerful and enduring structures that were not going to simply fade away with the end of the war. Instead, they became the instrumentalities through which both military and civilian developments would materialize during peacetime.

In this context, technological systems such as nuclear power become a source of governing power and authority over key aspects of society—they become what Winner and others call *sociotechnical regimes*: "...[E]ach significant area of technical/functional organization in modern society can be seen as a kind of regime…under which we are obliged to live. Thus, there are a number of regimes…in energy production and distribution, in petroleum, coal, hydroelectricity, nuclear power, etc., each with a form that can be scrutinized for the politics of its structural properties" (Winner, 1986: 54-55).

The building of the physical infrastructure and institutional architecture that came to embody the commitment to nuclear power in the United States is a fascinating story, much too long to be adequately presented here. Instead, we have made "sketches" of it to illustrate both a regime in its ascendancy and a system of electricity production and distribution that was progressively reconstituted to reflect the complexion of this regime. We will demonstrate how, time and again, the rise of nuclear power in the United States has progressively destabilized the electricity system and made it more vulnerable to both internal hazards and external threats. And, in the process, it has progressively destabilized U.S. and international geopolitical security.

The Great Nuclear Bandwagon: Wobbly, but Still Rolling

A Tale of Two Blackouts

On a hot August afternoon in 2003, 50 million people in eight Midwestern and Northeastern states and Ontario, Canada lost electricity due to a cascading blackout.[1] Within minutes, 508 generating units at 265 power plants were taken offline.[2] It took up to four days to restore power, and some units were out of service for up to two weeks. As the nation's worst power outage, its comparison with the nation's second-worst outage—the "great Northeast blackout" of 1965—is instructive. That event had affected 30 million people in six states and portions of Ontario. Then, as now, the fact that "the North American power grid is one large, interconnected machine" (U.S.–Canada Power System Outage Task Force, 2004: 5), was central to the fact that both blackouts cascaded far beyond the immediate area in which the problem originated. As Perrow (1984) has observed, such is the nature of complex, tightly coupled systems. Unlike the 2003 outage, in the 1965 incident all power was restored within thirteen hours. A key difference: the blackout of 1965 involved no nuclear power plants.

The Role of Nuclear Power in the 2003 Blackout. An international team appointed to investigate the 2003 blackout chose, for the most part, to limit its inquiry to events on that fateful day, and its determination of blame to one power company—FirstEnergy Corporation of Akron, Ohio, and the region's electric reliability organization, the Midwest Independent System Operator (MISO). FirstEnergy was already a "poster child" for utility mismanagement, owing to a twenty-six-month outage at its Davis-Besse nuclear plant, which will be discussed shortly. The plant's outage removed up to 877 MWe (megawatts electric) of generating capacity from FirstEnergy's system,[3] unquestionably compromising the utility's ability to reliably meet peak load demand on the day of the blackout, August 14, 2003.

Despite these circumstances, the Davis-Besse outage is scarcely mentioned in the report, and is only indirectly linked to the problems FirstEnergy experienced on August 14. Nor is the unexpected outage a day before the blackout of another, even larger, nuclear plant—the 1,090 MWe Donald C. Cook unit 2 operated by neighboring utility American Electric Power—factored into the stresses placed on the regional system. The task force noted that system operators "take into account the unavailability of such units and any transmission facilities known to be out of service in the day-ahead planning studies they perform to ensure a secure system for the next day" (2004: 25-26). But because the Cook reactor had just gone out of service the day before, MISO's "day-ahead" market planning would have been extra challenging. Nonetheless, the task force categorically dismissed any such notion: "The unavailability of these generation units did not cause the blackout" (2004: 26).

Nowhere does the report fault the nearly 17,000 MWe of nuclear-generated electricity, both in the United States and nearby Toronto, Canada—more than 27 percent of the total electrical output affected by the blackout—for greatly prolonging the duration of the outages in some places. The investigating team went to some length, in fact, to exonerate nuclear power of any culpability in the blackout at all (U.S.–Canada Power System Outage Task Force, 2004: 119):

> The NWG [Nuclear Working Group] found no evidence that the shutdown of U.S. nuclear power plants triggered the outage or inappropriately contributed to its spread (i.e., to an extent beyond the normal tripping of the plants at expected conditions). All nine plants tripped...in a manner consistent with the plant designs. All nine plants safely shut down. All safety functions were effectively accomplished, with few problems, and the plants were maintained in a safe shutdown condition until their restart.

In the task force's view, the nuclear plants that were tripped out of service on August 14 performed exactly as they were supposed to. Yet there is more to the story: these plants may not have *triggered* the outage or contributed to its *spread*—terms which conveniently delimit the analysis—but they most definitely contributed to its *length*. Of the nine U.S. reactors involved in the blackout, the earliest any of them was back on line was August 17.[4] This is because most nuclear power plants, especially those of U.S. design, go to complete shutdown mode when they are tripped off.[5] Once in complete shutdown, it typically takes a minimum of three days to bring them back to full power. And if the shutdown process itself has caused any problems, or maintenance has been planned for the near future—for instance, to refuel—the maintenance will be moved up so as to take advantage of the shutdown, which is actually quite rational. The only problem is that it can extend the reactor's shutdown period by a week or more.

It is revealing to juxtapose the 2003 blackout task force's exoneration of nuclear power with the findings of the 1965 blackout investigation team. One 1965 recommendation stands out in particular: "industry should reevaluate the comparative usefulness of...fast-starting generators for use in emergencies and *place a greater value on them as compared to the slower-starting...steam power plants, either conventional or nuclear*" [emphasis added] (Federal Power Commission, 1965: 26). Moreover, the 1965 team concluded that it would be preferable to have a larger number of smaller generators than a smaller number of larger ones, "because a large number of units can increase generation simultaneously and supply a greater amount of power more quickly than a single unit with the same amount of reserve in total..." (1965: 26). But these recommendations were not in accord with the electric power industry's massive scale-up, already materializing, to nuclear power and other large-scale steam generator projects. This scale-up has resulted in a system that has become increasingly vulnerable to power disruptions. It has also made the system unnecessarily vulnerable to terrorist attacks, by constructing a group of inviting targets with the capacity for widespread devastation.

Other Systemic Disruptions Related to Nuclear Power. The 2003 blackout was not the first time that nuclear power caused, or at least aggravated, systemic power disruptions, nor was it the first time that its role in so doing was denied by the nuclear power regime. In the summer of 1968, just three years after the 1965 blackout, with more than six dozen commercial reactors already either announced, under construction, or actually operating, power disruptions began occurring in various parts of the country with increasing regularity, as rising demand for electricity outpaced the addition of new supply.[6] These disruptions involved a new phenomenon: "brownouts." Brownouts are voltage reductions, usually initiated by utilities, to bring electricity usage in line with supply. The term gained immediate currency; as with blackouts, brownouts were an eery reminder that the once-reliable grid was vulnerable to disruption and even failure. Brownouts, along with "rolling blackouts"—controlled temporary blackouts to certain customers or areas—and conservation measures, were used by the utilities in an effort to keep the system from destabilizing. Paradoxically, such measures were themselves a form of system instability. By the fall of 1973, the nominal beginning of the energy crisis of the 1970s, a well-documented crisis in the electric power system had already been underway for at least three years.

A key cause was that a number of major nuclear reactor projects missed, by wide margins, their expected completion dates. Additionally, the reactors which were on line were plagued with problems so much of the time that their average capacity factor—actual electrical output as a percentage of rated capacity- was less than 60 percent.[7] These conditions had the effect of further destabilizing a system that was already in trouble.

Such occurrences were, and are, far more than aberrations in an otherwise stable and reliable system; rather, they are endemic to the system, and have greatly contributed to its chronic *instability*. The question then arises: if nuclear power itself has been so prone to instability, and has made the entire electricity system more vulnerable to disruptions, how has it come to play such a vital role in the U.S. energy system, accounting for 20 percent of all electricity generated? This is especially perplexing, given that it was a technology that solved no critical problem in the energy system when it was introduced, and, in fact, took many years—and billions of public and private research, design, and development dollars—before the electric utilities would embrace it. To understand such a conundrum, it is necessary to view the development of nuclear power not merely as the Herculean construction of a vast energy-producing apparatus, but also as the construction of a vastly powerful *governing regime*. What follows is a sketch of how the political economy of nuclear power was created, the problems and failures it incurred along the way and the resultant impact it has come to have on both energy and national security.

'Too Cheap to Meter:' A Brief History of Nuclear Power

The promise of nuclear power—like the wildly optimistic promises of most modern technologies—had been that it would someday produce electricity, in the words of AEC Chairman Lewis Strauss, "too cheap to meter" (Ford, 1986: 50). The *real* story of nuclear power provides sobering testimony for how divergent the unfolding of a technology can actually be from the promises laid out for it.

Military Selection of a Technology. The genesis of a number of key technologies can be traced to military purposes, going as far back as the beginning of the country's existence.[8] In no other case, however, has the U.S. government's commitment been as massive and urgent as it was in the development of nuclear energy. This commitment was first embodied in the Manhattan Project, the U.S. government's monumental initiative during World War II to develop the atom bomb.

Most accounts of the history of the civilian use of atomic energy are traced to President Dwight D. Eisenhower's "Atoms for Peace" initiative announced in 1953. However, even before World War II ended in August 1945, conscious efforts were already underway to chart nuclear energy's peacetime direction.[9] Once the war ended, the pace of these efforts quickened, propelled by the momentum of the contractual and advisory relationships forged in order to produce the bomb.

Brigadier General Leslie Groves, the Manhattan Project's commanding officer, preferred to execute research, manufacturing, construction and management contracts with "a few of the nation's largest and best qualified companies and universities." He believed this "was the most expeditious and effective way to develop, design and produce atomic bombs" (Orlans, 1967: 5). Significantly, electrical equipment manufacturers General Electric and Westinghouse and construction companies Bechtel and Stone and Webster— firms which subsequently dominated the manufacture and installation of commercial nuclear power plants—were prominent among them.

Two things are noteworthy about the plans for the peacetime stewardship of nuclear fission. One is the remarkable continuity in the recommendations, from the original advisory committees in 1944 and 1945, to the policies and programs for governing nuclear energy eventually pursued by the U.S. government. Key outcomes of this work included the establishment of a national system of nuclear research laboratories, the early research, design, and development of electricity-producing reactors and the establishment of the Atomic Energy Commission (AEC) and the International Atomic Energy Agency (IAEA). The other point concerns the institutional composition of these committees: they brought together science, academia, the military and corporate business in an unprecedented way, forging a template for the subsequent governance of nuclear energy.

'Atoms for Peace:' Moral Imperative or National Security Imperative? When President Eisenhower announced his "Atoms for Peace" initiative in December 1953 before the U.N. General Assembly, he singled out electricity production: "A special purpose would be to provide abundant electrical energy in the power-starved areas of the world. Thus the contributing powers would be dedicating some of their strength to serve the needs rather than the fears of mankind" (National Archives and Records Administration). Statements like this gave the initiative the tone of a *moral imperative.* It has also been frequently claimed that this was a way of assuaging guilt for the use of nuclear weapons on two civilian targets, Hiroshima and Nagasaki, during World War II.[10]

However, it has been even more persuasively argued that Atoms for Peace reflected a *national security* imperative: keenly aware that a desperate nuclear arms race had already begun, Eisenhower believed that any hope of controlling nuclear technology for national defense purposes would require a bold strategic overture that allowed other countries to have access to it for legitimate civilian, but not military, purposes. That was both the genius and, as events have unfolded, the undoing of the plan (Bergeron, 2002: 18-20).

Converting the Agnostics: A Regime in the Making. Civilian nuclear power did not spring to life upon Eisenhower's proclamation; that was still another ten years away. It took approximately eighteen years from the earliest implementation of a civilian nuclear power development program before the electric utility industry was willing to embrace it.[11] This demonstrates the industry's reticence about accepting this new technology. Aside from the fact this was a largely unproven technology, there was also the fact that "...there was no shortage of fuel looming in the near future. The nuclear power industry was not born out of a desperate need of the electricity producers to find an alternative to traditional energy sources" (Basalla, 1988: 167). Even the Atomic Energy Commission had concluded, in a 1959 briefing for President Eisenhower, that: "For our own economy, with but few exceptions, we do not need atomic energy power in the foreseeable future" (Balogh, 1991, quoted in Cohn, 1997: 22).

It took the enactment of three major national laws, the near-complete blurring of the distinction between public and private interest, more than $2 billion in public subsidies, approximately $1 billion more in corporate subsidies, and the fundamental revision of the norms by which risks and losses are indemnified to induce the commercialization of nuclear power. It may endure as one of the most protracted and expensive marketing campaigns ever waged, and it's not over yet.

The three federal laws were the Atomic Energy Act of 1954, the Price-Anderson Indemnity Act of 1957, and the Private Ownership of Special Nuclear Materials Act of 1964. The Atomic Energy Act of 1954 (Public Law 83-703) revised the Atomic Energy Act of 1946 (Public Law 79-585) by allowing private firms to own reactor facilities, with the government retaining ownership of the nuclear fuel (Melosi, 1985: 231). With passage of the Private Ownership of Special Nuclear Materials Act of 1964 (Public Law 88-489) private firms were even allowed to own the fuel.

During the mid-1950s, the fledgling nuclear power industry maintained a steady drum beat of a consistent message: there would be no commercialization of nuclear power without government action to limit or subsidize private liability. The Atomic Industrial Forum, an industry trade group, made the remarkable claim that "the problem of liability for catastrophic accidents was a 'serious immediate threat to the vital national interest' of establishing a nuclear power industry" (Morone and Woodhouse, 1989: 54). The mind-boggling contention that the privatization of nuclear power required the socialization of its risk was not seriously challenged. Ultimately, the Price Anderson Indemnity Act of 1957, (Public Law 85-256), amended the Atomic Energy Act of 1954 to limit private industry's liability in the event of an accident at a nuclear power plant.[12] While hearings on the act were being held in 1957, the Brookhaven National Laboratory produced a study estimating that as many as 3,400 deaths, 43,000 injuries, and up to $7 billion in damages could be expected in a "worst-case" nuclear accident. The study's findings were essentially ignored in subsequent Congressional deliberations on the bill.

Meanwhile, both the government and the reactor manufacturers were underwriting the research, design, and development of a number of reactor designs and technologies. All told, some $2 billion was expended by the government on the development of civilian nuclear power between 1948 and

1965.[13] The reactor manufacturers, principally General Electric and Westinghouse, also underwrote reactor design and development costs. The largest nuclear power R&D initiative was the Power Reactor Demonstration Program, which ran from 1955 until around 1965. A major objective of this program was to induce industrial participation (Morone and Woodhouse, 1989: 52-57). Although some electric utilities participated in the program, they were largely unwilling to order nuclear plants of their own accord, given the abundant supplies of relatively inexpensive conventional fuels like coal, oil, and natural gas.

The Unbearable Lightness of Light Water. Key decisions about the design of reactors intended for commercialization were made even as the Power Reactor Demonstration Program was commencing. The chosen technology of *light water,* which uses ordinary water as a coolant, also requires the use of enriched uranium. Enriched uranium has a higher proportion of U-235 in a given volume of U-238 than occurs in nature; without enrichment the fission process is not strong enough to continue in a light water reactor. Morone and Woodhouse argue that the light water technology was chosen *not* because of its superior safety characteristics or cost-effectiveness, but because it was already being used in naval propulsion, under the direction of Admiral Hyman Rickover (1989: 29-46). While a number of other reactor designs continued to be tested under the Power Reactor Development Program, the fruits of this work were largely ignored: virtually all U.S. reactors, and most of those in other parts of the world, use the light water design. Morone and Woodhouse view the selection of light water as an "historical accident;" were it not for Rickover, a much safer reactor design might well have been adopted (1989:104-111).

Aside from safety considerations, one of the most serious consequences of the decision to use enriched uranium in nearly all U.S. reactors and most of those in the rest of the world, has been to facilitate the global proliferation of nuclear weapons. This point will be addressed later in the chapter.

The 'Great Bandwagon Market' for Nuclear Plants. A major turning point in the utilities' acceptance of nuclear power came with the announcement of the Oyster Creek nuclear plant near Toms River, New Jersey, in December 1963. Oyster Creek, the largest reactor facility yet constructed, was the first of ultimately thirteen reactors installed by General Electric or Westinghouse at a set contract price. Since the contracts also called for the manufacturers to ready the facilities for operation, they were called "turnkey" plants. Unknown to the utilities that purchased them—and to all *prospective* nuclear utilities—these plants were sold at a price considerably below their actual cost. A subsequent RAND analysis estimated that altogether, these "loss leaders" cost their manufacturers close to $1 billion (Munson, 1985: 116). Had the actual costs been known at the time, one utility executive has reported, the utilities would never have made a commercial commitment to the technology (Rudolph and Ridley, 1986).

Instead, the turnkey plants led utility executives to believe that nuclear power had become cost-competitive with conventional power. This belief unleashed what Philip Sporn, former president of American Electric Power Company, referred to as a "great bandwagon market" for the technology (Bupp and Derian, 1981: 49). The phenomenon developed with such intensity that Bupp and Derian have characterized it as *"intoxication by light water"* (1981: 75-76). The number of orders for nuclear reactors ballooned from 11 during 1963-65 to 65 during 1966-67 (U.S. Energy Information Administration). But because these ensuing orders were no longer under the turnkey arrangement, something else ballooned as well: their price tags.

The Bandwagon Develops a Wobbly Wheel: Construction Delays and Rapidly Rising Costs. Of the 53 commercial nuclear reactors expected to come on line between 1967 and 1973, not one was finished on schedule. Consequently, their generating capacity was not available to help meet the rapidly increasing peak summer electricity demand. This placed added strains on an already-strained system, as mentioned earlier. These stresses are evident in the national grid's *capacity margins* during this time.[14] The electric power industry views a capacity margin of 15 percent as minimally acceptable. Table 1 shows the effect of delayed nuclear projects on generating capacity margins for the summers of 1968 to 1973. It is clear from these data that, had the reactors been in operation by their originally scheduled dates, the ability to meet peak summer demand during these years would not have been nearly as tenuous, especially after 1970.

Table 5.1

The Effect of Nuclear Project Delays on Peak Summer Generating Capacity Margins, for Major Systems in the Contiguous United States, 1968 – 1973

Year	Generating Capacity Margin (percent of capacity)	Total Capacity of Delayed Nuclear Reactors (MWe)[1]	Capacity Margin if Delayed Capacity Were Counted (percent of capacity)
1968	13.7	1,100	14.1
1969	13.6	4,100	14.8
1970	12.1	5,700	13.7
1971	12.3	11,400	15.2
1972	15.8	19,800	20.0
1973	13.5	26,500	18.9

[1]Includes all projects which should have been in service for that summer. Since a number of delays spanned more than one summer, they are counted in each summer that was missed.

Sources: Energy Information Administration, *Annual Energy Review* 2002; Federal Power Commission, *Electric Power Statistics* 1968-1973; *Nuclear News* (August 1980); International Atomic Energy Agency

With the system's margins stretched so thin (according to the industry's own standard), warnings of impending summer blackouts and brownouts became a regular feature of newspapers and other media organs. These warnings reached a crescendo by the summer of 1970, when capacity margins were at their lowest. An editorial in the *New York Times* in July of that year observed:

> Far from disappearing, the national power crisis shows signs of becoming a permanent feature of the American scene for the next decade if not longer....This nation's entire economy and way of life have been built on the assumption of a limitless supply of cheap electricity. That assumption has now become unjustified.... (7/3/1970: 24)

The editorial was published more than three years before the Arab oil embargo, widely viewed as the beginning of the energy crisis of the 1970s. Yet it referred to the problems in the electricity system as a "national power crisis."

Ironically, the electric utility industry, along with the manufacturers of both power plants and major home appliances,[15] had become victims of their own success: their campaign to promote the increased use of electric appliances—especially air conditioning and electric space heating—had worked so well that they were unable to keep up with the increased demand. Their failure to meet this demand, exacerbated by the nuclear plant delays, led to planned and unplanned disruptions of electric service. In this failure, they violated two of the central tenets of what Winner (1982) has called the "implicit social contract" around electricity: "Producers of [electricity] agree to supply safe, reliable, abundant energy at a reasonable price. The rest of society agrees to pay the going rate and let producers go about their business" (1982: 272). By the end of the 1970s, the electric power industry had essentially violated *all* of the conditions of the social contract, and consumers were no longer inclined to either pay the going rate *or* let them go about their business.

A key problem behind efforts to bring the nuclear plants on line in a timely and reliable way was that engineers in the nuclear power industry had assumed, as an article of faith, that *economies of scale* would allow progressively larger reactors and plants to be installed at decreasing costs in time and money per megawatt of capacity and be operated more efficiently. They had this faith despite very little actual experience with the technology. Accordingly, the first wave of commercial reactors exceeded the scale of their prototypes by as much as ten times or more.[16] What occurred completely contradicted their expectations: as the reactors escalated in size and scale, delays in their construction ballooned, as figure 5.1 demonstrates.

The difficulties were not limited to the effects of plant completion delays: even as completed reactors came on line, they were far less reliable than expected and therefore further contributed to disruptions in power. As Komanoff (1981) has observed, "Until the mid-1970s, utilities and the Atomic

Figure 5.1
Reactor Size and Construction Delays, 1968-1973
(expected vs. actual, in months)*

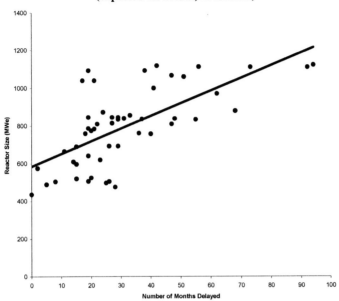

*Excludes the Fort St. Vrain (CO) and Diablo Canyon 1 (CA) reactors.
Sources: Nuclear News; International Atomic Energy Agency

Energy Commission (AEC) generally assumed that nuclear plants would operate at 80 percent capacity factors" (1981: 247). Since they actually operated at less than 60 percent on average, they provided 25 percent less power
to the grid than had been anticipated.

The problem was even more acute for the larger reactors increasingly being ordered: the average capacity factor for those greater than 800 MWe was
54 percent, substantially lower than the 66 percent for those less than 800
MWe (1981: 249). Once again, the great increases in power plant scale during the 1960s and 1970s were implicated as a primary cause of performance
shortfalls in the electricity system. In all such cases, the relative lack of
experience with large reactors was a key issue.

The conditions that led to extended plant construction delays produced
another problem: their rapidly rising costs. Komanoff demonstrated that, contrary to industry expectations, the cost of nuclear power during the 1970s
categorically surpassed coal by substantial amounts.[17] He found that the real
construction cost of a typical coal plant, with appropriate emissions equipment installed, increased 68 percent, while the real construction cost of a
typical nuclear plant increased 142 percent.

By isolating various cost factors, Komanoff was able to determine that "design and equipment changes to reduce the hazards of nuclear power generation underlay most of the real...increases in nuclear costs" (1981: 7).[18] He attributed this to his *sector size hypothesis:* the nuclear power industry was obligated to "prevent total accident and environmental risks from expanding in proportion to the growth of [the nuclear power] sector" (1981: 2). That is, to contain the *total* risk to society of nuclear power, as the number of reactors and plants increased, the amount of additional risk that each one posed had to be decreased, thereby adding to its cost. This hypothesis located the responsibility for increasingly stringent—and costly—regulatory standards with the nuclear power regime's own expansion rather than with regulation-happy government bureaucrats.

A Second Wobbly Wheel: Plant Cancellations. The year 1974 was a year of great paradox: a report would later describe it as the "high-water mark in terms of the [electric utility] industry's commitment to future additions to nuclear plant capacity" (U.S. Energy Information Administration, April 1983). The report then proceeded to document how 1974 also marked the beginning of a fateful ebb in the nuclear plant construction program. For only the second time in the seventeen-year history of commercial nuclear power, a number of previously ordered units were cancelled. By the beginning of 1979, even before the accident at Three Mile Island, 53 orders had been terminated. Ultimately, 104 commercial reactors would be cancelled—just as many as are currently licensed (Nuclear Energy Institute; Nuclear Regulatory Commission). No new orders have been placed since 1978.[19]

'Then Came Three Mile Island:' Safety Issues Cause a Third Wheel to Wobble. If it wasn't already clear by early 1979 that the nuclear power regime was spinning out of control, the worst accident at a U.S. nuclear plant dispelled any doubt. Among three scenarios of the risks of a major nuclear reactor accident presented on March 9, 1979 to NRC commissioner Peter Bradford, was the following one: "The probability is less than 0.05 that the next major accident occurs within the next 21 reactor years" (U.S. Nuclear Regulatory Commission, cited in Riccio, 2001).[20] Less than three weeks later, on March 28, 1979, a major accident occurred at the Three Mile Island Unit 2 reactor. A variety of errors and malfunctions caused a "routine incident" to become a partial meltdown; about half of the reactor core melted, some 20 tons of which formed into a puddle in the bottom of the reactor vessel.[21] About ten million curies of radioactivity were released into the environment, and nearly 150,000 people living near the reactor in the Harrisburg, PA area were evacuated (Lochbaum, 2004: 5).

There is no question that the TMI accident was a pivotal event in the status of nuclear power in the United States. It was a bizarre case of life imitating art: the movie, "The China Syndrome," had opened just twelve days earlier. In one exchange in the movie, set in a nuclear plant somewhere in California, a reporter asks a plant safety engineer how large an area might be affected if a meltdown were to occur. His response: "an area the size of Pennsylvania."[22]

Despite the fact that Unit 2 at Three Mile Island ultimately did what it was designed to do—contain a catastrophic event at a nuclear plant—Morone and Woodhouse noted that (1989: 97-98):

> ...Three Mile Island badly damaged the credibility of the nuclear enterprise. It vividly and starkly demonstrated that unanticipated things could go wrong in a reactor.... In terms of nuclear power's *political* safety [emphasis added], TMI was a disaster. For the lesson the news media and the public learned from it was based not on what actually happened, (which is to say very little), but on what might have happened. Unanticipated mistakes were made, design flaws exacerbated the problem, unforeseen damage to the reactor core resulted and public officials and regulatory agencies showed themselves to be confused and uncertain. All this made the possibility of a catastrophe much more real to the public than it had ever seemed before.

When the accident at the Chernobyl plant in the Ukraine occurred seven years after TMI, it merely cemented in the American public's mind how dangerous a technology nuclear power was. As Morone and Woodhouse observed, "Where Three Mile Island was a reminder that something might happen, at Chernobyl something did happen. The potential for catastrophe that underlay the public rejection of nuclear power was fully realized" (1989: 100).

'Living La Vida LOCA:' Other Accidents, Near-Accidents, and Accidents in the Making. Long before the TMI accident and ever since, accidents and equipment failures have occurred at nuclear plants that have involved at least some of the same characteristics as the events that came together on March 28, 1979. According to the Union of Concerned Scientists (UCS), between 1988 and 1998 "U.S. nuclear plants...reported more than 200 events very much like the one that triggered the TMI accident. The cooling water for the reactor core was unexpectedly lost in each of these events" (Lochbaum, December, 1998).[23] Why these events did not lead to a TMI-type accident has been attributed by the UCS to luck.

There have been a handful of other major accidents in the United States, including the partial meltdown of the Fermi fast breeder reactor, thirty miles from Detroit in 1966, and a cable fire at the Brown's Ferry (Alabama) unit 1 reactor, that burned uncontrollably for seven and a half hours. It burned through "so many electrical control cables that all of the safety equipment installed to provide cooling water to the reactor was rendered inoperative" (Ford, 1986: 219). According to Ford, "T.V.A. nuclear engineers said privately that a meltdown was avoided 'by sheer luck'" (1986: 220). Sheer luck, it seems, has played a large role in the avoidance of more major reactor accidents like Three Mile Island.

There have been, as well, a number of safety problems that were accidents in the making. Most of these involved the failure or near-failure of specific components and systems, notably the development of cracks in critical places in reactor pressure vessels, cooling system tubes, steam pipes, and the like.[24] In some instances, these led to ruptures; in others, they were detected before ruptures occurred. The process by which metal surfaces, welded seams, nozzles, and joints crack in such an environment, where there are high levels of neutron bombardment from the fissioning nuclear fuel, combined with intense heat (approximately 300° C or 520° F) and constant high pressures, (two tons per square inch or more), is called *embrittlement*.[25] If an area on a reactor vessel becomes sufficiently embrittled, the vessel will crack and, if the crack penetrates through the entire thickness of the vessel wall, it will experience a sudden loss of coolant accident (LOCA), with potentially catastrophic consequences.

Another major problem has involved the development of cracks in, and potential leakage of coolant water through, control rod drive mechanism (CRDM) nozzles on the reactor vessel heads of the 69 pressurized water reactors currently in service in the United States.[26] This is the problem that occurred at the Davis-Besse plant owned by FirstEnergy of Ohio, and the reason it was unavailable on August 14, 2003, the day of the greatest blackout in U.S. history. By the time FirstEnergy employees examined the reactor vessel's head after its shutdown in February 2002, they found that wet boric acid residue left from the leaking coolant had eaten through the head's six inch-thick carbon steel outer casing, creating a gaping seven-inch by five-inch hole.[27] All that stood between that hole and a catastrophic loss of coolant accident, (and probable partial or complete meltdown), was the 3/16-inch thick stainless steel reactor vessel liner, that was bulging into the hole—a result of the 2,200 psi pressure inside the reactor vessel.[28] FirstEnergy subsequently reported to the NRC that debris in the containment structure would have most likely blocked critical water inlets in the reactor's emergency core cooling system. With the emergency core cooling system largely inoperable, the chances of a reactor core melt would have been quite high (Lochbaum, 2004). After a twenty-six-month outage for the major repairs, Davis-Besse was returned to service in April 2004.

Since 1984, twenty-seven reactors—one quarter of the entire U.S. fleet—have been shut down for a year or longer for safety repairs (Lochbaum, 2004: 13). The average length of time for these shutdowns has been well over two years. When any plant is shut down, replacement power must be purchased by the plant operator, usually at a premium. For FirstEnergy, the total cost of the Davis-Besse outage was just under $650 million, half of which went to purchasing replacement power. As a result of Davis-Besse, FirstEnergy had its bond ratings lowered by three major rating firms (FirstEnergy, 2003: 24). This has undoubtedly led to higher financing costs. It may have also placed pressure on the company to cut other costs.[29]

Taken together, the various design flaws, equipment failures, operator errors, near-accidents (including accidents in the making) and actual accidents that have been part of the nuclear power experience can be viewed as a gamble imposed on society, a gamble involving huge and largely hidden costs. David Lochbaum of the Union of Concerned Scientists likens it to playing a slot machine at a gambling casino (December, 1998):

> At a casino, a jackpot occurs when three spinning wheels on a slot machine all stop in a certain combination. A nuclear power plant can be compared to a slot machine having an event wheel, an equipment wheel and a worker performance wheel. Sometimes the event wheel stops on some initiating event such as "fire," "broken pipe" or "loss of power." Sometimes the equipment wheel stops on "failure." Sometimes the worker performance wheel stops on "mistake." At Three Mile Island, the wheels stopped on "loss of feedwater," "failure" and "mistake" to produce a major reactor accident.... The abundance of initiating events, equipment failures and worker mistakes demonstrates that the wheels still stop frequently on these symbols. The TMI accident demonstrated that the wheels can line up for a major reactor accident.

When the "right" wheels line up in a slot machine, it leads to fortune. When the "right" wheels line up at a nuclear power plant, however, it can lead to disaster.

The NRC: Nuclear Power's Fourth Wobbly Wheel. The Nuclear Regulatory Commission was created by the Energy Reorganization Act of 1974 (Pub.L. 93-438). The intent was for it "to be less protective and more aggressive in regulating the [nuclear power] industry than its predecessor, the [Atomic Energy Commission], had been" (Rosenbaum, 1987: 143).[30] In its emergence from the dismantled AEC, the NRC inherited the AEC's mixed legacy of safety regulation at nuclear facilities. On the bright side was the former agency's philosophy of "defense in depth" with regard to the design and installation of reactor safety systems, principally the requirements that reactors be installed inside robust containment structures, and that they have emergency core cooling systems (Bergeron, 2002: 39-40; Ford, 1986: 90-91). One of the most dubious legacies has been the agency's reliance on industry claims and assurances concerning reactor safety measures, meanwhile downplaying, disregarding or even overruling the findings of the agency's own safety experts and researchers, and those of the national research labs like Oak Ridge and Sandia.[31] It has led one prominent critic to accuse the NRC of "regulatory malpractice" (Lochbaum, 2003).

This dubious legacy has overshadowed NRC performance across the years. A report by the General Accounting Office, undertaken after a highly publicized series of safety and management breaches at Northeast Utilities' Millstone plant in Connecticut in 1996, concluded: "There are a number of instances in which NRC has neither taken aggressive enforcement action nor held nuclear plant licensees accountable for correcting their problems on a timely basis. NRC's practice of giving licensees extensive time to fix their problems allows nuclear plants to continue to operate and the problems to grow worse" (May, 1997: 19).

Just four months after the GAO report was released, in September 1997, both units of the Donald C. Cook plant in southwestern Michigan were shut down after their emergency core cooling systems were declared inoperable. A "cascade of problems" with safety equipment and systems was so extensive that these units remained down for the next three years (Galbraith, 5/31/2000). A *South Bend* (IN) *Tribune* investigation, published in June, 2000, concluded that (Galbraith, 6/1/2000):

> Cook officials failed to address safety concerns for years, and the NRC had to be prodded to enforce its own rules. For the record, Cook voluntarily shut down both reactors and the NRC kept them down while the company retooled internally and embarked on a $574 million project to identify and fix problems. Yet it took a nuclear watchdog group and a pair of whistleblowers from distant plants to make the case that Cook was unfit, by NRC standards, to sustain a large-break, loss-of-coolant accident in either of its oval containment structures next to Lake Michigan.

The case of Davis-Besse's "hole in its head," a hazard that the NRC had long known about, wasn't taken seriously until February, 2001, when cracks were found to have encircled the bases of the control rod drive mechanism (CDRM) nozzles on the reactor head of the Oconee (South Carolina) nuclear plant. It took the NRC six months to issue a bulletin requiring owners of "highly susceptible" pressurized water reactors—like Davis-Besse—to undertake proper inspections of the CRDMs by that December. FirstEnergy failed to perform the inspection by the deadline. A shutdown order was recommended by the NRC's technical staff, but the agency's politically appointed commission decided instead to negotiate a compromise with the utility that allowed it to operate the reactor for another six weeks, until a scheduled refueling shutdown. A high-risk potential loss of coolant accident was downplayed by the agency's leaders, who, its critics charge, did not follow their own policies and procedures. In a scathing critique, the Union of Concerned Scientists referred to the agency's handling of the incident and others like it as "dangerously irresponsible" (UCS, 2002).

This pattern of NRC regulatory laxity in the face of nuclear plant operator intransigence continues into the present. This is best exemplified by the well-documented case of the Salem-Hope Creek, NJ nuclear generating complex that includes the Hope Creek and Salem I and II reactors, owned and operated by PSEG Nuclear (soon to be merged with Exelon). The second-largest generating complex in the country has been plagued with a number of equipment, safety, and management problems over the years, with the third forced shutdown in less than a year occurring in June, 2005. At least two of these problems, a ruptured steam pipe and a malfunctioning coolant water recirculation pump, were potentially catastrophic. Even before the third incident, which involved an abnormally large leak of radioactive coolant water, Delaware's congressional delegation had requested that the Government Accountability Office assess the effectiveness of NRC's reactor oversight process, stating: "In light of recent events at Hope Creek, we ask that your review take the performance at this plant into account." (Montgomery, 4/16/2005: B1). All of this occurred in the context of heightened scrutiny of the complex by the NRC, dating back to August, 2004.

Of greater concern than any individual incident, none of which has yet led to a serious accident, is what has been alleged to be the absence of a "safety conscious work environment" at the complex. This was the reason, after years of equipment problems, safety concerns, and management lapses that the NRC had finally agreed to place the complex and its operator under heightened scrutiny. But it was not without some additional prodding: David Lochbaum, nuclear physicist and safety expert for the Union of Concerned Scientists, had noted months earlier that "the safety culture at Salem and Hope Creek today is just as bad as that at Millstone and Davis-Besse" (Lochbaum, 3/28/2004), and that "the very same safety problems that NRC required to be corrected in 1998 before Salem Unit 1 could restart now afflict both Salem reactors and Hope Creek, yet NRC allows all three reactors to continue operating" (6/21/2004).

In early August, 2005, citing "PSEG Nuclear's inconsistent progress and 'frequent' staff and equipment problems...," NRC Region I Director Samuel J. Collins recommended to the Commission that heightened oversight of the Salem-Hope Creek complex be extended for another year (Montgomery, 8/6/2005: B1). This is probably of little consolation to several former PSEG Nuclear employees who lost their jobs attempting to call senior management's attention to precisely these types of problems. One of them—Dr. Nancy Harvin—filed a "whistle-blower" discrimination complaint for wrongful (i.e., retaliatory) termination with the NRC. For its part, the NRC dragged its investigation out many months beyond its own internal time limits.[32]

Such is the great nuclear bandwagon—wobbling from the combined impact of numerous problems throughout its existence but still rolling. In the fourth section, we will return to this metaphor as we describe the nuclear power regime's plans for its renewal. Before that, we turn to an assessment of the *external* threats facing this wobbling construction, principally those associated with global terrorism.

Nuclear Terrorism and the Response of the U.S. Nuclear Power Establishment

The terrorist attacks on U.S targets on September 11, 2001 and the worldwide increase in violent anti-Western extremism in the twenty-first century have brought attention to a hitherto little noted layer of nuclear power's hidden costs to society. More than any other energy source (and most other industrial activities) commercial nuclear power could provide potent means for terrorists to inflict massive casualties on civilian populations. Even if such deadly attacks do not occur or do not succeed, society must inevitably incur significant monetary costs simply because of policies and programs implemented to defend against them. Further, there may be other intangible costs in the form of psychological stress on citizens (particularly those living near nuclear power plants) erosion of personal liberties, and compromises to important democratic institutions.

A full accounting of all these costs requires a realistic assessment of how the commercial nuclear power regime might provide ways for terrorists to attack and kill innocent civilians in large numbers.

The Nature of the Terrorist Threat

There are numerous intersections between the nuclear electric power regime and the potential for serious terrorist attacks within the United States, ranging from the subtle (nuclear power's role in the proliferation of uranium enrichment technology) to the obvious (attacks on nuclear power plants causing a core meltdown). Assessing which are the most serious threats and which most require immediate societal action requires analysis of many different dimensions.

In the words of terrorism expert Bruce Hoffman (2002: 63),

> the terrorist act is conceived and executed in a manner that simultaneously reflects the terrorist group's particular aims and motivations, fits its resources and capabilities and takes into account the "target audience" at whom the act is directed.

An evaluation of threats would, therefore, be difficult without first attempting to characterize the nature of the adversary. Terrorist acts can emerge from a variety of motivations, as illustrated by the violence associated with opposition to the war in Vietnam and the bombing of the federal building in Oklahoma City. But for the United States today, the movement of concern is specifically the anti-western Islamic extremism represented by (but not solely consisting of) the Al Qaeda organization and its affiliates.

It is reasonable to expect that the most significant threats will have many of the characteristics of previous attacks attributed to Al Qaeda:

- Targets chosen because they have symbolic significance for the extremist movement;
- Methods of attack chosen to cause the maximum number of civilian deaths and a maximum degree of fear and tension within the society (keeping in mind that the goal is to energize the Islamic world against western influence and to weaken the western world's will to fight or to continue to impose western values on the Islamic world);

- Meticulous, long-term planning;
- Use of a relatively small cadre (dozens at most) of extremely dedicated, highly trained attackers who are willing to die in the attack;
- A "stateless" organizational base, which implies limited access to high technology and limited ability to manufacture complex devices;
- Limited ability to hold and defend positions once attack has begun—hence the need for surprise and rapid accomplishment of the intended damage.

In this section, these characteristics will be used as a screening tool for assessing the likelihood and destructiveness of a number of different types of terrorist threat. However, we should keep in mind that these assumptions, while simplifying the analysis, also may compromise it. It is certainly true that, looking farther into the future, the nature of potential terrorist threats might be quite different. Hoffman (2002: 65) says,

> Noted terrorism scholar David Rapoport...estimates that the life expectancy of at least 90 percent of terrorist organizations is less than one year and that nearly half of those that make it that far cease to exist within a decade.

Thus it is reasonable to expect that at some point in the future the threat from Al Qaeda and its allies may be significantly diminished. However, other terrorist movements will ineluctably arise, so the vulnerabilities to be discussed here will no doubt persist unless ameliorative action is taken.

Methods of Exploiting Nuclear Power Technology for Terrorist Purposes

There are various ways that nuclear power technology could be exploited by dedicated and highly motivated terrorists to cause massive harm to civilians. The threats to be addressed here are:

1. Proliferation of uranium enrichment technology;
2. The "dirty bomb" and attacks on fuel shipments;
3. Attacks on nuclear power plants;
4. Attacks on spent fuel storage facilities.

Each pathway is different in terms of likelihood of the attempt, likelihood of success, potential extent of damage, and the effectiveness of the procedural and physical barriers in place. Moreover, there are differences in the degree to which each category of threat is properly seen as a derivative of the commercial nuclear industry and therefore one of the hidden costs of the regime, that is our present focus.

Proliferation of Uranium Enrichment Technology. As discussed earlier, the nuclear power industry developed around a reactor design pioneered by the U.S. Navy that used enriched uranium as the fuel and ordinary (light) water as the coolant. The problem with that choice has always been that worldwide promotion of nuclear power based on enriched uranium fuel could lead to the worldwide spread of enrichment technology, which could be used for enriching uranium to the high levels needed for nuclear weapons.

Eisenhower's answer to this concern was famously naive: he proposed in his Atoms for Peace program that administrative controls could ensure that the then secret enrichment technology would remain under American military control. About that he was also famously wrong,[33] and uranium enrichment is today carried out in many industrialized countries of the world. For the most part, because of the vast international network of export controls and facility inspections by the International Atomic Energy Agency, these non-military fuel enrichment plants are not being diverted into production of highly enriched uranium (HEU). But there are signs that the uncontrolled spread of enrichment technology may now be occurring possibly leading to a black market in weapons-grade enriched uranium and bombs made with it (Swedish Nuclear Power Institute, 2002).

In early 2004, Pakistan's top nuclear scientist, A.Q. Khan, admitted to providing plans, specifications and components of enrichment technology to North Korea, Iran, and Libya, all of which had ambitions to develop nuclear weapons (Rohde and Sanger, 2004). Subsequent investigations showed that Khan had stolen a classified technology developed by the commercial European consortium Urenco, whose main business is enriching uranium for power reactors all over the world.[34]

In the 1970s Urenco's laboratories in the Netherlands developed a state-of-the-art gas centrifuge design intended to allow the Europeans to compete with the United States in the lucrative commercial fuel enrichment business. Because of international concern about proliferation of nuclear weapons, the centrifuge factory was supposed to be highly secure but in practice the atmosphere there was, in the words of *Christian Science Monitor*'s Peter Grier (2004), "relaxed:"

> The centrifuge building housed a snack shop, and workers with full clearance routinely filtered through—including a well-liked metallurgist named Abdul Qadeer Khan.

Khan abruptly left Urenco in 1976, and on the basis of the drawings and specifications he had stolen, Pakistan built an enrichment facility that eventually produced the HEU it needed for its small nuclear arsenal, first demonstrated in 1998. Thus the earlier fears that a nuclear power industry based on enriched fuel could lead to proliferation of nuclear weapons were shown to be all too justified.

And the proliferation has continued. With Khan's assistance, North Korea also built a uranium enrichment facility believed to have produced enough material for several nuclear weapons. Iran and Libya proceeded with enrichment operations that have recently been disclosed and that may have been intended to supply materials for weapons. (Following the discoveries, both have vowed not to pursue this path, but Iran's actual intentions remain highly suspect.)[35]

Investigations following these disclosures have shown that the black market in enrichment technology did not begin with A. Q. Khan. *The New York Times* reported (Smith, 2004),

> The records show that industry scientists and Western intelligence agencies have known for decades that nuclear technology was pouring out of Europe despite national export control efforts to contain it.
> Many of the names that have turned up among lists of suppliers and middlemen who fed equipment, materials and knowledge to nuclear programs in Pakistan and other aspiring nuclear nations are well-known players in Europe's enrichment industry...

These developments are dangerous, certainly, because the more nuclear-armed nations there are, the more likely that a nuclear war might break out. But there is another danger—that terrorist groups will find it easier to obtain nuclear weapons. It has long been understood that nations possessing nuclear weapons have a natural reluctance to use them because of the fear of retaliation in kind. Terrorist groups, particularly those motivated by religious extremism, are less inhibited in this regard (Stern, 1999:7).

With as little as 50 kilograms of HEU, it would not be difficult for a terrorist group to construct a crude, but highly destructive, nuclear weapon (Swedish Nuclear Power Inspectorate, 2004). In contrast, building a plutonium weapon is probably beyond the capabilities of any non-state group for the foreseeable future. As a former head of Los Alamos National Laboratory has said, "If somebody tells you that making a plutonium implosion weapon is easy, he is wrong. And if somebody tells you that making an improvised nuclear device with highly enriched uranium is difficult, he is even more wrong" (Harold Agnew, quoted in Garwin, 2002).

The great fear among terrorism specialists is that anti-western terrorist groups may be able to obtain HEU (or operational nuclear weapons, for that matter) from states that are sympathetic to their cause. The explosion of even a small nuclear weapon in a U.S. city would be a cataclysm of unprecedented proportions. Even a 1 kiloton (kt) device (about 1/10 the size of the bombs that destroyed Hiroshima and Nagasaki and about 1/150 the typical size in the U.S. or Russian strategic arsenal) would, if detonated in the middle of New York City, kill about 200,000 people within a week. A 10 kt device would kill perhaps five times that many (Garwin, 2002). The effects on the U.S. economy and society and on the world as a whole are simply beyond prediction, if not beyond contemplation.

This connection between the current activities of the commercial nuclear power industry and potentially devastating terrorist attacks on U.S. cities is not as direct as some of the threats to be discussed below but the inherent destructive potential of such attacks is so great that this risk must be seen as one of the most serious hidden costs of nuclear power.

Current U.S. policy on nuclear nonproliferation is exacerbating this risk. Since the end of the cold war the United States has been backing away from its longstanding commitment to prevent nuclear weapons proliferation throughout the world. For decades the U.S. nonproliferation program followed two parallel tracks: first, incentives for non-weapons states to remain so, and second, voluntary restraints in its own nuclear weapons activities. Both strategies reflect the terms of the Nuclear Non-Proliferation Treaty. But in recent years many of the restraints have been abandoned and plans to abandon even more have been announced.[36]

Since the 9/11, 2001 attacks and the revelations about the weapons programs of Pakistan, North Korea, Libya, and Iran, the United States has been aggressive in its efforts to curb the spread of nuclear weapons, achieving some degree of success with Libya, failing utterly with Pakistan and North Korea and obtaining ambiguous results with Iran. In light of the recent movement of U.S. nuclear weapons policies away from restraint and towards a more aggressive posture, potential proliferators will be inclined to see the U.S. nonproliferation stance as two-faced and unilateral. As a consequence, international efforts to prevent the spread of weapons and weapons technology to nations as well as to terrorists will be impeded.

The "Dirty Bomb and Attacks on Fuel Shipments. The possibility that a terrorist group could wreak havoc in a major city by detonating conventional explosives heavily laced with radioactive material has received a great deal of press attention, partly because detailed plans on how to make such "dirty bombs" were found in Al Qaeda's caves in Afghanistan. Additional attention to the threat has arisen because the U.S. Attorney General decided to incarcerate Jose Padilla, an American citizen, for pursuing the idea. The threat has also garnered a great deal of attention from terrorism experts because preventing such an act seems, over the long run, very difficult (Nartker, 2002).

The difficulty is that there are so many ways that a terrorist could obtain significant quantities (tens of grams for example) of highly radioactive material. One of the greatest concerns is "sealed sources," which are canisters containing refined radioactive materials used in a variety of industrial and scientific activities. Such materials are stored with moderate, but not heavy, security precautions in thousands of facilities throughout the United States (Kelly, 2002). The packaging of the materials is designed to protect workers, so the terrorists, too, might not be exposed to excessive radiation until, perhaps, the dirty bomb was assembled and detonated.

Fortunately, the destructive potential of such a device is not expected to be high in terms of fatalities. Jessica Stern (2002) states,

Dirty bombs are far more frightening than lethal. Numerous studies by government and non-government scientists have shown that a dirty bomb would kill only people in the immediate vicinity of the explosion. While people living downwind of the blast would be exposed to additional radiation, there would be very few additional cancer deaths, probably undetectable in the statistical noise.

Dirty bombs are nonetheless a cause of concern because of the societal and economic disruption they could cause. Large areas (many city blocks, for example) would have to be evacuated, and casualties from panic during such an evacuation might even exceed those from the radiation itself. Restoration of the evacuated areas to productive use would be problematic, since there are no developed technologies (besides demolition) for restoring radioactively contaminated urban facilities to the high standards that the Environmental Protection Agency has established for around the clock habitation (Kelly, 2002).

The direct connection between dirty bombs and the commercial nuclear power industry is weak. Though opinions vary among experts on how attractive a dirty bomb might be to terrorists, there is little disagreement that the use of spent fuel (the most radioactive product of nuclear power) for such a purpose would be highly impractical. Unshielded spent fuel rods are so radioactive that they are considered "self-protecting," meaning that a person who removed a rod from a shipping cask or a spent fuel repository would be quickly incapacitated and soon die from a massive dose of radioactivity.

It is for similar reasons that sabotage, or hijacking, of spent fuel shipments are believed to be an unlikely method for a terrorist attack (despite the fact that the NRC halted all such shipments for almost two years after the 9/11 attacks (Ramstack, 2003)). To be sure, there is enough radioactive material in one shipping cask to kill hundreds of thousands of people, in principle. But anyone who somehow succeeded in opening a fuel transport cask and removing some of the spent fuel would be incapacitated by the symptoms of radiation sickness so quickly that no practical advantage could be taken of the material.

Moreover, the casks are very tough, having been designed for extremely bad highway or railway accidents and extreme fire conditions. It is possible that terrorists could cause a bad enough accident that the casks might be breached or penetrate a shipping cask with an armor-piercing rocket. However, the consequences would probably be far less than that of the dirty bomb discussed above, because wide dispersal of the radioactive material is unlikely (GAO, 2003). Evacuation and decontamination would incur significant economic costs and no doubt produce substantial public anxiety, but there would be few if any casualties due to released radiation.

Attacks on Nuclear Power Plants. The 9/11 attacks prompted almost immediate speculation that nuclear power plants were highly vulnerable to hijacked commercial aircraft piloted by suicidal terrorists. These concerns were elevated by President Bush's State of the Union announcement that plans for nuclear power plants were found in Al Qaeda caves in Afghanistan (Meyer and Zitner, 2002). In 2004, the 9/11 Committee staff report revealed that an early version of the 9/11 attack plan included crashing airliners into nuclear power plants (National Commission on Terrorist Attacks on the United States, 2004). The greatest fear is that a fully fueled jumbo jet flown at high speed directly into the containment building of a nuclear reactor could smash a hole through the thick walls and spew tons of aviation fuel into the building. Damage to the reactor from the resulting fires and from missiles produced by the impact could cause the reactor to melt down. The result would be a massive release of radioactivity and, with the containment building penetrated, an extremely radioactive cloud of gases and fine particles would be released into the atmosphere. Such a plume could expose downwind populations to lethal doses and result in thousands, tens of thousands, or even hundreds of thousands of deaths, mostly due to latent cancers (Hirsch, 2002).

The nuclear power industry and the NRC aggressively dispute such speculations, characterizing their power plants as "hard targets" that would survive such impacts (Mintz, 2002) and insisting that the main thing needed is to prevent terrorists from hijacking airliners in the first place (Global Security Newswire, 2002). To bolster public confidence in the intrinsic protection provided by the containment building, the Nuclear Energy Institute (NEI), a lobbying group for the industry, sponsored a scientific study of an airliner crashing into the thick concrete walls of a containment building and widely proclaimed that the study's results showed there was no problem. But critics pointed out major flaws in the NEI study, claiming that numerous optimistic assumptions in the calculations biased the results (Hirsch et al., 2003). They also pointed out that there are critical facilities in nuclear power plants (like the control room), that are *outside* the containment building and, hence, not protected by all that concrete and steel.

The responsibility for sorting out such conflicting claims falls on the NRC, which has announced plans to carry out a program of "confirmatory research" on whether nuclear power plants are vulnerable to airliner impact. But it is doubtful that the results of such research will quell the controversy, because too many critics of the agency, like NEI itself, see it as a defender of the industry. For many years the NRC has addressed a variety of complex reactor safety issues with programs of "confirmatory research" that are designed to appear scientific and objective, but that are often intended only to "confirm" pre-determined conclusions that are favorable to the industry.[37] The absence of an objective process to resolve technical questions about hazards to the public from reactor operation is a fundamental policy issue on many levels.

One of the most difficult questions regarding vulnerability to airline impacts is whether a core meltdown would occur even if the containment building was penetrated and jet fuel burned inside. Some experts warn that the greater danger is from an armed attack by a small ground force of highly trained and highly motivated terrorists. Once inside the plant boundaries and in control of certain key locations, they could force a core meltdown and breach of containment by manipulating or destroying a small set of reactor control and safety systems. It is significant that only two core meltdowns have occurred in commercial power reactors—Three Mile Island and Chernobyl—and unsafe operator actions were the principal cause in both cases (Bergeron, 2002: 47 and 49).

Historically, the NRC's answer to such a possibility was to require plant owners to maintain a security program adequate to repel the so-called design basis threat, or DBT. But even before the 9/11 attacks NRC's requirements were often criticized as being too weak. For example, a maximum of three armed attackers was assumed for the DBT, and they were assumed to have only small arms, not more powerful weapons like rocket propelled grenades (Hirsch, 2002).

Enforcement of these security requirements was notoriously weak prior to the 9/11 events. The NRC's own force-on-force exercises at power plants in the 1990s resulted in a failure rate of almost 50 percent, even though the security forces at the plants were given six months advance warning of the dates the mock attacks were to occur. This poor showing was a source of great consternation among the nuclear utilities, that successfully pressured the NRC to cancel the force-on-force program in 1998 (only to reinstate it almost immediately in reaction to bad press (Hirsch, 2002)).

The 9/11 attacks forced the NRC to reconsider what kind of sabotage threats should be considered credible, and in April 2003, the agency issued a revised DBT postulating a larger and better armed attack force. However, the details of the new requirement are classified. Not surprisingly, NRC critics have expressed skepticism about the new requirements, and charge that the parameters of the new DBT were arrived at by considering what existing plant security forces could handle rather than objectively evaluating what type of attack was really credible (Weil, 2003).

The secrecy now associated with NRC's deliberations and decisions about nuclear power plant security, along with the agency's long record of bending to industry pressure to keep costs down, make it virtually impossible for outsiders to assess risk to the public due to terrorist attacks on commercial nuclear reactors. It is possible that the risk is unacceptably high, and the NRC should do more, but it is also possible that the upgraded protection is sufficient and additional resources would be better spent on other vulnerabilities.

From a public policy perspective, this is an intolerable dilemma rooted in the lack of credibility of the NRC as an objective guardian of public safety. Industry critic Daniel Hirsch (2002) states,

Put bluntly, the NRC is arguably the most captured regulatory agency in the federal government, a creature of the industry it is intended to regulate. Efforts to separate its promotional and regulatory functions, which led to the breakup of the Atomic Energy Commission in the mid-1970s, have failed utterly. The NRC's principal interest is in assisting the industry, keeping regulatory burdens and expenses to a bare minimum, and helping to jumpstart the nuclear enterprise.

Attacks on Spent Fuel Storage Facilities. One of the many unfortunate consequences of the U.S. government's pursuit of nuclear power before working out its difficulties is the accumulation of spent fuel rods at each power plant in the country. Fuel rods become unusable in nuclear reactors after two years or so because of the buildup of highly radioactive fission products (which are the atoms resulting when uranium nuclei split into pieces). These contaminants eventually interfere with the operation of the nuclear core, so the rods must be removed periodically and replaced with fresh ones. But because the federal government and the nuclear industry have not been able to establish suitable permanent storage facilities for the spent rods, the power plants themselves are now *de facto* waste repositories. Most of the fuel ever burned at each plant is still on site, either suspended in large pools of water, which act to keep the self-heating rods cool, or housed in dry casks, which are air-cooled.

When spent fuel pools were seen simply as interim storage, they were expected to contain only a modest number of rods arranged in an "open rack" configuration. If all the water was drained out the temperature of the rods would increase, but since they were widely spaced, they would not get hot enough to be dangerous. As the number of rods at each site relentlessly climbed, the NRC took the position that such a "loss of coolant" accident was so unlikely that plant owners were allowed to reconfigure the arrangement of rods from the original concept to much more densely packed arrangements.

However, if, somehow, the water in the pool does drain out, the tighter packing diminishes the ability of natural air circulation to keep the rods cool. Various studies have shown that in the absence of water the rods would heat up to the ignition point and begin to burn. A large fire could ensue, lofting enormous amounts of radioactive material into the atmosphere. The result would be exposure of many people in the surrounding area to dangerous, possibly fatal, doses of radiation. As with the terrorist-induced core-melt accident discussed above, the deaths would occur over a period of time, primarily in the form of latent cancers. A 1997 study by Brookhaven National Laboratory estimated that the number of cancer fatalities from such an event could be as high as 28,000 (Alvarez, 2002).

NRC's calculation of a very low probability for a loss of coolant *accident* may be valid but it is irrelevant in regard to the possibility that terrorists could *intentionally cause* such an event. These pools are located outside the containment building and hence may be more vulnerable to attacks by aircraft impact or armed attack than the reactor itself.

In 2003 an independent scientific study of the dangers inherent in U.S. spent fuel pools was published in the journal *Science and Global Security* (Alvarez et al., 2003). It warned of the vulnerability of these facilities to terrorist attack and presented numerous calculations to evaluate whether the fuel rods would ignite, the possible extent of radioactive contamination downwind of the fire, and the number of latent cancer deaths that might be expected. The study went beyond just analysis; it proposed concrete actions to remedy the situation. Over a ten-year period, most of the fuel in the densely packed water pools could be moved to dry cask storage, that is much less vulnerable to terrorist attack. Then the water pools could be restored to their original open-rack configuration, also much less vulnerable. The cost would be substantial—$3.5 billion to $7 billion for the U.S. reactor fleet—but might be partially paid from the huge unspent fund set aside for the (still nonexistent) permanent waste repository. The end result would be the removal of an important public vulnerability to terrorism.

NRC's reaction to the *Science and Global Security* article was prompt and predictable. It is also a telling indication of the paralysis of the nuclear enterprise in the United States. The NRC's six-page rebuttal (NRC, 2003) concluded:

> NRC does not believe that the fundamental recommendation of this paper, namely that all spent fuel more than five-years-old be placed in dry casks through a crash ten-year program costing many billions of dollars, is at all justified. Spent fuel stored, in both wet and dry storage configurations, is safe and measures are in place to adequately protect the public.

The rebuttal also pointed out that much of the independent study was based on earlier NRC research and that the NRC was in the process of carrying out additional research that would "update" the older results and show, essentially, that there was nothing to worry about. Unfortunately for the scientific process, the results of the new work would be classified.

It is impossible to know who is right in such an argument. The NRC has a multi-million dollar annual research budget, almost all of it derived from operating fees paid by the nuclear industry. This funding is contracted out on a variety of specific projects to universities, the Department of Energy's national laboratories, and private research firms. The research program primarily targets technical questions that bear heavily on controversial reactor safety issues. Since the early 1990s (when the agency's funding became almost entirely fee-based) much of the research has been carefully designed to confirm pre-determined conclusions favorable to the nuclear industry's interests. Though mostly conducted by outside research groups, the work on the most controversial issues is carefully overseen on a day-to-day basis by politically-attuned managers at the NRC.[38] Independent analysts cannot compete in such a lopsided contest. But their message should be heard objectively, not reflexively attacked.

The controversy over whether spent fuel storage facilities are vulnerable to terrorist attacks has also exposed a deep problem related to nuclear power: the conflict between the Federal government, on one side, and states and municipalities on the other, regarding jurisdiction over nuclear waste transportation and storage. In November 2001, the owner of the Diablo Canyon nuclear power plant in southern California asked the NRC for permission to construct a dry cask spent fuel storage facility near the plant. Local anti-nuclear groups formally protested, saying that the environmental assessments performed by the plant owner and the NRC did not consider the possibility of terrorist attacks. But the NRC maintained that such events were "speculative" and "worst case scenarios" and, hence, need not be addressed.

In 2004, the attorney general of the state of California, along with the attorneys general of three other states, joined a lawsuit against NRC in federal court to require that local citizens and their representatives have a say in what level of protection against terrorist attacks is established at the new facility. But the NRC nonetheless proceeded to grant the new license (Sneed, 2004). It can do this because the Atomic Energy Act assigns to the NRC sole authority on decisions related to the safety of civilian nuclear operations, so that the normal checks and balances inherent in the interplay among federal, state, and local governments have been removed.

The Accountability Crisis

Assessing how and where future terrorist attacks might occur is extremely difficult, but when the potential targets under consideration are nuclear power plants, or their spent fuel repositories, there are added problems. The unique properties of the nuclear energy enterprise create substantial barriers to objective assessment of such threats. The central problem might be called a crisis of accountability.

Normally, decisions affecting the health and welfare of millions of citizens are arrived at through complex processes incorporating institutional and individual accountability as well as a set of checks and balances to assure the final decisions are, on average, honest and objective. Today's nuclear enterprise lacks the centering processes that lead to good public policy.

- Because of the Price Anderson Act, insurers are sheltered from the costs of the worst types of nuclear disasters and, hence, do not play the normal role of underwriters—providing realistic assessments of risk.
- Because of deregulation, many of the corporations owning nuclear power plants are shells with few capital assets other than the plants themselves. This, too, diminishes accountability.
- Because of the Atomic Energy Act's sweeping delegation of authority to the NRC, state and local governments are constrained in their efforts to ensure proper protection of their citizens from harm.

- Because the Nuclear Regulatory Commission is an autonomous bureaucracy whose senior leaders benefit from serving the interests of the industry far more than from ensuring objective analysis, the agency's staff often work towards obscuring risks rather than clarifying them.

In the final section of this chapter we consider the implications, for both U.S. energy security and national security, of the risks and vulnerabilities to which we have drawn attention in this and the preceding sections.

Implications for Energy and National Security

'Déjà vu All Over Again:' Things Will Be Different This Time: Preparing for the "Second Coming" of Nuclear Power

It is against the backdrop of the metaphorical rickety bandwagon with four wobbling wheels that nuclear power's protagonists have, for a decade or more, been calling for the "second coming" of nuclear power.[39] If they succeed, they hope to reverse the fortunes of what has been variously called "The Failed Promise of Nuclear Power" (Bupp and Derian, 1981), the "Collapse of an Industry" (Campbell, 1988) and "The Demise of Nuclear Energy" (Morone and Woodhouse, 1989).

Nuclear Power 2010. This is the name the Bush administration has given to their plans for breathing new life into the nuclear power project. Like nearly everything else about the technology, this plan conveys a vision of nuclear power's future that is not the U.S. Government's alone. In fact, the membership of the Near Term Deployment Group (NTDG) that formulated it reads like an "institutional Who's Who" of the nuclear power regime.

Declaring nuclear power to be "safe, clean and economical" and that "[t]he performance of nuclear plants in the United States is excellent" (DOE, 2001: iv, 1), the report sets forth the near-term plan for deployment of what are referred to as "Generation IV" reactors.[40] Although the NTDG stressed that any subsequently selected reactor designs must be cost-competitive in an environment of electricity deregulation, government support is deemed essential, in the form of "leadership, effective policy, efficient regulatory approvals, and cost sharing of generic and one-time costs" (2001: 1).

For a private sector industry claiming to have matured, this degree of proposed taxpayer largesse is remarkable, though not unprecedented. Its rationale, as Deputy Secretary of Energy Kyle E. McSlarrow stated it, is simple: "Few utilities are interested in making investments in billions of dollars in a new power plant if they can't be certain that they can operate the plant on a predictable schedule—or, in a worst case, if there is a prospect that they won't be able to operate at all" (7/13/2004). Utility reticence to invest in nuclear power is uncannily familiar.

Putting aside for the moment the various unresolved problems and issues which continue to plague the technology, there is compelling evidence that the terrorist attacks of September 2001 have altered public perceptions of the safety of nuclear power installations, and the corresponding support for building more of them. Perhaps even more important than public perceptions, which are, after all, subject to the vicissitudes of time and public relations efforts, is the more objective assessment of the vulnerability of these installations. And this assessment, presented in the preceding section, does not reveal a system well-suited for optimal security in an age of global terrorism.

Then there are the various unresolved problems and issues. Prominent among them is the as-yet unresolved matter of the long-term secure disposition of high-level radioactive waste, particularly spent reactor fuel. One stumbling block centers on the government's unwillingness to guarantee the structural integrity of the concrete storage canisters for more than 10,000 years. Yet the waste placed in them will remain radioactive for the next 240,000 years. Even if these problems are somehow solved, there is still a basic limiting factor: the Yucca Mountain facility would be full within the next several decades, *just handling the waste from the existing reactors.*

There is a more fundamental problem still: nuclear power has *never* been economically competitive, if the term means anything resembling a true market test. Aside from the monumental benefits of the Price Anderson act discussed earlier, there is the estimated $86 billion in "stranded costs" associated with nonproductive utility investments in nuclear facilities, much of which they have been allowed to recover from ratepayers. Being able to be compensated by one's customers for poor business performance is not usually the way of the marketplace. Now, this same group of institutional actors claims that it needs additional government assistance to develop prototypes for a whole new generation of nuclear reactors—in order to find ones that can be "economically competitive."

Add to this the safety challenges posed by a progressively aging fleet of existing reactors. Amazingly, a growing number of them have already had their operating licenses extended by the NRC for another twenty years, with many more applications flooding in. Among those expected to be submitted is one for the Davis-Besse plant, now that it has a new head, and the Hope Creek and Salem I and II reactors at Lower Alloways Creek, NJ.[41] In the face of operating experience that has indicated a reactor lifecycle considerably shorter than the original license duration of forty years, operators are now being given permission to run their reactors—barring a catastrophic incident of course—for 50 percent longer, up to sixty years.

Conclusions

The nuclear power enterprise has failed the terms of any reasonable "social contract" regarding energy supply to the American society. The roots of its failure can be traced to the special protections set in place by an alliance of industry and government proponents to ensure the enterprise would thrive despite its manifest difficulties. In Section 2, we showed that this "great nuclear bandwagon" developed, and continues to exhibit, a range of internal problems that have rendered it unstable. And in Section 3 we showed that the enterprise as currently configured is both vulnerable to exploitation by anti-American terrorists, and incapable of properly dealing with this challenge.

These weaknesses reflect the unusual and unfortunate history of commercial nuclear power in the United States, a history that began with an unprecedented government incubation of an unproven technology and that has culminated in an imposing political economy that is self-propagating and resistant to change. As unfortunate as this history may be, we cannot at this point erase its very real consequences; if nothing else, the presence on the landscape of 103 operating reactors is a fact that must be acknowledged.

Technology such as nuclear power cannot be uninvented, but it can be reinvented. And, as some European countries have shown, it can also be phased out—if that is seen to be in the best interests of society. But this or any other option should be the product of a careful deliberative process—one that not only looks at the environmental or economic impacts of this technology but at the political texture of the institutions it embodies as well. In doing so, we can be guided by Winner's wisdom (1986: 55):

> The important task becomes…one of evaluating the material and social infrastructures specific technologies create for our life's activity. We should try to imagine and seek to build technical regimes compatible with freedom, social justice and other key political ends.…If it is clear that the social contract implicitly created by implementing a particular generic variety of technology is incompatible with the kind of society we deliberately choose—that is, if we are confronted with an inherently political technology of an unfriendly sort—then that kind of device or system ought to be excluded from society altogether.

The challenge is to begin the process.

Notes

1.   A *cascading* blackout occurs when a surge of power spills over—cascades—from one system to another, taking out power plants and lines in rapid succession.
2.   The entire blackout actually took several hours—the "minutes" reference pertains only to its "cascade stage." See U.S.–Canada Power System Outage Task Force, "Final Report on the August 14, 2003 Blackout in the United States and Canada: Causes and Recommendations" (2004: 73-91).

3. This is enough electricity to serve the populations of Toledo and Cleveland combined -two cities which were affected by the blackout.
4. Two of the nine reactors -Perry and Indian Point 3- took a week or longer to return to service. (Perry is owned by FirstEnergy.)
5. For helpful descriptions of the different design and operational features of U.S. and Canadian nuclear power plants, see U.S.-Canada Power System Outage Task Force, 2004: 123.
6. This is also the year in which the North American Electric Reliability Council (NERC) was "voluntarily" established by the utility industry "to insure maintenance of reliable supplies of electricity and to prevent small power shortages from cascading into major blackouts" (*New York Times*, 6/12/1968: 61).
7. To be considered "good" a plant's capacity factor should be at least 80 percent (Komanoff, 1981).
8. See Basalla, *The Evolution of Technology* (1988: 167). Also see Hughes, *American Genesis: A Century of Invention and Technological Enthusiasm* (1989).
9. One of two committees established in July, 1944, to contemplate post-war scenarios for nuclear energy concluded that the United States "should encourage fundamental research and industrial development [of nuclear energy] both of which were essential to maintaining the advanced scientific and technical position that national defense demanded" (Hewlett and Anderson, 1962: 325). A "blue ribbon" Interim Committee was appointed by President Truman the following spring (1945), to make "recommendations on postwar research, development and control, including whatever legislation they judged necessary" (1962: 353). They were advised by some of the most prominent Manhattan Project scientists, as well as by key industrialists, representing such firms as Westinghouse.
10. In 1963, David Lilienthal, the first chairman of the AEC, said "We were grimly determined to prove that this discovery was not just a weapon. This led to…a wishful elevation of the 'sunny side' of the Atom" (Lilienthal, 1963: 103).
11. The eighteen-year span begins with 1948, when the first reactor development program was initiated, to 1966, when the first sizable batch of orders for commercial nuclear reactors-20-were placed by the utilities (Morone and Woodhouse, 1989; U.S. Energy Information Administration, 2002).
12. As originally passed, Price-Anderson required reactor operators to secure up to $60 million in private liability insurance while the government assumed up to a limit of $500 million more. The law has been amended or extended on several occasions, most recently in the Energy Policy Act of 2005, which extends the protection until 2025. See NRC, "Fact Sheet on Nuclear Insurance and Disaster Relief Funds" (http://www.nrc.gov/reading-rm/doc-collections/fact-sheets/funds.html).
13. Amounts are in *current* dollars—valued in the years in which the money was spent.
14. Capacity margin—the difference between dependable capacity and projected peak load, divided by the dependable capacity- is an important indicator of plant reliability.
15. General Electric and Westinghouse were, and are, manufacturers of both power generating equipment and household appliances.
16. See Morone and Woodhouse (1989: 47-66).
17. This was true even with safety and environmental costs factored in for both technologies and controlling for inflation and interest costs, both of which were high and unstable during that period.
18. There is a wealth of informative data analysis in Komanoff's chapter 10 (1981: 227-245), especially Table 10.1 on p. 228 and Table 10.4 on p. 236.

19. That may soon change, based on the filing of the first wave of Early Site Permits with the NRC by a small group of nuclear utilities seeking to build new facilities and the more recent announcement, by a consortium of seven power companies and reactor manufacturers, of their intent to initiate the application process for the possible construction of one or more new plants (Francis, 2004; Broad, 2004).

20. A "reactor year" is the number of reactors in operation times years. At that time, there were 70 units operating (including the ill-fated TMI unit 2). Therefore, 21 reactor years would have taken about 4 months (0.3 year). So the prediction was a less than five percent chance of a major accident within the following 4 months.

21. That a routine incident could lead to such an outcome is what is behind Perrow's (1984) conception of "normal accidents." Bergeron (2002: 45-48) presents a thorough description of the events of the accident and its investigation.

22. A lively and contentious debate has developed in the ensuing years about how "realistic" the movie portrayal was. A number of antinuclear and environmental groups have weighed in on one side, and the Nuclear Energy Institute has weighed in on the other. A number of web sites present these conflicting sides. See, for example, http://www.animatedsoftware.com/hotwords/meltdown/meltdown.htm and http://www.nei.org/doc.asp?docid=565.

23. The sudden loss of reactor cooling water is known as a loss of coolant accident, or "LOCA."

24. The reactor pressure vessel contains the reactor core, the apparatus which holds the uranium fuel rods and control rods, thereby controlling the fission process. Coolant water flows through this vessel to maintain a safe temperature.

25. For an informative essay on embrittlement, see Odette and Lucas (2001).

26. The CRDM nozzles guide the reactor's control rods. Their proper functioning is essential to the modulation of the nuclear fission process. Any damage to these mechanisms could therefore lead to catastrophic results.

27. Boric acid is used as an additive in the coolant water of pressurized water reactors. Boric acid has been found to be corrosive to ferritic steel. This is why the boric acid deposits accumulated from coolant that leaked from three control rod drive mechanisms on the Davis-Besse reactor pressure vessel head wound up eating through the head's six-inch thick steel. See Oak Ridge National Laboratory Review (1/04: http://www.ornl.gov/info/ornlreview/v37_1_04/article_06.shtml#top)

28. An analysis conducted by the NRC's Office of Research, in collaboration with the Oak Ridge National Laboratory, determined that the liner would have burst open at that point within as little as two more months, (Lochbaum, May, 2004; ORL, January, 2004).

29. At a time of sharply declining profit—themselves a consequence of the plant's shutdown—this added expense was clearly taking a toll. Whether it affected company maintenance operations can only be speculated. However, FirstEnergy's failure to maintain proper "vegetation management" (i.e., tree-trimming) was cited as a central cause in the original line failure that ultimately led to the blackout. See U.S. – Canada Power System Outage Task Force, "Final Report on the August 14, 2003 Blackout in the United States and Canada: Causes and Recommendations" (April 2004: 58-60).

30. The Atomic Energy Commission's longstanding "dual responsibility" of both promoting and regulating civilian nuclear power had been a major factor in Congress dissolving the agency and creating two separate agencies: the NRC, responsible for regulation and the Energy Research and Development Administration (ERDA), responsible for research, development and promotion of nuclear and other energy technologies.

31. This pattern led to two major policy decisions on key safety concerns while the AEC was still in existence, the consequences of which were inherited. One dealt with the adequacy of emergency core cooling systems—systems that were supposed to kick in following a sudden loss of coolant accident, such as a pipe bursting, to prevent a core meltdown. The other dealt with the adequacy of "pressure suppression" systems introduced by both GE and Westinghouse into their reactor designs as a means of avoiding the construction of more robust—and expensive—containment structures. See Ford (1986: 91-130, 191-192) and Bergeron (2002: 43-75).

32. Dr. Harvin's complaint was turned down as unsubstantiable by the NRC on April 5, 2005. She has since filed a civil lawsuit against PSEG Nuclear under New Jersey's whistle-blower protection law.

33. For some details of the early collapse of Eisenhower's strategy of keeping uranium enrichment secret and American, see Bergeron (2002).

34. Urenco is a major partner in the consortium planning to construct a nuclear fuel enrichment plant in New Mexico.

35. In September 2004, the *Guardian* (U.K.) reported that "The U.S., Israel and the Europeans all claim that Iran is covertly engaged in building a nuclear weapon," and that Israel has threatened a pre-emptive strike against Iranian nuclear facilities (MacAskill, et al., 2005).

36. For example, in 1999, the U.S. reversed course and decided not to endorse the Comprehensive Test Ban Treaty. In 2000, the U.S. abandoned negotiations with Russia on START III exactly at the point in time that final agreement was within reach (Woolf, 2001). (The substitute Moscow Agreement of 2002 was a pale and cynical replacement.) In 2002, the U.S. announced that several non-weapons states were now considered fair game for U.S. nuclear strikes, thus abandoning a longstanding commitment never to target such nations with nuclear bombs (Kralev, 2002). In 2003, the U.S. began using commercial nuclear reactors to produce nuclear weapons material, thus abandoning the "no dual use" policy for such reactors that was followed for nearly fifty years (Bergeron, 2004). And in 2004, the Energy Department continued to plan a new factory to produce nuclear weapons and to design smaller and more "usable" bombs (Fleck, 2004).

37. See, for example, the discussion of one such contentious issue in Bergeron (2002), Chapter 3.

38. See, for example, the discussion of the "Direct Containment Heating" issue in Bergeron (2002: 55-75).

39. See, for example, Numark and Terry (2003).

40. The Nuclear Energy Institute (NEI), some of the members of which also serve on the NTDG, has been simultaneously promoting its "Vision 2020" initiative, which calls for "the addition of 50,000 megawatts of electricity to the U.S. power supply from new nuclear plants and an additional 10,000 megawatts from improvements to existing nuclear plants" (http://www.nei.org/index.asp?catnum=2&catid=143, accessed 7/19/2004). This equates to approximately 50 new nuclear plants, assuming an average size of 1,000 MWe each.

41. See NRC, "Future Submittals of Applications" (*http://www.nrc.gov/reactors/operating/licensing/renewal/applications.html#underreview*)

References

Abrams, S. (2002). quoted in Radiological Weapons: 'Dirty Bomb' Conference Set for Next March. *Global Security Newswire*, November 14, 2002.

Alvarez, R, et al. (2003). Reducing the Hazards from Stored Spent Power-Reactor Fuel in the United States. *Science and Global Security.* 11, 1.

Alvarez, R. (2002). What About the Spent Fuel? *Bulletin of the Atomic Scientists.* January/February, 45.

Basalla, G. (1988). *The Evolution of Technology.* Cambridge (U.K.): Cambridge University Press.

Bergeron, K. (2004). The Death of No-dual-use. *Bulletin of the Atomic Scientists.* January/February, 15.

_____. (2002). *Tritium on Ice: The Dangerous New Alliance of Nuclear Weapons and Nuclear Power.* Cambridge, MA: MIT Press.

Broad, W. J. (2004, May 25). Nuclear Weapons in Iran: Plowshare or Sword? *The New York Times.*

Bupp, I. C. and Derian, J. (1981). *The Failed Promise of Nuclear Power: The Story of Light Water.* New York: Basic Books.

Byrne, J., and Rich, D. (1986). In Search of the Abundant Energy Machine. In J. Byrne and D.Rich (Eds.). *The Politics of Energy Research and Development.* Energy Policy Studies Volume 3. New Brunswick, NJ: Transaction Books.

Campbell, J.L. (1988). Collapse of an Industry: Nuclear Power and the Contradiction of U.S. Policy. Ithaca, NY: Cornell University Press.

Cohn, S. M.. (1997). *Too Cheap to Meter: An Economic and Philosophical Analysis of the Nuclear Dream.* Albany, NY: State University of New York Press.

Eisenhower, D. D. (1953). Peaceful Uses of Atomic Energy. Address to the General Assembly of the United Nations, December 8, 1953. Washington, DC: National Archives and Records Administration.

Federal Power Commission. (1965). *Northeast Power Failure: A Report to the President.* Washington, DC: U. S. Government Printing Office.

FirstEnergy Corporation. (2003). Management Discussion. *Annual Report 2003.*

Fleck, J. (2004, June 4). Plan Slashes Nuclear Arsenal. *Albuquerque Journal.*

Ford, D. (1986). *Meltdown: The Secret Papers of the Atomic Energy Commission.* New York: Simon and Schuster.

Francis, D. R. (2004, March 29). After Nuclear's Meltdown, a Cautious Revival. *Christian Science Monitor.* Retrieved on 6/13/2004. Available at http://www.csmonitor.com/index.html.

Galbraith, M. S. (2000, May 30). Peeling Layers off the Onion. *South Bend Tribune.* Retrieved on 7/11/2004. Available at http://www.southbendtribune.com/local/fission.html.

Garwin, R. L. (2002). Nuclear and Biological Megaterrorism. 27th Session of the International Seminars on Planetary Emergencies. Erice, Sicily. August 21.

Global Security Newswire. (2002, August 16). Threat Assessment: Nuclear Power Plants at Low Risk, NRC Says.

Grier, P. (2004, Mach 2). The spread of nuclear know-how. *Christian Science Monitor,* C1.

Hewlett, R. G., and Anderson, Jr, O. E. (1962). *The New World, 1939/1946.* University Park, PA: Pennsylvania State University Press.

Hirsch, D., Lochbaum, D., and Lyman, E.. (2003). The NRC's Dirty Little Secret. *Bulletin of the Atomic Scientists,* May/June, 44.

Hirsch, D. (2002). The NRC: What Me Worry? *Bulletin of the Atomic Scientists,* January/February.

Hoffman, B. (2002). The Mind of the Terrorist. In H. W. Kushner (Ed). *Essential Readings on Political Terrorism.* Lincoln, NE: Gordian Knot Books.

Hughes, T. P. (1989). *American Genesis: A Century of Invention and Technological Enthusiasm 1870-1970.* New York: Viking Penguin.

Kelly, H. (2002). Dirty Bombs: Response to a Threat. *Public Interest Report, 55*(2), 1.

Komanoff, C. (1981). *Power Plant Cost Escalation.* New York: Van Nostrand Reinhold.

Kralev, N. (2002, February 22). U.S. drops pledge on nukes. *Washington Times.*

Lilienthal, D.E. (1963). Change, Hope, and the Bomb. Princeton, NJ: Princeton University Press.

Lochbaum, D. (2004). *U.S. Nuclear Plants in the 21ˢᵗ Century: The Risk of a Lifetime.* Cambridge, MA: UCS Publications.

———. (2004). Same Problems At Same Nuclear Plant Deserve Same Protection For The Public (Personal Communication, June 21, 2004). Retrieved July 17, 2005. Available at http://www.ucsusa.org/clean_energy/nuclear_safety/page.cfm?pageID=1802

———. (2004). Remarks by David Lochbaum, Nuclear Safety Engineer, about Safety Culture at the UNPLUG Salem Rally, on March 28, 2004. Retrieved July 17, 2005. Available at http://www.ucsusa.org/clean_energy/nuclear_safety page.cfm?pageID=1802.

———. (2003). Regulatory Malpractice: NRC'S 'Handling' of the PWR Containment Sump Problem. Union of Concerned Scientists. Retrieved on 7/8/2004. Available at http://www.ucsusa.org/clean_energy/nuclear_safety/.

———. (1998). Nuclear Plant Safety: Will the Luck Run Out? Union of Concerned Scientists. Retrieved on 7/8/2004. Available at http://www.ucsusa.org/clean_energy/nuclear_safety/.

MacAskill, E., Naji, K., and McGreal, C. (2005, September 9). U.K. Sets Iran Deadline to End Nuclear Bomb Work. *The Guardian.*

Melosi, M. V. (1985). *Coping with Abundance: Energy and Environment in Industrial America.* Philadelphia: Temple University Press.

Meyer, J., and Zitner, A. (2002, January 30). Troops Uncovered Diagrams for Major U.S. Targets, Bush Says. *Los Angeles Times,* A1.

Mintz, J. (2002, December 26). Nuclear Plants Are Secure, Study Says. *Washington Post.* A2.

Montgomery, J. (2005, August 6). Regulators Eye Keeping Close Watch on PSEG - 'Heightened' Safety Supervision Recommended into Next Year. *The News Journal,* B1.

———. (2005, April 16). Probe of nuclear overseer wanted—Plant troubles spur lawmakers' request. *News Journal,* B1.

Morone, J. G., and Woodhouse, E. J. (1989). *The Demise of Nuclear Energy? Lessons for Democratic Control of Technology.* New Haven, CT: Yale University Press.

Munson, R. (1985). *The Power Makers.* Emmaus, PA: Rodale Press.

Nartker, M. (2002, November 18). Radiological Weapons: 'Dirty Bomb' Attack Is 40 Percent Probability, Expert Says. *Global Security Newswire.*

National Commission on Terrorist Attacks on the United States. (2004, June 16). Outline of the 9/11 Plot: Staff Statement No. 16.

New York Times. (1968, June 12). Electric Utilities Form Group; New England Affiliation Slated, 61, 69.

———. (1970, July 3). Power Policy Needed, 24.

Numark, N., and Terry, M. (2003). Is a Second Coming Nigh? *Nuclear Engineering International,* October, 38-40.

Oak Ridge National Laboratory. (2004). Staying in the Comfort Zone. *Oak Ridge National Laboratory Review*: 37 (1). Retrieved on May 25, 2004. Available at http://www.ornl.gov/info/ornlreview/v37_1_04/

Odette, G. R., and Lucas, G. E. (2001). Embrittlement of Nuclear Reactor Pressure Vessels. *JOMMM: The Member Journal of the Minerals, Metals & Materials Society*, *53* (7), 18-22.

Orlans, H. (1967). *Contracting for Atoms*. Washington, DC: Brookings Institution.

Perrow, C. (1984). *Normal Accidents: Living with High-Risk Technologies*. New York: Basic Books.

Ramstack, T. (2003, July 25). Department of Energy Lifts Moratorium on Shipping Nuclear Waste. *Washington Times*.

Riccio, J. (2001). *Risky Business: The Probability and Consequences of a Nuclear Accident*. Greenpeace U.S.. Retrieved on 7/5/2004. Available at http://www.greenpeaceusa.org/reports/.

Rohde, D., and Sanger, D. E. (2004, February 2). Key Pakistani Is Said to Admit Atom Transfers. *The New York Times*, A1.

Rosenbaum, W. A. (1987). Energy, Politics, and Public Policy. Washington, DC: Congressional Quarterly Press.

Rudolph, R., and Ridley, S.. (1986). *Power Struggle*. New York: Harper and Row.

Smith, C. S. (2004, February 19). Roots of Pakistan Atomic Scandal Traced to Europe. *The New York Times*.

Sneed, D. (2004, March 24). NRC Approves Fuel Storage Site at Diablo Canyon, Calif., Nuclear Plant. *San Luis Obispo Tribune*.

Stern, J. (2002, June 11). A Rational Response to Dirty Bombs. *Financial Times*.

Stern, J. (1999). *The Ultimate Terrorists*. Cambridge, MA: Harvard University Press.

Swedish Nuclear Power Inspectorate. (2002). Eliminating Stockpiles of Highly Enriched Uranium.

Union of Concerned Scientists. (2002). Davis-Besse: The Reactor with a Hole in Its Head. Retrieved on 7/8/2004. Available at http://www.ucsusa.org/clean_energy/nuclear_safety/.

U.S. – Canada Power System Outage Task Force. (2004). *Final Report on the August 14, 2003 Blackout in the United States and Canada: Causes and Recommendations*. Washington, DC: U.S. Government Printing Office.

(U.S.) Congress. Senate. Committee on Energy and Natural Resources. (2004, July 13). *Hearings on the Role of Nuclear Power in National Energy Policy*. 108th Congress, 2nd Session.

(U.S.) DOE (Department of Energy), Office of Nuclear Energy, Science and Technology. (2001). *A Roadmap to Deploy New Nuclear Power Plants in the United States by 2010: Volume I, Summary Report*. Washington, DC: U.S. Government Printing Office.

(U.S.) EIA (Energy Information Administration). (2002). Nuclear Power Plant Operations, 1957-2002. *Annual Energy Review 2002*. Table 9.2, 257.

———. (1983). *Nuclear Plant Cancellations: Causes, Costs, and Consequences*. Washington, DC: U.S. Government Printing Office.

(U.S.) GAO (General Accounting Office). (2003). *Spent Nuclear Fuel: Options Exist to Further Enhance Security*. (GAO-03-426): August 14. Washington, DC: U.S. Government Accounting Office.

———. (1997). *Nuclear Regulation: Preventing Problem Plants Requires More Effective NRC Action*. (GAO/RCED-97-145): May 30. Washington, DC: U.S. Government Accounting Office.

(U.S.) NRC (Nuclear Regulatory Commission). (2003). Fact Sheet on NRC Review of Paper on Reducing Hazards From Stored Spent Nuclear Fuel, August 2003. Available at www.nrc.gov.

Wald, M. L. (2004, April 26). Energy Providers Seek Grant as Step to Build Nuclear Plant. *The New York Times*. Retrieved on July 19, 2004. Available at http://www.nytimes.com/.

Weil, J. (2003, May 5). NRC Issues Trio of Security Orders, Including One Revising the DBT. *Inside NRC.*
Winner, L. (1986). *The Whale and the Reactor: A Search for Limits in an Age of High Technology.* Chicago, IL: University of Chicago Press.
Winner, L. (1982). Energy Regimes and the Ideology of Efficiency. In G. H. Daniels and M. H. Rose (Eds.), *Energy and Transport: Historical Perspectives on Policy Issues* (pp. 261-286). Beverly Hills: Sage Publications.
Winner, L. (1977). *Autonomous Technology: Technics-out-of-control as a Theme in Political Thought.* Cambridge, MA: MIT Press.
Woolf, A. F. (2001). *Nuclear Arms Control: The U.S.-Russia Agenda.* Congressional Research Service Report IB98030 (updated October 15, 2001): CRS-8.

Energy and Globalization

6

The Political Economy of Electricity Liberalization

Navroz K. Dubash and James H. Williams

Introduction

The electric power industry around the world is undergoing dramatic changes. Over the last fifteen years, under the banner of "electricity reform," (or liberalization, or restructuring), most countries have enacted market-oriented changes in the laws and institutions governing the sector. Despite enormous differences between developing and industrialized countries in the goals and institutional context of these changes, in the 1990s electricity reform coalesced into a narrowly technocratic, and somewhat improbably uniform, prescription for national policy. With little reference to national circumstances, the "standard prescription," (as even its proponents refer to it), describes a sequence of steps for the replacement of state or regulated monopolies with competing private firms, the establishment of competitive markets, and the introduction of independent regulation (Hunt, 2002: 5).

In industrialized countries, reform is justified as a way of squeezing additional efficiency gains out of essentially well-functioning systems. In developing countries, the rationale is more often stated in negative terms: the need to transform a state-owned system that is variously debt-ridden, insolvent, a drain on state finances, inefficient, polluting, corrupt, or a tool of political patronage. In both industrialized and developing countries, electricity reform is mostly an expert discourse dominated by the discipline of economics, that supplies both the terms of the analysis and the measures of success.

As we argue in this paper, the economics-focused discourse on electricity reform results is in a distressingly narrow perspective. Debatable ideas with limited empirical grounding are frequently implemented on the basis of ideology alone. Moreover, advocates of liberalization seldom consider the idea that electricity is embedded in a larger political and social fabric when de-

155

signing market-oriented reforms. This paper examines electricity reform through a broader lens, contemplating both changes in the institutions that comprise electricity systems and the interaction of these changes with the political/economic environments in which they are embedded. From this vantage point, questions about economic outcomes are important, but so, too, are questions about political structures and motivations, underlying assumptions and the role of electricity in society.

In the following section we take a closer look at some of the key problems of standard prescription electricity reform in practice, and at the narrow conceptual foundations on which it rests. While it is not possible here to undertake a comprehensive critique, we do describe some of the main reasons that the model should be subject to more robust debate than is typically the case. We then depart from the narrow confines of the standard prescription to examine electricity reform from a broader perspective, that of electricity as a social project. Here, questions of governance, equity, environment and geopolitics take center stage. How, we ask, does standard prescription electricity reform hold up as a model judged against these broader concerns? We conclude with some observations on the future of electricity reform.

Electricity Reform and its Discontents

Electricity reform became a global phenomenon in the 1990s, spreading rapidly in both industrialized and developing countries. By the end of the decade most industrialized countries and about seventy developing countries had undertaken some kind of reform (ESMAP, 1999; Bacon and Besant-Jones, 2001). That the scope and sequence of these reforms differed from place to place is less remarkable than the widespread acceptance of the need for reform, and the principles underlying it; among which were the political and financial elites worldwide who had for decades supported the public power model. It is true that many state utilities were in poor financial and technical condition, especially in developing and transitional countries, yet this only partly explains the stampede effect, since the cookie-cutter reforms adopted were seldom targeted solutions for the sector problems and national conditions in question.

First implemented in Pinochet's Chile in the early 1980s, electricity reform was an outgrowth of the global juggernaut of liberalized trade, investment, and regulatory policies launched in the Reagan-Thatcher era. In the United States, key legislation enabling electricity deregulation was approved in 1992 (Hirsh, 1999). About this time, international financial institutions led by the World Bank abandoned the state-led development approach of many decades, and adopted the standard prescription of electricity reform as a prerequisite to lending for electricity development (World Bank, 1993). Coupled with other features of "Roaring Nineties" globalization—the emergence of aggressive new commercial interests (such as Enron) in the traditionally staid public utility field, strong-armed persuasion by the home governments of those commercial interests and unprecedented international capital flows—these measures placed immense pressure on governments to liberalize their power sectors (Stiglitz, 2003). In developing countries with poorly-performing electricity industries, or even with well-managed industries but in the throes of debt-driven national fiscal crises, liberalization represented an internationally sanctioned solution to seemingly intractable problems (Williams and Ghanadan, 2005).

There have been bumps in the path of electricity reform's implementation: most notoriously the California electricity crisis of 2000-2001, in which an economic superpower was brought to its knees by the machinations of private companies in newly deregulated electricity markets. In many places, as results on the ground have diverged from theoretical predictions, reform has stalled or moved in unexpected directions and among electricity scholars, new thinking has started to emerge (Von Hirschhausen and Opitz, 2001; Dubash, 2002; Jamasb, 2002; Phadke and Rajan, 2003; Wamukonya, 2003a; Blauvelt, 2004; Lave, Apt and Blumsack, 2004; Williams and Dubash, 2004). Unfortunately, in most places few policy makers and even fewer members of the general public are in a position to interpret either the theoretical arguments or the empirical results; there is little understanding of what electricity reform is, what it implies, or what the alternatives might be. More often than not, the response to setbacks is a recommendation for more of the same— privatization, competition, and regulation—but with greater dedication and intensity. As the discussion below suggests, however, this recommitment to the standard prescription is based on a very partial and limited perspective on electricity.

Privatization

Privatization is the leading edge of electricity reform.[1] Privatization in various forms, from the divestment of existing state utilities to investment in new generating plants by independent power producers (IPPs), has transferred control of some U.S. $1 trillion in electricity assets to private operators in forty countries (Phadke et al., 2003). Privatization in electricity, as in other industries, is said to be motivated by potential efficiency gains that result from a change in ownership. However, these arguments are often overblown, and, at minimum, fail to account for the broader institutional changes necessary to truly reform electricity. Indeed, while electricity privatization is usually rationalized on economic grounds, in reality it is often a political act, intended to overturn existing political-economic arrangements.

The economic argument for privatization usually rests on the premise the private sector, subject to the discipline of the market, is inherently more efficient than the public sector at producing goods and services (Pollitt, 1995: 1; Ingco, 1996: 732). The resulting improvement in efficiency is said to result in lower long-term costs, improving a country's overall macroeconomic performance and competitiveness in the global economy (Schipke, 2001: 1-7). In the electricity context, these claims are disputed, to say the least. A major study of ownership effects in the U.S. power industry showed no difference in cost of service between private and publicly owned utilities; in fact, public ownership had resulted in lower prices over a long period (Kwoka, 1996). Internationally, one comprehensive study covering fourteen countries found no ownership effect in economic or energy efficiency once load factor, age, technology, and country effects were taken into account (Pollitt, 1995: 187). In some cases privatization may improve efficiency, but this must be determined on a case-by-case basis in a manner that distinguishes the effects of ownership from other factors. It appears that incentive structures and management practices have a much stronger effect on power sector efficiency than ownership, per se.

Privatization is also promoted as essential for attracting investment capital, technology, and skills. Conversely, for governments with pressing macroeconomic concerns such as debt and fiscal constraints, being able to hand responsibility for profit, loss and risk to the private sector represents a relief of financial burdens, and the possibility of refocusing resources elsewhere. In the 1990s, this view underlay World Bank lending policies that promoted, and in some cases required, power sector privatization (World Bank, 1993; ADB, 1994). However, privatization alone by no means guarantees an influx of capital. Witness the investment boom and bust of the 1990s. During the early 1990s, private investment in developing country power sectors grew rapidly to exceed U.S. $40 billion annually (Izaguirre, 1998). Since about 2000, however, these investment streams have largely dried up, reflecting the shaky financial condition of the electricity industry worldwide (IEA, 2003; Lamech and Saeed, 2003; Manibog, 2003). Orissa, the first Indian state to privatize its power sector, is often cited as a cautionary tale of unmet promises of foreign investment in the wake of privatization (Kanungo Committee, 2001; Mahalingam, 2002; Kale, 2004).

More often than not, privatization efforts have deeper political underpinnings (Schipke, 2001). Privatization can be motivated by a government's need to obtain revenues that address short-term political problems—financial crises, unemployment, inflation—without the politically costly step of addressing the underlying causes of the problem. The privatization process often involves "ring-fencing" or "cherry-picking," in which segments of the industry that have good commercial potential are separated from segments that do not, making the former more attractive to buyers. Without strong transparency and oversight in place, this also facilitates insider privatization that bestows economic benefits on select groups, while leaving loss-making enterprises in the public sector. Potential beneficiaries often become strong proponents of privatization; it would be naïve to expect otherwise.

A worrisome potential implication of electricity privatization is that the enmeshing of politics and economics can lead to the creation of private monopolies that are restrained neither by adequate competition nor by effective regulation. In the case of Thailand, for example, the government has proposed privatizing the former state utility EGAT through a stock sale in which only a tiny elite fraction of the population is capable of participating (Greacen and Greacen, 2004). Since earlier plans for competition have been scrapped, and regulation of the EGAT monopoly at present appears weak by design, this could become a textbook example of electricity sector privatization gone awry, with Thai ratepayers potentially left responsible for the speculative excesses of a barely regulated semi-private monopoly (Schipke, 2001; Greacen and Greacen, 2004).

Privatization is also often motivated by yet another political imperative— reducing workforce in the power sector. Economists tend to applaud layoffs as an efficiency measure, while some critics argue that layoffs can, and do, undermine the performance and efficiency of electric utilities through loss of skilled personnel.[2] Whether or not overall efficiency benefits outweigh the loss of jobs in the sector, it is certainly the case that privatization is often undertaken to reduce the political strength of organized labor. In the archetypal case of electricity privatization—the U.K.—undermining the political power of unions was a central and well-publicized motivation of the Thatcher government (Martin, 1993; Emmons, 2000).

Competition

Competition is the Holy Grail of electricity reform. Since the 1970s, reform advocates have argued that electricity supply should no longer be considered a natural monopoly to be regulated by the state, but rather a commodity subject to competition and market forces. Competitive electricity markets are said to promote socially optimal prices and send correct price signals to investors, eliminating the need for most forms of government intervention in the sector, such as planning and tariff-setting. In practice there are different types and degrees of competition, including at both the wholesale and retail level. Wholesale competition includes such limited forms as "single buyer" arrangements in which otherwise traditional integrated utilities purchase a portion of their power from IPPs rather than their own generators; another example is bilateral forward contracts negotiated between a single supplier and a single purchaser. Usually, however, the ultimate goal of electricity reform in advanced economies is to achieve full, real-time competition among multiple suppliers and purchasers, in which prices are determined by the laws of supply and demand in spot and futures markets rather than set by flesh and blood regulators.[3]

However, electricity is unlike other commodities in that it cannot be easily stored and supply must meet demand at all times for the system as a whole to continue operating. Because of this, in conditions of shortage, suppliers may be able to exercise market power, charging exorbitant prices for the final increment of power needed to keep the system running. As a consequence, countries with characteristics such as pre-existing capacity and transmission shortages, small geographic size (which favors natural monopoly) and a small number of large generators, are all poor candidates for competitive real-time electricity markets (Huneault, 2001: 26; Woo, Lloyd and Tishler, 2003: 1104). Just as important, even where conditions appear to be favorable, such markets are vastly complicated to set up, operate and oversee.

The case for competition often rests on the argument that it will inevitably wring out cost reductions that will benefit the public through lower prices. The results of competitive electricity markets in this regard have been mixed at best, and in the worst cases, such as California in 2000-2001, quite bad indeed. As one study of competitive generation markets in the U.K., Norway, Alberta (Canada), and California puts it, in each case competitive markets "failed to deliver reliable service at low and stable prices" (Woo et al., 2003: 1108). As a result, government bodies in each country curtailed the competitive experiment by the imposition of price caps and other regulatory controls. The reasons for these failures included market power, strategic bidding, and lack of response to price spikes by customers. As the world now knows, in California these problems were compounded by illegal manipulation at the hands of Enron Corporation and other merchant generators, resulting in blackouts, the bankruptcy of the state's largest utility and costs to ratepayers and taxpayers in excess of U.S. $30 billion (Duane, 2002; Lockyer, 2004) .

There are cases in which wholesale electricity prices have declined with competition, but these results must be viewed with some caution. For example, in the U.K. and Australia, declining cost trends had already begun prior to reforms and were largely due to fuel prices that were dropping for reasons unrelated to the electricity market (Green, 1998: 10; Sharma, 2003: 1098). In the U.K., official studies of market abuses showed that producer cost savings of 40 to 50 percent were not being passed on to consumers but rather retained as excess profits.[4] As a result, in 2001 the vaunted U.K. power pool that has served as the world's most frequently copied model for wholesale markets, was transformed into a new system that abandoned pools in favor of a bilateral trading system (Woo et al., 2003: 1112).

Competition also faces formidable and still unresolved long-term problems in terms of planning, coordination, reliability, and investment in new transmission and generating capacity. These problems did not exist when individual utilities were responsible for all these functions within their service areas. Transmission congestion is a case in point. Traditionally, the amount of trading between utility service areas was small, and interconnections were seen primarily as pathways to provide backup sources of power in case of shortages and emergencies. With the advent of high-volume electricity trading in competitive markets, formerly adequate transmission capacity is stretched to the limit, and sometimes, beyond (Lerner, 2003). As high profile blackouts related to transmission congestion in the U.S. and Europe in 2003 indicated, the putative benefits of competition may not outweigh the loss of reliability and added coordination costs required in a competitive system (Loehr, 1998; Mountford and Austria, 1999; Casazza and Loehr, 2000; Lerner, 2003). Also under-appreciated is that the pursuit of competition has a high-opportunity cost, as promising regulatory-based approaches, such as integrated resource planning (IRP) and performance based regulation (PBR), are often shelved in the transition to competition.

Economists tend to see difficulties such as market power, congestion and long-term investment as problems that can be solved through appropriate market design (Hunt, 2002; Stoft, 2002). Often lost in the effort to develop sophisticated market design solutions, however, is the much more fundamental requirement for the political capacity to defy powerful interests that wish to shape institutions and rules to their advantage. A wide range of seemingly technical questions are charged with the prospect of profit- or loss-making, and hence, with scope for political chicanery. For example, before competition can take place industries must be "restructured," which involves dismantling utility monopolies into component functions and auctioning them off to competing firms. But in this process, who will bear the burden of uneconomic investments by the incumbent utility, known as "stranded costs?" How will their assets be fairly valued and divested? Perhaps most far reaching, how can the independence and effectiveness of the market referees who will make such decisions be assured? The economic theory of electricity markets has grown increasingly sophisticated, but the intricacy of proposed solutions itself highlights the question of the state's ability to implement them in real economies and real political cultures. To compare idealized competitive markets to the gritty workings and failures of regulated and state-run systems may be appealing but it can also be a dangerous illusion.

Regulation

Regulation is an essential plank of the standard model, notwithstanding the popular conflation of reform with "deregulation." What regulation means in practice depends on the type of reform and the role of the regulator. In the neo-liberal standard model of a fully competitive system, prices and investment decisions are determined by the market, and the function of regulators is to act as "hands-off" market referees. In the current environment that tends toward privatized utilities in uncompetitive markets, a regulatory tariff-setting and planning regime with strong enforcement capabilities, similar to the traditional U.S. system, is more often the goal. Effective regulation is indispensable if electricity reform is not to be a license for predatory practices by private firms. But establishing successful regulatory regimes poses major challenges for countries in which independent regulation is an institutional novelty. For most developing countries prior to electricity reform, regulatory functions were integrated into the same state utilities and ministries responsible for electricity production, not independent watchdog organizations.

In the U.S., regulation has been referred to as the "halfway house" of American political economy, meaning that the regulatory regime plays a fundamental role in the balancing of public and private interests (Reagan, 1987: 9). In this view, regulation is not merely an instrumental approach to economic efficiency, but an explicitly political process that allocates resources according to social values in the negotiation of conflicting interests. At the same time, this process is (in theory) conducted in a rule-governed manner that is accountable to the public but insulated from undue influence by interested parties, public or private. Not surprisingly, despite the seemingly technocratic nature of regulatory decision-making, regulatory processes are very much shaped by national histories.

American regulation, which is a global point of reference, is an historical product of American institutions and political traditions. Its legal foundations can be traced to English jurisprudence.[5] Its political rationale rests on the philosophies of federalism and separation of powers of the American Founders (Wilson, 1980: viii). And it owes its specific institutional forms to a century of democratic debate and struggle at the state and federal level, driven initially by public backlash against the monopolistic practices of railroads in the Gilded Age (Rudolph and Ridley, 1986; Hirsh, 1999; Palast, Oppenheim and MacGregor, 2003). Other countries face the challenge of building regulatory systems on a very different base of institutions and traditions.

Regulation is not an easy task in any political context. American regulator Alfred Kahn once joked that "those whom the gods would destroy, they first make regulators."[6] In electricity, regulators must strike a delicate balance between the financial viability of suppliers, prices to consumers, and a host of public policy concerns such as access, cross-subsidies, and pollution. Historically, success in this task has depended on three institutional attributes strongly shaped by political context: independence, accountability, and competence. These are challenging attributes to institutionalize, and arguably more so in developing countries.

Regulatory independence is challenged on one hand by private industry interests with money and skill and, on the other, by governments wary of permitting independent bodies to make decisions in a vital and politically sensitive sector. The challenges of ensuring independent funding for regulators, and of finding independent staff in a context where regulators formerly worked in ministries or private utilities and still have colleagues there, are also not trivial. Accountability is confounded by overlapping and possibly contradictory obligations to elected leaders, private utilities, and the public. In particular, accountability to the public can be a difficult-to-enforce abstraction. Yet, as Palast et al. (2003) argue, accountability to the public, enabled by transparent and democratic processes, is the main guarantor of efficient regulation and deterrent of corruption. Finally, regulators must be sufficiently competent to manage the complicated technical and institutional problems of electricity regulation (Kahn, 1991). Competence demands a clear mandate and jurisdiction, financial and technical resources, enforcement powers, and skilled personnel. Whether cash-strapped governments will commit the necessary resources to build competent regulatory organizations is an open question.

The three elements of the standard prescription—privatization, competition, and regulation—are far from universally accepted, empirically tested, technical solutions to power sector problems in every country. This is not to say that these prescriptions are always wrong or never appropriate, but they do require far greater discussion and location in national context than the current cookie-cutter approach to electricity reform allows for. Indeed, taken together, the elements of the standard prescription are theoretically debatable, empirically murky, and imply complex transformations of economies, societies and polities. Most problematically, they rest on a very limited view of electricity's role in society and politics, and thus fail to anticipate the full impact of reform efforts, let alone signal a trajectory toward social transformation. To do so requires a broader perspective.

Electricity Reform as a Social Project

The significance of electricity for industrial society is beyond dispute. Electricity is a precondition for industrial development and even for agricultural production. Lifestyles everywhere have increasingly come to depend on adequate and reliable electricity, a dependence exacerbated by the spread of information technology as the underpinning of organizational systems. In developing countries, the arrival of electricity provides the conditions for a release from drudgery and the potential for enhanced access to health facilities and education.

Too often, however, the centrality of electricity to modern society is misused to limit critical debate on the political economy of electricity. To ensure that the lights come on when we flick a switch, we are often told it is unproductive, impolite, and even unpatriotic to question how many thousands are to be displaced in order to build a dam, what is to be done with nuclear waste, or who will benefit and who will lose out with a particular tariff structure. In contrast to this uncritical approach, understanding electricity as a social project requires an examination of how electricity is embedded into social, political and environmental contexts, and its impacts in these domains. In this section, we examine electricity reform through this wider lens.

To think of electricity as a social project means to acknowledge electricity's transformative potential and to recognize a substantial measure of intentionality in how it is directed. How societies define the role of electricity within a broader social vision, how they organize and manage the industry, and how they evaluate the trade-offs between different production and consumption choices in service of a social vision, are all proper subjects of deliberation. However, a robust and democratic decision-making process is a precondition for such debate. Governance of electricity is, therefore, the starting point of our exploration. In the discussion below, we argue that electricity reform narrows the exercise of collective public choice, by transforming the role of members of the public from citizen to consumer.

This narrowing excludes consideration of important social objectives that deserve to be central to decision-making around electricity, particularly equity and the environment. There is a near total absence in the reform literature on the equity implications of the standard model. Yet, economic efficiency, the core objective of the standard model, often pulls in a quite different direction from equity. An explicit discussion of the trade-offs between the two is essential for a more complete and honest policy dialogue on electricity. Environmental implications too, are remarkably absent from the standard model, despite the enormous environmental footprint of the electricity sector. Any vision of a sustainable future can hardly afford to ignore the environmental consequences of electricity systems.

Finally, electricity is not only important for national politics but is increasingly a factor on the global political stage. Electricity has implications for international cooperation and conflict through the upstream linkages of fuel supplies and, at the downstream end, through environmental impacts and growing international electricity trade. Yet, viewed through a financial and technical lens, the geopolitics of electricity reform are nearly invisible.

The sections that follow elaborate these four themes that are central to electricity as a social project.

Governance: The Scope for Democratic Control by the Public

By changing ownership from public to private, shifting scales of operation, introducing new actors, and changing the relationship between users and providers, electricity reform will certainly lead to new forms of governance, whether by design or by default. What is the nature of these governance forms and what scope remains for democratic control by the public? To what extent is the vision of decentralized service delivery likely, and to what extent does it support democratization of electricity? How does governance of electricity at national and sub-national levels interface with emergent regimes of global governance? And with what effect?

Before exploring these questions, it is worth delving a little deeper into the ubiquitous, but vaguely defined term, "governance." A scan of the voluminous literature suggests that contemporary discussions of "governance" usually stress decision-making processes; that is, the literature addresses *how* decisions are made, but with attention to a broader set of actors than just government.[7] The perception that communities, NGOs and the private sector are important and legitimate actors in decision-making is now embedded in the notion of governance.[8] As a corollary, the ability to participate in the process of governing need not rest only in formal authority, but can also derive from norms, institutionalized rules, and understandings between networks of actors. This broader notion of governance promises more robust decision mechanisms, a broader base of information, and multiple and complementary mechanisms of accountability.

Does electricity reform support and embrace this broader construction of governance? At first glance it would seem so. In the world of vertically-integrated public power, the state provided electricity as part of a social compact with the public. While this compact provided a strong basis for accountability, its instrument—the vote—is a particularly blunt one; electricity is not the only service the state provides, and voting patterns are blurred by many issues other than electricity. The reform prescription of privatization, unbundling (as a prelude to competition) and regulation, promises a greater diversity of actors in the sector and more direct vehicles for accountability, particularly for the consumer. Based on these arguments, electricity reform is often promoted as a governance-enhancing effort.

However, this argument rests on a particularly narrow and apolitical view of governance that stresses consumer protection over citizen intervention. It also is not supported by the actual practices of electricity reform in many countries, which have neither stressed better governance in their design, nor practiced it in implementation. These points are argued more completely below.

By shifting responsibility for service provision away from a vast and seemingly opaque state to differentiated corporate entities, electricity reform seemingly gives the end-user greater scope for holding service providers accountable. But at the same time, it changes the nature of the relationship between service provider and user. While electricity provision is an unambiguously political issue under public ownership, it is precisely this political nature that is blurred under privatization and restructuring. As Wood (2004) perceptively notes, electricity reform transforms accountability to the public as a whole into accountability to individual customers. The result is a fractured social geography that isolates individual consumers, likely limiting the scope of their interaction to electricity providers. While isolated customers are expected only to engage private utilities through the medium of the monthly bill and the customer complaint center, a politicized public, operating to enforce a social compact, could justifiably voice views on the entire spectrum of issues surrounding electricity provision.[9]

The governance impacts of fragmenting the public into household-sized units rather than a collective actor, and restricting the range of legitimate public concerns in the operation of the power sector, are exacerbated by other reform trends. Importantly, the finance-driven logic of reform places great importance on accountability to investors, which is often linked to the development of laws and regulations to protect property rights. As a result, at the same time governments are more isolated from public concerns, they are often more closely engaged with the demands of private financial interests. Much of the discussion of reform in developing countries revolves around the failure of reforms to improve either customer service on the one hand, or investor protections on the other. Yet, even should these problems be solved eventually, the slanting of governance toward powerful private (and quite often foreign) interests, and away from the ordinary non-shareholder public, would be a highly problematic reform outcome.

Precisely these sorts of concerns have provoked citizen activism on a range of electricity-related issues, particularly during the 1990s. Perceived issues of mismanagement, corruption, and lack of responsible decision-making have repeatedly been associated with private power projects. Well-known examples include campaigns to expose the cost to the public—in terms of expensive power, unwarranted state financial burdens, and deeply flawed processes—of Enron's Dabhol power project in India and the Paiton project in Indonesia (Mehta, 1999; Seymour and Sari, 2002). Questions of full financial disclosure have often been at the root of such controversies. Private utilities, often backed by governments, declare that financial details, including the terms of power purchase agreements, must be kept confidential to protect their commercial interest. But in the absence of financial information, it is near impossible to challenge utilities' claims regarding returns and profit. These battles have been fought with private utilities and with government ministries, as well as in the court of public opinion through the media. More recently, with the establishment of regulators in several countries, this critical debate has moved to the regulatory arena (Palast et al., 2003). The record of citizen intervention under public monopoly convincingly demonstrates that accountability can and should operate through a far broader set of mechanisms than the vote alone. Whether under pre-reform public ownership and monopoly, or under a post-reform privatized sector and regulated market, governance is more about political accountability than consumer protection per se.

Not surprisingly, the transition from politicized public to de-politicized customer has not gone smoothly. Ultimately, customer concerns have a great deal to do with what happens upstream of the meter. The details of contracts for electricity generation, processes of tariff setting and subsidy provision, the efficiency and adequacy of the transmission and distribution system, and a host of related issues are salient to the customer's experience. Indeed, issues of this sort that were hotly contested under public power have not gone away, and neither has public attention. In this sense, while the actors have expanded in number, and while significant new arenas of contestation have emerged—notably regulation—governance, whether under public monopoly or private ownership and competition, requires concern with very similar issues.

That liberalization and reform processes have led to public unrest in several countries likely has much to do with the stealth and secrecy with which liberalizers have undertaken reform, especially in the developing world (Dubash, 2002). In Argentina, for example, electricity reform was managed by a coterie of technocrats, without public discussion or scope for input (Bouille, Dubrovsky and Maurer, 2002). Where reformers attempt engagement with the public, it most often consists of "education" aimed at convincing customers to accept the wisdom of higher tariffs in the short run (Wood, 2004). Electricity reform so undertaken is not open to scrutiny and challenge. Reforms are typically based on a narrow intellectual base dominated by economic and technical perspectives; other concerns may well be areas of citizen interest and action—such as environmental and social issues—but they have no space in reform formulations. In Argentina, to return to the example above, reforms resulted directly in a highly regressive tariff structure, that was reversed in the face of popular unrest. As this example suggests, electricity liberalization that is not buttressed by a democratic process may be more subject to public challenge later on.

At the same time, many reformers are likely engaged in an exercise of cynical realism, implementing reform in a stealthy manner. Democratic process would involve taking on the challenging task of explicit discussions with and concessions to organized labor in the electricity industry, often the most vocal and best-organized opponents of reform. More broadly, it would require convincing the public that they will receive the benefits of reform in the short- to medium-term, and that broader public concerns will indeed be addressed. However, especially in developing countries, governments have implemented electricity reform in the context of financial strain and crisis, often with the explicit motivation of attracting private investment (Dubash, 2002). Simultaneously keeping promises of short run returns to private capital and short-term gains to the public is an insurmountable challenge in the absence of substantial public coffers with which to pay for both. More often than not, the public is asked to pay up front in the form of higher tariffs for unspecified future benefits of reform. For this reason, democratic process and scrutiny offers a real challenge to the reform agenda, at least in the developing world.[10]

At minimum, a democratically constituted type of electricity reform would force an explicit discussion of the distribution of costs and benefits of liberalization, and the timeframes associated with each. Central to such a discussion are procedural rights, (or lack thereof), that enable engagement in electricity governance.[11] Drawing from Principle 10 of the Rio Declaration, these rights are succinctly summarized as pertaining to access to information, participation in decision-making, and accountability for enforcement.[12] Acceptance of these rights would provide the basis for governance through a more effective public voice, allowing public advocates to focus on developing the capacity to engage in debate, rather than fighting to win the right to even participate in debate. Significantly, the importance of procedural rights cuts across both the traditional and post-reform versions of organizing the electricity sector.

Procedural rights are, however, the route to a vastly more complex system of governance, the challenges of which should not be underestimated.[13] Rights to information and participation can lead to an avalanche of information and opportunities, well beyond the processing capacities of civil society organizations or other representatives of the public interest. To return to a prominent theme in our discussion of regulation, the capacity of civil society groups to engage at multiple levels—legislative, regulatory and operational—is central to the governance of electricity. Even if the capacity issue is managed, there is a risk that the pendulum may swing too far away from the state. Particularly worrisome is the prospect that bureaucracies could abdicate their responsibilities in favor of what Graham (2002) calls a new "technopopulism"—citizens performing what has been the role of regulators, encouraged by an information technology, enabled trend toward disclosure.

If the coincidence of electricity reform and democratization for the sector as a whole seems overstated, the prospects appear somewhat more promising *if* one believes that sector reform will promote decentralized electricity provision. The vision of local communities sustainably and equitably running small scale generating technologies—either independently or connected to the grid—could seem to promise a better governed sector driven by local needs and controlled by local processes.

However, the sustainable energy agenda has by no means won broad global approval among self-described progressives. Green energy advocates, particularly in the U.S., argue with some justification that their vision also supports democratic values by reversing a century long trend toward greater centralization in control over energy (Rudolph et al., 1986; Berman and O'Connor, 1997; Hirsh, 1999). Dismantling utilities and forcing them to face competition, in this view, is profoundly empowering and democratizing. By contrast, civil society organizations in developing countries are deeply skeptical about unbundling and privatization of public utilities that they fear will remove electricity from public control and place it in the hands of powerful corporations who are beyond the scope of weak and nascent regulatory bodies to control.[14] In this view, decentralization could result in energy anarchy rather than energy democracy.

Moreover, unbundling and privatization associated with electricity reform are certainly consistent with concentrated ownership and control over electricity, raising the likelihood of anti-competitive outcomes. Indeed, the number of corporations worldwide that have the financial reach and technical expertise to take on and manage generation and distribution businesses in various parts of the world are rather few. Drawing again from India, liberalization has attracted two dominant domestic corporate houses that are likely to carve up and share most of India's electricity sector in the coming years (*Business Today*, 2004). The global water sector presents an extreme picture of just how concentrated the market for public service delivery can be; two French firms currently control 70 percent of the global private water market, affecting 215 million consumers (Hall, 2002).

Electricity reform holds the possibility for centralization through another avenue—globalizing the scale of control over electricity. Specifically, electricity reform, particularly the privatization of public utilities, potentially subjects electricity provision to globally negotiated disciplines on investment. Under these disciplines, states are prohibited from discriminating between foreign and domestic investment or setting performance benchmarks inconsistent with investment disciplines. Forms of domestic regulation may be restricted to those that are "least trade distorting," considerably constraining the domestic governance (Cho and Dubash, 2003). For example, current efforts by Denmark and the U.S. state of Arizona to promote a home-grown renewable energy industry might be inconsistent with a global investment framework. So might efforts to create rural cooperatives that favor community investment, such as that which led to the successful rural electrification drive in the United States.

As this brief review suggests, the links between institutional changes in the electricity sector and likely governance arrangements are considerably muddled. Platitudes that automatically link electricity reform with democratization have a certain rhetorical appeal but are weakly grounded in both theory and practice. Instead, the lasting governance legacy of electricity reform may well be an underlying shift from political citizen to apolitical consumer, restricting the scope for democratic intervention on critical environmental and social concerns.

Equity in Electricity Reform: Affordability, Access, Labor

The language of efficiency drives the practice and discourse of electricity sector reform worldwide. Advocates argue that by increasing efficiency and reducing costs reform will expand the total size of the pie, allowing for all to gain. While this may be true in some situations, in many cases there are real losers from electricity reforms, losers who are by no means compensated by winners. Indeed, reformers are often motivated by a perception that the legacy of electricity as a public service has burdened the sector with a social conscience it is not equipped to bear; reform is an opportunity to shed this burden. And while it is true that many past problematic policies have been justified in the name of equity, the reformers' doctrinaire application of neo-classic economic principles, to the exclusion of any mechanism of explicit social choice, seems an over-reaction. In this section, we suggest that the efficiency goals of electricity reform are in frequent and structural tension with the goal of building equitable societies.

The antagonism between equity and efficiency in electricity reform is perhaps most startlingly brought to light by the issue of expanding access to electricity to include the urban and rural poor. From within the reform logic, it makes perfect sense to sideline electricity access. Expanding access requires extending the grid or deploying distributed technologies to populations that are only able to consume small amounts of electricity, are politically disorganized, or are expensive to serve due to spatial dispersion. When assessed against the reform metrics of cost recovery, increased efficiency and fiscal sustainability, access, and particularly rural access, looks like a losing proposition. Consequently, the academic and policy debate around reforms is content to focus on institutional change in existing electricity systems. In many developing countries, this focus excludes a substantial proportion of the population that is unconnected to the electricity grid. In several African countries, such as Ethiopia, Uganda, Tanzania and Kenya, electrification levels are below 10 percent.[15] Even at the high end of this range, a decision to focus on electricity reform without a parallel focus on increasing access is startling and ethically problematic.

The evidence from reforming countries reinforces the perception that electricity access is not part of the agenda. As a study of Bolivia's reform experience concluded, "it seems evident that the necessary expansion of the grid to connect the poor will not take place as a result of privatization and restructuring" (ESMAP, 2000). An official review of the first state to undertake restructuring in India (Orissa) damningly stated that "rural electrification seems to have been the worst casualty of the reforms process" (Kanungo Committee, 2001).

In the few cases where electricity access has been added on to reform programs, it has required a departure from the reform logic, and critically, a political acceptance that expansion of access is a public responsibility. Specifically, governments have had to step in and play a steering role, by earmarking and allocating subsidies, and by purposefully providing incentives to private actors to undertake expansion of electricity access or by stimulating new institutions to take up the challenge. In Chile, Guatemala, and Nicaragua, for example, dedicated funds are intended to entice private players to enter rural electricity markets (Jadresic, 2000; Wamukonya, 2003b). Historical experience from the industrialized world bears out the need for dedicated focus backed by political attention and public funding. In the U.S., rural electrification took off only after a decade-long political struggle over the appropriate role for the state in rural electrification. Once a public role was accepted and defined, the U.S. Rural Electrification Administration managed to stimulate rapid electrification across the U.S. using a model of rural cooperatives, backed by financial and technical assistance (Brown, 1980).

Presently, the struggle to attract investment capital and to improve profitability dominates electricity politics in most developing countries, paving the way for an exclusionary and narrow reform approach. Even in countries such as South Africa, where equity and black empowerment drive the post-apartheid political agenda, early drafts of an electricity distribution reform design (produced by a consultant) provided no explicit proposals for rural access and black empowerment. Only after active intervention at the cabinet level was the plan reworked to place a priority on electricity access (Philpott and Clark, 2002). In countries where the political context is less overtly and forcefully solicitous of the poor and the marginal, the challenge of reshaping the homogenous and hegemonic discourse of electricity reform must surely be considerably harder.

By contrast to access, issues of affordability do occasionally force their way into restructuring debates, driven by political organizing and unrest in urban areas. The immediate context for agitation is often the fraught issue of electricity subsidies. In developing countries or economies in transition, electricity prices are likely to go up as a result of reforms aimed at achieving economic sustainability, and the burden on low-income and vulnerable groups can be considerable. In Bulgaria, for instance, old-age pensioners pay 14 percent of their household budget—the second highest share of expenditure—for electricity, and increases in electricity prices hit them particularly hard (Doukov, Dubash, and Petkova, 2002). In other cases, low-income groups have been implicitly subsidized through permitted non-payment of bills, a practice inevitably and abruptly halted by the introduction of commercial business practice. These transition costs can be extremely burdensome. For example, in South Africa, 2 million people have been evicted for non-payment of utility bills, leading to a massive resistance movement (McDonald and Pape, 2002: 162).

The observation that subsidies—explicit or implicit—have been poorly targeted and wastefully disbursed in many cases, while substantially correct, has led to a broad dismissal of any and all role for subsidized electricity. The reform prescription typically calls for removal of subsidies in the short run, promising only improved service quality in the long run. Faced with a history of unresponsive electricity providers, this bargain has not been credible or politically palatable in many countries. Efforts at subsidy removal tied to reform have led to unrest in a broad range of countries from India to Ghana to Poland,[16] where reforms led to tariff increases by a factor of 35. [17]

Beyond subsidies, the reform approach promises to turn the link between social benefits and electricity prices on its head. Instead of starting from the premise that electricity is a basic service that needs to be subsidized, the reform approach suggests that electricity is a commodity that should be priced to maximize efficient use. The latter application of economic principles to electricity would result in a tariff structure that charges the highest prices to the consumers with the most inelastic demand; a practice with the potential to hit the poor hardest. In Thailand, for example, proposals to this effect were a central part of consultants' prescriptions, which quickly foundered on the rocks of political reality (Greacen et al., 2004). In brief, the reform prescription of economic orthodoxy has frequently run aground on the political issues of distribution and equity.

Even in cases where electricity reform does appear to have resulted in cost savings, and therefore, potential benefits for consumers, these gains are seldom without costs, which are often unaccounted for. In California, deregulation was driven by industry desire to avoid paying for high cost generation capacity, particularly nuclear plants and by electricity suppliers and traders who sought opportunities for greater profit. Ultimately, the "stranded costs" of expensive power were placed on consumers, who also bore the risk of market manipulation and regulatory failure—a risk that ultimately placed huge burdens on the state exchequer and contributed to political instability (Duane, 2002; Gamson, 2002). In the U.K., efficiency gains were achieved, in part, on the backs of coal miners who lost their jobs as part of the "dash to gas." However, neither coal miners nor the general public received the benefit of efficiency gains. Instead, shareholders of private utilities have reaped the bulk of the gains and power purchasers are paying more than they likely would have paid under public ownership and vertical integration (Newbery and Pollitt, 1997). In Argentina, tariff reforms in keeping with economic orthodoxy led to low-income families paying 40 percent more than high-income families in absolute terms, reversing the pre-reform pattern of cheaper electricity for poorer households (Bouille et al., 2002). In all of these cases, distributional issues were entirely ignored in the design of reforms.

Perhaps most discussed, but arguably most intractable, among social issues arising from reforms are the concerns of labor, for efficiency in reforming electricity systems is often won at the cost of jobs. In Western Europe, for example, 212,000 jobs were reported lost in the electricity sector from 1990 to 1995, a 17 percent loss. Of this the U.K. accounted for almost half—a loss of 42 percent for the sector in that country (Hall, 1999). While it is hard to deny that public utilities in many countries have become over-staffed, particularly in the developing world, it is also true that the social dislocation and instability associated with large-scale lay-offs are considerable. At minimum, there is a case for internalizing these costs through mitigation programs such as retraining and voluntary retirement schemes, which should figure prominently in reform debates.

While affordability, access and labor concerns are often muted at best in electricity reform debates, reform advocates do marshal one powerful equity-based argument for reforms—electricity reform will lead to a healthier fiscal situation and release money in the state budget for social expenditures such as health care, and education. In parts of South Asia, Central Asia, Africa, and Eastern Europe, the argument indeed has some merit, for subsidies to the electricity sector account for a substantial component of fiscal stress. In India, for example, subsidies to the State Electricity Boards accounted for an average of 23 percent of the states' fiscal deficit in 2001-2002.[18] If reform led to a decrease in these subsidies, and if the savings were allocated to social expenditures, this would be a powerful pro-equity, pro-reform argument.

However, to presume that money saved from the electricity sector, if any, will necessarily go to socially important expenditures ignores the complex political economy of national budget processes. A study of post-reform states in Central Asia and Eastern Europe shows that although sector deficits fell as public companies were taken off the books through privatization, the impact on the overall deficit is ambiguous and hard to measure (World Bank, 2004). Moreover, the savings from lower electricity sector deficits did not translate to higher social spending, perhaps because it was used toward prior obligations or to buffer the impact of higher tariffs. The complex link between electricity and a country's fiscal situation punctuates the broader argument being made here: whether through price, access, labor, or fiscal expenditures, electricity reform has broader political ramifications that will define winners and losers. These discussions should be explicit, rather than buried under a façade of techno-economic objectivity.

Environmental Factors: Marginal to Globalized Energy

If it is often the case that politically potent social concerns are marginal in electricity reform processes, seemingly abstract environmental concerns are even more distant. In a decade and more of electricity reform, there is little evidence that a vision of transformation to an environmentally and socially sustainable electricity future has been reflected in electricity reform templates, nor that reform designers are even peripherally aware of such ambitions. If electricity futures can be characterized by a bipolar distinction between globalized energy that is intertwined with financial globalization, and sustainable energy that celebrates the local and environmentally clean, then electricity reform is clearly bound up with the politics of globalized energy.

This observation is powerfully illustrated by studies of the decision-making process that underlies electricity reform and of their impacts (Dubash, 2002; Wamukonya, 2003a; World Bank, 2003). For example, there are few reports of environmental advocates, scholars, or even environment ministries playing any substantive role in electricity reform dialogues. Instead, electricity futures have been debated in entirely different arenas—ministries of power and finance. The exclusion of environmental concerns belies the reality of the electricity sector's considerable environmental footprint (Holdren and Smith, 2000). Local, regional, and global air pollution from fossil fuel burning, submergence of lands behind dams and nuclear fuel disposal, to name but a few issues, are globally manifest concerns that together compose an environmental headache arguably unrivalled by any other sector.

The exclusion of environmental concerns from electricity reform is a function of both local and global politics. Whether driven by debt, as in much of Latin America, or by short-term fiscal crises, as in South Asia, or by larger macroeconomic financial crisis as in South-East Asia, reforms of electricity are overwhelmingly dictated by financial considerations (Dubash, 2002). Often, electricity sector reform falls under the broader umbrella of economic "adjustment" and international donor agencies play a correspondingly prominent role. Financial concerns thus are necessarily vaulted to the top of governmental priorities—either because of creditor pressures for repayment or donor agency conditionalities. Faced with citizen unrest over rising tariffs or uncertain service, management of the social pain that often accompanies economic adjustment is the second priority of governments, often as a matter of political survival. Thus politically squeezed, environmental concerns are crowded out of electricity reform debates.

For electricity reform insiders, this lack of attention to environmental issues is not a problem. They argue that environmental benefits will be a fortunate byproduct of economic gains: competition will generate pressures for efficiency gains up the electricity chain from distribution to generation; privatization will give birth to companies best able to act on those pressures; and these more technically efficient systems will waste less electricity and use less fuel, resulting in environmental gains (Joskow, 1998). This argument has some merit, particularly in countries where electricity systems are wasteful, and where a lack of either effective regulatory oversight or commercial pressure has led to a pattern of inefficiency. However, the conclusion that often follows, that there is no need for additional intentional focus on environmental issues, is misguided. The competition pressure linkage is but one pathway that links electricity and environmental outcomes, and there are several others that may lead to different and contradictory outcomes, particularly over a longer time scale.[19]

First, there is a simple price effect. If electricity prices increase as a result of reform, as is likely in developing countries, electricity consumption will decrease with attendant environmental gains (even if social losses). In industrialized countries, the converse is likely to occur.

Second, the price effect may be reduced or reversed by a substitution effect. If the price of electricity increases, consumers may substitute toward relatively dirty fuels such as kerosene for lighting and cooking, and coal for heating.

Third, reform could result in shifts in generation technology choices, with ambiguous environmental outcomes. For example, market arrangements organized around price bids for power supply may favor old coal generation plants, whose costs have been amortized. The choice of fuels may also be affected in unpredictable ways. For example, Australia moved to cheaper, lower quality coal following liberalization, resulting in increased CO_2 emissions from the power sector (Sharma, 2003). On the other hand, there has been a documented "dash to gas," a relatively clean fuel, after the introduction of competitive markets in the U.K., in part due to the low construction costs and short lead times of small gas-fired plants (Parker, 1996). If gas supplies fail to keep pace with demand and result in a price spike, the environmental gains of more gas-based generation could rapidly be reversed.

Fourth, on the demand side, there are both theoretical reasons to expect electricity reform prescriptions will erect barriers to end-use energy efficiency, and empirical evidence to suggest this outcome has already occurred. Theoretically, unbundling electricity into constituent parts increases transactions costs in realizing end-use efficiency programs, and creates scope for free riders. Empirically, in the post-reform period, utilities in many industrialized countries have shown little interest in delivering energy efficiency services.[20] Where investments in energy efficiency have continued, it is because of specific government interventions.

Finally, environmental choices are often implicitly embedded in economic regulatory decisions. For example, regulator decisions that link profits to electricity sold act as a brake on energy efficiency, while profits linked to revenues do not have this effect. Significantly, environmental choices can also be explicitly embedded in regulation or promoted through stand-alone policies, and the choice to do so is a political one. For example, the U.K. has had a tax on fossil fuel generation for the purpose of supporting non-fossil fuel energy sources. Regulatory measures such as a "renewable portfolio standard," which requires electricity providers to purchase a proportion of their electricity from renewable sources, have been adopted in several European countries and American states. Integrated resource planning (IRP), a tool originally developed under the vertically integrated regulated approach to electricity, could also be fruitfully used in a competitive framework (Regulatory Assistance Project, 1994; D'Sa, 2005) Notably, the limited proactive

measures taken so far have been restricted almost entirely to the industrialized world, or to a few middle-income countries such as Brazil, which has a
requirement that a proportion of revenues be spent on energy conservation.

Given the current politics of reform, which favors short-term financial
considerations first, and social obligations second, environmental considerations will continue to be an afterthought at best. This is particularly true of
the developing world. In some industrialized countries, particularly those of
Northern Europe, proactive measures such as renewable portfolio standards
or dedicated charges, do play some mitigative role. In the short- and medium-
term, therefore, it seems near inevitable the environmental impact of electricity reform will be determined by the additive impact of the various pathways
elucidated above, the direction of which will be highly context-dependent,
modified slightly by marginal proactive measures in some countries.

What would it take to transform the politics of electricity reform so as to
place environmental issues near the center of reform design? There are currently two realms of political action related, but by no means coincident, that
have the potential to drag the electricity debate in a different direction. The
first is the looming issue of global climate change. The second is a burgeoning movement of activists and technologists, recently joined by selective
businesses, to advocate for a decentralized and renewable energy future.

Despite the fact that the electricity sector, (including heat production),
accounts for some 38 percent of global carbon emissions (Dubash, 2002),
climate change receives scarcely a mention in most reform designs.[21] Conversely, it is only in recent years electricity reform has figured as an important
arena worthy of urgent intervention in global climate change negotiations. In
part, this divorce may be due to the unfortunate deadlock at global climate
negotiations over political commitments to greenhouse gas commitments,
even while national decisions about policies that affect those commitments
move ahead.

While in Europe climate policy does factor in electricity policy, in the
United States, the national political refusal to accept global restrictions on
emissions translates into a refusal to even consider climate impacts in national decisions of global environmental significance. In the developing
world, internalization of climate concerns in national policy is restricted by
fears of opening the door to green conditionality. In addition, developing
countries worry about eroding the agreement enshrined in the 1992 Framework Convention on Climate Change that responsibility is "common but
differentiated" among industrialized and developing countries, with the former
taking the lead. In brief, the South has been understandably unwilling to
sacrifice equity and sovereignty at the altar of international environmental
cooperation (Agarwal, Narain and Sharma, 2002). One proposed southern
alternative, to allocate equal per capita entitlements to the biosphere's ab-
sorptive capacity—a "global commons"—has been rejected by industrial-

ized countries. Given this deadlock, the climate issue has, so far, failed to spur to reconsideration of electricity reform, with the possible exception of the European Union.[22]

The sustainable energy movement, for lack of a better term, is intrinsically closer to electricity reform debates. Advocates of green energy are eloquent and passionate in its pursuit, and view the transition to a decentralized and renewable energy future as only a matter of time.[23] This agenda has recently gained considerable political momentum. At the World Summit on Sustainable Development at Johannesburg in 2003, a call for global agreement on renewable energy targets was narrowly defeated, echoing the divisions in the climate debate. Undeterred, governmental and non-governmental advocates of renewable energy technologies have sponsored high profile global events at which to pursue their agenda. For example, the International Conference for Renewable Energies, held in Bonn, June 2004, resulted in a political declaration of support for renewable energy and an action program comprising voluntary commitments.[24] These international efforts, however, risk running against the rock of domestic politics. If environmental issues get little traction in domestic electricity debates, there is little reason to expect that a global writ will displace these politics. To do so will likely take either coercion or money; both are unlikely. Coercion would arouse a politically unsustainable backlash, and the recent history of global environmental politics suggests a sufficient infusion of money is highly unlikely. More generally, the climate issue points to a much broader set of geopolitical concerns around electricity.

Electricity Reform and International Politics

Oil supplies are widely known to be a focus of geopolitical competition and conflict, but it is less known that electricity has the potential to follow suit (Yergin, 1991; Klare, 2001). Internationalization of electricity—the transfer across national borders of electric power and the fuel required to generate it and in some cases of capital and ownership—makes electricity vulnerable to many of the same kinds of strategic concerns already seen with oil: disruption of supply, volatile prices, and struggle over control of resources and infrastructures. While the internationalization of electricity is much less extensive than the oil trade, there have been several recent cases that demonstrate the potential for electricity to appear as either a weapon or a casualty of conflict. In 2001, for example, Russia cut off electricity supplies to both Georgia and Ukraine in a conflict over debt (Wendlandt, 2001). In the same year, separatist violence in the Indonesian province of Aceh halted the delivery of liquefied natural gas to Tokyo Electric Company for six months, forcing it to scramble for gas to run its generating plants and creating a national scare in Japan (Harrison, 2003).

Given that electricity is being internationalized and thus increasingly exposes countries to regional and global competition, does electricity liberalization, per se, have any geopolitical implications? The California electricity crisis of 2000-2001, while not itself international, provides a provocative perspective on this question. Powerful Texas companies closely allied politically with the Republican Party and the Bush Administration played a central role in the crisis. The El Paso Corporation manipulated natural gas supplies to send the price of California's main power generation fuel soaring, while Enron (along with other Texas companies, such as Reliant and Dynegy) manipulated wholesale electricity prices. The result cost California tens of billions of dollars, bankrupted the largest state utility, destroyed the state's credit rating, and led ultimately to the recall of a Democratic governor and his replacement with a Republican (Duane, 2002). None of this would have been possible under the former regulated power system. Academics may bristle at using California to suggest that a sovereign government might be destabilized through a liberalized electricity sector, but it seems unlikely that any national leader contemplating electricity reform in his or her own country would have failed to consider this instructive possibility.

The geopolitical implications of electricity reform clearly depend on the circumstances and the kind of reform involved, such as whether it is limited reform or the full standard model. Equally clearly, changing the public-private balance in the control of electricity has the potential to be expressed in geo-politically significant ways. For example, there is a strong movement throughout Asia toward natural gas as a preferred fuel for generating electricity, for reasons of economy and environment. Yet natural gas is closely linked to oil and fraught with many of the same concerns. Governments, in the interest of energy security, may, therefore, make different decisions regarding natural gas than a fully privatized sector, for instance, by subsidizing domestic production or paying more to diversify fuel supplies than would profit-maximizing private companies. China has already shown itself willing to pay a premium to bring gas pipelines from Russia, Central Asia, and Xinjiang as insurance against volatile Middle East and Persian Gulf supplies (Harrison, 2003). The geopolitical linkage to electricity also works in the opposite direction: electricity liberalization is an avenue that can bring regional and global actors into domestic politics. For example, electricity liberalization provided an avenue for the IMF and World Bank to dictate national policy in Thailand and South Korea in the aftermath of the Asian crisis, demanding the privatization of state electricity assets (Byrne et al. 2004; Greacen et al., 2004). At least in Thailand, this has produced a neo-nationalist backlash, itself a geopolitical issue.

Several important proposals for electricity cooperation at the Asian sub-regional level have emerged in the last few years, for which electricity liberalization has significant implications. In Northeast Asia, countries are investigating interconnecting their power grids to share electricity, and constructing pipelines to bring Russian natural gas to China, Japan, and South Korea. The most controversial of the proposed projects involves a pipeline and high-voltage transmission route from Russia down the Korean peninsula. Beyond any potential economic benefit, this project represents a cooperative regional approach to solving the North Korean nuclear threat. In return for letting the lines pass through its territory, North Korea would gain access to energy supplies and infrastructure improvements that are the key to its economic recovery, and, hopefully, to its peaceful integration in the region. The U.S., however, has forbidden the involvement of American companies or multilateral lenders in these projects. Under these conditions, and with a legacy of hostility and mistrust among the countries involved, Northeast Asian electrical unification is unlikely to happen without strong government leadership among all parties and the collective development of a regional governance regime. As a key Chinese energy official observed, "[a] comprehensive regional approach accepted by all of us would be much better than letting the vagaries of the marketplace decide what happens...It would be much better if we adopt a regional approach" (Harrison, 2003: 36; Von Hippel and Williams, 2003).

Electric grid integration is also being discussed in Southeast Asia, under the auspices of the Asian Development Bank's Greater Mekong Subregion (GMS) project. The GMS project is seeking to create a liberalized regional electricity market, centered on a regional grid that would have as its backbone a series of new hydroelectric dams along the Mekong and its tributaries. Most of the electricity would likely go to Bangkok and large cities in eastern China, while the dams would be constructed in rural Vietnam, Laos, Cambodia, Burma, and southwestern China. The GMS project is being vigorously opposed by NGOs throughout the region, who believe it will do enormous ecological and cultural damage in poor hinterlands while benefiting financiers and industrial consumers in wealthy cities (Hirsch, 1996; Hirsch, 1999; ADB, 2002; Yu, 2002; ADB, 2003; IRN, 2003; Yu, 2003; England, 2004). Geo-politically, the GMS project raises the prospect of privatized power sectors in dominant regional states—in this case, China and Thailand—externalizing the environmental and social consequences of electricity production onto weaker, poorer countries.

A similar "electricity resource colony" relationship has been suggested regarding hydroelectric and natural gas production in South Asia's poorest countries—Nepal, Bhutan, and Bangladesh—for delivery to urban consumers in wealthier countries, especially India (Gunasekera and Najam, 2003). In both Southeast and South Asia, electricity liberalization could thus become an avenue for inequitable relationships among countries, as well as within them. Objections over transboundary social justice have joined with concerns over prices in unregulated spot markets to slow the planned Central

American Electrical Interconnection (SIEPAC) (McIlhenny, 2004). Concerns a few foreign-owned firms may come to dominate regional interconnections have already been validated in South America's Southern Cone, where the Chilean firm Enresis controls not only more than half the Chilean supply but also the supplies to substantial fractions of Colombia, Argentina, Peru, and Brazil (Bouille and Wamukonya, 2003).

It has long been argued that commerce is the main alternative to war. Oil expert Daniel Yergin and others have urgently reprised this argument regarding rising Asian oil demand and Middle East oil. Conflict over oil, they say, will only be avoided by liberalizing markets and thinking in geoeconomic rather than geostrategic terms (Yergin, Eklof and Edwards, 1998; Salameh, 2003; Yergin and Stoppard, 2003). Yet for electricity, in the examples given above, this would not seem to be the case. In Northeast Asia, it is precisely geo-strategic thinking that will lead nations to build a cooperative regional electricity system, if it is to be built; in South and Southeast Asia, market-led integration of power systems may lead to inequitable and ultimately conflict-ridden relations among nations. In the case of privatizing nuclear electricity, it would be absurd to consider it primarily in economic terms; in the age of proliferation and terrorism, strategic considerations are paramount. There is, of course, an alternative to the organization of international relations along either military-strategic lines or market-dominant lines, that the war versus commerce narrative fails to mention, and that is cooperative international governance. Indeed, for many aspects of global dilemma that bear strongly on electricity, such as climate protection and avoiding nuclear proliferation, this seems the only viable option, present U.S. policy notwithstanding. Liberalized electricity may play a role in avoiding conflict, but in many cases will do so only when it is explicitly shaped to serve such ends. Geopolitics is a topic that should be centrally included in the public debate over electricity reform in the many places where the linkages are real and the stakes are high.

Conclusion

Electricity liberalization aims at delivering electricity from the realm of social and political negotiation to the realm of market transactions. Historically, social negotiation over electricity has resulted in a stable social compact, which took different institutional forms in different political contexts. In the U.S., for example, it took the form of a regulatory bargain, whereby private utilities were allowed a stable profit in return for guaranteed social obligation. In much of the rest of the world, it took the form of state-owned and vertically integrated utilities charged with providing electricity in the public interest. Public ownership also allowed electricity to be used as an instrument of state policy, an allowance that extended to electricity as a support for industrial development, agricultural growth and rural electrification. Electricity became a potent symbol of what the state could do for the citizen, and, in return, electricity became an instrument of state legitimacy. The standard model of reform seeks to end all these long-standing relations, and replace them with a series of disconnected relations between a customer and a profit-minded provider. In short, electricity reform seeks to disembed electricity from its social and political context.

There is no doubt that the electricity sector is in crisis in many countries. The critics of state-led, vertically integrated, electricity correctly point to financially insolvent, technically inefficient, and administratively non-transparent electricity sectors in many parts of the world—particularly the developing world. This failure to deliver the service effectively has weakened the social compact at the heart of publicly provided electricity. But public power has not failed everywhere; it has failed where the broader political and social institutions in which electricity is embedded have failed. A failure of public provision of electricity is frequently a symptom of a larger failure of the state.

Ironically, liberalized electricity is no less dependent on robust public institutions than is electricity as a public charge, as the challenges of establishing competition and regulation discussed here suggest. But the standard model was not designed to address broader institutional breakdown. Instead, it emerged in industrialized countries where electricity organized around a social compact was working quite well. Electricity liberalization, then, cannot be credibly invoked as a phenomenon that responds to the weakening of state-led and socially embedded electricity.

Instead, electricity reform is better understood as response to burgeoning financial pressures—fiscal crises, debt burdens, and macroeconomic adjustment—in developing countries, and an attempt to extract marginal efficiency gains in industrialized countries. In addition, there is an irreducibly ideological driver to electricity reform—a belief that electricity is a business and bureaucrats do not belong in business. From this ideological perspective, electricity reform is also a mechanism to liberate opportunities for profit, both by the electricity industry, and by electricity consuming industry, typically large industrial companies. The electricity industry sees vast new markets opening in the emerging world, if electricity can be pried free from the state grasp. And, indeed, if the result is better quality electricity, more efficient systems, and faster rates of electrification, it may well be worth abandoning what is a crumbling social compact. However, the experience so far suggests that neither weak political and social institutions nor markets will be able to guarantee this favorable outcome. For industrial consumers, abandoning the social compact allows them to maximally leverage their position as lucrative and valuable base-load customers to win lower prices. However, as discussed here, lower cost electricity may come at the price of more unstable and lower quality electricity; the bargain may well prove to be Faustian.

As the uncertainties and potential costs of the standard model have become more apparent, many countries have witnessed problems in implementing the model and growing political resistance, leading to a decreased pace of liberalization. There is no longer a consensus acceptance of the standard prescription as the path to reform, nor a consensus vision of the ultimate destination. In Thailand, a drive to electricity markets has morphed into electricity development as an instrument of regional economic power. In India, a far-reaching Electricity Act lies dormant, as the government grapples with ways of containing the political tensions that full implementation of the Act would unleash. The World Bank has replaced its privatization imperative of the 1990s with the more ambiguous call to "public-private partnerships" in its latest infrastructure plan. In many countries the reality of 2005 is an electricity sector that is neither the old state system nor a fully liberalized, well-functioning market, but an unwieldy hybrid of the two.

This new, hybrid ground promises to be more fertile terrain for consideration of the larger social project of electricity. Commercial concerns will not go away, and, indeed, they should not. But the growing realization of the importance of regulation, the need for active oversight over competitive processes, and the reinforced public perception of electricity as something more than a commodity has signaled the resilience of the state as an important actor in electricity. Bringing the state back into electricity forces a debate on its legitimate role and its limits, a discussion which firmly re-embeds electricity in the political process.

This process of re-embedding is a potential vehicle for creating democratic space around the future of electricity. Once the economic absolutes of the standard model are left behind, there is far greater space to debate how, as societies, we wish to govern electricity and in the service of which objectives. One important, and necessary, legacy of the rise of liberalized electricity is the importance of respecting its commercial constraints, and this, too, must continue to form part of the discussion.

Although democratic space for consideration of electricity as a social project has broadened, social capacity to occupy that space remains limited. This is particularly true in the developing world, where the bulk of electricity expansion will take place in the coming decades. For electricity reform to be seized as a broader project of social change will require far greater capacity and engagement of civil society groups and consumers. The case for incorporation of a broader environmental set of objectives into electricity reform, in particular, remains very thinly made.

How hybrid institutions of electricity will evolve is an open question, subject to both global and domestic forces. In most countries, however, those institutions are being forged now, providing an opportunity to shape them around a broader vision of electricity that accounts for objectives beyond narrow economic and commercial ones.

Notes

1. Exceptions are the United States, Germany and Japan, which have traditionally had private utilities operating within the limits of a governmental regulatory regime.
2. For a typical description of the benefits of workforce reduction, see Joskow (2000: 122). For an opposing view, see Palast et al. (2003: 80-81).
3. A vast literature exists on this topic. See Hunt (2002) or Stoft (2002).
4. Office of Gas and Electricity Markets, *Introduction of the Market Abuse Condition into the Licences of Certain Generators: Second Submission to the Competition Commission*, London: OFGEM, 2000, cited in Woo et al., (2003: 1111).
5. Charles F. Phillips, *The Economics of Regulation*, Homewood, IL: Richard D. Irwin, (1969: p.54-57), cited in Hirsh (1999: p.16).
6. Cited in Hirsh (1999: 225).
7. See for example, a special issue of the *International Social Science Journal* on governance, March 1998, and Rhodes (1996).
8. Often, governance is reduced to the conditions necessary to provide a stable environment for investment and the functioning of business. Here, governance becomes centrally about the sanctity of contracts, stability of regulations and stable mechanisms of internal corporate governance. Form this perspective, governance is about accountability of governments to corporations and of corporations to their shareholders. Since it entirely excludes the broader public this is a far more narrow use of the term governance than is adopted in this paper. For efforts to draw this distinction, see Wood (2004) and Prayas (2004).
9. While it is possible that retail competition will someday allow ordinary small consumers the option to "exit" their utility and move to another provider, this has so far rarely occurred in industrialized countries, and seems unrealistic to expecet in the developing world.
10. In the industrialized world, the story may be somewhat different. State finances may be less constrained, utility financial conditions are likely to be more stable, and tariffs are generally already at cost recovery levels, reducing the need for short-term increases.
11. For a recent effort to think through procedural rights in electricity, see World Resources Institute, National Institute of Public Finance and Policy, and Prayas-Pune (2004).
12. For an effort to operationalize this approach to environmental decision-making more generally, see Petkova et al. (2002).
13. For a warning about reliance on "democracy by disclosure" see Graham (2002).
14. For an illustration of this view, see the compilation of papers edited by Prayas Energy Group, Transnational Institute and Focus on the Global South, from a workshop on Asia Power Sector Reforms, Bangkok, Thailand, 7-10 October, 2002.
15. Estimates of electrification range widely across sources, which in itself speaks to the lack of concerted attention to electricity access in Africa.
16. See examples in Dubash (2002) and Wamukonya (2003c).
17. Calculated by R. Ghanadan; sources: Krishnaswamy and Stuggins (2003) and IEA (2003).
18. Computed by authors from Government of India Planning Commission data.
19. The following discussion draws on several studies that explore the links between environmental outcomes and electricity reform: Burtraw et al. (2000), USAID (1998a; 1998b, 1998c), Dubash (2004), Martinot (2000), Kozloff (1998) and Hamrin (2002).

20. In particular, see the case studies reported in USAID (1998c).
21. The Central and Eastern European region is an exception but even in these cases the environmental agenda was driven by broader political and economic concerns. For example, the insertion of climate concerns into electricity debates in Bulgaria was stimulated by questions of accession to the European Union and related environmental requirements (Doukov, Dubash, and Petkova, 2002).
22. For a summary of recent steps in the EU linking climate and electricity, see http://www.climnet.org/EUenergy/liberalisation.html.
23. See, for example, Dunn (2000), Vaitheeswaran (2003).
24. Reports of a high level conference at Bonn in June 2004 are available at www.renewables2004.de.

References

ADB (2003). *Greater Mekong Subregion, Ninth Meeting of the Experts Group on Power Interconnection and Trade (EGP-9), Guangzhou, PRC, 18 November 2003, Summary of Proceedings*. Manila: Asian Development Bank.

———. (2002). *GMS Countries Close to Finalizing Both the Master Plan on Power Interconnection and the Agreement on Power Trade*: Asian Development Bank. Available at http://www.adb.org/GMS/GMS-SA-energy.asp#ener-5.

———. (1994). *Bank Policy Initiatives for the Energy Sector*. Manila, Philippines: Asian Development Bank.

Agarwal, A., Narain, S., and Sharma, A. (2002). The Global Commons and Environmental Justice - Climate Change. In J. Byrne, L. Glover and C. Martinez, (Eds.), *Environmental Justice: Discourses in International Political Economy*. New Brunswick, NJ: Transaction Publishers.

Bacon, R. W., and Besant-Jones, J. (2001). Global Electric Power Reform, Privatization and Liberalization of the Electric Power Industry in Developing Countries. *Annual Review of Energy and the Environment*, 26, 331-359.

Berman, D. M., and O'Connor, J. T. (1997). *Who Owns the Sun? People, Politics, and the Struggle for a Solar Economy*. White River Junction, VT: Chelsea Green.

Blauvelt, E. C. (2004). Deregulation: Magic or Mayhem? *Electricity Journal, 17*(7), 39-47.

Bouille, D., Dubrovsky, H., and Maurer, C. (2002). Argentina: Market-Driven Reform of the Electricity Sector. In Navroz K. Dubash, (Ed.), *Power Politics : Equity and Environment in Electricity Reform*. Washington, DC: World Resources Institute.

Bouille, D., and Wamukonya, N. (2003). Power Sector Reforms in Latin America: A Retrospective Agenda. In N. Wamukonya, (Ed.), *Electricity Reform: Social and Environmental Challenges*. Roskilde, Denmark: United Nations Environment Programme.

Brown, D. C. (1980). *Electricity for Rural America : The Fight for the REA*. Westport, CT: Greenwood Press.

Burtraw, D., Palmer, K., and Heintzelman. (2000). Electriciy Restructuring: Consequences and Opportunities for the Environment. Washington, DC: Resources for the Future.

Business Today (2004, April 13). Anil Ambani's Power Play.

Byrne, J., Glover, L., Lee, H., Wang, Y-D., and Yu, J. (2004). Electricity Reform at a Crossroads: Problems in South Korea's Power Liberalization Strategy. *Pacific Affairs, 77*(3), 493-516.

Casazza, J., and Loehr, G. (Eds.) (2000). *The Evolution of Electric Power Transmission under Deregulation: Selected Readings*. Piscataway, NJ: IEEE.

Cho, A., and Dubash, N. K. (2003). *Will Investment Rules Shrink Policy Space for Sustainable Development? Evidence from the Electricity Sector.* Geneva: South Center.

D'Sa, A. (2005). Integrated Resource Planning and Power Sector Reform in Developing Countries. *Energy Policy, 33*(10), 1271 - 1285.

Doukav, D., Dubash, N. K., and Petkova, E.. (2002). Supply-led Versus Efficiency-led Electricity Reform. In N. K. Dubash (Ed.), *Power Politics: Equity and Environment in Electricity Reform.* Washington, DC: World Resources Institute.

Duane, T. (2002). Regulation's Rationale: Learning from the California Energy Crisis. *Yale Journal on Regulation, 19*(2), 471-540.

Dubash, N. K. (2004). Electric Power Reform: Social and Environmental Issues. In C. Cleveland (Ed.), *Encyclopaedia of Energy.* Elsevier.

Dubash, N. K. (Ed.). (2002). *Power Politics: Equity and Environment in Electricity Reform.* Washington, DC, World Resources Institute.

Dunn, S. (2000). *Micropower: The Next Electrical Era.* Washington D.C.: Worldwatch Institute.

Emmons, W. (2000). *The Evolving Bargain: Strategic Implications of Deregulation and Privatization,* Cambridge, MA: Harvard Business School Press.

England, V. (2004, April 4). Big Brother, Little Cousins. *Standard.*

ESMAP. (2000). *Introducing Competition into the Electricity Supply Industry in Developing Countries: Lessons from Bolivia.* Washington, DC: Energy Sector Management Assistance Program, World Bank.

——. (1999). *Global Energy Sector Reform in Developing Countries: A Scorecard.* Washington, DC: Energy Sector Management Assistance Program, World Bank.

Gamson, D. (2002). The California Conundrum: Rates, Reliability and the Environment under Electricity Restructuring in California. In M. Harriss, (Ed.), *Energy Market Restructuring and the Environment.* Lanham, MD: University Press of America.

Graham, M. (2002). *Democracy by Disclosure: The Rise of Technopopulism.* Washington, DC: Brookings Institution Press.

Greacen, C. S., and Greacen, C. (2004). Thailand's Electricity Reforms: Privatization of Benefits and Socialization of Costs and Risks. *Pacific Affairs, 77*(3), 517-542.

Green, R. (1998). England and Wales - A Competitive Electricity Market? *Program on Workable Energy Regulation* PWP #60.

Gunasekera, K, and Najam, A. (2003). Energy Security in South Asia: A Multiple Frameworks Analysis. In A. Najam, (Ed.) *Non-Traditional Threats to Security in South Asia: Environment and Security.* Lanham, MD: University Press of America.

Hall, D. (2002). *The Water Multinationals – Financial and Other Problems.* London: Public Services International Research Unit.

——. (1999). *Electricity Restructuring, Privatisation and Liberalisation: Some International Experiences.* London: Public Services International Research Unit.

Hamrin, (2002). Policy Options for Building Environmental Protection into the Restructuring Process. In M. H. Lanham, (Ed.), *Energy Market Restructuring and the Environment.* MD: University Press of America.

Harrison, S. S. (2003). Gas and Geopolitics in Northeast Asia: Pipelines, Regional Stability, and the Korean Nuclear Crisis. *World Policy Journal, 19*(4), 23-36.

Hirsch, P. (1999). Beyond the nation state: natural resource conflict and 'national interest' in Mekong hydropower development. *Golden Gate Law Review, 29*(3), 399-414.

——. (1996). Large dams, restructuring and regional integration in Southeast Asia. *Asia Pacific Viewpoint, 37*(1), 1-20.

Hirsh, R. F. (1999). *Power loss : the origins of deregulation and restructuring in the American electric utility system.* Cambridge, MA: MIT Press.

Holdren, J. P., and Smith, K. R. (2000). Energy, the Environment, and Health. In UNDESA UNDP, WEC, (Eds.), *World Energy Assessment,: Energy and the Challenge of Sustainability.* New York: UNDP.

Huneault, M. (2001). Electricity Deregulation: Doubts Brought On by the California Debacle. *IEEE Canadian Review.*

Hunt, S. (2002). *Making Competition Work in Electricity.* New York: J. Wiley.

IEA (2003). *World Energy Investment Outlook 2003.* Paris: International Energy Agency.

Ingco, S. P. (1996). Structural Changes in the Power Sector in Asia: Improving Profitability. *Energy Policy, 24*(8), 723-733.

IRN (2003). *Trading Away the Future: The Mekong Power Grid.* Berkeley, CA: International Rivers Network.

Izaguirre, A. K. (1998). *Private Participation in the Electricity Sector — Recent Trends, Note No. 154.* Washington DC: World Bank.

Jadresic, A. (2000). *Auctioning Subsidies for Rural Electrification in Chile.* Washington DC: The World Bank.

Jamasb, T. (2002). *Reform and Regulation of the Electricity Sectors in Developing Countries.* Cambridge: University of Cambridge.

Joskow, P. L. (2000). Deregulation and Regulatory Reform in the U.S. Electric Power Sector. In S. Peltzman and C. Winston, (Eds.), *Deregulation of Network Industries: The Next Steps.* Washington, DC: Brookings Institution Press.

———. (1998). Electricity Sectors in Transition. *Energy Journal, 19*(2), 25-52.

Kahn, E. (1991). *Electric Utility Planning and Regulation.* Washington, DC and Berkeley, CA: American Council for an Energy-Efficient Economy and University-wide Energy Research Group University of California.

Kale, S. S. (2004). Current Reforms: The Politics of Policy Change in India's Electricity Sector. *Pacific Affairs, 77*(3), 467-491.

Kanungo Committee (2001). *Report of the Committee on Power Sector Reforms in Orissa.* Bhubaneshwar, Orissa: Government of Orissa.

Klare, M. T. (2001). *Resource Wars: The New Landscape of Global Conflict.* New York: Henry Holt and Company.

Kozloff, K. (1998). Electricity Sector Reform In Developing Countries: Implications for Renewable Energy. Washington, DC: Renewable Energy Power Project.

Krishnaswamy V., and Stuggins, G. (2003) Private sector participation in the power sector in Europe and Central Asia : Lessons from the last decade. World Bank working paper no. 8. Washington, DC: World Bank.

Kwoka, J. E. (1996). *Power Structure: Ownership, Integration, and Competition in the U.S. Electricity Industry.* Boston: Kluwer Academic Publishers.

Lamech, R., and Saeed, K. (2003). *What International Investors Look for When Investing in Developing Countries: Results from a Survey of International Investors in the Power Sector.* Washington, DC: World Bank.

Lave, L. B., Apt, J., and Blumsack, S. (2004). Rethinking Electricity Deregulation. *The Electricity Journal, 17*(8), 11-26.

Lerner, E. (2003). What's Wrong with the Electric Grid? *Industrial Physicist, 9*(5), 8-13.

Lockyer, B. (2004). *Attorney General's Energy White Paper: A Law Enforcement Perspective on the California Energy Crisis.* Sacramento, CA: State of California.

Loehr, G. (1998, April 15). Ten Myths About Electric Deregulation. *Public Utilities Fortnightly.*

Mahalingam, S. (2002). A reform fiasco in Orissa. *Frontline* 19(10). May 11-24, 2002.

Manibog, F. R. (2003). *Power for Development : A Review of the World Bank Group's Experience with Private Participation in the Electricity Sector.* Washington, DC: World Bank.

Martin, B. (1993). *In thePublic Interest? :Privatization and Public Sector Reform.* Atlantic Highlands, NJ: Zed Books.

Martinot, E.. (2000). Power Sector Reform and Environment: A Role for the GEF? Washington DC: Global Environment Facility.

McDonald, D. A., and Pape, J. (2002). *Cost Recovery and Service Delivery in South Africa.* Cape Town: Human Sciences Research Council.

McElhinny, V. (2004). Update on PPP Energy Integration Initiative (SIEPAC). InterAction IDB Civil Society Initiative, March 12, 2004. Available at http://www.interaction.org/idb.

Mehta, A. (1999). *Power Play: A Study of the Enron Project.* Mumbai: Orient Longman Ltd.

Mountford, J. D., and Austria, R. R. (1999). Keeping the Lights On! *IEEE Spectrum.* June 1999.

Newbery, D. M., and Pollitt, M. G. (1997). *The Restructuring and Privatization of the U.K. Electricity Supply — Was it Worth It?* Washington. DC: World Bank.

Palast, G., Oppenheim, J., and MacGregor, T. (2003). *Democracy and Regulation : How the Public Can Govern Essential Services.* London and Sterling, VA: Pluto Press.

Parker, M. (1996). Effects on Demands for Fossil Fuels. In J. Surrey, (Ed.), The British Electricity Privatization Experiment: The Record, the Issues, the Lessons. London: Earthscan.

Petkova, E., Maurer, C., Henninger, N., and Irwin, F. with Coyle, J., and Hoff, G. (2002). *Closing the Gap: Information, Participation and Justice in Decision-Making for the Environment.* Washington, DC: World Resources Institute.

Phadke, A., and Rajan, S. C. (2003). Electricity Reforms in India: Not Too Late to Go Back to the Drawing Board. *Economic and Political Weekly, 38*(29).

Philpott, J., and Clark, A. (2002). South Africa: Electricity Reform with a Human Face? In N. K. Dubash, (Ed.), *Power Politics: Equity and Environment in Electricity Reform.* Washington, DC: World Resources Institute.

Pollitt, M. G. (1995). *Ownership and Performance in Electric Utilities : The International Evidence on Privatization and Efficiency.* Oxford: Oxford University Press.

Prayas. (2004). "Beyond State and Market." *Seminar* (541).

Reagan, M. D. (1987). *Regulation: The Politics of Policy.* Boston, MA: Little Brown.

Regulatory Assistance Project. (1994). *IRP and Competition.* Available at http://www.rapmaine.org/irp.html.

Rhodes, R. A. W. (1996). The New Governance: Governing without Government. *Political Studies,* XLIV, 652-667.

Rudolph, R., and Ridley, S. (1986). *Power Struggle : The Hundred-Year War over Electricity.* New York: Harper & Row.

Salameh, M. G. (2003). Quest for Middle East Oil: the U.S. versus the Asia-Pacific Region. *Energy Policy, 31*(11), 1085-1091.

Schipke, A. (2001). *Why Do Governments Divest? : The Macroeconomics of Privatization.* Berlin, New York: Springer.

Seymour, F., and Sari, A. P. (2002). Indonesia: Electricity Reform Under Economic Crisis. In N. K. Dubash, (Ed.), *Power Politics : Equity and Environment in Electricity Reform.* Washington, DC: World Resources Institute.

Sharma, D. (2003). The Multidimensionality of Electricity Reform - An Autralian Perspective. *Energy Policy, 31*(11), 1093-1102.

Stiglitz, J. E. (2003). *The Roaring Nineties: A New History of the World's Most Prosperous Decade.* New York: W.W. Norton.

Stoft, S. (2002). *Power System Economics: Designing Markets for Electricity.* New York: John Wiley & Sons.

USAID. (1998a). Case Studies of the Effects of Power Sector Reform on Energy Efficiency. Washington DC: USAID.

———. (1998b). The Environmental Implications of Power Sector Reform in Developing Countries. Washington, DC: USAID.

———. (1998c). Promoting Energy Efficiency in Reforming Electricity Markets. Washington D.C.: USAID.

Vaitheeswaran, V. (2003). Power to the People: How the Coming Energy Revolution will Transform an Industry, Change our Lives, and Maybe Even Save the Planet. New York: Farrar, Straus and Giroux.

Von Hippel, D., and Williams, J. H. (2003). *Environmental Issues for Regional Power Systems in Northeast Asia*. Third Workshop on Power Grid Interconnection in Northeast Asia, Vladivostok, Russia.

Von Hirschhausen, C., and Opitz, P. (2001). *Power Utility Re-Regulation in East European and CIS Transformation Countries (1990-1999): An Institutional Interpretation*. Cambridge, MA.

Wamukonya, N., (Ed.) (2003a). *Electricity Reform: Social and Environmental Challenges*. Roskilde, Denmark, United Nations Environment Programme.

———. (2003b). Power Sector Reform in Developing Countries: Mismatched Agendas. *Energy Policy, 31*(12), 1273-89.

———. (2003c). Some Emerging Lessons in the Reform of the African Power Sector. In N. Wamukonya, (Ed.), *Electricity Reform: Social and Environmental Challenges*. Roskilde, Denmark: United Nations Environment Programme.

Wendlandt, A. (2001, April 9). High Politics Help Grease the Wheels of Trade. *Financial Times*.

Williams, J. H., and Dubash, N. K. (2004). Asian Electricity Reform in Historical Perspective: Special issue on The Political Economy of Electricity Reform in Asia. *Pacific Affairs, 77*(3), 411 - 436.

Williams, J. H., and Ghanadan, R.. (2005). Electricity Reform in Developing and Transition Countries: A Reappraisal. *Energy*.

Wilson, J. Q. (1980). *The Politics of regulation*. New York: Basic Books.

Woo, C. K., Lloyd, D., and Tishler, A. (2003). Electricity market reform failures: U.K., Norway, Alberta and California. *Energy Policy, 31*(11), 1103-1115.

Wood, D. (2004). *Taking Power: Political and Social Dynamics of the Energy Sector*. Public Understanding and Participation Energy Symposium, Capetown, South Africa.

World Bank. (2004). *Power's Promise: Electricity Reforms in Eastern Europe and Central Asia*. Washington, DC: World Bank.

———. (2003). *Private Sector Development in the Electric Power Sector*. Washington, DC: Operations Evaluation Department, World Bank.

———. (1993). The World Bank's Role in the Electric Power Sector : Policies for Effective Institutional, Regulatory, and Financial Reform. Washington, DC: World Bank.

World Resources Institute, National Institute of Public Finance and Policy, and Prayas-Pune. (2004). Governance of the Electricity Sector in Asia:Benchmarking Best Practice and Promoting Accountability in the Electricity Sector. Available at http://electricitygovernance.wri.org

Yergin, D., Eklof, D., and Edwards, J. (1998). Fueling Asia's Recovery. *Foreign Affairs 77*(2).

Yergin, D. (1991). *The Prize: The Epic Quest for Oil, Money, and Power*. New York: Simon and Schuster.

Yergin, D., and Stoppard, M. (2003). "The Next Prize." *Foreign Affairs, 82*(6).

Yu, X. (2003). Regional Cooperation and Energy Development in the Greater Mekong Subregion. *Energy Policy* 31, 1221-1234.
——. (2002, November 13). Change Flows Down the Mekong. *Bangkok Post.*

7

The World Bank's Support for Large Dams:
A Case of Institutional Amnesia?

Peter Bosshard

Introduction

Large dams have for decades symbolized a centralized, capital-intensive, top-down development paradigm. They also illustrate the changing development policies of the World Bank. With more than 550 such projects financed over its 60-year history, the multilateral development bank is the world's premier promoter of large dams. After experiencing a series of high-profile development disasters, the Bank became increasingly cautious about financing large dams and other controversial infrastructure projects in the mid-1990s. Other financial institutions followed suit. As a consequence, the rate of global dam building dropped significantly in the 1990s.

Borrowing governments soon charged the World Bank had become too risk-averse and that detailed environmental, social, procurement, and fiduciary policies made doing business with the Bank too cumbersome. At the same time, the dwindling support for brick-and-mortar infrastructure projects reduced the Bank's lending particularly for middle-income countries, and the Bank became concerned that reduced lending would decrease its revenues, its relevance, and political clout.

In response to these concerns and pressures, the World Bank officially adopted a new high-risk strategy in February 2003, and decided to reengage in financing large dams and other contentious infrastructure projects. In July 2003, the Bank launched a new Infrastructure Action Plan, which included a series of measures to expand the Bank's support for infrastructure projects. In 2004, the Bank's management also proposed measures to simplify and weaken social and environmental safeguard policies in an attempt to expedite the approval of infrastructure projects, particularly in middle-income countries.

This chapter addresses the following questions: What is the social, environmental and economic track record of large dams? What factors have motivated the changing attitudes of the World Bank and other institutions towards large dam projects? And how is the bank integrating the lessons of past experiences as it moves back into large dams?

In addressing these questions, the paper focuses on the experience of India. India is one of the world's most important dam-building countries, and the Bank's role in Indian water and power projects has always been contentious. India has often been a trend-setter for the World Bank's water and power sector strategies and the Indian government is a strong supporter of the institution's new high-risk approach. Presently, the main authors of high-risk strategy are directly responsible for the World Bank's dam-building program in India.

The Large Dams Debate

In large parts of the world, rainfall is unevenly distributed throughout the year and mankind has tried to store water in reservoirs for more than 5,000 years. The technical capacity for hydroelectric generation has only increased the impulse to subdue rivers, channelling their natural energy into exploitable electricity. By the end of the twentieth century, more than 45,000 large dams had been built worldwide.[1] China (with no less than 22,000 large dams) the United States, India, Spain and Japan account for the biggest number of such structures. All but 5,000 of the world's 45,000 large dams were built after 1949. Dam building reached its peak during the 1970s. Currently, around 160 to 320 large dams are built every year.

The Services that Dams Perform

Large dams are built to provide water for irrigation, supply water for human and industrial uses, provide flood protection and generate hydropower. To a lesser extent, dams have been built to improve river navigation. Once built, their reservoirs have also been used for recreational purposes and aquaculture; many dams are multi-purpose projects.[2]

The majority of all large dams provide water for irrigation. Irrigated agriculture accounts for about 40 percent of the world's agricultural production. An estimated 30 to 40 percent of irrigated lands rely on dams, and so dams are estimated to contribute to up to 12 to 16 percent of the world's food production (World Commission on Dams, 2001: 12ff). About 12 percent of all large dams are built for water supply (World Commission on Dams, 2001: 14ff).

Many of the world's largest dam projects are built to generate hydropower. Hydropower currently provides 19 percent of the world's electricity supply— an amount of energy equivalent to roughly 6 percent of the world's oil production. Hydropower supplies more than 90 percent of all electric power in 24 countries (World Commission on Dams, 2001: 14). While roughly 13 percent of the world's large dams have flood management functions, this intention often works at cross purposes with the generation of hydropower. Governments around the world are increasingly de-emphasizing the role of large dams in the management of floods in favor of increasing electricity generation.

The Findings of the World Commission on Dams

For many decades, large dams have given concrete shape to the development aspirations of governments around the world. "They are concrete, rock and earth expressions of the dominant ideology of the technological age," comments Patrick McCully in *Silenced Rivers*: "icons of economic development and scientific progress to match nuclear bombs and motor cars" (McCully, 2001: 2ff). In 1954, India's Prime Minister, Jawaharlal Nehru, called large dams "a symbol of a nation's will to march forward with strength, determination, and courage." Since 1954, however, this optimism has waned. Numerous case studies have demonstrated that the benefits of large dams are routinely overestimated, while their costs tend to be underestimated. "I have begun to think that we are suffering from what we may call the 'disease of gigantism,'" Nehru said in 1958.

The most comprehensive evaluation of the development impacts of large dams was carried out by the independent, broad-based World Commission on Dams (WCD) in 1997 to 2000. Published in November 2000, the report's findings are summarized by the following (World Commission on Dams, 2001: xxviii):

> Dams have made an important and significant contribution to human development, and the benefits derived from them have been considerable. In too many cases an unacceptable and often unnecessary price has been paid to secure those benefits, especially in social and environmental terms, by people displaced, by communities downstream, by taxpayers and by the natural environment. Lack of equity in the distribution of benefits has called into question the value of many dams in meting water and energy development needs when compared with the alternatives.

According to the WCD report, large dams have displaced 40 to 80 million people. In addition, millions of people have been affected by the loss of land and fisheries, by the disappearance of flood-recession agriculture, and by water-borne diseases such as malaria that are spread by the construction of large dams. The beneficiaries of large dams are usually not identical with the groups that are negatively affected by them, and, so, dams in a sense, take away resources from one sector of the population and allocate them to another. Poor, politically powerless, rural communities, including indigenous peoples, have been particularly negatively affected by large dams. According to the WCD report, the failure to adequately resettle and rehabilitate affected people displaced by dams has led "to the impoverishment and suffering of millions" (World Commission on Dams, 2001: 31).

The effects of large dams are not limited to the direct social impacts. The WCD report found large dams had "extensive impacts on rivers, watersheds and aquatic ecosystems" and that efforts to mitigate such environmental impacts have generally failed (World Commission on Dams, 2001: 31). As Patrick McCully notes, a dam can be regarded "as a huge, long-term and largely irreversible environmental experiment without a control" (McCully, 2001: 31). Large dams have flooded a land area of at least 400,000 square kilometres, often containing some of the world's most diverse ecosystems. Dams have also fragmented the ecosystems of 60 percent of the world's rivers, while irrigation has resulted in the water-logging and salinization of large tracts of land.

In addition to these social and environmental challenges, dams have often failed to achieve their purported goals. The WCD report noted that "a considerable portion of dams fail[ed] to deliver on their overall objectives and many [fell] short of specific targets" (World Commission on Dams, 2001: 38). Large dams often experienced marked construction delays and cost overruns. On average, the 81 dams the Commission studied in more detail showed cost overruns of 56 percent (World Commission on Dams, 2001).

The WCD report confirmed the existence of many alternative solutions to the problems of agriculture, water supply, flood management, and electricity generation. Yet decision-making in the water and power sectors is distorted by what the report calls the "political economy of large dams" (World Commission on Dams, 2001: 168):

> As a development choice, large dams often became a focal point for the interests of politicians, dominant and centralised government agencies, international financing agencies and the dam building industry....There has been a generalised failure to recognise affected people and empower them to participate in the decision-making process.

In other words, the WCD conclusions reinforced the notion that mainstream approaches to financing large dam projects ignored significant social and environmental impacts and violated principles of democratic governance.

Resistance Against Large Dams

Because of significant social and environmental impacts, large dam projects have engendered resistance since the nineteenth century. In many countries, the opposition against large dams spawned wider movements for environmental protection, civil rights, and democratization. In the 1980s and early 1990s, groups fighting against large dams created one of the first prominent international NGO networks.

The international network fighting destructive large dams soon turned out to be remarkably effective. Projects such as Sardar Sarovar in the Narmada Valley (India), Yacyreta on the Parana (Argentina/Paraguay), Arun III (Nepal), Three Gorges on the Yangtze River (China), Bakun in the rainforest of Sarawak (Malaysia), and Ilisu in Southeast Anatolia (Turkey) became the symbols of the unsustainable policies and lacking standards of governments, equipment suppliers, engineering companies, the World Bank, export credit agencies and private investors.

Social movements and international NGO networks succeeded in stopping, or at least suspending, the construction of many high-profile dam projects, including Sardar Sarovar, Yacyreta, Arun III, Bakun, and Ilisu. They also managed to translate the public concerns about large dams into pressure for institutional reforms at the World Bank and other dam building institutions.

During the 1960s, 1970s and 1980s, more than 4,000 new large dams were commissioned per decade. This figure fell to just over 2,000 in the 1990s (McCully, 2001: xxviii). Developers found it particularly difficult to attract public or private finance for large hydropower projects. Indeed, this very deadlock encouraged private sector companies, governments and the World Bank to embrace the idea of an independent evaluation that led to the creation of the World Commission on Dams.

The World Bank's Love-Hate Affair with Large Dams

The attitude towards large dams symbolizes development paradigms generally; and this is even more true for the World Bank. The financial institution has funded more than 550 dams in its sixty years history. These dams received at least $86 billion (in 2004 dollars) in World Bank loans and credits and displaced at least 10 million people (Sklar and McCully, 1994: 37). John Briscoe, the Bank's senior water adviser, commented in 2003 lending for big dams accounted for about 10 percent of the institution's portfolio but 95 percent of its headaches (*The Economist,* 2003: 7).

Regarding the Bank and other important financiers of large dams, the WCD report found their influence to be even greater than might be reflected by the numbers above (World Commission on Dams, 2001: 171):

Although the proportion of investment in dams directly financed by bilaterals and multilaterals was perhaps less than 15%, these institutions played a key strategic role globally in spreading the technology, lending legitimacy to emerging dam projects, training future engineers and government agencies, and leading financing agreements.

Projects such as Tarbela in Pakistan, Kedung Ombo in Indonesia and Yacyreta in Argentina/Paraguay illustrate the technical problems, corruption, cost overruns, and social and environmental problems of dams financed by the World Bank. NGO criticisms and public concerns culminated in the Sardar Saorvar project on the Narmada River in India. "It seems clear that engineering and economic imperatives have driven the Project to the exclusion of human and environmental concerns," noted an independent review of the Sardar Sarovar project, commissioned by the World Bank, itself. The review continued: "As a result, benefits tend to be overstated, while social and environmental costs are frequently understated. Assertions have been substituted for analysis"("Sardar Sarovar: The Report of the Independent Commission," 1992: xxiv). In March 1993, the Bank withdrew from the project in the Narmada Valley under strong international public pressure.

As a consequence of the disastrous experience with the Sardar Sarovar dam in India's Narmada valley, the World Bank grew more cautious. It greatly reduced its funding for large dams in the mid-1990s, and created an Inspection Panel as a mechanism of increased accountability in 1994. In 1997, the Bank also agreed to co-sponsor the WCD process. As a consequence of this growing caution and accountability, the number of destructive new dam projects decreased significantly after the mid-1990s.

A 'Top-Down,' Bureaucratic and Fragmentary Approach

The World Bank's growing prudence regarding large dams and other high-risk infrastructure projects was not motivated solely by social and environmental criticisms. The Bank also realized that in many countries, efficiency improvements and a better management of existing infrastructure made more economic sense than financing new projects within an inefficient system.

In 2002, the Bank's Operations Evaluation Department (OED) evaluated the institution's water sector strategy in India. The evaluation found that "performance of completed water projects has been unsatisfactory because of over-optimistic appraisal and state's unwillingness to tackle institutional and financial reform," and that "much still remains to be done on developing sustainable mechanisms for water allocation and management" (Pitman, 2002: 7).

The findings of the 2002 review deserve to be quoted in some detail. OED found (Pitman, 2002: 4 – 5):

> Past approaches in India have been to develop water resources rather than to manage them efficiently.....Accountability is missing. The approaches have been top-down, bureaucratic and fragmentary, rather than participatory, client-oriented and integrated. Most users and beneficiaries have been excluded from decision-making and have no incentive to participate and improve service delivery. There are negligible incentives for government agencies to deliver adequate or quality services. This sets up a vicious circle of poor service, reluctance to pay, and insufficient income for operation and maintenance (O&M) that further reduces efficient service....In the long run, the gap between growing demand and inelastic supplies must be closed by increasing managerial efficiency, rather than developing new supplies.

The World Bank came to similar conclusions when it reviewed its water sector operations in India in 1991 and 1998 (Pitman, 2002: 18):

> Unfortunately, however, the findings of the [1998] sector review are almost identical to those of the 1991 review: the top-down, supply-oriented and fragmentary development framework still persists and present institutional arrangements do not enable comprehensive allocation, planning and management of water.

In February 2003, the Bank adopted a new Water Resources Sector Strategy with an emphasis on 'high risk/high reward' infrastructure investments. OED's 2002 evaluation of the Indian water sector was supposed to serve as an input into this new sector strategy, but did not support such an approach. To the contrary, the evaluation concluded (Pitman, 2002: 29):

> The Bank's current water sector operations have moved away from new construction and are focusing on making existing infrastructure work efficiently, and this is most appropriate given the poverty alleviation mission of the Bank.

Clearly, experiences on the ground did not justify the adoption of a new infrastructure strategy that focused on high-risk investments.

'No Point Investing in Generation'

Experiences in the power sector are similar to those of the water sector. In early 2001, OED evaluated the Bank's power sector strategy in India during the period between 1978 and 1998. As with the water sector, this review criticized the strategy of rapid generating capacity expansion that the Bank had pursued until the early 1990s. It found that (World Bank, 2001a):

> Until 1993, Bank energy lending largely followed the government's lead, supporting expansion of productive capacity through large-scale projects implemented by central or state monopolies....That the lending program was *irrelevant* to the Bank's broader goals of making the power sector sustainable became increasingly evident in the early 1990s....Institutional performance declined throughout the 1980s and 1990s. Many states had distribution losses of 40 percent and more.

In October 2001, the World Bank's country director, Edwin Lim, gave a critical overview of the problems in India's power sector. "There must be some [$4 to 6 billion] flowing every year into the pockets of individuals and institutions through theft, graft and corruption in the power distribution sector," Lim said. "The most important, and most challenging element, of power sector reforms is to combat this widespread theft, graft and corruption. This will require nothing less than a new governance system in the power sector" (Lim, 2001: 3). "There is no point investing in generation if the power does not reach the consumer," the International Finance Corporation's country director Bernard Pasquier commented in December 2000.[3] "Unless we fix distribution, no other problem in the power sector can be solved," India's Power Minister Suresh Prabhu agreed in September 2001.[4]

The need to shift away from physical investments in the power sector was also reflected in OED's latest Country Assistance Evaluation for India in 2002. This evaluation included the following "major lesson" (World Bank, 2002a: 65):

> Projects that focus on physical investments, with the primary objective of increasing energy production, facilitate the continuation of inappropriate and unsustainable sector policies....Although physical investments in energy infrastructure projects may be efficient, in the narrow sense that they are supporting the least-cost energy development program, these investments are unlikely to effectively utilize the country's limited resources where prices are far below real costs.

As a consequence, the recommendations of the evaluation report included the following (World Bank, 2002a: 65):

> The Bank should not support power generation projects (including private power projects) that supply power to inefficient, loss-making distribution entities, even if the generation company is itself efficient.

The World Bank's response to the inefficiencies in the power sector was to promote private sector participation and privatization. The trailblazer for this approach was, again, India. The Bank stopped financing power plants in this country in 1993. Starting with a power sector loan for the state of Orissa, the Bank in 1996 began lending for the corporatization and privatization of the power sector, particularly of electricity distribution. This approach was soon adopted in many other Indian states and countries that were prepared to follow the Bank's path of privatizing the power sector and the provision of infrastructure services more generally.

Back to Bricks and Mortar

Private investors were expected to fill the gap left by the Bank's withdrawal from brick-and-mortar infrastructure finance. By the end of the 1990s, it became increasingly clear the interest of private companies in investing in the transport, water supply, and electricity sectors of poor countries was very limited. Under these circumstances, important factions within the Bank's Board of Directors and management were unhappy with the institution's increased social and environmental prudence. They argued that the Bank had become too risk-averse, and that the social and environmental safeguard policies made doing business with the Bank too cumbersome (World Bank, 2001a).

In late 2000, the pendulum began to swing back. A strategic reorientation was expressed in several overlapping initiatives: a renewed commitment to financing projects with high social and environmental risks, a plan to return to financing brick and mortar infrastructure projects, and a weakening of the social and environmental standards applied in Bank projects in order to increase and expedite lending.

A New High-Risk Strategy

Under pressure from conservative member governments—particularly India, China, and the United States—Bank management returned to what it described as a "high risk/high reward" strategy. In late 2002 and early 2003, an internal task force officially embraced the new strategy and proposed measures by which the Bank's management could better support staff that took on new high-risk projects.

This strategy was first embodied in a new Water Resources Sector Strategy (WRSS) that the Board of Directors adopted in February 2003. The Strategy claims that the performance of dam projects has improved significantly in recent years, and that it is important for the Bank to be involved in such projects in order to get acquainted with best practices. The strategy asserts that "low-cost, often community based solutions" and "'easy and cheap' options" have been "mostly exploited," suggesting that, consequentially, the Bank needs to "re-engage with high risk/high reward hydraulic infrastructure"—in other words, with large dams (World Bank, 2003f: 3).

The Infrastructure Action Plan

In July 2003, the Board of Directors adopted a new Infrastructure Action Plan, which aims at significantly increasing infrastructure lending over two to three years. The Plan includes the following elements (among others) (World Bank, 2003a):

- The standardization of country-wide infrastructure assessments (the so-called Recent Economic Developments in Infrastructure or REDIs);
- An increased budget for the development of infrastructure projects;
- The simplification of internal processes, including the application of safeguard policies;
- The preparation of new lending instruments, including "sustainable subsidies for private provision";
- The implementation of 'high risk/high reward' projects.

The Bank's management expected an increase in the volume of new infrastructure investment from $5.4 billion in Fiscal Year 2003 to $6 billion in FY 2004 and about $6.5 to 7.0 billion in FY 2005. IFC expected total commitments in infrastructure to increase from $650 million in FY 2003 to about $1 billion in FY 2004 (World Bank, 2004c).

Public Subsidies for Private Investors

In February 2004, the Bank Group published a Guidance Note on the role of the state and the private sector in power projects in the context of the IAP (see World Bank, 2004f). The Bank planned to prepare similar draft notes on the water supply, sanitation, transport, gas and telecom sectors by the end of April 2004. The Board of Director's Committee on Development Effectiveness (CODE) had requested the preparation of such notes to clarify the Bank's response to the dwindling interest of the private sector in developing infrastructure projects.

The power sector Guidance Note emphasizes the attraction of private investors through "well-designed subsidies" in the form of "output-based aid" (World Bank, 2004f: 5). It does not discuss the fundamental problems of socializing private costs through public subsidies. The report does not address consistent problems of fraud, deceit and corruption in private power projects or the urgent need for transparency and accountability in this sector.

A 2003 internal evaluation of private sector development in the electric power sector (PSDE) recommended the following: "In its future PSDE interventions, the WBG should give greater emphasis to the mainstreaming of the poverty reduction and environmental objectives...that are at the core of the WBG's overall energy strategy" (World Bank, 2003d: 57). The new Guidance Note, however, disregards this recommendation, and gives short shrift to the social and environmental issues in the power sector.

The Guidance Note supports public subsidies and guarantees for private power projects. It generally discourages World Bank support for power generation projects that are controlled by the state. Notably exceptional, however, is support for state-owned hydropower projects. The report states (World Bank, 2004f: 11):

> New, large, and complex hydropower projects that have strong economic justification will usually require significant public investment. Compared to thermal generation, hydro projects have very different risk and benefit profiles and, accordingly, a much greater public financing role. These include the geological and hydrological risks, the long-lived nature of the assets, and the fact that many hydropower projects are multipurpose projects providing public goods such as flood control and drought protection. The Bank should support dams that are economically well justified, and should ensure that all such projects meet the good environmental and social practices which have been developed by the industry in recent decades.

In April 2004, the Bank's management published a similar Guidance Note on the role of the public and private sectors in water supply and sanitation investment. This document encourages support both for both private operators and "well-performing publicly owned and operated utilities" (World Bank, 2003b: 14, see also World Bank, 2002b). It makes the case for attracting private investment through long-term public subsidies. Like the power sector note, the document does not discuss sobering experiences with profiteering private operators that have not bothered to fulfil their contractual obligations in privatized water supply programs.

It seems the only lesson the Bank draws from the crisis of private power and water sector development is to call for public subsidies for private investors. In social and environmental terms, it seems to limit its role to ensuring that projects meet the "good practices which have been developed by the industry in recent decades" (World Bank, 2002c). This is a role the private sector can certainly play without the World Bank.

A Slow Start

As an initial measure, the Bank's administrative budget for the development of infrastructure projects was increased by $8 million. The institution started hiring new infrastructure experts to make up for the attrition in this sector in the past few years. In September 2003, the Bank also hosted a meeting with twelve other international financial institutions to coordinate the development of infrastructure projects.

When the IAP was adopted, the Bank planned to prepare REDI studies for ten countries by June of 2004. According to a confidential Board document, the Bank planned to carry out such studies in Vietnam, Indonesia, the Philippines, Mongolia, Colombia, Peru, Bosnia, Bulgaria, Palestine, Morocco, and one Indian state in FY 2004. Plans for FY 2005 included REDIs in India, Madagascar, Mauritania and Senegal (see World Bank, 2004c).

In May 2004, the office of the Bank's vice president for infrastructure informed International Rivers Network (IRN) that "work on the REDIs got underway later than expected due to administrative and budgetary delays" (Uku, 2004). The Bank hoped studies for Colombia and Indonesia, and possibly for Gaza, the African region and Eastern Europe, would be completed by the end of summer 2004.

Social and Environmental Standards on the Block

The Bank's record of dealing with high risk, particularly in dam projects, is bleak. Re-engaging in high-risk projects would require a strengthening of the policies and institutional capacities that allow the Bank to assess, avoid and mitigate social and environmental risks. Yet the opposite is taking place. Since the early 1990s, the World Bank has not strengthened its capacity to deal with risk. In November 2000, the Bank accepted the general strategic priorities of the World Commission on Dams in order to improve decision-making on water and power sector projects. The Bank did not, however, adopt any of the WCD's specific recommendations in the form of binding policies. And it weakened its safeguard policies in important aspects when it converted them into a shorter format after 1996.

Several internal evaluations by the Operations Evaluation Department concluded that the Bank has failed to mainstream social and environmental concerns into its decision-making processes. The OED also found that the quality of environmental assessments has deteriorated in recent years (see, for example, World Bank, 2002c). Furthermore, the World Bank has never produced any evidence that high risks in its projects effectively translate into high rewards. Instead, with specific regard for large dam projects, the OED and the WCD that found cost overruns were considerably higher than those of other infrastructure projects and that overall, the performance of large dams did not keep up with the stated objectives in terms of power generation and irrigation. This resulted in low rewards despite high risks (International Rivers Network, 2003).

Moving Away from World Bank Safeguards

Since 2002, Bank management has been discussing ways to speed up lending by relying on national social and environmental procedures and standards rather than the Bank's own safeguard policies in certain countries. In September 2003, the Bank's Managing Director sent a memorandum to all Bank staff urging them to process investment projects within twelve months (Zhang, 2003). This would be a significant development as between 1998 to 2003, the average preparation time for investment loans was 21 months (World Bank, 2003c: 2).

The shift toward the use of national safeguard policies appeared to take on an added urgency because of a sharp drop in World Bank lending to middle-income countries since the late 1990s. This drop was caused not so much by cumbersome safeguard policies but by the Bank's withdrawal from brick-and-mortar infrastructure projects. With an average of $11.6 billion per year, lending of IBRD resources in the FY 2000 to 2003 period was only about half as high as in FY 1999, and 26 percent lower than in the 1990 to 1997 period (World Bank, 2004b: 11).

In spring 2004, Bank management prepared a new middle-income country strategy to address decreased lending levels. The document explicitly recommended a weakening of the Bank's own standards. Under the heading, "remove obstacles to timely quality lending," the strategy proposed "that the Bank *accelerate the ongoing initiative to rely on certified national and safeguard systems in countries, and sectors within countries, where such systems are found satisfactory to the Bank"* (World Bank, 2004b: 24 – 25, emphasis in original).

In parallel, the Bank's management prepared discussion notes for the use of national safeguard systems rather than the Bank's own operational policies in all (and not just middle-income) countries in April and October 2004

(World Bank, 2004h, 2004d). According to these papers, the Bank will rely on national safeguard systems in future Bank projects if these systems are considered equivalent with a brief synthesis of the objectives and operational principles of the Bank's own operational policies.

The proposed approach will significantly weaken the policies implemented in Bank projects for several reasons. The synthesis prepared by Bank management does not contain many key elements of the Bank policies. According to an analysis prepared by the Center on International Environmental Law, the synthesis will weaken existing Bank policies in about 150 instances, and strengthen them in about twenty instances (World Bank, 2004e). Furthermore, the Bank will consider national policies equivalent even if required improvements are only being planned and have not yet been implemented. Once national systems have been accepted as being equivalent, the Inspection Panel will no longer be allowed to investigate the violation of binding Bank policies in projects but will need to use the national systems as its point of reference (International Rivers Network, 2005a).

In January 2005, 200 NGOs from fifty-eight countries protested against the proposed weakening of the policies used in Bank projects and the weakening of the Bank's accountability, in a letter to the Board of Directors. Still, the Board approved the proposed approach in February 2005. The approach will be tested in eight to twelve projects in a two-year pilot phase before it will be finalized.

Even before accepting the underlying strategy, the Board of Directors approved a pilot project for the use of national safeguard systems in Mexico in June 2004. The infrastructure project in the Mexican state of Guanajuato was expected to have negative environmental impacts and to cause involuntary resettlement. Yet Mexico's environmental assessment standards are considerably weaker than the World Bank's policy, and Mexico does not have a law on involuntary resettlement.

Safeguard policies—An Obstacle to Increased Lending in India?

The World Bank's lending targets for India are ambitious. Reaching them may require a weakening of safeguard standards. A confidential Regional Briefing on the South Asia Region that the Board of Directors discussed in February 2004 announced the following implication for the use of the Bank's safeguard policies (World Bank, 2004i: 4):

> Increased willingness to borrow IBRD (mainly by India and Pakistan) would require implementing changes to some of our processes (e.g., safeguards, procurements, use of repeater projects). To achieve these ambitious targets we will (…) make increased use of (and actively supporting [sic] development and effective implementation of) national fiduciary and safeguard policies.

The draft of the World Bank's new Country Assistance Strategy for India in June 2004 also announced "efforts to change the way that the Bank does business in India—seeking to harmonize Bank safeguard and fiduciary requirements... as far as possible around the policies adopted by GoI [the Government of India] and state governments" (World Bank, 2004a: paragraph 43).

World Bank evaluations have consistently found that the implementation of environmental and social standards in India is weak. The 2002 Country Assistance Evaluation stated (World Bank, 2002a: 70):

> Monitoring and enforcement of environmental standards is lagging and undermines the whole regulatory effort. Indian environmental legislation is comprehensive, but its enforcement is weak.

In its recommendations on energy sector operations, the report proposed that "[m]onitoring and supervision of environmental and social compliance agreements should be made a central issue in the Bank's ongoing dialogue with national and local governments" (World Bank, 2002a: 66). In 2002, another OED report found that "the Bank still has good reasons to be wary of projects involving resettlement" (Pitman, 2002: 26). The World Bank has so far not produced any evidence that would document the political will of Indian authorities to strengthen their compliance with existing social and environmental standards, national or otherwise.

A Flawed Concept of Country Ownership

The Infrastructure Action Plan stresses the importance of country ownership for infrastructure development. Yet Bank management seems to have a flawed concept of country ownership. It appears to equate this concept with government ownership, and government ownership with ownership by the infrastructure ministries. Decades of experience show that such a perspective is too narrow. Environmental ministries, academic institutions, non-governmental organizations, other civil society groups and most importantly, the social sectors that are marginalized in the formal political process must also be able to bring in their expertise and interests.

Infrastructure projects are often developed in a biased way by governments and financial institutions. The interests of politicians, governments, aid bureaucracies, and equipment suppliers favor the promotion of new investments over the improved management of existing infrastructure. The huge inefficiencies that usually exist in water and power supply are often not addressed even if such measures would be more cost-effective than building new infrastructure. Needs and options are not assessed in a balanced, participatory, and accountable way. Planning processes are skewed in favor of centralized, capital-intensive, top-down investment projects. Foreign consultants that are subsidized through trust funds are favored over domestic expertise and, in turn, entrench a bias for imported equipment. Finally, the promotion of privatization and the control of planning processes by national elites discriminate against infrastructure services that are identified and developed by poor communities.

Based on data from seven Latin American countries, Prof. Felix Rioja of the Georgia State University observes the following (Rioja, 1999: 12):

> The construction of new, highly visible infrastructure projects has received great attention in many countries. Maintaining infrastructure has generally been neglected. ...Most new public projects are financed by international donor aid. Maintenance expenditures, on the other hand, are mostly financed by taxation. Hence new investments receive a preferential treatment from the government. ...Simply shifting 20% of donor aid to filling potholes [used by the author as a short term for infrastructure maintenance] can raise GDP and welfare about 15% in the long run. Hence, filling potholes deserves much more attention than it has received.

New Guidelines on Options Assessment

On paper, the World Bank has embraced some best practice recommendations on developing power and water projects. In response to the WCD report, the Bank accepted the Commission's strategic priorities, including the principles of "Gaining Public Acceptance" and "Comprehensive Options Assessment." In July 2003, the World Bank published a sourcebook on the assessment of options in the water and energy sectors (World Bank, 2003e). The sourcebook proposes the following "principles to guide public decisions:" 1) create an enabling environment; 2) involve all relevant stakeholders; 3) assess all options strategically and comprehensively; and 4) reach a decision.

According to a Bank sourcebook (World Bank, 2003e: 1),

> stakeholder involvement and the assessment of options are important elements in the preparation of World Bank supported water resources and energy projects, and should be prominent topics in the dialogue between the Bank and developing countries....The emphasis on a systematic upstream assessment of options means that stakeholders should be involved in sectoral and basin-level planning activities....Sector plans...will no longer be just technical exercises undertaken solely by professionals.

The slow progress in preparing the fundamental REDI studies (see above) raises questions about the World Bank's seriousness in assessing all needs and options before financing new infrastructure projects. The role of country ownership and options assessments in the Bank's new plans for infrastructure projects in India will be analyzed below.

The World Bank's Infrastructure Plans in India

India is a good test case for the implementation of the Bank's new water and infrastructure strategies. With a total of $59 billion, the country was the largest single recipient of cumulative World Bank lending in June 2003. Until 1992, India was also the Bank's biggest borrower for water sector projects. Developments in the India portfolio have often brought about important shifts in the Bank's infrastructure policies.

India—The High-Risk Approach

The Indian government is one of the strongest promoters of the Infrastructure Action Plan and the return to a high-risk strategy within the World Bank. Praful Patel, the main author of the Bank's "high risk/high reward" strategy, is now the Vice President for South Asia and John Briscoe, the main author of the new water sector strategy, is the new senior water advisor for this region (in addition to sharing the job of senior water advisor for the whole Bank). Barry Trembath, the Bank's lead power engineer for East Asia and the Pacific, noted that the Vice President for South Asia was "very much involved in the Water Resources Sector Strategy and advocating this approach would be pushing this new philosophy very hard and very quickly" (2003).

India is also one of the world's major dam building countries. In 1994, 4,300 large dams were in place or under construction in India. Numerous case studies have demonstrated that large dams have an abysmal social, environmental and economic track record in this country. According to estimates large dams have submerged an area of about 37,500 square kilometres and have displaced at least 42 million people in India (World Commission on Dams, 2001). After 1980, the World Bank funded ten hydropower projects in India, including controversial schemes such as Sardar Sarovar and Nathpa Jhakri. During this period, power was the Bank's most important sector in India, and accounted for 28 percent of total lending in 1986 to 1990.

A History of Non-Compliance

Following high-profile problems of non-compliance, and in response to strong public pressure, the World Bank withdrew from the Sardar Sarovar dam in the Narmada Valley in March 1993. The following year, the Bank created the Inspection Panel in order to deal with future cases of policy non-compliance. After the Sardar Sarovar experience, the institution stopped funding large dams in India, and drastically reduced financing for dams worldwide.

Earlier high-risk projects in India share a long and unresolved social and environmental legacy. The World Bank is formally responsible for the compliance of projects with its operational policies until the loans and credits have been repaid. Despite this requirement, an OED report on India's energy sector found the following in 1999: "Legally, loan/credit agreements are valid until the loan/credit has been repaid. In practice, the Bank has not exercised its remedies beyond the closing date of the loan/credit" (World Bank, 1999: 18). The report proposed (World Bank, 1999: 26):

> Monitoring and supervision of environmental compliance agreements should be made a central issue in the Bank's ongoing dialogue with the national and local governments.... For environmentally sensitive energy projects, the Bank should continue to review the performance of the state environmental institutions until the loan is repaid.

However, the World Bank refuses to accept this responsibility for existing high-risk projects such as Sardar Sarovar. It is ironic that at the same time, the Bank is planning to invest in a new generation of high-risk projects.

Doubling Infrastructure Lending for India

Among the World Bank's targets for increased infrastructure lending is the Indian government, which has committed to a huge acceleration in dam construction. In May 2003, it announced plans to increase the country's hydropower capacity by 50,000 megawatts over ten years at an estimated cost of $50 billion. As a first step, the government commissioned pre-feasibility studies for 162 new hydropower projects. The Common Minimum Program of the coalition government led by the Congress Party also attaches "the highest priority to the development and expansion of physical infrastructure," including irrigation and power. The Program does not mention dams explicitly, but building large dams has always been a multi-partisan consensus in India.

The plans of the successive Indian governments fit in well with the World Bank's new high-risk strategy. According to an internal Bank document, "India has asked the Bank to scale up its lending assistance from around $1.5 billion a year (50 percent IBRD) to about $3.0 billion a year—with most of the increment coming from IBRD for infrastructure" (World Bank, 2004i: 3). In December 2003, the World Bank announced that it would double its lending for India within two years and that most additional lending would fund infrastructure development. As part of its new focus on energy, the Bank was considering support for transmission, rural electrification and hydropower projects. As the *Economic Times* quoted an unnamed Bank official on December 7, 2003, "the Indian government wants our help in constructing several dams in the Himalayan region from Himachal to Arunachal Pradesh, and we are finalising those."

After the national elections of May 2004, the World Bank prepared a new India Country Assistance Strategy (CAS) for the period, 2005 to 2008. While the CAS process is supposed to be country driven, a power sector manager of the World Bank advised representatives of the dam industry and governments at a hydropower conference in November 2003: "Insist on [the development of hydropower] in the country assistance strategy talks, as this is where projects enter the pipeline" (*Hydropower and Dams*, 2003).

In June 2004, the Bank published a consultation draft of the new CAS. The draft strategy announced "the Bank will work with GoI and its PSUs [public sector utilities] to seek possible new avenues for support on a modest scale for hydropower development" (World Bank, 2004a: paragraph 109). According to the CAS, the Bank plans to extend an IBRD loan of $400 million for a new hydropower project in India in 2006 and an IBRD partial risk guarantee of $150 million for another hydropower project in 2008 (World Bank, 2004a: Annex B3). The Strategy was approved by the Board in August 2004.

NHPC—A Partner for the World Bank?

The National Hydro-Electric Power Corporation (NHPC) is India's largest central government institution that develops and operates hydropower projects. It was set up in 1975 and develops projects that are located in sensitive areas (such as Jammu and Kashmir) or are politically particularly well-connected. NHPC's chief managing director Yogendra Prasad is known as an ardent opponent of the WCD recommendations, and a strong critic of the environmental clearance process and the role of NGOs in India. In January 2000, Prasad made the following comments about the role of non-governmental organizations (Prasad, 2002):

> The most tiring and trying ordeal awaiting NHPC will be to meet the challenges of anti-development anachronistic obscurantism obstructing the attempts to reap benefits from bounties of Nature and to keep the poor tribals always in loin cloths, fig leaves and bare tops.

On February 15, 2004, an unnamed Bank official stated in the *Economic Times*: "We are in the process of identifying possible hydro projects and talks are on with power corporations. The bank will work only with agencies that hold track records of good technical, financial, environmental and social performance. The agencies have to adhere to the international standard." The Bank official commented on the performance of NHPC as follows: "The NHPC is moving towards global corporate performance standards and is improving its financial performance. This is recognized by the market. We have done due diligence on the corporation and are impressed by the progress."

The draft CAS of June 2004 also claimed: "While for many years the hydropower business in India had a poor reputation, some major actors (including NHPC) have started to improve their environmental and social safeguard practices" (World Bank, 2004a: paragraph 109). The Bank did not offer any evidence for this assertion.

In early 2004, senior water advisor John Briscoe and other Bank officials visited NHPC's Narmada Sagar project in the Narmada valley and dam projects in Himachal Pradesh. In April 2004, they also visited dams in the Northeastern state of Arunachal Pradesh, including NHPC's 1000 megawatt Middle Siang project. According to Michael Carter, the World Bank country director in India, the Bank delegation was invited by NHPC to visit Narmada Sagar "to become familiar with NHPC's current activities and its techniques for managing large construction projects. That was of interest to us, because we are considering the possibility (although, again, at a very early stage) of IBRD/IDA support for some hydropower development by NHPC if it can meet our standards, although not in the Narmada basin" (Carter, 2004).

Narmada Sagar—A Model for the World Bank?

In a meeting with Himanshu Thakkar of SANDRP and Peter Bosshard of International Rivers Network (IRN) on February 3, 2004, John Briscoe was not prepared to comment on the Narmada Sagar project or other projects that he and fellow Bank officials had visited in recent weeks. In a conversation with Shalmali Guttal of Focus on the Global South on March 17, 2004, Briscoe said that Narmada Sagar was a remarkable project because it was being completed ahead of time. He also argued that India's hydropower industry had much improved its standards regarding resettlement issues, and Narmada Sagar was a good example of this.

The following excerpts from articles in local Indian newspapers shed some light on the resettlement standards applied in the Narmada Sagar (or Indira Sagar) project, and the tactics that NHPC uses to speed up project construction:

- The administration has disconnected the power supply and has uprooted the handpumps supplying drinking water in four villages to be affected by the submergence of the Indira Sagar project. All the villagers have been terrorized by these actions of the administration....Terrorized villagers told *Bhaskar* the administration is threatening the people at gun point and is bent up on emptying the villages through threats even though the issue of compensation is yet to be resolved....The administration has earlier on removed the school, Panchayat, janpad, police station, bank etc. facilities and has either auctioned or demolished the buildings housing these in villages Ladwa, Saria, Navghat, Abhava, Badkeshwar (Dianik Bhaskar, 2002 translated by Shripad Dharmadhikary).
- The administration has once again created havoc and come down heavily on several of the villages in Harsud tehsil including Baladi affected by the Indira Sagar Project. On one hand, several shops, houses have been smashed up and damaged, on the other hand about 100 men of the SAF [Special Armed Force] and the police staged a march past in the Baladi and nearby villages to create an atmosphere of fear and terror so people get frightened and run away fast (Dianik Bhaskar, 2003 translated by Shripad Dharmadhikary).[5]

Enter ADB, IFC, and MIGA

In January 2004, the Asian Development Bank announced the preparation of a technical assistance project to the tune of $400,000 for "Hydropower Development" in India. According to the project officer, the ADB is considering technical assistance "to undertake due diligence and various review work" for the Loharinag-Pala and the Tapoyan-Vishnugad hydropower projects in the state of Utaranchal (Abeygunawardena, 2004). Loharinag-Pala and Tapoyan-Vishnugad are two projects of 520 and 360 megawatts that are being developed by India's National Thermal Power Corporation (NTPC).

The ADB has so far never financed dam projects in India directly. The ADB and the World Bank have a reputation of avoiding cooperation in India and other countries, and it is noteworthy that ADB plans to support NTPC dams, while the World Bank primarily appears to examine cooperation with NHPC. In March 2004, the World Bank and ADB also announced major increases in their support for infrastructure projects in Pakistan, with a primary focus on the water and power sectors.

The World Bank's management expects to identify and approve new dam projects in India within a year. IFC and MIGA, the Bank Group's private sector finance and guarantee institutions, can act more quickly by supporting projects being developed by private investors. In October 2004, the International Finance Corporation approved support for the Allain Duhangan hydroelectric power project, a run-of-river scheme that is being developed by an Indian company in Himachal Pradesh. Allain Duhangan is IFC's first dam project in India. Representatives of the affected communities challenged the project with a complaint to IFC's Compliance Advisor/Ombudsman.

In January 2004, NGOs learned that MIGA was considering support for the Omkareshwar dam project on the Narmada River. If built, Omkareshwar will displace an estimated 50,000 people. Construction has started but so far, no environmental impact assessment has been carried out, and no resettlement action plan has been prepared. In March 2004, Bank Group country director Michael Carter confirmed that MIGA had received an application in December 2003, and was reviewing support for the Omkareshwar project (Carter, 2004). One month later, NGOs were informed that the Agency had turned down this application for social and environmental reasons.

No Learning From Past Experience

"There is no point investing in generation if the power does not reach the consumer," IFC's country director for India commented in December 2000. Recent evaluations of the World Bank's sector strategies also concluded that a rapid expansion of power generation and water supply did not make sense within inefficient sector environments. But the Bank's new sector strategies in India do not reflect these lessons of past experience.

A Case of Institutional Amnesia

On February 3, 2004, Himanshu Thakkar of SANDRP and Peter Bosshard of IRN met with John Briscoe, the World Bank's senior water advisor, and other officials of the Bank's Delhi office. The purpose of the meeting was to learn more about how the IAP and the new water sector strategy were being implemented in India, and how the Bank was learning from past experience in doing so.

The World Bank's OED found in 2002 the growing gap between supply and demand in India's water sector "must be closed by increasing managerial efficiency, rather than developing new supplies." Did the World Bank officials who were responsible for designing and implementing the new water sector strategy agree with this assessment? At the meeting of February 3, John Briscoe said he had never heard about this evaluation. This is particularly surprising since the evaluation was an input into the new water sector strategy Briscoe had prepared one year earlier. In his meeting with NGO representatives, the senior water advisor first argued that multilateral development banks should only finance new investments, while maintenance should be left to the government. After further consideration, John Briscoe was not prepared to take a position on whether the Bank's water sector strategy should shift its focus towards new investments or better management. "The World Bank will finance whatever makes sense, including large infrastructure," he said evasively.

The 2002 OED review deplored the Bank's lacking interest in learning from past experience. "It is surprising that the Bank has shown so little interest in, and has not been willing to commit resources to, systematic evaluation of project implementation and impact," the review quotes the Indian water sector expert A. Vaidyanathan as saying. "Institutionalized learning from experience is conspicuous by its absence" (World Bank, 2002a: 22). "The lessons from past experience are well known, yet they are generally ignored in the design of new operations," the Bank's own Quality Assurance Group (QAG) commented already in 1997 (World Bank, 1997: 15). The approach of the Bank's management to infrastructure lending in India confirms this finding. The new high-risk strategy is the latest example of what the QAG termed the World Bank's "institutional amnesia."

Pouring More Dollars into a Cracked Vessel?

The critique of the World Bank's institutional amnesia is mirrored in a report that the Water Supply and Sanitation Collaborative Council (WSSCC) published in March 2004. The WSSCC was created in 1990 through a mandate from the UN General Assembly. On March 18, 2004, WSSCC's chair Jan Pronk commented: "Today the key issue in water and sanitation is not, primarily, the availability of resources. It is the willingness on the part of those who allocate those resources to learn the lessons of both past failures and current successes." And the WSSCC argued in a press release on the same day (WSSCC, 2004):

> From India to Bolivia, Kenya to Nepal can be found the ruins of now-defunct water and sanitation programmes that have never yielded more than a fraction of the benefits expected.... [S]imply pouring billions more dollars into a cracked vessel will not lead to the achievement of the Millenium Development Goals but to more years of failure and frustration. Similarly, increasing the funds available for further large-scale, delivery-oriented infrastructure will achieve very little without a re-think of how and for whom such funds are to be spent.

The Assessment of Options: "Washington Speak" and India Action

The World Bank's infrastructure strategy for India is not based on lessons from the past. Does it at least incorporate the best practice recommendations of the Infrastructure Action Plan and other recent Bank documents on the water sector? According to the IAP, support for new infrastructure and water sector projects should begin through a systematic assessment of a country's infrastructure situation in the form of a so-called REDI. The representatives of the Bank's Delhi office were not aware of this process, and said that the India Department was not carrying out such an assessment. "This is Washington speak," John Briscoe argued.[6]

No Balanced Assessment of Options

The Bank's new options assessment sourcebook recommends that lending operations in the water and energy sectors be based on a balanced, participatory assessment of all options, including policy and institutional changes. Again, the World Bank officials in February 2004 said that they had not read this sourcebook and John Briscoe claimed that its recommendations represented only the opinion of its author, and not the Bank's. India was a sovereign country, the senior water advisor argued. Options assessments were carried out by the government before the World Bank got involved, and so "the recommendations of the sourcebook are not going to happen in India." This contrasts sharply with the Bank's earlier, detailed analyses of the irrationalities in India's water and power planning systems.

The management of the Bank's South Asia Region intends to increase its focus on the political economy of decision-making. In February 2004, the regional management claimed that "the Bank's increased concern for political economy issues implies a better awareness of how resources—including those arising from Bank support—are allocated, especially through informal systems in society" (World Bank, 2004g). The decision to simply delegate options assessment in the infrastructure sector to the Indian government contradicts this claim.

Alessandro Palmieri, the Bank's lead dams specialist and the main author of the new sourcebook on options assessment, agreed that this document "reflect[ed] only the opinions of the authors." (The sourcebook itself does not carry any such disclaimer.) Palmieri argued since the sourcebook did not constitute formal Bank policy, he did not expect any follow-up activities, and discussing the implementation of its recommendations made "no sense" (Palmieri, 2004). This is disturbing. In public, the sourcebook is presented as "one of the cornerstones of the Bank's Dams Planning, Management and Action Plan" (*Comprehensive Options Assessment of Dams and Their Alternatives*, 2003: 50). More generally, the Bank management has, for many years, insisted on following best practices in its operations, rather than adopting new binding policies. The complete lack of commitment to implementing the recommendations of the options assessment sourcebook puts this approach into question.

The Bhakra Dam—Another Model in Crisis

In his meeting with the NGO representatives, John Briscoe argued that "there has been a sea-change in the mindset of dam builders regarding resettlement for dam projects." Briscoe was not prepared to comment on the Narmada Sagar project or other projects that he had visited in recent weeks. When challenged to mention projects that expressed the improved social and environmental standards of dam building in India, the senior water advisor referred to the Bhakra dam as the only example.

The reference to the Bhakra dam as the prime example of how the standards of dam building in India have improved is telling. For one thing, Bhakra was built in the 1950s, and can certainly not serve as an example of improvements in recent decades. More importantly, the project is an example of the unsustainable policies that have led India's agriculture into a serious social, environmental, and economic crisis. Bhakra is a multipurpose dam on the Sutlej River often credited for turning the states of Punjab and Haryana into India's breadbasket and rice bowl, and for overcoming India's food crisis. Yet a report by Shripad Dharmadhikary of the NGO, Manthan Adhyayan Kendra, belies these claims. According to Dharmadhikary's research, the benefits attributed to Bhakra appear to be both exaggerated and fundamentally unsustainable. In addition, the serious social and environmental problems of the project are still unresolved fifty years after its completion. It is amazing that the World Bank still uses the outlived Bhakra project as the model for the social and environmental impacts of large dams.

The agriculture of the Punjab and Haryana is in deep crisis. In this system, Dharmadhikary concludes, "there will be a short-lived burst of prosperity, followed by permanent devastation. Somewhat like a supernova" (Dharmadhikary, 2005: 9). In comparison, a massive, decentralized program to harvest rainwater, manage watersheds, and conserve soil and water would protect India's environmental resources and increase the productivity of vast land areas. It would also employ large numbers of people and would put purchasing power into the hands of India's poor. This would create a market demand for the food surpluses that can currently not be sold.

Conclusion

India is an important test case for the implementation of the Infrastructure Action Plan and the World Bank's new high-risk strategy more generally. The current plans for increased infrastructure financing in this country suggest that the IAP has been taken hostage by the vested interests of dam-building bureaucracies. The new dam-building plans ignore important lessons of the past. According to the Bank's own evaluations of the water and power sectors in India, improving the efficiency of the existing infrastructure would be more relevant for the Bank's broader development goals than financing new sources of supply within an unsustainable sector environment.

The new dam building plans also ignore the current best practice recommendations for a balanced and participatory assessment of all available options, as defined in the IAP, the strategic priorities of the World Commission on Dams, and the Bank's recent options assessment sourcebook. By limiting the concept of government ownership to ownership by the ministries responsible for infrastructure development, the Bank management defies decades of experience.

The Bank management seems prepared to tinker with the institution's binding safeguard policies in order to achieve its ambitious lending targets. Management proposes relying increasingly on domestic social and environmental policies in Bank projects, although the Bank's evaluations have found that the enforcement of the existing environmental standards in India is seriously deficient.

'To be Hypocritical and Get Away with It'

Robert Hunter Wade, a professor at the London School of Economics, interprets the institutional changes of James D. Wolfensohn's presidency as an attempt to de-link the political agenda of the World Bank from its operational strategy. While the political agenda—including concerns like participation and the social and environmental safeguard policies—is targeted at a critical global public, the operational units have been strengthened to serve the interests of Southern governments. The effect of the reforms was for the Bank to "decoupl[e] itself internally so as to allow its parts to say and do things with different parties that if spot-lit all at once would seem inconsistent. The reform, in other words, was a way to institutionalize the capacity to be hypocritical and get away with it" (Wade, 2001: 2).

The World Bank's new infrastructure plans for India are a stark example for this institutional hypocrisy. The Bank has carried out evaluations producing self-critical findings on its past water and power sector strategies in India. It has announced its support for the strategic priorities of the World Commission on Dams, and has published a sourcebook on the balanced assessment of options that reflects these priorities. Yet in actual practice, the Bank's renewed push to promote large dams does not integrate the lessons of past experience, and leading Bank representatives even dismiss the institution's best practice guidelines as "Washington speak."

The World Bank's current course of action will make it more difficult to achieve the Millennium Development Goals. It will fuel further conflict, and will prolong the deadlock in important sectors. It will block the promotion of alternative approaches to infrastructure that are socially and environmentally sustainable and can provide a long-term basis for economic development.

Infrastructure finance will only contribute to poverty reduction if the political economy of the sector is clearly recognized. Infrastructure development should start with the needs and initiatives of the poor, and not the interests of governments, aid bureaucracies, and corporations. The World Bank should be less risk averse when supporting innovative technologies and processes that address the needs of the poor. Since the Bank has not learned the lessons of past experience, and has not strengthened its capacity to deal with risk, it should not engage in social and environmental high-risk projects as it expands its lending for infrastructure projects.

Notes

1. According to the generally accepted definition by the International Commission on Large Dams, dams are considered large if they have a height of more than 15 meters, or if they have a height of 5-15 meters and a reservoir volume of more than 3 million square meters.
2. For an introduction to the issues posed by large dams, see McCully (2001) and World Commission on Dams (2001).
3. Bernard Pasquier quoted in Power Line, December 2000.
4. Suresh Prabhu quoted in Power Line, September 2001.
5. For an eyewitness account of the resettlement policies applied in the Narmada Sagar project, see Manthan Adhyayan Kendra. (2002).
6. According to a confidential Board document, a REDI is planned in India in FY 2005. See the section on the implementation of the IAP above.

References

Abeygunawardena, P. (2004). Personal Communication to Himanshu Thakkar of SANDRP, March 31, 2004.

Carter, M. (2004). Personal Communication to Dana Clark of the International Accountability Project, March 11, 2004.

Center for International Environmental Law. (2004). *Matrix of World Bank Operational Principles, Draft.*

Comprehensive Options Assessment of Dams and Their Alternatives. (2003). Geneva: Dams and Development Project.

Dharmadhikary, S. (2005). Unraveling Bhakra. Manthan Adhyayan Kendra.

Dianik Bhaskar. (2003, January 8).

———. (2002, December 13).

Hydropower and Dams. (2003, June).

International Rivers Network. (2005a). *NGO Concerns on the Use of National Safeguard Systems in World Bank Projects.* Berkeley, CA: International Rivers Network.

———. (2005b). *NGO Comments on the Use of Country Systems in Bank Operations.* Berkeley, California: International Rivers Network.

———. (2003). *Gambling with People's Lives.* Berkeley, California: Environmental Defense, Friends of the Earth, International Rivers Network.

Lim, E. R. (2001). Plenary Address. *Conference on Distribution Reforms.*

Manthan Adhyayan Kendra. (2002). *Jabgaon - Displacement without Rehabilitation.*

McCully, P. (2001). *Silenced Rivers: The Ecology and Politics of Large Dams.* New York: Zed Books.

Palmieri, A. (2004). Personal communication to Peter Bosshard, IRN.

Pitman, G. T. K. (2002). *India: World Bank Assistance for Water Resources Management.* Washington, DC: World Bank.

Prasad, Y. (2002, January 1). The Future of Hydropower is Bright. *Indian Express.*

Rioja, F. K. (1999). Filling Potholes: Macroeconomic Effects of Maintenance vs. New Investments in Public Infrastructure.

Sardar Sarovar: The Report of the Independent Commission. (1992).

Sklar, L., and McCully, P. (1994). *Damming the Rivers: The World Bank's Lending for Large Dams.* Berkeley, California: International Rivers Network.

The Economist. (2003, July 19). Damming Evidence. *The Economist,* 7.

Uku, R. (2004). Personal communication to Peter Bosshard, IRN.

Wade, R. H. (2001). The US Role in the Malaise at the World Bank: Get up, Gulliver!

Water Supply and Sanitation Collaborative Council. (2004). Press Release.

World Bank. (2004a). *Country Assistance Strategy of the World Bank Group for India: Public Consultation Draft.* Washington, DC: World Bank.

———. (2004b). *Enhancing World Bank Support to Middle Income Countries.* Washington, DC: World Bank.

———. (2004c). *Infrastructure Action Plan Update: Part II.* Washington, DC: World Bank.

———. (2004d). *Issues in Using Country Systems in Bank Operations.* Washington, DC: World Bank.

———. (2004e). *Matrix of World Bank Operational Principles.* Washington, DC: World Bank.

———. (2004f). *Public and Private Sector Roles in the Supply of Electricity Services: Operational Guidance to the World Bank Group Staff.* Washington, DC: World Bank.

———. (2004g). *South Asia Region Responses to Directors Questions and Comments on Informal Board Briefing*. Washington, DC: World Bank.

———. (2004h). *Use of Country Systems - Operationalizing the Approach*. Washington, DC: World Bank.

———. (2004i). *World Bank Group Briefing to the Executive Directors: Scaling up Our Support to Meet the MDGs, South Asia Region: Background Documentation, Informal Board Discussion*. Washington, DC: World Bank.

———. (2003a). *Infrastructure Action Plan*. Washington, DC: World Bank.

———. (2003b). *Operational Guide for World Bank Group Staff: Public and Private Sector Roles in Water Supply and Sanitation*. Washington, DC: World Bank.

———. (2003c). *Operations Policy and Country Services: Streamlined Processing for Qualifying Investment Projects*. Washington, DC: World Bank.

———. (2003d). *Power for Development: A Review of the World Bank Group's Experience with Private Participation in the Electricity Sector*. Washington, DC: World Bank.

———. (2003e). *Stakeholder Involvement in Options Assessment: Promoting Dialogue in Meeting Water and Energy Needs: A Sourcebook*. Washington, DC: World Bank.

———. (2003f). *Water Resources Sector Strategy: Strategic Directions for World Bank Engagement*. Washington, DC: World Bank.

———. (2002a). *India: The Challenges of Development: Overview of Sectoral Assistance Evaluations: An OED Country Assistance Evaluation*. Washington, DC: World Bank.

———. (2002b). *Operational Guide for World Bank Group Staff: Public and Private Sector Roles in Water Supply and Sanitation*. Washington, DC: World Bank.

———. (2002c). *Promoting Environmental Sustainability in Development*. Washington, DC: World Bank.

———. (2001a). *Cost of Doing Business: Fiduciary and Safeguard Policies and Compliance*. Washington, DC: World Bank.

———. (1999). *Meeting India's Energy Needs (1978 - 1999): A Country Sector Review*. Washington, DC: World Bank.

———. (1997). *Quality Assurance Group: Portfolio Improvement Program - Draft Internal Report*. Washington, DC: World Bank.

World Commission on Dams. (2001). *Dams and Development*. Washington, DC: Earthscan Publications Ltd. Available online at http://www.dams.org.

Zhang, S. (2003). *Memorandum to OVPS*.

Energy and Environment

8

Can Geosequestration Save
the Coal Industry?

Mark Diesendorf

Introduction

There is archaeological evidence that coal was used in the Bronze Age, 3,000 to 4,000 years ago, in ancient China and in Roman Britain. But over the millennia, while human and animal labor and wood burning were the principal energy sources, coal played a minor role. In the pre-industrial age, reflected in the novels of Thomas Hardy and the paintings of the Old Masters, energy supply was local and distributed over land and waterways.

The growth of coal mining and use was driven by the growth of technology. Steam powered machines were introduced around 1770, commercial revolving wheel cutters in 1868 and the longwall cutter, originally driven by compressed air, in 1891. Bulldozers, mechanical shovels and eventually giant dredges, for open-cut coalmining, were introduced in the twentieth century, when coal became the principal fuel for electricity generation. The use of large coal-fired power stations, rated at 1,000 megawatts or more and located in coal-mining areas, has shaped a centralized electricity grid based on high-voltage transmission lines that transport high-grade energy from mine to city.

Associated with coal's large contributions to energy supply and the economy, are very large impacts on the natural environment, health and society. The coal industry also wields great political power. It is perceived to have a strong influence on the policies and processes of many governments, international organizations and local communities.

This chapter reviews briefly the environmental, health and social impacts of the coal industry and its political power. It then examines critically the potential role of a new technology offering the possibility of entrenching coal for the next several centuries allowed by coal reserves. If successful, the technology would do this by reducing coal's biggest impact, its major contri-

221

bution to global climate change resulting from the emission of the greenhouse gas, carbon dioxide (CO_2), when coal is combusted. The technology involves the capture of CO_2 and its injection into geological formations deep underground, where it would be sequestered from the atmosphere for thousands of years. This is called 'geosequestration' or 'CO_2 capture and storage' (CCS). Our critical examination asks:

- What are the environmental, health and social impacts of geosequestration?
- What is it likely to cost?
- When could it feasibly make a large contribution to electricity generation?
- What is its role in diverting resources away from existing technologies for the efficient use of energy and renewable sources of energy?
- Is the prospect of geosequestration drawing attention away from ongoing programs to build many more conventional, dirty, coal-fired power stations.

In this chapter Australia, the world's largest coal exporter and the fourth largest coal producer, is treated as a case study.

Coal Production and Consumption

In 2002 total global production of coal of all types amounted to 4.78 billion tons with energy content of 102×10^{18} joules. Coal consumption, which was approximately the same as production, was responsible for the emission of 9.1 billion tons of carbon dioxide (CO_2), the principal greenhouse gas (U.S. EIA, 2004).

Globally the main coal producers in 2002 were China, U.S., India, Australia, Russia, South Africa, Germany, and Poland, in that order (see table 8.1). The biggest coal exporter was Australia. These are the countries where we expect the coal industry to be the most politically powerful. This is certainly the case for Australia, as will be discussed below.

Coal is the leading source of electricity generation in both OECD and non-OECD countries. Table 8.2 shows the high dependence upon coal for electricity generation in several countries. Coal is also combusted directly in the smelting of aluminium and other metals, and in steel and cement works. In cities in several developing countries, coal is still widely used as a fuel for residential heating.

Impacts of Coal Use

Coal is one of the most damaging sources of environmental pollutants used by humankind. Every stage of coal use—from mining, to washing, to transportation, to burning and to disposing of the wastes—brings substantial environmental and health damage, and social impacts:

Table 8.1

The World's Largest Coal Producing and Consuming Countries, 2002

Country	Coal production (million tons)	Coal consumption (million tons)
China	1430	1060
U.S.	996	818
India	358	247
Australia	344	98
Russia	236	No data (former U.S.S.R. 612)
South Africa	223	130
Germany	210	371
Poland	162	136

Source: U.S. EIA (2004), Tables 25 and 14. We have converted the EIA data from short tons to tons.

Table 8.2

Percentage of Electricity Generated from Coal in Selected Countries

Country	Year	Percent of electricity from coal	Trend since 1990
Poland	2000	96	steady at saturation
South Africa	2000	92	steady
Australia	2000	78	steady
P.R. China	1999	75	small increase
India	1999	75	increase
Czech Republic	2000	73	steady
Germany	2000	53	fallen slightly
U.S.	2000	52	steady
Denmark	2000	47	fallen greatly as use of gas & wind increase
Korea	2000	42	big increase
U.K.	2001	37	fallen rapidly since 1986

Sources: International Energy Agency reports; U.S. EIA (2004).

- Greenhouse gases are emitted from combustion and mining.
- Air is polluted from combustion, mining and transportation.
- Water is diverted from drinking, agricultural and ecological uses.
- Water is polluted from mining, coal washing and combustion.
- Land is degraded from mining, pollution from combustion, and the disposal of solid wastes.
- Coalmining is still one of the most dangerous occupations, even in industrialized countries.
- Coalmining and coal-fired electricity foster centralized energy production and use, thus supporting a system that is vulnerable to disruption from natural causes, electrical instabilities and sabotage.
- The industry is losing jobs rapidly and, in particular, local jobs in regional centers and rural areas.

In the early 1990s the coal industry's public relations arm coined the phrase "clean coal," creating the false impression in the public mind that existing sources of coal and coal-burning technologies produce little pollution. When challenged, the coal industry in Australia explained that "clean coal" was used to describe Australian coals because they are low in sulfur and hence, lower in air pollution than coals burned in several other parts of the world. In the late 1990s the term "clean coal" was extended to hypothetical coal-burning processes in which carbon dioxide is captured and buried, glossing over the situation that this may take several decades to implement on a commercial scale, (see below). "Clean coal" lobbies tend to ignore all except the first two impacts listed in the previous paragraph.

Greenhouse Gas Emissions

Carbon dioxide emissions from various types of power station and fuel are shown in figure 8.1. Coal is the highest CO_2 emitter per unit of electricity sent out. Of the various types of coal, brown coal, or lignite, is the worst in this respect. Black coal power stations, with ordinary boilers burning pulverized fuel, emit about 1000 tons CO_2/MWh sent out, while those with supercritical boilers emit about 800 tons CO_2/MWh sent out. The power stations with geosequestration are all hypothetical.

Air Pollution

Over the past two centuries, many communities in coalmining and coal burning regions have suffered from extreme air pollution. The infamous London smogs of the nineteenth and twentieth centuries killed many thousands of people until domestic coal burning was banned in the 1950s. Similar zones of great danger existed in eastern Europe until some years after the fall of communism in the 1980s. Beijing was one of the most polluted cities in the world until it was awarded the 2008 Olympics; then coal burning was banned inside the third-ring road and within two years citizens were saying, in wonder, they could see the stars at night. But several other regions of China, India and other Third World countries are still shrouded in the poisonous veils produced by extracting and burning coal.

Even in highly developed countries, such as the U.S. and Australia, coal burning is still a big emitter of sulfur dioxide, nitrogen oxides, fluoride, hydrochloric acid, boron, particulate matter, mercury, and sulfuric acid. Nitrogen oxides or NOx are toxic to humans and other animals, are one of the main contributors to the production of ozone and, hence, smog, and are an important source of acid rain. Sulfur dioxide is toxic to humans and other animals and is an important source of acid rain.[1] This is a web-based gateway to internationally peer reviewed information on chemicals commonly used

Figure 8.1

CO_2 Emissions from Various Power Stations with Various Fuels

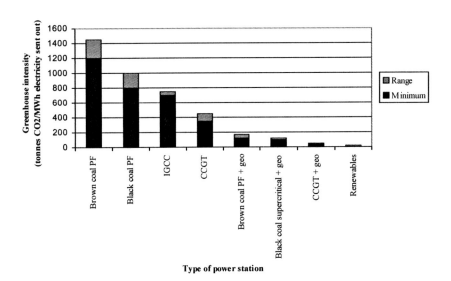

Sources: This author's results. Emissions from some specific Australian power stations were either obtained directly from annual or environmental reports of electricity generation utilities or, in cases where coal consumption data are published, by calculation using CO_2 emission factors of Australian fuels and point-source energy content of fuel (Australian Government, 2004c, Table 1). Emissions from hypothetical power stations with geosequestration from Freund and Davison (2002) and other published desktop studies assuming capture of 80-90 percent of CO_2 emissions.

Notes:

"PF" denotes "pulverized fuel," the standard type of coal-fired power station.

"IGCC" is "Integrated Gasification Combined Cycle," a new type of coal-fired power station that is not currently competitive with PF types;

"CCGT" denotes "Combined Cycle Gas Turbine," the most efficient existing type of base-load gas-fired power station.

"Geo" denotes "geosequestration."

"Renewables" in this figure comprise wind power and certain types of bioenergy. Renewable energy has been assigned nominal CO_2 emissions under assumption that energy use for manufacturing power plant comes from predominantly fossil fuels.

throughout the world, which may also occur as contaminants in the environment and food. Coal-fired power stations also emit low-level ionizing radiation, which is potential cause of small numbers of cancers, genetic defects and possibly heart disease each year (UNSCEAR, 2000).

Water Pollution and Water Take

The production, transportation, washing, storage and burning of coal can have significant effects on surface and underground water bodies.

In particular, coal washery waste discharge, amounting to tens of millions of tons per year, pollutes water as well as the area of land used for storage in tailings dams. A little of this waste, which is about 40 percent coal, is beginning to be used as a fuel source, (e.g., Redbank power station in the Hunter Valley of Australia), but this is hardly a solution to a massive problem.

Some large coal-fired power stations take tens of millions of tons per year of fresh water from rivers and lakes for cooling purposes. This competes with drinking and agricultural uses and ecological flow requirements of rivers. It is technically possible, and in some cases economically feasible, to design any new coal-fired power stations to be either air-cooled, like one of Queensland's newest power stations, Millmerran, or, in the case of coastal power stations, cooled with sea water.

Discharging warm cooling water from power stations into rivers and lakes lifts the ambient water temperature and so is a hazard to ecosystems as well.

Land Degradation and Impacts on Biodiversity

Contrary to the notion that 'out of sight is out of mind', modern underground coalmining is collapsing the land surface, opening up large cracks in streambeds, and draining rock pools and wetlands. Creeks and rivers that were once pristine and supported healthy ecosystems, are now dry, dead zones. Underground mining is also releasing pollution in the form of methane gas to the surface and cracking key water supply structures (Colong Foundation for Wilderness, 2004).

Open-cut coalmining takes even larger areas of land. The land area used per kilowatt-hour of electricity generated is much larger than that used by wind power or rooftop solar photovoltaics or bioenergy based on agricultural crop residues rather than dedicated energy crops. If open-cut mining takes place in land that was previously pasture or open woodland, it is possible to restore it after mining has been completed to something superficially resembling a pasture or open woodland. In practice land rehabilitation costs money, and some coalmining corporations are failing to fulfill their contracts by undertaking the necessary rehabilitation. In Queensland, Australia, the situation was exposed by a whistleblower, Jim Leggate, who revealed that his

State Government Department, charged with the regulation of the mining industry, had adopted a policy of non-enforcement of those regulations (Whistleblowers Australia, 2005). The result was a potential taxpayer bill, now about $2 billion, to avoid environmental harm that mining companies were being allowed to impose on Queenslanders.

Open-cut coalmines also may release vast quantities of dust, some of which comprises fine particles. Although this is normally controlled to some extent by water sprays, it is still an environmental and health problem. In the mid-1990s epidemiological research (see, e.g., Pope et. al., 1995) revealed that the health hazards of inhaling fine particles may be much greater than previously thought and that there may be no safe threshold. Particles of more than 10 micrometers (millionth of a meter) in diameter are mostly stopped in the nose and throat and appear less harmful. Between 2.5 and 10 micrometer, the particles penetrate into the bronchi and bronchioles of the lungs and are regarded as more harmful. Particles smaller than 2.5 micrometer (known as PM2.5 or fine particles) penetrate so deeply into the lungs that they reach the alveoli and so could be even more dangerous. Many national pollution inventories report on PM10 (particles up to 10 micrometer in diameter), but very few report on PM2.5.

The adverse health effects of fine particles include:

- Toxic effects by absorption of the dust into the blood (eg from lead, cadmium, zinc);
- Allergic or hypersensitivity effects (eg from some woods, flour grains, chemicals);
- Bacterial and fungal infections (from live organisms);
- Fibrosis (eg from asbestos, quartz);
- Cancer (eg from asbestos, chromates);
- Irritation of mucous membranes (eg from acids and alkalis);
- Long-term deleterious effect on lung function causing marginally increased death rates and sickness in sensitive people.

Local communities in coal-burning regions are becoming increasingly concerned about fly ash, which is both toxic and carcinogenic, containing fine particles, heavy metals, arsenic, fluoride, boron, molybdenum and low-level radioactivity. Current practice is to dump it in unlined landfills, such as depleted open-cut coalmines, instead of ensuring the prevention of leaching and wind-blown escapes. Fly ash is sometimes used in concrete, but since it is radioactive, it may be a low-level health hazard when the concrete is used for homes and offices.

Occupational Health and Safety

Despite the advances of modern technology, underground coalmining is still one of the most dangerous and unhealthy of all occupations. Coalminers are at high risk of suffering from several different types of respiratory disease, from explosions and fires caused by methane gas, from collapse of underground tunnels, and from poisonous fumes and noise.

In Australia. a study by the National Occupational Health and Safety Commission (1998) found that from 1989 to 1992 the mining industry had the third highest rate of traumatic deaths, after the forestry and fishing industries. The mining death rate was thirty-six deaths per 100,000 people per year, which was seven times that of all industries taken together. The box below offers an abridged extract from a description of one tragic event:

Prosecutions Over Australian Mine Disaster Fail to Address Underlying Safety Issues

By Terry Cook
26 April 2000

Two years after a judicial inquiry into the deaths of four miners at the Gretley coalmine, the government in the Australian state of New South Wales has begun prosecuting the mine operator Newcastle Wallsend Coal Company, its parent company Oakbridge Pty Ltd and several of its managerial staff.

The four men -John Hunter, 36, Edward Batterham, 48, Mark Kaiser, 29, and Damon Murray, 19- were killed on November 14, 1996, when the mining machine they were operating cut into an adjacent disused mine shaft that was filled with water. They had no way of escaping the powerful inrush of water and were drowned....

Even if found guilty, the [managers] only face fines and the loss of their mining licenses. The company could also be fined. The government has not brought criminal charges despite evidence at the previous inquiry showing that a series of company decisions had severely compromised safety in the mine and led directly to the disaster which claimed the four lives.

Justice James ... Staunton was compelled to admit that there was evidence of "widespread and serious shortcomings at every level of management of the Newcastle Coal Company...."

Source: http://www.wsws.org/sections/category/workers/au-mines.shtml

---

In China, where Dickensian conditions are still prevalent, tens of thousands of coalminers are killed in "accidents" every year.

Assessing the Public Health Impact

The public health impacts of coal burning depend on the concentrations, daily doses, periods of exposure, and environmental and lifestyle factors such as smoking, alcohol consumption and exercise. Not every individual reacts in the same way to hazardous chemical and physical agents. Even a few heavy smokers and drinkers live to a ripe old age; however, statistically, their chances are much worse than those of non-smokers and moderate drinkers. It must be recognized that there is generally insufficient data on the effects of low levels of exposure received over long periods of time. Rigorous epidemiological studies are few and far between. It is the rare acute cases of illness and environmental disaster that tend to be reported in the medical literature and the media.

Nevertheless, in recent years there has been progress in the analysis of the health impacts and *external* costs (costs of environmental and health damage not taken into account in the market prices) of energy supply in the U.S. and EU. These costs are based on the full fuel cycles (e.g., from the mining of coal through to the disposal of fly ash from a coal-fired power station). The calculations use Life Cycle Assessment and trace the main pathways of the pollutants from the points of emission to the various receptors (people, soils, crops, forests, buildings, etc.). The most comprehensive set of studies to date is the ExterneE project carried out in the late 1990s on behalf of the European Commission (ExternE, 1998; Rabl and Spadaro, 2000). There is of course much uncertainty in such calculations and the 1998 ExternE studies can be considered to be very cautious and conservative, because:

- They focus on the impacts of the well-known air pollutants, oxides of nitrogen and sulfur, to which they add the impacts of fine particles and aerosols which became pollutants of concern in the mid-1990s. They omit health hazards that they cannot quantify, such as those of heavy metals, volatile organic compounds (VOCs), fluoride, land degradation and waste management.[2]
- They consider only the impacts of the most modern combined-cycle power stations, with flue gas desulfurization (i.e. collection of SO_2 emissions from smokestacks) electrostatic precipitators, (to collect dust from smokestacks), and low NO_x emissions. They point out that, for many existing power stations, the emissions of NO_2 and SO_2 can be several times higher.
- They calculate the monetary value of deaths from air pollution by multiplying the reduction of life expectancy by the monetary value of life per year. Most earlier studies obtained much higher values by multiplying the number of deaths by the monetary value of a statistical life.
- The results are calculated for an average population density of 80 persons/ km^2 and should be rescaled according to average population of the region of interest.

With these assumptions, ExternE's calculated external costs of new European fossil-fuelled power stations, as reviewed by Rabl and Spadaro (2000), are shown in figure 8.2. The range of typical retail electricity prices in Europe is 4 to 8 Euro cents/kWh and so including the calculated external cost in the price of coal electricity could double or even triple the current retail price.

Figure 8.2
Typical Damage Costs of New Baseload Coal and Gas-Fired Power Stations Assuming Average European Conditions.

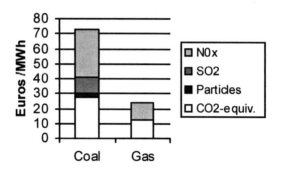

Source: Rabl and Spadaro (2000).

Note: These external costs are additional to the economic costs of generation. 1 Euro = 1.23 U.S.$ on 1 October 2004.

The ExterneE studies found that the external costs of wind power, photovoltaic electricity and some types of biomass energy are negligible compared with those of fossil fuels. However, some other forms of biomass energy may have impacts up to about half those of natural gas.

Scale, Centralization and Job Creation

Throughout the twentieth century coal-fired electricity has driven an increasing centralization of the electricity grid, with economies-of-scale driving the construction of ever-larger power stations at coalfields, the largest rated at several thousand megawatts. From these power stations, electricity is transported via high-voltage transmission lines to cities and large industrial electricity consumers. Such a centralized network is very vulnerable to disruption resulting from natural causes (storms, lightning, wildfires, floods) as well as instabilities in the transmission system and sabotage.

The construction of modern coalmining equipment and major components of power stations, such as 660 MW turbogenerators, has also become highly centralized. With the rise of automation, there have been substantial job losses in both coalmining and electricity generation in several industrialised countries (Dunn, 1999):

> Worldwide, only about 10 million coal mining jobs remain, making up one-third of all mining jobs and accounting for one-third of 1 percent of the global workforce. In industrial nations, the coal mining industry is no longer a major employer, and employment is falling even where production or exports are rising.

As a specific example, in Australia employment in coalmining has decreased by 45 percent since its peak in the mid-1980s, although the quantity of coal mined has increased substantially. Employment in electricity generation has fallen by 50 percent since the early 1990s, although the quantity of electricity generated has increased substantially (Diesendorf, 2004a).

In contrast, the lowest cost renewable energy power stations, powered by wind and biomass, are typically rated at 1 to 200 MW and require a much more distributed grid network. The scale of these renewable energy technologies means that in some cases they can be financed locally and that many components can be manufactured locally. Thus there is more local control over the technologies, more local employment creation and more benefits flow to the regions where they are manufactured and installed. For instance, wind farms currently being built in Australia have an Australian content (in dollar terms) of about 50 percent and this is expected to increase to about 80 percent if the Mandatory Renewable Energy Target is increased. With this level of local content wind power creates four to six times the number of local jobs per MWh generated compared with coal electricity, which has an Australian content (in dollar terms) of about 26 percent (MacGill, Watt and Passey, 2002; Diesendorf, 2004a).

Some economists argue that coal electricity has fewer jobs because it is more economically efficient and this is the reason why coal-fired electricity is cheaper than wind power. However, even if wind power becomes much more economically efficient over the next ten to twenty years, to that the extent that the number of *global* jobs in wind power per MWh declines to that of coal electricity, the point is that the smaller scale of wind power entails that small economies, such as those of Denmark and Australia, will always gain more *local* employment per MWh from wind power. Furthermore, the low price of coal electricity is in large measure due to the fact that it does not include the environmental and health costs that it imposes. If these are taken into account, they can lift the price of coal electricity to a level far above that of wind power and bioelectricity, as has been suggested above.

Political Influence of the Coal Industry

One measure of the political power of the coal industry is the magnitude of subsidies it receives. De Moor (2001) has estimated that the global energy sector receives over $240 billion per annum in subsidies to fossil fuels. Of this, coal receives $53 billion per annum. This estimate includes coal's share in the subsidies for electricity generation in OECD countries but not in non-OECD countries. In Western Europe and Japan, Anderson (1995) has estimated that subsidies to coal production in 1991 to 1992 were equivalent to providing a domestic producer price that is more than three times the import price in Belgium, Germany and Japan, two times in Spain and 40 percent higher in France and the U.K. Furthermore, assistance per coalminer was about $90,000 per year in Belgium and West Germany, $38,000 per year in U.K. and over $100,000 in France (expressed in U.S. 1990s dollars). In the U.S., Senate Energy Bills S.597 and S.14 provided coal subsidies in the fiscal year 2003 of $4.8 billion, comprising $2.2 billion for tax breaks and $2.8 billion for direct subsidies. This does not include R and D funding which is also measured in billions.

Why does such a large and wealthy industry receive such large subsidies? The literature on subsidies and extortionary trade policies commences with the premise that governments behave in ways to maximize their chances of remaining in office. They can deliver large and concentrated benefits to well organized groups and impose costs on other less organized groups in a dispersed way, so that each loser loses only a little (Anderson, 1995). The coal industry and its allies can afford to make large political donations and to foster links with publishers and journalists gaining them extensive, positive, media coverage. The community at-large is often unaware of the magnitude of the subsidies. Coalmining unions are often found to be in alliance with management on issues not involving occupational health and safety. In coalmining regions, this alliance can be translated into strong political influence at both State/Provincial and Federal Government levels.

In Australia coal is so cheap to mine that producer subsidies are less important than subsidies to large consumers, such as aluminium smelting (Riedy and Diesendorf, 2003). Instead of receiving producer subsidies, the coal industry is given a dominant role in the formulation of national energy policy. For instance, in June 2004 the Australian Government (2004a) released its Energy White Paper, that supported a big investment in geosequestration and little for renewable energy. At the launch of the White Paper, the Industry Minister set the context:

> The coal industry produces 80 per cent of our energy and the reality is that Australia will continue to rely on fossil fuels for the bulk of its expanding power requirements, for as long as the reserves last.

Subsequently the Australian Broadcasting Corporation's Investigative Unit obtained leaked meeting minutes, emails and memos that suggest that, behind the scenes, the fossil fuels industry influenced strongly the content of that White Paper (ABC, 2004). The ABC reported that the Industry Minister had formed a secret advisory group to assist him on the development of policy. The group of twelve companies, known as the Lower Emissions Technical Advisory Group (LETAG), comprised among others the major fossil fuel producers—Exxon Mobil, Rio Tinto, BHP Billiton—and big fossil fuel users and generators—Alcoa, Holden, Boral, Amcor, Energex, Edison Mission, and Origin Energy. They worked directly with the Government to develop the energy plan. It was something that the Government was not keen to publicize. According to notes taken by one of the executives during a LETAG meeting, the Minister stressed the need for absolute confidentiality, saying that if the renewable energy industry found out, there would be a huge outcry. The ABC also obtained the minutes of a LETAG meeting during which the General Manager of the Energy Futures branch of Federal Government's Department of the Industry stated that the government was seeking to adjust policy so that it supports and accommodates industry's direction (ABC, 2004).

In a big coal-producing country as Australia, such apparent collusion between the fossil fuel industry and government is not new. In the 1990s, I was one of the representatives of the environmental NGOs on a group convened by the Australian Government to (nominally) advise on the development of a macro-economic model of greenhouse response called MEGABARE. Our advice was ignored and the structure of the completed model and the presentation of the results of the modelling were biased so that it exaggerated the costs of reducing greenhouse gas emissions and ignored the benefits (Diesendorf, 1998). MEGABARE was used widely by the Australian Government in the international forum; for example, during negotiations on the Kyoto Protocol to support the government's position in opposition to international greenhouse abatement targets and especially the Kyoto Protocol. In particular, MEGABARE, and its successor GIGABARE, were used as a basis for special pleading by the Australian Government that, as a 'fossil fuel dependent country,' Australia's target should involve an increase in emissions.

Subsequently, it was revealed our advisory group was a sham and that there was a secret Steering Committee convened by the Australian Bureau of Agricultural and Resource Economics (ABARE) comprising mainly representatives of large fossil fuel producers and consumers, including Rio Tinto, BHP, Australian Coal Association, Australian Aluminium Council, Texaco, Mobil, and Exxon. The fee for membership of this inner group was Aus. $50,000 and ABARE did not reveal the source of the funding for its modelling in the publications of the results (Commonwealth Ombudsman, 1998). In recruiting members of the Steering Committee, ABARE explicitly stated that "the benefit to your organisation of participating in this project" includes "influencing policy debate."

There were international links. According to RJ Smith from the Competitive Enterprise Institute of Washington, DC, the head of ABARE presented the MEGABARE model at a conference in Washington, DC on July 15, 1997 that was designed to develop strategies to oppose the Kyoto Protocol (Interview with RJ Smith cited in Burton, 1997, p.1).

Nowadays the ongoing work of lobbying the Australia Government to oppose ratification of the Kyoto Protocol and any substantial actions to reduce greenhouse gas emissions is conducted *inter alia* by the Australian Industry Greenhouse Network, www.aign.net. Its membership is drawn mainly from the big greenhouse gas-emitting industries: coal, oil, motor vehicles, cement and minerals. In the U.S., AIGN has a wide range of counterparts—a sample is included in Table 3.

Table 8.3
Selected Organizations Promoting Coal and
Growth in Energy Consumption in the U.S. and Australia

Organization	Web address	Mission (from Website) & comments
U.S.		
Center for Energy and Economic Development (CEED)	www.ceednet.org/index.asp	"To foster the long-term viability of coal-based electricity generation in America"
American Coal Foundation	www.teachcoal.org/aboutus.ht ml	"To develop, produce and disseminate coal-related educational materials and programs designed for teachers and students."
Americans for Balanced Energy Choices (ABEC)	www.balancedenergy.org/abou t_abec.asp	"To promote a dialogue with community leaders across the U.S. on issues involving America's growing demand for electricity"
Coalition for Affordable and Reliable Energy (CARE)	www.careenergy.com/about/in dex.asp	(To ensure) "the availability of affordable and reliable supplies of energy for America's families and businesses"
Global Climate Coalition	www.globalclimate.org	Deactivated since it has achieved its mission to stop the U.S. from ratifying Kyoto Protocol and accepting mandatory cuts in greenhouse gas emissions.
Australia		
Australian Coal Assocation	www.australiancoal.com.au	"representing the interests of the black coal producers in New South Wales and Queensland, the states that produce 98 percent of Australia's black coal."
Australian Industry Greenhouse Network	www.aign.net	Even this is obscure: e.g., "(members) have an interest in better understanding the climate change issue; contributing to the climate change policy debate; and see value in collaborative industry action on climate change policy issues."
Australian Aluminium Council	www.aluminium.org.au	One aim is "to encourage the growth of the aluminium industry in Australia and in the use of aluminium in Australia and overseas". In practice the council is one of the principal campaigners against Australia ratifying the Kyoto Protocol. (In Australia, unlike the rest of the world, most aluminium is manufactured using coal-fired electricity.)

Based on their own websites and media reports, the methods used by these organizations include:

• lobbying politicians, public officials and decision-makers in business;
• media campaigns; dissemination of other information and educational materials;
• commissioning computer modelling of greenhouse response;
• conference presentations;
• organization of conferences, workshops, seminars and public meetings;
• funding of scientific research, "think tanks" and public opinion "surveys";
• creation and ongoing funding of "NGOs."

Outcomes of the political influence of the coal industry, together with its allies among the other fossil fuel and coal-based aluminium industries, in both U.S. and Australia, have been substantial. As of 1 October 2004, the U.S. and Australia are the only two Annex 1 countries (apart from Monaco and Liechtenstein) to refuse to ratify the Kyoto Protocol. Energy policy, backed up with very large amounts of government funding, is targeted at geosequestration in both countries, with minimal funding for efficient energy use and renewable energy. The U.S. FutureGEN project has allocated $1 billion to build a pilot coal-fired power station of 275 MW with separation and geosequestration of at least 90 percent of the CO_2 produced. In Australia there are three Cooperative Research Centres for fossil fuels, one of which is devoted to geosequestration, but none for renewable energy.

So, despite the environmental, health and social problems of coal use outlined above, the coal industry is enjoying strong support from energy sector lobbyists, public officials and politicians, especially in the U.S. and Australia. An important technical element in this support is the possibility that the separation and geosequestration of CO_2 may become a commercial reality in the future. Therefore, the next section of this chapter reviews the technology, impacts, costs and development timescale of this technology.

Geosequestration

Science and Technology of Geosequestration

For several years the oil and gas industry has been investigating the potential of geosequestration to reduce CO_2 emissions in many natural gas fields where CO_2 occurs naturally mixed with methane, the main constituent of natural gas. Several scenarios for future energy systems, with much lower rates of CO_2 emissions than existing energy supply mixes, assign an important role to natural gas as a transitional fuel to a sustainable energy future based primarily upon renewable energy sources used efficiently (e.g., Saddler, Diesendorf and Denniss, 2004, for Australia; Torrie, Parfett and Steenhof,

2002, for Canada). Natural gas is a much cleaner fuel than coal, in terms of greenhouse gas emissions, air and water pollution, land degradation, and occupational health and safety. But the emission of CO_2 from some gas fields offsets a significant part of the greenhouse benefit of burning the natural gas extracted from those fields, compared with coal. So, we recognize that geosequestration may be essential at some natural gas fields.

Fortunately, it is generally simpler and cheaper to implement geosequestration at natural gas fields than at coal-fired power stations. The latter case involves either converting coal to a gas before combustion and then extracting the CO_2, or capturing the CO_2 from the stream of combustion gases in the smokestack of a conventional power station that burns pulverized coal. Then the CO_2 must be compressed, requiring much energy, piped from the point of production to the geosequestration site, and then injected into a suitable geological formation at least 800 meters deep underground. The capture of CO_2 is the most complex and difficult step. On the other hand, it is the security of the final geosequestration step that is most uncertain and risky over the long term.

Capturing CO_2 from *existing* power stations requires the use of expensive equipment and large quantities of energy, thus reducing overall power station efficiency. For these reasons, retrofitting existing power stations to capture CO_2 is not considered by the industry and research communities to be the lowest cost route to geosequestration. A very large research effort is, therefore, being committed to new coal utilization technologies that would reduce the cost and complexity of capturing CO_2. Technologies that could be applied directly to electricity generation include integrated gasification combined cycle (IGCC) and oxy-fuel combustion. The production of hydrogen or liquid fuels from coal could also be associated with CO_2 capture. IGCC is, perhaps, the most advanced of these but it is still much more expensive than conventional (pulverized fuel) coal-fired generation and requires further technical improvements.

In general, the main barriers to large-scale application of geosequestration are the immaturity of the technology, the energy penalty, the costs of capture, and the currently unquantified risks of the escape of CO_2 from underground stores. Reducing those risks to a very low level may entail substantial costs.

In Australia a technology road-mapping exercise set 2014 to 2015 as the earliest possible date for operation of the first pilot-scale coal-fired electricity generation project with geosequestration in the Southern Hemisphere. Given the size and complexity of the technology development task required, this may be optimistic. With larger financial resources, the U.S. $1 billion FutureGEN project is likely to be the global first.

For future commercial operation, much scientific and engineering research is still required on the long-term containment of CO_2, the consequences of breaching of containment and the reduction of costs of the capture and burial of CO_2. This means that a wide range of disciplines and specific areas of expert knowledge are required, such as ecology, chemistry, geology, physical geography, various branches of engineering, risk analysis and economics. It is suggested that research topics include:

- Conditions favoring natural containment of CO_2 and breaches of natural stores;
- How to assess suitability of potential stores for injected CO_2;
- Leakage pathways from underground stores to the surface;
- Risk of large releases from all types of underground stores;
- Mechanisms of storage and release of CO_2 in saline aquifers and deep coal seams. In particular, conditions under which CO_2 forms stable solids in these stores;
- Methods of monitoring containment in all types of underground stores.
- Impacts of CO_2 on fresh water and shallow sea ecosystems and soil and subsoil micro-organisms;
- For geosequestration under the ocean bed, research on seamount ecosystems: species, ecosystems structure and function.

Environmental, Health and Social Impacts of Geosequestration

There is quite a large body of experience in transporting gases in pipelines or large tankers and storing them underground. CO_2 is easier to handle than methane, the major constituent of natural gas, because CO_2 does not burn or explode. The main dangers of geosequestration (summarized in Table 4) would result from escapes of large volumes from underground stores. For economic reasons, stores are likely to be quite large and so the possibility of large escapes is a real concern. Presumably, stores where CO_2 becomes bound underground as limestone or other minerals would have negligible risk of large releases. But such stores may be hard to find. The majority of stores, where CO_2 would be stored as a liquid under pressure, are likely to be much less secure.

Since oil and gas fields are quite well understood, proponents of geosequestration argue that large escapes from these stores will be rare, provided sensible procedures are established. For example, if a store was previously a gas well, the CO_2 pressure in the store would have to be constrained to remain below the previous gas pressure in the store. However, just because oil and gas (and the CO_2 that is often found associated with them) have been contained for millions of years, it cannot be assumed that reinjected CO_2 will be securely contained. This will depend upon whether the integrity of the store has been damaged by the large number of wells drilled into it and by structural changes in the walls of the store resulting from the extraction of oil or gas.

Table 8.4
Summary of Potential Environmental and Health Impacts of Geosequestration

Risk	Impact
Escape of CO_2 into the atmosphere	Contribution to global climate change via greenhouse effect. Asphyxiation of humans & animals in low-lying areas
Escape of CO_2 into waterways	Acidification of waterways and impacts on biodiversity
Escape of CO_2 into soils	Damage to soil ecosystems
Escape of CO_2 from under sea-bed	Damage to seamount ecosystems
Pushing brine from saline aquifers to the surface	Contamination of drinking water; dryland salinity of soil

A sufficiently large release of CO_2 from a store into the atmosphere would increase the anthropogenic greenhouse effect and, hence, increase global climate change. Furthermore, since CO_2 is heavier than air, the sudden emergence of a large volume of CO_2 at a point on the Earth's surface could result in low-lying areas near the breach filling with CO_2 and people becoming asphyxiated. A natural example occurred at Lake Nyos in Cameroon in 1986, when the volcanic crater lake suddenly emitted very large quantities of CO_2. An invisible cloud, estimated at 50 m thick, poured over the rim of the crater, filled the valleys below to a range of 25 km, and killed 1,700 people and thousands of cattle.

On a smaller scale, this kind of event could occur more commonly as a result of breaching of an above-ground or near-surface store or a pipeline. Both slow leaks and sudden escapes resulting from (say) earth tremors or sabotage could be a problem. The siting and protection of above-ground and near-surface CO_2 stores and pipelines would be a key factor in minimizing the occurrence such events. As always, developers will be tempted to cut corners in order to reduce costs. In practice, industry in general—and the energy industry in particular—has tended to locate hazardous installations near low-income and minority communities.

Because scientific knowledge of CO_2 storage in saline aquifers and deep coalmines is quite rudimentary at present, a premature rush into their use could be much more risky than using oil and gas wells. The only large trial conducted to date in the U.S., of pumping CO_2 down into deep coal deposits for the purpose of Enhanced Coal Bed Methane Recovery (ECBMR), caused swelling of the coal matrix (Wildenborg and Van der Meer, 2002). This could result in cracks developing in the coal and surrounding rock and hence the release both CO_2 and coal-bed methane into the atmosphere.

Even before CO_2 reaches the atmosphere, sudden escapes and slow leakage could impact on ground water, surface waterways, soils, subsoil and biodiversity. In water, CO_2 dissolves partially to form carbonic acid and the resulting decrease in pH could have a wide range of adverse impacts on living organisms. Impacts on soil microbes and soil ecosystems in general could be profound. Even less well understood are subsoil microbial systems and their possible responses to CO_2 (Johnston and Santillo, 2002).

The breaching of CO_2 reservoirs under the seabed could impact strongly on seamount ecosystems. Previously it was thought that the ocean bed was low in biodiversity. But, recently, seamounts rising 1000 meters or more above the ocean bottom have begun to be studied. They are rich in biodiversity, containing many species new to science, highly productive, and highly vulnerable to disturbance (Johnston and Santillo, 2002). Storage in international territory under the seabed is, presumably, restricted by the London Convention.

Theoretically it may be possible with detailed investigation of potential stores, well-designed technologies, management systems, laws and policing of those laws, the risks of severe adverse environmental and health hazards of geosequestration could be reduced to very low levels. Then, the principal hazards remaining would be those of coalmining and the non-greenhouse impacts of coal burning. However, safety may come at a high economic cost.

Cost of Geosequestration

Figure 8.3 shows the current costs of avoiding emission of a ton of CO_2 from an existing best-practice pulverized fuel coal-fired power station, and by using several existing commercial technologies (efficient energy use, Combined Cycle Gas Turbine, [CCGT], biomass and wind) and by using two different types of hypothetical coal-fired power stations with geosequestration. The black bars give minimum values and the gray bars give the approximate range of uncertainty.

In practice, costs of both fossil and renewable power vary significantly between countries and between regions of countries and so figure 8.3 can only be considered to be a rough guide. More precise costs, including those of transmission, must be calculated for particular regions. For the existing technologies in figure 8.3, cost estimates come from Saddler, Diesendorf, and Denniss (2004) for Australia, with 1 AUD = 0.7 x 1 U.S.D. For existing technologies, the uncertainty range reflects mainly the range of scales and sites. For instance, a 100 MW wind farm at an excellent site could generate electricity at U.S. $35 to 40/MWh (U.S. 3.5-4.0 c/kWh). However, a 20 MW wind farm at a medium wind site may generate at U.S. $50/MWh (U.S. 5 c/kWh). The minimum bioelectricity costs come from landfill gas and biomass residues, while the maximum come from dedicated energy crops without other economically viable products (e.g., activated charcoal, eucalyptus oil) At the time of writing, there are large differences between countries and regions in the costs of generating electricity from natural gas and coal. The CCGT values in figure 8.3 reflect Australian natural gas prices in September 2004 that

Fig. 8.3
Typical Costs of Avoiding Emission of a Tonne of CO_2

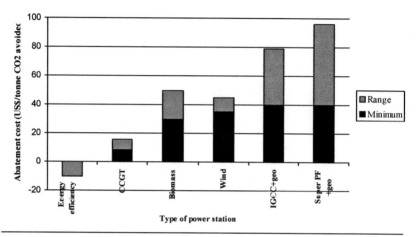

Sources: See text.

Note: It is assumed the avoided CO_2 emission is from a new conventional, pulverised fuel, black coal power station without geosequestration. This power station has a greenhouse intensity of 80 kg CO_2/MWh electricity sent out and a generation cost of U.S. $25/MWh. The abatement costs shown in Fig. 3 are *additional* to the cost of the conventional coal power station. 'Geo' denotes geosequestration. 'Super PF' denotes a conventional pulverized fuel coal-fired power station with a supercritical boiler.

were far below those in the U.S. at the same time. For efficient energy use, we assume that costs vary between negative and zero, depending upon the degree of implementation.

For the two hypothetical coal-fired power stations with geosequestration in figure 8.3, one is an Integrated Gasification Combined Cycle (IGCC) power station and the other is a new supercritical pulverized fuel power station. Since there is no commercial geosequestration, the large uncertainty bands represent genuine uncertainty in costs rather than variation resulting from scale or site. At the present level of uncertainty, it is unclear which of the two geosequestration options shown here will be cheaper. IGCC is currently the option most favored by geosequestration researchers. Its power station is expected to be more expensive than the supercritical pulverized fuel power station, but its cost of separating CO_2 is expected to be less. It is assumed that CO_2 is transported only 100 km by pipeline from production point to store. Cost estimates are taken from Freund and Davison (2002) supplemented with other international sources. For geosequestration in oil fields that are almost exhausted, there may be some economic value in injecting CO_2 for enhanced oil recovery that would offset at least part of the costs.

Figure 8.3 represents *actual* costs for the existing technologies (efficient energy use, CCGT, biomass and wind) and *current estimates* of future costs for the two coal technologies with geosequestration. All these costs can be expected to decline over the next two decades. However, the costs of renewable energy technologies have been declining steadily over the past two decades and this trend is expected to continue as the scale of production continues to increase and improvements, already achieved in R and D, are commercialized. For instance, projections by both a government-owned corporation (Short and Dickson, 2003) and industry (Mallon and Reardon, 2004) researchers suggest that wind power at excellent sites may be competitive with conventional coal-fired electricity in eastern Australia costing about U.S. $25/MWh by 2020. On the other hand, coal-fired electricity with geosequestration is likely to cost *at least* U.S. $40/MWh, above that of conventional coal-fired electricity and even the $40/MWh minimum level shown in figure 8.3 is unlikely to be achieved by 2020.

What Could Geosequestration Achieve and When?

Geosequestration offers the possibility of capturing and storing 80 to 90 percent of CO_2 emitted from new coal-fired power stations in the long term. However, it would not reduce significantly any of the other environmental, health or social impacts of coal-fired electricity—namely air and water pollution, high water use, land degradation, occupation health and safety hazards, vulnerability to disruption and job losses from automation.

Geosequestration would take several decades to make a significant reduction in CO_2 emissions. Saddler, Riedy and Passey (2004) have developed a spreadsheet model to estimate the potential for geosequestration to reduce emissions from coal-fired electricity generation in Australia. The model assumes that geosequestration is technically feasible, capable of long-term storage, environmentally safe and commercially viable. Demonstration power stations are assumed to be built between 2016 and 2020, with "commercial viability" (whatever that means) being achieved in 2020. Geosequestration is applied only to new plant, in States where large underground storage sites are known to exist, and modeling is extended out to 2030. The remainder of this section quotes directly the results from the executive summary of Saddler, Riedy and Passey (2004), with some shortening, and with references and parentheses added:

> It was found that use of CCS (CO_2 capture and storage) alone would reduce emissions by about 9 % percent in 2030, and cumulative emissions from 2005 to 2030 by only 2.4%. percent. A scenario with modestly increased energy efficiency, corresponding to the efficiency potential assumed in the Australian Energy White Paper (Australian Government, 2004a), could reduce emissions in 2030 by about the same amount, and cumulative emissions by twice as much. This would be achieved at zero or even negative cost.

If gas-fired generation and renewable energy were built instead of new coal-fired generation, to achieve the same cumulative abatement, by 2030, as CCS, would require only a doubling of the current very modest MRET (Mandatory Renewable Energy Target, currently only 9500 GWh/year) target, and double that of additional gas-fired generation.

Scenarios that include more extensive energy efficiency improvements, though still well within identified technical potential, combined with use of gas-fired generation and renewables instead of new coal-fired plant, could reduce emissions in 2030 by more than five times as much as CCS alone, and cumulative emissions by ten times as much.

The key to these results is that end-use efficiency, gas-fired generation, wind power and some types of bioenergy are currently commercially available, and so do not have to wait until 2020. While it is possible CCS may be an effective abatement option after 2030, use of currently available technologies will reduce emissions much sooner and at lower cost, and make any abatement task for CCS easier.

In practice, in countries that have placed strong emphasis on geosequestration in their energy policies, plans for new, conventional, dirty, coal-fired power stations are proceeding apace. In the U.S. about 100 such power stations are in various stages of development. Assuming that seventy-two of these projects survive public opposition, the U.S. would emit an additional 209 to 275 million tons of CO_2 per year from coal by 2012 (Clayton, 2004). This corresponds to an increase of 9 to 12 percent in the U.S. 2002 CO_2-equivalent emissions from electricity generation (U.S. EPA, 2004). In four out of Australia's six states, there are proposals for a total of three new conventional black coal-fired power stations and one major refurbishment of a very old and dirty brown coal station (Diesendorf 2005 a,b,c; 2004b) amounting to an additional 32 million tons per year of CO_2 emissions by 2010. This corresponds to a 17.6 percent increase in the Australian 2002 CO_2 emissions from electricity generation (Australian Government, 2004b).

This situation suggests that the possibility of large-scale geosequestration, three or more decades in the future, is being used to deflect attention away from the current reality of business-as-usual. Thus, geosequestration is less about sustainable development and more about sustaining the coal industry by greening its image.

Conclusion

The coal industry has strong political influence and has built up a network of supporting organizations that lobby government and other decision-makers, gain extensive positive media coverage, disseminate information in schools, obtain grants and subsidies, perform R and D, and present a high profile at professional and other conferences. With its substantial human and financial resources, the coal industry is promoting geosequestration as a means of ensuring that future electricity generation systems will still be highly dependent upon coal.

Geosequestration of CO_2 emissions from coal-fired power stations could possibly begin to make a significant contribution to greenhouse gas abatement after 2030. But, even then, it cannot reduce any of the other environmental and health impacts of coal use: air and water pollution, large water use, land degradation, biodiversity loss and occupational health and safety hazards. Furthermore, geosequestration introduces new environmental and health hazards. If the coal industry is successful in establishing large-scale geosequestration, people will continue to suffer these impacts and the citizens of countries with high coal use may be forced to pay very large subsidies for geosequestration, either through the taxation system or through high electricity prices.

Geosequestration may never become economically competitive with a mix of efficient energy use, natural gas and lower-cost renewable energy sources such wind power and bioenergy from crop residues. Despite that situation, the *possibility* of geosequestration in the future is being used to divert funding away from cleaner technologies that are more cost effective now, notably efficient energy use and renewable energy, and to deflect attention away from current proposals to build many more conventional dirty coal-fired power stations.

Between now and 2030 (Saddler, Riedy and Passey, 2004) and possibly by 2050 (Saddler, Diesendorf and Denniss, 2004), much greater reductions in CO_2 emissions from electricity generation could be achieved in Australia more cheaply from a combination of efficient energy use, solar hot water, natural gas, wind power and bioenergy based on crop residues. In Canada, which currently generates only about 15 percent of its electricity from coal, an 86 percent reduction on CO_2-equivalent greenhouse gas emissions from electricity generation could be achieved by 2030, using existing technologies (Torrie, Parfett, and Steenhof, 2002: 109-110).

Efficient energy use, in particular, offers a myriad of technologies that can reduce energy wastage and emissions at no net cost and with very low environmental and health impacts. Wind and bioenergy require a more distributed energy supply system than the current highly centralized system based on large coal-fired power stations and, in some countries, nuclear power stations. In the age of terrorism, a distributed system is more secure and resilient than a centralized system. Distributed energy systems also create much more local employment than centralized systems.

While there are future potential roles for geosequestration, especially for reducing CO_2 emissions at gas fields, it is unwise for governments to allocate to geosequestration the major part of their funding for future energy supply and demand management systems. Efficient energy use and several renewable energy technologies could make large contributions in the short and medium term (by 2020). Indeed, it has been argued that the additional costs of renewable energy sources could be funded from the savings from efficient energy use, so that the transition to a sustainable energy future could possibly be made at no net cost (Saddler, Diesendorf and Denniss, 2004; Torrie, Parfett and Steenhof, 2002). Current proposals for new or refurbished conventional coal-fired power stations in Australia could be cost-effectively replaced with a mix of efficient energy use, renewable energy and natural gas stations by 2010 (Diesendorf, 2005a,b,c; 2004b).

Some government action and up-front funding is required to facilitate the transition process under current circumstances where the environmental and health costs of burning fossil fuels have not been internalized in prices. It is unfortunate that the two industrialized countries that are refusing to ratify the Kyoto Protocol, the U.S. and Australia, are directing very large resources into geosequestration while doing very little to reduce their greenhouse gas emissions. The U.S. has the world's highest total emissions and Australia has the world's highest per capita emissions. The U.S. Government and Congress have already delayed extension of the production tax credit for wind power for all of 2004, thus undermining the U.S. wind power industry. The Australian Government has refused to expand the tiny Mandatory Renewable Energy Target (MRET) which gives a subsidy of a small fraction of 1 c/kWh to accredited renewable energy sources.

The pathway to a sustainable energy future must involve such initial stimuli and more: either a carbon levy or tradeable emission permits with cap and trade. This would be an economically rational means of allocating resources between coal with geosequestration on one hand, and efficient energy use with renewable energy and natural gas on the other hand.

Notes

1. For details of the hazards of chemicals in the environment, see the IPCS INCHEM website, http://www.inchem.org (accessed 15 December 2005).
2. Impacts of ozone are included in those of nitrogen dioxide. The impacts of mercury and lead have not yet been quantified.

References

ABC. (2004, September 7). Story broadcast on Australian Broadcasting Corporation national radio. Available at http://www.abc.net.au/pm/content/2004/s1194166.htm.

Anderson, K. (1995). The political economy of coal subsidies in Europe. *Energy Policy*, 23, 485-496.

Australia: National Occupational Health and Safety Commission. (1998). *Work-related traumatic fatalities in Australia, 1989 to 1992*. Retrieved on January 3, 2005. Available at http://www.nohsc.gov.au/Statistics/publications/#relatedfatalaties.

Australian Government. (2004a). *Securing Australia's Energy Future*. Canberra: Department of Prime Minister and Cabinet. Retrieved on January 2, 2005. Available at http://www.pmc.gov.au/publications/energy_future/index.htm.

——. (2004b). *National Greenhouse Gas Inventory 2002*, Canberra: Australian Greenhouse Office. Table 4. Retrieved on January 2, 2005. Available at http://www.greenhouse.gov.au/inventory/2002/pubs/inventory2002parta.pdf.

——. (2004c). *AGO Factors and Methods Workbook*. Canberra: Australian Greenhouse Office, Table 1. Retrieved on January 3, 2005. Available at www.greenhouse.gov.au/workbook.

Burton, B. (1997). WMC's campaign to scuttle binding targets. *Mining Monitor*, 2(4),1. Australia: Mineral Policy Institute. Retrieved October 2004. Available at www.mpi.org.au.

Clayton, M. (2004, December 23). New coal plants 'bury' Kyoto. *Christian Science Monitor*. Retrieved on January 2, 2005. Available at http://www.csmonitor.com/2004/1223/p01s04-sten.html.

Colong Foundation for Wilderness. (2004). Retrieved September 2004. Available at www.colongwilderness.org.au.

Commonwealth Ombudsman. (1998). Ombudsman releases ABARE investigation report. Media release, Canberra, 4 February.

De Moor, A. (2001). Towards a grand deal on subsidies and climate change. *Natural Resources Forum, 25*(2), 167-176.

Diesendorf, M. (2005a). Towards a clean energy future for Queensland. A report for the Clean Energy Future Group in collaboration with Queensland Conservation Council. November. Available at www.wwf.org.au/.

——. (2005b). Towards a clean energy future for Western Australia. A report for the Clean Energy Future Group in collaboration with the Conservation Council of Western Australia. Available at www.wwf.org.au/.

——. (2005c). Towards a clean energy future for New South Wales. A report for the Clean Energy Future Group. Available at www.wwf.org.au/.

——. (2004a). Comparison of Employment Potential of the Coal and Wind Power Industries. *International Journal of Environment, Workplace and Employment* 1, 82-90.

——. (2004b). Towards a clean energy future for Victoria. A report for the Clean Energy Future Group in collaboration with Environment Victoria. November. Available at www.wwf.org.au/.

——. (1998). Australian economic models of greenhouse abatement. *Environmental Science and Policy*, 1, 1-12.

Dunn, S (1999). King Coal's Weakening Grip on Power: Worldwatch Institute, September/October.

ExternE. (1998). *ExternE: Externalities of Energy. New results 1998*. Luxembourg & Belgium: European Commission, Directorate-General XII, Sci. Res. & Dev.. See also http://ExternE.jrc.es/.

Freund, P., and Davison, J. (2002). *General overview of costs*. IPCC workshop on carbon dioxide capture and storage. Regina, Canada, November. Available at www.climatepolicy.info/ipcc/index.html.

Johnston, P., and Santillo, D. (2002). *Carbon capture and sequestration: potential environmental impacts*. IPCC workshop on carbon dioxide capture and storage, Regina, Canada, November. Available at www.climatepolicy.info/ipcc/index.html.

MacGill, I., Watt, M., and Passey, R. (2002). *The economic development potential and job creation potential of renewable energy: Australian case studies*. Commissioned by Australian Cooperative Research Centre for Renewable Energy Policy Group, Australian Ecogeneration Association and Renewable Energy Generators Association.

Mallon, K., and Reardon, J. (2004). *Cost convergence of wind power and conventional generation in Australia.* Melbourne: Australian Wind Energy Association. Available at www.auswea.org.au.

Pope, C.A., Thun, M. J., Namboodri, M. M., et al. (1995). Particulate air pollution as a predictor of mortality in a prospective study of U.S. adults. *American Journal of Respiratory Critical Care Medicine*, 151, 669-674.

Rabl, A., and Spadaro, J. V. (2000). Public health impact of air pollution and implications for the energy system. *Annual Review of Energy & Environment*, 25, 601-627.

Riedy, C., and Diesendorf, M. (2003). Financial subsidies to the Australian fossil fuel industry. *Energy Policy*, 31, 125-137.

Saddler, H., Diesendorf, M., and Denniss, R. (2004). *A Clean Energy Future for Australia*, Sydney: Clean Energy Future Group. Available at www.wwf.org.au.

Saddler, H., Riedy, C., and Passey, R. (2004). *Geosequestration: What is it and how much can it contribute to a sustainable energy policy for Australia?* Discussion Paper No. 72. Canberra: Australia Institute.

Short, C., and Dickson, A. (2003). *Excluding technologies from the Mandatory Renewable Energy Target.* ABARE eReport 03.12, Canberra: AbareEconomics, June, Table 10.

Torrie, R., Parfett, R., and Steenhof, P. (2002). *Kyoto and Beyond: The low-emission path to innovation and efficiency.* Canada. Available at www.torriesmith.com.

United Nations Scientific Committee on the Effects of Atomic Radiation (UNSCEAR). (2000). *Sources and Effects of Ionizing Radiation, 1: Sources. Annex B: Exposures from natural radiation sources* (pp.109-10; 136-8). Available at http://www.unscear.org/reports/2000_1.html.

U.S. EIA. (2004). Energy Information Administration of U.S. Department of Energy. Retrieved on October 1, 2004. Available at www.eia.doe.gov/emeu/iea/coal.html.

U.S. Environmental Protection Agency. (2004). *Inventory of U.S. Greenhouse Gas Emissions and sinks: 1990-2002.* Washington, DC: Environmental Protection Agency, Table 3.6. Retrieved on January 2, 2005. Available at www.epa.gov/globalwarming/publications/emissions.

Whistleblowers Australia. (2005). Whistleblower cases of national significance and the case of Mr Jim Leggate. Available at http://www.uow.edu.au/arts/sts/bmartin/dissent/contacts/au_wba.

Wildenborg, A. F. B., and Van der Meer, L.G. H. (2002). *The use of oil, gas and coal fields as CO_2 sinks.* IPCC Workshop on carbon dioxide capture and storage, Regina, Canada, November. Retrieved on October 1, 2004. Available at www.climatepolicy.info/ipcc/index.html.

9

From Love-ins to Logos: Charting the Demise of Renewable Energy as a Social Movement

Leigh Glover

Having been a part of the general environmental movement that saw renewable energy as the promise of a new future and now seeing that future being owned by British Petroleum, General Electric, Royal Dutch Shell, and other corporate giants responsible for the devastation wrought by their promotion of fossil fuel and nuclear energy use, it is difficult to regard the emerging sustainable energy era with unbridled enthusiasm. It appears that these corporations can buy renewable energy businesses more easily than homeowners can purchase the equipment. At a time when global energy use is at its highest levels ever and forecast to continue rising (IEA, 2004; UNDP et al., 2000), environmentalists and staid international institutions alike are eagerly anticipating the solar economy (Flavin and Lenssen, 1994; Scheer, 2002; Brown, 2003; World Bank, 2004). Somewhere along the line, renewable energy went from the domain of counter culture to corporate mainstay, from communes to communication strategies, from naturalism to natural capitalism, and from love-ins to logos.

Renewable energy once offered an alternative social future, characterized as the "soft energy path." Amory Lovins' 1979 landmark text set the bar for energy sustainability and despite the furnace-load of works on renewable energy since that time, in many respects Lovins' basic case has not been surpassed.[1, 2] *Soft Energy Paths* provided a clear, thorough, and explicit account of the social values and implications associated with a renewable energy future. Compared to the conventional energy-society order, the alternative promised to be more democratic, less militarized, less hazardous, more flexible, more efficient in its uses of energy and capital, and more open to options and choices in the social sphere. As befits a work of this reputation and influence, many scholars depict *Soft Energy Paths* as the starting point of the renewable energy movement. But this work also marks the onset of the demise of renewable energy as a social movement, conveniently establishing the division between the "counter culture" movement and the arrival of the "corporate culture" project. Since then, there are precious few considerations of renewable energy as a social initiative. Today, discussion of an energy counter culture is almost completely moribund. Modestly, we seek to give the original idea of soft energy paths its due.

Searching for the Roots of the Alternative Energy Revolution

When the background of renewable energy is being considered, it is often projected as a mostly technical matter. If social influences are admitted, renewable energy is generally understood as a mainstay of environmentalism or as arising in specific response to the global oil supply crises of the 1970s. In this offhand treatment, much about the social implications of renewable energy is made amenable to rewriting.

This received wisdom is misleading, both about environmental thought and specifically about renewable energy. Western environmentalism can trace its roots to diverse places and times—from Romantic poets, eastern philosophy, the arts and crafts movement, communtarianism, and the science of ecology, to the ecological practices of indigenous peoples—all with some legitimacy.[3] But there is a tendency to mix social movements with intellectual and conceptual sources in these accounts, and no doubt this author is as guilty as anyone in this regard. However, academic accounts emphasize the intellectual, political, and organizational aspects of this history, while neglecting its social and cultural formation. Only recently, have some accounts begun to filter through, but precious few are interested in these historical dimensions of environmentalism.[4] In a cultural sense, the conservative charge that the baby boomer generation is obsessed with its own interests and claims for itself social reforms that belong to earlier times may be made to good effect. However, making the environment into an identifiable political theme is unequivocally the product of the era of the 1960s and 1970s. There was no term for 'environmentalism' prior to the 1960s because there was no broad social movement that could be identified with this interest. Before the 1960s the public debates were of the preservationist/conservationist stripe and generally applied to public land use. All sorts of important ideas and theories about the environment flourished prior to the 1960s in the developed and developing world, but they simply didn't register as particularly important in mainstream politics. That panoply of decisions about land use and management that European settlers faced in the New World and modernizers faced in the Old World, and which have largely determined today's human shaping of the world landscapes, did not involve the type of political disputation to which we have become accustomed in contemporary times. For it was in the counter culture era of social change that the diverse sources of environmentalism were mixed and came to influence mainstream political agendas, the formation of environmental interest groups, and established party politics. Indeed, what other period of the twentieth century would have ranged so widely, eclectically, and creatively in considering social alternatives?

Contemporary renewable energy technologies were researched and developed effectively beginning in that era. Much of the early experimentation with sustainable energy was outside the state and corporate spheres, conducted in personal, communal, and academic contexts. A small amount of post-war experimentation was greatly supplemented by an explosion of activity in the later 1960s. The business sector became involved in the development and manufacture of commercial products toward the latter part of this period, most notably where this involved discrete machinery or components (wind turbines, solar cells, and solar thermal heaters). Renewable energy companies were usually small and independent of conventional energy corporations and utilities. Applications of the technology were isolated, small, privately or communally owned, usually domestic or agricultural, and often "hobbyist" in character. Alternative technologies of greatest interest at the time were amenable to investigation and application with low levels of investment: PV, small wind, small hydro, and bio-digestion. On the other hand, technologies such as tidal power and geothermal energy were in the inaccessible "big science" league.

Alternative energy was effectively a subculture in this period, much of it independent of government and corporate involvement. There was widespread information on these technologies through various outlets, including magazines (for example, in the U.S., *Organic Gardening and Farming, Environment Action Bulletin,* and *Home Power*) and importantly, through the social network of the counter culture. Much individual experimentation took place and there was great innovation. As with many nascent technologies, amateur curiosity was an initial motivation, and little capital was involved. With the OPEC oil embargo of the 1970s, renewable energy garnered wider attention, and the interest of governments and the scientific establishment validated the potential of this technology as a "solution to the energy crisis." And this same decade essentially marked the end of renewable energy's first phase.

If we allow that technology has social roots (Winner, 1977, 1986; Bijker et al., 1987; McGinn, 1990), and that renewable energy expanded outside obvious corporate and state sponsorship (Butti, 1980), then what social forces and social goals shaped this technology? Renewable energy received its first widespread applications and use in the industrial economies through the followers of alternative lifestyles. Today this phrase invites derision and has been co-opted to serve a number of political interests, but at the time it meant those wanting to live outside the mainstream. Rejecting the confines of conventional life in the developed world, individuals and groups experimented with a variety of alternative social choices in living arrangements, property ownership, farming, material consumption, entertainment, drugs, marriage, education, transport, health, religion, and a plethora of other dimensions of social life. It was always loose, as social movements are want to be, and difficult to fix in any absolute sense.

So let's begin here by affirming the counter culture movement as the source of the idea that social change in the developed world could be brought about by a shift to alternative energy. Certainly, its ideas about society and nature were drawn from many places, but this social movement forged the concept that alternative energy technology could make modern society afresh.

Breaking Free

Central to the counter culture was the belief that if an individual or group wants to live outside the influence of corporate and state culture, they must separate as many dimensions of their lives from those influences as they can (Roszak, 1995). As well as the better-known rejections of capitalism, sexism, racism, nationalism, militarism and promotion of indigenous rights, racial equality, and equal opportunity, there was an understanding that separation and independence involves making active choices about technology. Partly this course departs from instrumental rationality, for the social benefits of these choices were always multifarious, interlinked, and bound into visions about a coherent social life.

What was so offensive about the conventional energy system? For a start, its ownership and control was in the hands of large corporations and states. In every way, it was of great scale and beyond the comprehension of the general public, capable of being operated only by skilled and elite technicians and employees of these large enterprises. Its interests were not primarily in the public good, but in the profit and power of its owners and controllers. Great social apparatuses were constructed to ensure the security of its facilities and capital, and these security and economic dimensions were part of national governments that were essentially militaristic. Power plants and associated energy facilities were harmful to the environment—especially dangerous in the case of nuclear power—and aesthetically offensive. Conventional energy systems were monuments to exploitative social hierarchies, unresponsive to social needs and uncaring of their environmental impacts, and were part of a rampant industrialism inimical to the human prospect. At its extreme, the counter culture rejected the conventional energy system and, importantly, everything it stood for.[5]

Alternative energy offered a means to escape the state- and corporate-managed energy systems, to tread lightly on the earth, to be independent, to be rooted in a local ecology, to link to other alternative technologies, to offer social benefits, and to be peaceful. It is worth remembering that the movement for renewable energy was driven forward by fear and loathing over the burgeoning nuclear energy industry, which was the epitome of all that the counter culture rejected (Lovins and Price, 1980).

Langdon's Winner's insight that technology is politics (1977) may now be passé, even though it remains accurate. Ownership, design, control, autonomy, and responsibility associated with any technology are not fixed by the character of the technology but reflect social settings. Just because renewable energy was envisaged as part of a program of social reform by the counter culture (although that perhaps formalizes matters excessively), does not mean that these politics are axiomatically transferred when the ownership, production, design, and control of that technology passes from individual and local hands into those of states and corporations. But it does mean that it is unlikely the technology will retain its original politics intact.

Renewable energy technologies were possessed of particular attributes that offered to deliver a different kind of society than the one plugged into the conventional energy system. Lovins suggested five foundations of the 'soft path' (1979: 38-39):

1) Renewable energy flows rather than stocks;
2) Diverse, modest, and specifically applied sources;
3) Flexible and relatively low technology;
4) Output matched in scale and distribution to end uses; and
5) Energy quality matched to end-use needs.

Central to the social goal of alternative energy technologies was that they conveyed autonomy to their users. Renewable energy held the promise of being 'off the grid,' detached from power lines, pipelines, and 'big oil.' Basically, its users would be able to understand and control their own systems, fix and maintain them using basic skills, create no pollution and impinge on no one else, live free of monthly utility bills and high energy costs, and erode support for the state- and corporate-managed energy system. Soft energy paths were to involve decentralized approaches and diverse forms of technology and energy sources. These technologies were to meet energy needs by matching their scale and aligning energy quality to the task involved. They were to be reliable and adaptable to a variety of tasks and circumstances. And because they were not part of the centralized energy system, they possessed a number of economic advantages over the fossil fuel and nuclear energy system, including much lower capital investment, minimal transmission and distribution costs, no need for reserve capacities, no risks of massive overcapacity or mistimed capacity additions, and no compulsion to organize communities to capture available economies of scale.

Critically, renewable energy sources were not meant as a substitute for conventional energy sources and were not sought as a means to meet the demands of a mass consumption lifestyle. Rather, renewable energy systems were designed to meet modest needs and small energy services. In this way, the conventional energy system and all that it entailed was to be obviated and in its place an alternative way of meeting energy needs established; sustainable energy systems were meant to wholly replace the conventional energy system, which provided nothing the counter culture needed, and for which there were clear alternatives.

In this way, renewable energy was the technical means to social ends. Renewable energy could satisfy these ends in ways that both pre-modern energy systems and the conventional energy system had failed. Although there was some interest in lessons from the past and from the developing world, the cause of renewable energy in the West was progressive, built on the advances offered by new forms of technology, or by novel applications of existing technologies to provide energy service needs. As a problem of technology and society, renewable energy may have been promulgated by the counter culture as being 'closer to the earth,' but for the most part it promised environmentalism of a modern kind. The utopian claims made for the social advantages of renewable energy were often grounded in technological positivism, anticipating social transformation from technological change. Still, the counter culture was clear that the socially beneficent technology would be built on small scale, locally managed platforms that would not attract multinational corporations, but would instead stimulate an 'eco-economy' of modest size (Brown, 2001, carries forward this idea).

Thinking Globally and Acting Universally

Some energy visionaries saw renewable technology's eventual universal adoption as evolving through small successes until everyone would be using alternative energy. It was an alternative after all, so it made sense to contemplate the complete demise of conventional energy and arrival of sustainable energy. Lovins (1979) had placed a transition zone between the hard and soft energy paths in which fossil fuels, nuclear power, and renewables might coexist. But he was confident this would not last long. Somewhere in the transition, we offer, is where the social promise for renewable energy starts to go badly wrong.

So what is the significance of the global aspirations for advocates of renewable energy? Firstly, advocates such as Lovins challenged the conventional energy system on its own terms, by finding ways to prove renewable energy was cheaper than fossil fuels and should therefore be the sensible choice for states and energy consumers. That it was safer than nuclear energy was also an argument of the day, but one that, in the post-Chernobyl era, drifted away.

Secondly, these advocates sought to make the transition as palatable as possible by suggesting that, while the results of the sustainable energy future would produce utopian expressions of individual freedom, democratic collective action, and environmental responsibility, it would seemingly not require wholesale overhaul of modernity's social institutions. Renewable energy would prompt revolutionary change, but a radical revolution, such as one that would end capitalism, wouldn't be necessary to bring it to fruition.[6] The justification for renewable energy's superior rationality advanced by Lovins and others was explicitly conservative, expressing a faith in the inherent judgment of economic and social institutions to recognize the virtues of a sustainable future, once freed from government and market failures of various types (Hawken, 1993; Hawken et al., 1999). With loss of demand and removal of the drip of state subsidy, the conventional energy system would wither and the transition to the soft energy path would result from the rationality of the dominant economic and political institutions.

Thirdly, renewables advocates wanted to use the same instruments that created the fossil fuel and nuclear energy system to promote the renewable energy system, especially state assistance for renewable energy. To their credit, these advocates usually combined the arguments for renewable energy with the causes of improved energy efficiency and energy conservation. But although such market governance had failed to protect community and ecological values in its design of the conventional energy system, it would be essential for introducing a renewables-based economy (and indeed, this has proved to be the case).

Embedded in these strategies were a number of implications.

- For renewable energy to be widely taken up without disrupting existing state and corporate power, existing utilities and fossil fuel companies would have to be the purveyors of renewable energy. States would have to oversee and manage this process. Either that, or there would have to be a proliferation of small firms willing to resist the appeal of economies of scale.
- If renewable technologies were going to be used in this way, then renewable energy had to become part of the existing system. The matter of phasing and integrating them into the existing system became an economic and technological problem of great complexity. This transition, therefore, implies a hybrid system that features the use of both conventional and renewable energy.
- State decisions would effectively become the tool for controlling the characteristics of the emerging system, principally in determining the ways and the rate at which it would support renewable energy technologies.
- Renewable technologies are given the role of an alternative fuel source within the conventional energy system and are assessed on criteria related to fuel sources. In order to fulfill their role as fuel source, renewable tech-

nologies would additionally meet requirements to efficiently integrate into the existing system.

Following David Nye (1999), we are reminded of the extent to which technological determinism has influenced our ways of considering the energy system. Surely, much of the optimism about the possibilities of a renewable energy transition was caught up in this mindset. The counter culture invested socially transformative power in the technology of renewable energy and gave less attention than it should have to the role of culture in creating, spreading, and developing technologies. Still, it was the transition thesis that created the possibility of a corporate- and state-brokered renewable energy future, not the counter culture's technological optimism.

Here Comes the Sun (Incorporated)

Into this scenario enters the political economy of conventional energy. Large fossil fuel corporations began buying renewable technology companies. Their leaders talked of a future beyond oil. Proving that life can be stranger than art, British Petroleum dubbed itself "BP – Beyond Petroleum," a move that some environmentalists found beyond perfidy.

Environmentalists divided over this development according to their ideologies. Pragmatists, for example, welcome the support that the renewables-based economy would receive from giant energy corporations, taking these developments as proof of the efficacy of the renewable energy cause (Flavin and Lenssen, 1994; Brown et al, 1991; Brown, 2004). On the other hand, skeptics have doubted that corporations will genuinely promote a renewables-based economy, and speculate that the corporate elite may even use their influence to slow its arrival (Scheer, 2002). All environmentalists accept that corporations are responding to the profit motive in their industry investments. Caution by both parties may be necessary at this stage, for although the energy giants have made considerable expenditures on renewable energy, these amounts are minor in their overall budgets and operations.[7]

More than the actual scale of corporate investment, at stake is what to make of a renewable energy future steered by corporate strategy and state policy. It is offered here that this development represents the "ecological modernization" of renewable energy.[8] While the state has dabbled in renewable technologies for quite some time, these efforts have been highly publicized *and* generally of little significance. Almost no national energy system in the developed world has managed to get beyond a couple of percent of its energy supplies or meet any significant portion of its major energy service needs from renewable sources. Yet, with the entry of large energy corporations into the field, the responsibility of the state is changed and its provider role for the interests of "capital-in-general" is evoked. Now the state will work more assiduously to provide the regulatory, policy, and political settings that will assist the development of the renewables-based economy. Doubtless the state's task of easing the way for renewable energy is made politically gentler if the conventional energy corporations also own the renewable energy enterprises.

One hallmark of ecological modernization is the cooperation between states, corporations, and arguably, NGO advocates. Some environmentalists and progressive corporations have taken to proclaiming the benefits of cooperation, and governments can often be found applauding the maturity of these decisions. Certainly, in renewable energy there has been plenty of "working together." A marriage of interests has always been likely between elements of the corporate sector and those environmentalists seeking national policy changes, because many environmental groups concentrating on national politics have mostly abandoned any prospect of widespread change through "bottom-up" civil society actions (Gottlieb, 2005). Reform of the energy sector has meant "solving the economic problem," and the solution has been to pursue economies of scale in production of renewable energy units, invest in technological improvements, and hack away at subsidies given to conventional energy or to acquire access to high subsidies for renewables. These strategies can be pursued simultaneously with civil society mobilization, but this nevertheless requires bringing the interests of the state and corporations to bear on the problem.

Technology Fine and Society Wrong?

Perhaps no cliché in contemporary renewable energy circles is more persistent and misleading than the saw that the technology problems have been solved, and the problems remain in social, political, and economic realms. This misunderstanding is responsible for an important part of the misdiagnosis about renewable energy. For a start, the formulation has it that the two dimensions of technical and social can be taken as compatible, that they can exist on common ground and concern the same world, as it were. Such an argument might have applied to the original goal for alternative energy, namely that it be part of a social goal, but that is not the case now.

Technically, the renewable energy problem that has been solved is how to meet isolated energy service needs at very modest scales, basically domestically or at the village level, without using or relying on fossil fuels. This was, if you like, the first goal of renewable energy and an array of technologies has been developed that meets this need. PV, very small wind turbines, micro hydro, solar thermal heating, biogas digesters, and passive solar design were essentially mature technologies at least two decades ago. This social solution is specifically workable for those in the counter culture willing to go "off-grid." But what about the middle-class—the dominant stratum in modern societies?

The current technology problem for renewable energy is one that focuses on the middle-class. What is that problem? Making renewable energy technology a substitute for the conventional energy system without disrupting the middle-class penchant for consumption. Optimists and promoters for renewable energy will immediately cite the rapid growth of wind energy, and describe how effectively large-scale wind turbines are being plugged in to meet the needs of baseload supply for regional electricity grids. A contrary view holds that what is being revealed more than opportunities for the technology are its limits; there are actually relatively few places with the kinds of wind characteristics suitable for large-scale units. Wind energy, the dashing prince of renewable technologies, turns out to realize an economy of scale in only a few places (often those of great scenic beauty both on- and off-shore), and has a disinclination to work everyday. Moreover, wind's arrival tends to upset some middle- (and upper-) class neighborhoods if it is thought to be obtrusive (see a special issue of the Boston College Environmental Affairs Law Review, 2004, for a review of opposition to the Cape Wind project).

For PV, the problems have been about designing systems that are indistinguishable from grid-derived electricity. Accordingly, the challenges have become not how to rig up an array of PV cells, but how to arrange the metering so the system is integrated into the existing grid and how to work out systems of accounting to capture its benefits. In this way, the applications for PV are supplemental to a grid connected user.[9] Ingenious as these solutions have been, they are essentially adaptations to make PV technologies perform in ways to meet the criteria set by grid-based electricity planners.

Scaling up renewable energy technologies to meet the demands of a conventional energy system has not been very successful for most sources. Renewable energy has its place in the conventional energy system, such as wind farms and building-integrated PV, but technologically it is a long way from meeting the primary energy needs of the developed world. When basic calculations are completed for the number of wind turbines or PV arrays needed to replace the world's coal-fired power stations, the resulting scenarios verge on nothing less than the bizarre.[10] Meeting current energy needs will necessitate the maturation of technologies, such as tidal power and various large-scale forms of solar concentrators, and the development of other technologies that are currently far from viable. And yet the renewables-based economy continues to be premised on the assumption that we have the available technology to meet global energy demands (see, e.g., Scheer, 2002).

For the technologically optimistic, the problem is social (taken to also include issues with political and economic dimensions). To reach a renewable energy future, therefore, requires a social setting in which today's residential, commercial, industrial, and transport demands for energy will be met by renewable energy sources. It is expected that renewable energy will serve as a substitute for existing energy services in every way. Renewable energy must be cheap, reliable, and safe, not polluting in ways that its consumers are likely to notice; it must be as abundant, available, and simple for consumers to use as existing energy systems.[11] Whatever is favored and desirable about fossil fuel energy systems, renewable energy must also meet, and hopefully exceed. No energy user today is expected to significantly change their patterns or levels of energy use in the new (but nevertheless modern) order.

Nearly every social, economic, and political problem diagnosed for the transition to a renewables-based future by moderns stems from this technological ideology. Firstly, there is the question of the reliability of supply (often associated with the problem of efficient energy storage). Renewable energy technologies for the most part are frequently characterized by intermittent or fluctuating levels of supply. For the counter culture's idea of renewable energy, reliability was not much of a problem as not all energy service needs are continuous or resolutely fixed in some way; most are flexible in a number of ways. But satisfying the middle-class brings forth the need to leave energy demands high and growing.

The counter culture's idea of renewable energy was for it to meet an energy service need and there can be a number of ways to meet any particular service, so that a user might have a choice of technologies that could be applied. That an energy source should be available continually in full and abundant supply may be an industrial requirement, but that is hardly the case for the smaller demands envisioned by the counter culture. Expectations that energy is always available, virtually without limit, without fluctuation, and without cessation is a system requirement of the conventional energy regime serving an insatiable middle-class thirst for energy.

Secondly, there is the thorny issue of the retail price of renewable energy. High costs for the production of energy from renewable sources seemingly reflects the immutable laws of economics, and so, renewable energy has to cross the price thresholds set by competing conventional fuel sources. A vast literature attests to the effect of supply and demand for renewable energy—most of it irrelevant to the central problems of the new economy. For renewable energy as a counter culture solution, the basis for comparison is not the cost of the energy, but the cost of the service that energy provides. But since the conventional energy system provides the criteria by which renewable energy is assessed in a middle-class society, we often don't compare the costs of energy services and energy users don't receive this information.

Even if we could carry out this comparison, it would be a concession that an economic comparison of price reflects a fair comparison of costs. Such a presumption is mostly absurd from the point of view of the counter culture. Uncounted costs of the conventional energy system include historical and current subsidies for fuel sources, environmental damage, social costs due to health threats, safety and security risks, and so on. What is considered as 'the market' for conventional energy fuels is an artifice reflecting only relatively minor and residual questions of marginal price after substantial state subsidies and historical support have worked their effect. Only from the viewpoint of the corporate- and state-managed energy system, replete with subsidy, must renewable energy beat the costs of conventional energy.

Thirdly, there are environmental protection requirements. For the counter culture's conception of renewable energy, this simply is not a major problem as none of the technologies are likely to be of great scale or involve especially toxic materials or processes. In order to meet the demands as a fuel source for the conventional system, however, renewable technologies must be large (as per the dictates of economy of scale), and must at the same time comply with environmental regulations. For example, large-scale hydropower isn't environmentally acceptable, even though it is the largest renewable energy source within the conventional energy system (McCully, 2001). In another case, one might examine the issue of the coastal locations of large wind turbines. By displacing conventional power plants and possibly nuclear facilities, wind turbines are an environmentally more desirable technology. Yet, socially and ecologically there can be objections to sources of our energy which redefine the landscape. When we make renewable energy match the needs of the conventional energy system, whatever social or ecological issues that need to be resolved for these technologies increase in scale along with the size of the units involved. That there could be environmental problems arising from the original generation of renewable energy technologies is contrary to their design imperatives, but entirely consistent with the consequences of large centralized renewables-based systems in service to modern society.

Fourthly, there is the issue of energy efficiency. Renewable energy can be highly efficient when applied directly to the energy service task as there are no distribution and transmission losses, less conversion losses from energy to task, and few reserve capacity requirements as energy is only used when needed. But when used as a fuel source in a centralized energy supply and distribution system, renewable energy is made as relatively inefficient as fossil fuels. Most of the advantages of renewable energy are lost when it fuels the conventional energy system and is built with excess capacity, transmitted with high losses, and so on. Several implications arise from this: for a start, renewable energy is hardly cheap when used inefficiently.

Renewable energy is currently in the process of being overhauled as a technology. Much of what was developed at the small scale is of no commercial use for large energy supply companies. A new generation of technologies is now being developed to serve quite different ends. Associated with the introduction of this technology is a new set of social issues. What renewable energy advocates seem to have overlooked is that the social and environmental benefits of the old technology are not necessarily characteristic of this new generation. These new technological developments have effectively closed off meaningful advances in the old technology in the developed world, so that designing technologies that people could buy and operate for their homes, farms, small factories, and commercial centers is no longer being pursued. Renewable energy technology is held in a cycle of perpetual disadvantage, whereby every successive advance to make it fit better into the conventional energy system creates a further set of obstacles that erode its original advantages over fossil fuels.

Why We Can't Get There From Here

Some might argue that the current energy order is actually a combination of corporate, state, and societal demands representing a practical (and effective) compromise. Contemporary conditions, in this way of thinking, would represent the precursor to a soft energy future—a kind of "third way" of energy politics, resolving the right wing (hard path) and left wing (soft path) orthodoxies through sensible compromise.[12] But this is a misleading formulation that papers over essential problems that the trend toward a "hard path renewable energy system" cannot resolve.

For a number of reasons, today's trends should not be taken as constituting a trajectory that will conclude in the achievement of a sustainable energy era. Firstly, the coming corporatist version of a soft energy future is premised on the view that renewable energy must meet all conventional energy needs—only better in nearly every way—and that we have the technology to do this. There is real doubt as to whether renewable energy technologies can meet existing and future energy needs of a corporate-led, middle-class-focused economy (which presumably include the commitment to economic growth). Total energy demand levels are high and efficiency is generally low in the developed world, and, in these circumstances, renewable energy cannot replace fossil fuels. Only by permanently curbing demand and greatly improving efficiency can there be any hope of a genuine renewables-based economy. The growth in size and efficiency of wind turbines, for example, will matter little if the overall growth in energy demand continues. Clearly then, the prospects for a soft energy future are tied to the prospects for a steady-state economy (or for those that don't follow Herman Daly,[13] an economy that can develop without increasing its material demands and waste products). Part of the problem here is that the corporate energy system is designed to promote growth and that renewable energy has been conscripted into this cause.

Second, the closer renewable technologies come to meeting this need of a substitute fuel source, the more they will replicate the problems of conventional energy. This paradox is an uncomfortable reality for environmentalists, but what are we going to say when someone proposes a mile-high wind turbine? There's a bind here in that meeting current energy needs under the conventional paradigm using renewable energy means big installations and plenty of them, and this just can't occur without significant social and environmental costs. Decisions over trading off large hydroelectric schemes for large coal-fired power stations might not offer a clear environmental choice, but these are the types of prospects looming in a corporate energy system that seeks to expand its renewables base. It is unclear, then, whether the new energy order will have the full support of mainstream environmentalists.

Third is the issue of the falling social barriers, particularly that of cost (or more precisely, retail price). Of course, if there were any reasonable accounting for the costs of conventional energy, then all sorts of options for renewable energy would already be widespread. Our prediction is that cost will prove to be a chimera and that lower prices for renewable energy will not result in its widespread adoption. Price is just one of many factors that have to be addressed in making renewable energy an acceptable fuel source for the corporate energy system; and in isolation, it will not prove decisive. In the history of the energy system, politics explains a great deal and price tends to reflect political decisions and circumstance, not vice versa. Thus growth in wind energy is often associated with its falling retail price, but governmental promotion of renewable energy created the market and made investment in wind energy secure, leading to economies of scale that have subsequently reduced the price. Using price to explain the condition of the energy system is simply "economism," with its absurd assumption of "perfect markets." Conventional wisdom holds that renewable energy has to compete with the costs of fossil fuels and nuclear energy, while it is offered here that costs merely reflect political decisions, so that when there is widespread political support for renewable energy, then it will be of an acceptable price (because politics, to put it crudely, decide what costs are counted). High costs of renewable energy serve as a rationale that, in turn, evokes a passive economy that serves to disguise an active set of political decisions.

I Can See for Miles and Miles

Hermann Scheer, Amory Lovins, and other pundits of a soft energy future, joined as they are by such august bodies of official energy wisdom as the IEA, are riding the wave of the ever-popular and optimistic field of future studies. Slightly off-putting is that the drumbeat for the forthcoming renewable energy revolution has been continuous since the 1970s oil crises, appearing in virtually every alternative energy journal every year in some form. As such, much of the talk of the forthcoming energy paradigm shift is propagandist and self-serving.

This apparent continuity in the faith of soft energy advocates held over these decades masks a basic discontinuity in the very character of that much portended future. How far renewable energy now seems from its roots in the counter culture and how little remembered this heritage has become. By consigning the counter culture to oblivion and wiping history clean of its imprint of an energy transformation carrying forward a program of social reform, these origins have been cast aside with other populist condemnations of the counter culture as hedonistic, utopian, and socialist.[14] Renewable energy today presents itself as the epitome of respectability, tied closely to professional cadres of technicians, scientists, and engineers, promoted by everyone from government agencies to business councils, and funded by shareholders and government grants. In effect, renewable energy has gone mainstream in every sense, transformed from a radical agenda to a conformist condition.

Having abandoned its romantic William Morris-esque stance, renewable energy's self-image is now that of high modernism, of the sleek white blades of wind turbines and the cool azure circuitry of the PV cell. Renewable energy has become the sort of high-technology modernism proposed by R. Buckminster Fuller (1971) and others within the "operating manual for space-ship earth" school of environmental managerialism[15] that in retrospect seems to share much with contemporary "ecological modernization." A contemporary generation could be forgiven for assuming that renewable energy was another benevolent product of those socially conscious corporations whose logos now adorn the "green" energy machinery of our time.

In that collection of generalizations about renewable energy as a social solution were concerns about: an increasing interdependency in society, its growing complexity and the need for greater social management, its vulnerability to failures, the need for increased security of centralized systems, rising social and economic risks of these big systems, the alienation of people from decisions that shape their lives, and the inefficiency and precariousness of large systems. Oddly, while the smaller and easier environmental concerns have tended to be swept up in state-sponsored ecological modernization, the social concerns of these nascent energy system critics withered. A possible exception to this generalization is the decline of nuclear energy in the developed world; despite an enormous effort by state powers to arrest decline, the industry barely made it out of the 1970s. This decline, however, was hardly motivated by the wider social implications of the industry; rather, the technology proved to be too dangerous and its energy outputs too expensive despite the staggering levels of public sector subsidy and vigorous efforts to convince the public of the industry's safety.[16]

That the use of renewable energy is increasing should not blind us to the fact that we are no closer to an alternative energy future than when the concept was promulgated almost three decades ago. Because the prospect of a vibrant and expanding nuclear energy industry was so appalling to environmentalists that the dilapidated condition of this completely state-subsidized industry has thrown the character of the fossil fuel component of the conventional energy system into lighter relief. And perhaps because some radical parts of the counter culture became transfused into wider social practice it is reasonable to consider that society took from these reformers those lessons that were most amenable and practical, and left the rest behind. Or it might be that vested interests allowed a degree of social and economic reforms in order to subvert more fundamental disruptions to political and economic elites (Byrne and Rich, 1983). And it may be that the transformation to an alternative energy system was a vision only suited to those who considered a revolution necessary.

Many explanations are possible, but one cannot escape the rude fact that no major changes to the conventional energy system occurred through these years of challenge. Deregulation? Privatization? System benefits charges? Renewable portfolio standards? These changes are minor, even inconsequential, administrative measures that the interests of the corporate energy system have accommodated. So far, reformers have managed to eke out such small concessions for renewable energy, and little else.

Before leaving this argument, the reader should not be under the impression that the political economy of corporate energy has exerted an iron grip over the attitudes, choices, and collective behavior of western society. Somewhere into this argument, and there is insufficient space here, we need to place renewable energy into the types of social change that have occurred, including changes to the broader economy and to lifestyles. On this count we risk technological determinism, but it is unavoidable. Corporate-managed, middle-class-based, consumer societies employ technologies to provide an array of services within the home, workplace, and in institutions. Modernization is more than the technologization of life, it also shapes social life toward the private, the insular, and the individual consumptive act. Yet this insularity for keeping comfortable, for earning a living, for entertainment, education, and whatever else, is often mistaken for independence. Such pseudo-independence is consumptive in nature, and the means for its production is outside the realm of consumption. Consumers in modern society, by definition, don't create the products and services they consume—they buy them.

A major misunderstanding about the contemporary effort to usher in sustainable energy systems lies in a failure to understand the basic interstices of corporatism, middle-class life, and consumerism. The middle-class has no interest in production and certainly does not equate the virtues of independence with being free to provide their own goods and services in energy or any other commodity. For the counter culture, the test of independence was whether the energy service is 'off the grid.' But the consumer-residents of corporate-managed societies are embedded in grids of an immense variety and complexity as necessary conditions of having access to mass consumption goods and services, of which electricity is but one. In this case, the growth of private consumption is made possible through the growth in the corporate economy, and the middle-class obliges by celebrating the greater opportunities to consume.

The Alternative Energy Logo

Here, then, is where renewable energy as a social solution has been doomed; renewable energy can be a productive technology that provides a service, but who in corporate-managed society wants independence in production? Almost no one in the developed world, it appears. To consider that there is a place for independent production of energy is completely counter to the mass consumption impulse of modernity. Provision of services by third parties, usually corporations and contractors, is the efficient (and profitable) preference of the contemporary order. Are we seriously considering that families who have service contracts for their water heaters and appliances, who have garages to service their cars, who use thermostats to control household temperatures, who use televisions and VCRs for entertainment, who operate computers and telephones in order to communicate with people and read items of interest, want to operate their own energy systems?

Crossing the divide of fossil fuel energy requires using the bridge of energy conservation and reduced consumption to reach a genuinely renewable energy-based society on the other side. Such a transition means tackling contemporary society's preference for abundance over sufficiency, for waste over frugality, for replacement over repair, and for frivolity over utility. Because a transformative renewable energy future cannot be premised on normal economic activity, the viability of the strategy rests on converting some of the core attributes of society. To date, the advocates of renewable energy have tended to look past this sociological condition and argue their case entirely on technological, economic, and ecological virtues.

In contrast, the renewable energy proposal seems essentially premised on consumer sovereignty when the dominant consumer preference is for mass consumption. Advocacy of a soft energy future embedded in current society seems to take the economic rationality of the individual consumer as the motive force for change, when attention should have been directed at collective scales of transformation.

So what is the current prospect for renewable energy on the broad scale for industrialized economies?

- Renewable energy systems will likely be owned by oligopolies (state and private) that control the world's fossil fuel, electric, and nuclear energy systems.

- Renewable energy, in its logo-friendly format, will be made compatible with the corporatist, neo-liberal ideology of the developed world and will become part of the process of economic globalization.
- Renewable energy will become part of the centralized system of energy production and distribution in which energy users' choices will be those dictated by consumer sovereignty; i.e., they will be completely dependent on the corporate-organized and -defined market for 'green energy' and the like.
- Renewable energy technologies will aspire to technological sophistication and will soon be understood and serviceable only by experts and managed by professionals.

Today, I cannot readily buy or order renewable energy systems suitable for my home. They are not offered for sale in the building supply superstores and my local builder doesn't know anything about them. After thirty years of advocacy, renewable energy is still a niche product. Yet what will be the transforming effect if, in the not too distant future, such systems are easily ordered (perhaps from the Internet)? Is anything more to be expected from the corporate vision of soft energy?

All through the landscape of modernity are textbook examples of urban sprawl, yet of this multitude of new housing estates, few homes, if any, exhibit a solar orientation or passive solar design or evidence of other renewable energy applications. Wherever the renewables-based economy is meant to be happening, there is not sign of it, except in utility-scale wind farms, industrial agriculture's development of biofuels, and giant office blocks ornamented with PV. Something has gone terribly wrong with the vision for a soft energy future. We passed the crossroads to a socially progressive alternative energy future some while ago. It was a small thoroughfare, poorly signposted, with an uncertain destination, and we were in a hurry at the time. We are at the point where renewable energy's future looms and we can still remember where that alternative pathway was, but few, it seems, are interested in looking back. It is almost laughable that some of us believed that alternative energy could usher in a convivial society, the conserver society, or the alternative society (Illich, 1980; Henderson, 1988).

Our soft energy future now shows every sign of being big, corporate-managed, state-subsidized, high technology-based, with modest amounts of renewable energy mixed with plenty of fossil fuel use. As befits the mass consumption mentality, citizens will neither own, control, understand, nor maintain the technology that produces this energy. They will not be considered responsible for its ecological effects, nor are they likely to reduce energy consumption or greatly increase the efficiency of its use; but they will be able to buy the logo of "green energy" from the same corporate governors who have traditionally managed energy affairs on their behalf. And who, in modern life, could want for anything else?

Notes

1. Discussion of the forthcoming renewables-based economy focuses on non-transport energy, and that of the hydrogen-solar economy includes transport. Advocates for hydrogen applications and integration of this technology into the solar economy represent perhaps the most obvious expression of the argument being advanced here, but with a critical difference: while there are available renewable technologies to satisfy one version of a sustainable energy future, the transport sector has never enjoyed widely-accepted technological alternatives to the fossil fuel-burning internal combustion engine. For this reason, our discussion is confined to energy use that for the large part does not concern transportation.

2. Although Lovins' account remains the best-known, many other contemporaneous reports and publications argued that the decline of the oil era was in sight (see, e.g., Stobaugh and Yergin's (1979) *Energy Future* for the Harvard Business School).

3. A number of excellent studies on these sources might be consulted (see, e.g., Dobson, 1990; Dryzek et al., 2003; Glacken, 1976; Ponting, 1993; O'Neil, 1993; and Pepper, 1996). Largely missing from these is the counter culture as a source of theory or practice. While philosophies and ideologies are easily amenable to representation and study, social movements and cultural phenomena are not. Unfortunately, environmental ideas have become fixed in family trees of ideology and derivation and divorced from their social context and the social movements that gave them meaning. This is not to say that the character of the counter culture didn't contribute to this problem, as it was so diverse and eclectic in its environmental views—to the extent that it may only be the amalgam of its views that is distinctive, rather than the creation of anything original.

4. Exceptions are Taylor (1995) and Gottleib (1997, 2005) on environmental movements.

5. Lovins' (1979: 148) original list of conventional energy's ill effects is a good representation of this rejection, albeit of a more somber and responsible cast, including among the conventional energy system's key problems its strong central control, bypassing of traditional market mechanisms, encouragement of suburbanization, distorted political structures and social priorities, increased bureaucratization and alienation, compromised professional ethics, reinforcement of national and international wealth inequity, militarization of civilian life, increased social and economic risks, eroded federalism, and elitist technological orientation that diminishes democracy.

6. Barry Commoner's (1977) *Poverty of Power: Energy and the Economic Crisis* certainly identifies capitalism and the profit motive as major causes of the U.S. crises in energy, economic performance, and environmental damage in the 1970s, and concludes by advocating the investigation of more central planning in energy, seemingly along the lines of some Western European nations. This, however, was about as far as Commoner ventured into the social realm and the work had surprisingly little content on renewable energy technologies.

7. Dunn and Flavin (2002: 41) report that "BP's $100-million annual investment in clean energy equals only about 1 percent of the company's overall expenditures of $12.5 billion."

8. After Hajer (1995), ecological modernization describes state activity to reconcile industrial economic functions with the protection of ecological values, and is exemplified by such initiatives as environmental protection laws and agencies.

9. Off-grid applications are often cited as a major opportunity for PV, which is a perfectly reasonable claim, but one that overlooks the fact that the overwhelming majority of PV-supplied electricity services provided to date are met within grids.
10. In 2002, the US consumed 3,858 TWh of electricity (IEA 2004). For the sake of argument assuming a solar array output of 1 MW over 10,000 square meters (with 12% module efficiency and service corridors of 1,700 square meters per MW) and that 1 MWp in U.S. on average produces around 1,600 MWh per year, some 24,000 square kilometers—an area the size of New Hampshire—would be required for 2,411 TWp PV. For wind, 200,000 square kilometers—an area the size of South Dakota or Nebraska—would be required, assuming 1 MW wind turbines with annual output of 3,416 MWh per turbine and with an area of 0.18 sq km per 1 MW wind (5.5 MW per sq. km). In the case of wind, North Dakota could supply U.S. electricity needs, but only if a massive transmission and distribution system covered the state. And then, the wind energy system would aggregate conversion losses greater than the existing system, a dubious indicator of progress.
11. Byrne and Rich (1983) long ago noted this basic conundrum in the modernist idea of a renewable energy future.
12. Apologies to Anthony Giddens (1998) *The Third Way: The Renewal of Social Democracy.*
13. Daly's case (1973, 1996) for the 'steady state economy' is well known in environmental politics and environmental economics.
14. Indeed, within the ranks of conservative pundits, this activity has seemingly kept many in gainful employment sheeting home all manner of social ills, from drug abuse to single motherhood, to a social movement whose members who never controlled any major corporate, educational, or government entity, major political party, or other major social institution.
15. For a while, 'spaceship earth' was a popular metaphor, used famously by Kenneth Boulding (1966), but also by Paul Ehrlich (1968), Barbara Ward (1968), and others. Fuller's own words in expressing the ethos of this approach cannot be improved upon (1971:120): "While no politician or political system can ever afford to yield understandably and enthusiastically to their adversaries and opposers, all politicians can and will yield enthusiastically to the computer's safe flight-controlling capabilities in bringing all of humanity in for a happy landing. So, planners, architects, and engineers, take the initiative. Go to work ...."
16. Perhaps the most obvious example is the U.S. nuclear power industry's reliance on the federal Price-Anderson Act that limits the public liability of nuclear plants in the case of an accident. Without this public subsidy to shoulder the potential costs of an accident above the nominal cap set by the Act, the industry simply couldn't afford insurance. In effect, the state acknowledges that the costs of an accident could exceed the value of the nuclear industry. For a fulsome discussion of these issues see Byrne and Hoffman (1996).

References

Bijker, W., Hughes, T., and Pinch, T. (Eds.). (1987). *The Social Construction of Technological Systems: New Directions in the Sociology and History of Technology.* Cambridge, MA: MIT Press.
Boston College Environmental Affairs Law Review, 31(2). (2004).
Boulding, K. (1966). The Economics of the Coming Spaceship Earth. In H. E. Jarrett (Ed.), *Environmental Quality in a Growing Economy.* Washington, DC: Resources for the Future.

Brown, L. (2004). *Europe Leading World into Age of Wind Energy*. Retrieved October 10, 2005. Available at www.earth-policy.org/Updates/Update37.htm.

Brown, L. (2003). *Plan B: Rescuing a Planet Under Stress and a Civilization in Trouble*. New York: W. W. Norton and Company.

Brown, L. (2001). *Eco-Economy: Building an Economy for the Earth*. New York: W. W. Norton and Company.

Brown, L., Flavin, C., and Postel, S. (1991). *Saving the Planet: How to Shape an Environmentally Substainable Global Economy*. New York: W. W. Norton and Company.

Butti, K. (1980). *A Golden Thread: 2500 Years of Solar Architecture and Technology*. New York: Van Nostrand Reinhold.

Byrne, J., and Hoffman, S. (Eds.). (1996). *Governing the Atom: The Politics of Risk*. New Brunswick, NJ and London: Transaction Publishers.

Byrne, J., and Rich, D. (1983). The Solar Energy Transition as a Problem of Political Economy. In D. Rich, J. M. Vogel, A. M. Barnett, and J. Byrne (Eds.), *The Solar Energy Transition: Implementations and Policy Implications—American Academy for the Advancement of Science Selected Symposium 74*. Boulder, CO: Westview.

Commoner, B. (1977). *The Poverty of Power: Energy and the Economic Crisis*. New York: Bantam Books.

Daly, H. E. (1996). *Beyond Growth: The Economics of Sustainable Development*. Boston, MA: Beacon Press.

Daly, H. E. (1973). *Toward a Steady-State Economy*. San Francisco, CA: W. H. Freeman.

Dobson, A. (1990). *Green Political Thought*. London: Unwin Hyman.

Dryzek, J. S., Downes D., Hunold, C., Schlosberg, D., and Hernes, H.-K. (2003). *Green States and Social Movements: Environmentalism in the United States, United Kingdom, Germany & Norway*. Oxford: Oxford University Press.

Dunn, S., and Flavin, C. (2002). Moving the climate agenda forward. In L. Starke (Ed.), *State of the World 2002: A Worldwatch Institute Report on Progress Toward a Sustainable Society*. New York, London: W. W. Norton. Pp. 24-50.

Ehrlich, P. (1968). *The Population Bomb*. Cutchogue, NY: Buccaneer Books.

Flavin, C. and Lenssen, N. (1994). *Power Surge: Guide to the Coming Energy Revolution*. New York: W. W. Norton and Company.

Fuller, R. B. (1971). *Operating Manual for Spaceship Earth*. New York, NY: Pocket Books.

Giddens, A. (1998). *The Third Way: The Renewal of Social Democracy*. Cambridge: Polity Press.

Glacken, C. (1976). *Traces on the Rhodian Shore: Nature and Culture in Western Thought from Ancient Times to the End of the Eighteenth Century*. Berkeley: University of California Press.

Gottlieb, R. (2005). *Forcing the Spring: The Transformation of the American Environmental Movement*. Washington, DC: Island Press.

Gottlieb, R. (Ed.) (1997). *The Ecological Community*. New York: Routledge.

Hajer, M. A. (1995). *The Politics of Environmental Discourse: Ecological Modernization and the Policy Process*. Oxford: Oxford University Press.

Hawken, P. (1993). *The Ecology of Commerce: A Declaration of Sustainability*. New York: Harper Business.

Hawken, P., A. Lovins, and L. H. Lovins (1999). *Natural Capitalism: Creating the NextIndustrial Revolution*. Boston: Little, Brown and Company.

Henderson, H. (1988). *The Politics of the Solar Age*. Indianapolis, Indiana: Knowledge Systems.

Illich, I. (1980). *Tools for Conviviality*. New York: Harper and Row.

International Energy Agency. (2004). *World Energy Outlook 2004*. Paris: International Energy Agency.

Lovins, A. B. (1979). *Soft Energy Paths: Toward a Durable Peace*. San Francisco, California: Harper Collins Publishers.

Lovins, A. B., and Price, J. H. (1980). *Non-Nuclear Futures: The Case for an Ethical Energy Strategy*. New York: Harper Colophon.

McCully, P. (2001). *Silenced Rivers: The Ecology and Politics of Large Dams*. New York: Zed Books.

McGinn, R. E. (1990). *Science, Technology, and Society*. New York: Prentice Hall.

Nye, D. E. (1999). *Consuming Power: A Social History of American Energies*. Cambridge: MIT Press.

O'Neill, J. (1993). *Ecology, Policy and Politics: Human Well-Being and the Natural World*. New York: Routledge.

Pepper, D. (1996). *Modern Environmentalism: An Introduction*. New York: Routledge.

Ponting, C. (1993). *A Green History of the World: The Environment and the Collapse of Great Civilizations*. New York: Penguin.

Roszak, T. (1995). *The Making of a Counter Culture: Reflections on the Technocratic*. Berkeley: University of California Press.

Scheer, H. (2002). *The Solar Economy: Renewable Energy for a Sustainable Global Future*. London: Earthscan.

Stobaugh, R. and Yergin, D. (Eds.). (1979). *Energy Future: Report of the Energy Project at the Harvard Business School*. New York: Vintage.

Taylor, B. R. (Ed.) (1995). *Ecological Resistance Movements: The Global Emergence of Radical and Popular Environmentalism*. Albany: State University of New York Press.

United Nations Development Programme, United Nations Department of Economic and Social Affairs, World Energy Council. (2000). *World Energy Assessment: Energy and the Challenge of Sustainability*. New York: UNDP.

Ward, B. (1968). *Spaceship Earth*. New York: Columbia University Press.

Winner, L. (1986). *The Whale and the Reactor*. Chicago: University of Chicago Press.

Winner, L. (1977). *Autonomous Technology: Technics Out-of-Control as a Theme in Political Thought*. Cambridge, MA: The MIT Press.

World Bank. (2004). *Sustainable Energy: Less Poverty, More Profits*. Washington, DC: World Bank.

Contributors

Kenneth D. Bergeron is an Albuquerque-based writer specializing in issues related to public safety and technology. As a physicist, he spent 25 years researching nuclear reactor safety (among other things) at the U.S. Department of Energy's Sandia National Laboratories. He is the author of *Tritium on Ice: The Dangerous New Alliance of Nuclear Weapons and Nuclear Power* (2002; paperback, 2004), awarded a Gold Medal by ForeWord Magazine for best book on Political Science.

Peter Bosshard is Policy Director of International Rivers Network, an international environmental and human rights organization based in Berkeley, California. Formerly Director of the Berne Declaration, a Swiss advocacy group, Bosshard has advocated for stricter social, environmental, and accountability standards for development finance since the early 1990s, and has coordinated high-profile campaigns on destructive infrastructure projects. Bosshard has published extensively on water and energy issues and was actively involved in the World Commission on Dams process.

John Byrne is Director and Distinguished Professor of Public Policy, Center for Energy and Environmental Policy, University of Delaware. He is also co-founder of the Joint Institute for a Sustainable Energy and Environmental Future, an innovative research and advocacy organization headquartered in Seoul, Korea. He is general editor of the Energy and Environmental Policy book series, published by Transaction Publishers. His recent books include *Energy Revolution* (co-author, 2004) and *Environmental Justice* (co-editor, 2002).

Joy Clancy is a Reader in Development Studies with the Technology and Sustainable Development Division, University of Twente, The Netherlands. She is a founding member of ENERGIA, the International Network on Gender and Sustainable Energy. Dr. Clancy's most recent publications in this area include *Gender Equity and Renewable Energies* (a Thematic Background Paper for the International Conference for Renewable Energies, Bonn, June 2004) and *The Gender Face of Energy* (co-authored with Margaret Skutsch).

Mark Diesendorf teaches at the Institute of Environmental Studies, University of New South Wales, in Sydney, Australia. He is also Adjunct Professor of Sustainability Policy at Murdoch University, Western Australia, Vice-President of the Australia-New Zealand Society for Ecological Economics, and Director of Sustainability Centre Pty Ltd (see www.sustainabilitycentre.com.au). He is co-editor of the book, *Human Ecology, Human Economy: Ideas for an Ecologically Sustainable Future*, and co-author of the national scenario study, *A Clean Energy Future for Australia* (2004).

Navroz K. Dubash is IDFC Chair Professor of Governance and Public Policy at the National Institute of Public Finance and Policy (New Delhi, India). His work focuses on the development of institutions and the design of governance mechanisms with particular relevance to electricity and water infrastructure. His areas of publication and expertise include the political economy of electricity restructuring, climate change policy, and mechanisms for democratic global governance. He is the editor of *Power Politics* (2002).

Leigh Glover is a Policy Fellow and Assistant Professor, Center for Energy and Environmental Policy, University of Delaware. He has published in the fields of energy and environmental policy, climate change, sustainable development, postmodernism and environmental politics, and worked for several years in Australian government on environmental and resource issues. Glover is co-editor of *Environmental Justice: Discourses in International Political Economy* (2002).

Michael T. Klare is the Five College Professor of Peace and World Security Studies (a joint appointment at Amherst, Hampshire, Mount Holyoke, and Smith Colleges and the University of Massachusetts at Amherst) and Director of the Five College Program in Peace and World Security Studies. He is the author of *Blood and Oil: The Dangers and Consequences of America's Growing Petroleum Dependency* (2004) and *Resource Wars: The New Landscape of Global Conflict* (2001). Klare is also the defense correspondent of *The Nation* magazine.

Joan Martinez-Alier is Professor of Economics and Economic History at the Universitat Autonoma de Barcelona. He is a Member of the Scientific Committee of the European Environment Agency and President (2006 and 2007) of the International Society for Ecological Economics. Martinez-Alier is the author of *Ecological Economics: Energy, Environment and Society* (1987) and *The Environmentalism of the Poor: A Study of Ecological Conflicts and Valuation* (2002).

Margaret Skutsch is a Senior Lecturer in Development Studies with the Technology and Sustainable Development Division, University of Twente, The Netherlands. Her research is focused on social and community forestry and on gender questions in development, energy, and forestry. She is scientific director of Kyoto: Think Global, Act Local, an international research program commissioned by the Dutch Ministry of Foreign Affairs. Her most recent publications in this area include *The Gender Face of Energy* (co-authored with Joy Clancy).

Noah Toly is a Research Fellow, Center for Energy and Environmental Policy, University of Delaware. He has published in the fields of energy and environmental policy, climate change, and biodiversity conservation, including "A Tale of Two Regimes: Instrumentality and Commons Access" and "Globalization and the Capitalization of Nature: A Political Ecology of Biodiversity in Mesoamerica" (both appear in the *Bulletin of Science, Technology, and Society*).

Young-Doo Wang is Associate Director of the Center for Energy and Environmental Policy and Director of the Environmental and Energy Policy Program at the University of Delaware. He is a co-founder of the Joint Institute for a Sustainable Energy and Environmental Future, which promotes peaceful and sustainable energy policy options in Northeast Asia. His most recent book in the energy field is *Energy Revolution: 21ˢᵗ Century Energy and Environmental Strategy* (co-authored, 2004).

James H. Williams is a lecturer and research associate in U.C. Berkeley's Energy and Resources Group and a consultant in California's electric power sector. His research focuses on the political economy of energy in Asia and the U.S. Publications include "Electricity Reform in Developing Countries: A Reappraisal" (*Energy – the International Journal,* in press); "The Political Economy of Electricity Reform in Asia" (*Pacific Affairs*) and "Fuel and Famine: Rural Energy Crisis in the Democratic People's Republic of Korea" (*Asian Perspective*).

Andrew D. Zimmerman's research concerns democratic control of large-scale technologies and the meaning and requirements of citizenship in this context. He is the author of "Toward a Democratic Ethic of Technological Governance" (*Science, Technology, & Human Values*) and has published frequently on "technological citizenship." He maintains a research affiliation with the University of Delaware's Center for Energy and Environmental Policy and serves in the academic administration of Delaware Technical & Community College.

Index

acid rain, 1, 4, 224.
Africa, 18, 48, 51, 53, 67-68, 71-72, 96,
100, 102-103, 106-108, 170, 173,
183n15, 201.
Agarwal, Anil, 37, 53, 177.
Atomic Energy Commission (AEC), 120-
121, 129, 140, 147n30.
Atoms for Peace, 119-120, 134.
Australia, 10, 160, 175, 221-246.

Basalla, George, 121, 146n8.
Beck, Ulrich, 6, 11.
Bergeron, Kenneth, 10, 120, 129, 139,
147n21, 148n31, 148n33, 148n36,
148n37, 148n38.
biodiversity, 1, 24n2, 55, 226, 238-239,
243.
biogas, 49, 54, 67, 73, 80, 255.
biomass, viii, 19, 36, 46-47, 56, 61-63,
66-67, 69-71, 77-80, 82, 84, 85n1,
85n5, 85n8, 230-231, 239, 240, 241.
Borgmann, Albert, 26n21.
Brazil, 48, 176, 180.
Brown, Lester, 15, 247, 252, 254.
Bush, President George H. W., 97-98.
Bush, President George W., 93, 98, 101-
105, 108, 138, 143, 178.
Byrne, John, viii, ix, xiin1, 9, 10, 11, 12,
25n8, 25n10, 25n12, 26n19, 115,
178, 262, 266n11, 266n16.

capitalism, ix, 3, 10, 12, 13, 16, 18-19,
21-24, 25n5, 26n22, 38, 40, 45, 247,
250, 253-254, 265n6.
Carter Doctrine, 93-111.
Central America, 47-48, 180.
Chernobyl, 9-10, 114, 127, 139, 252.
China, 5, 9, 47, 51, 56-57, 67-69, 72, 80,
178-179, 192, 195, 199, 222-224, 228.
Clancy, Joy, 70, 74, 75, 81.

class, 16, 18, 22, 40, 255-257, 259, 262.
clean coal. *See* coal: clean.
climate change, vii, ix, 1-2, 4, 7, 11, 13,
15, 16, 24n2, 53-54, 57, 70, 176, 180,
181n21, 181n22, 222, 234, 239.
Clinton, President William J., 98, 100-
101, 104.
coal, viii, 14-15, 36, 40, 42, 45-47, 51,
55-56, 66, 85n2, 85n5118, 122, 125,
172, 175, 221-246, 256, 260; clean,
3, 4-5, 224.
Colombia, 8, 47, 50-51, 57, 100, 102-
103, 106, 180, 201.
conflict, 1, 5, 7-8, 37, 56, 93-111, 113-
152, 177, 180.
corporatism, 9, 262.

dams. *See* hydropower.
Deffeyes, Kenneth, viii, 109n20.
democracy, 2-3, 13, 17, 20-21, 23, 25n16,
43, 56, 132, 162-165, 167-169, 178,
182, 183n13, 194, 24, 253, 265n5.
Denmark, 14, 15, 169, 223, 231.
Diesendorf, Mark, 231, 232, 233, 235,
239, 242, 243, 244.
Dubash, Navroz, 11, 157, 167, 169, 171,
175, 176, 183n16, 183n19.

ecological economics, 35-36, 53, 55.
ecological modernization, 4, 22, 254, 255,
261, 262, 265n8.
Ecuador, 47, 53, 56-57.
Eisenhower, President Dwight D., 96,
119-121, 134, 148n33.
electricity reform. *See* liberalization.
Ellul, Jacques, 16, 20.
energy; and climate change, *see* climate
change; and deforestation, 47-50, 67-
68; endosomatic, viii, xiin3, 35-37,
52, 55; exosomatic, viii, xiin3, 35-37,

273

52, 54-56; and pollution, ix, 1, 4-5,
49, 56, 174, 223-224, 226-227, 229,
236, 241, 243; and poverty, 17-18,
23, 35-60, 67-91, 197, 200, 215; resources, 7-8, 14, 17, 44, 48, 52, 95,
181, 195, 200; technology, vii-x, 5-7,
16-18, 20-21, 25n6, 25n7, 65, 68, 69,
71, 72, 74, 80, 81, 114, 119, 145,
158, 175, 221, 228, 249-256, 258-
259, 261, 263-264; and war, 1, 24n3,
41, 93-111, 135, 180.
environment; 47, 51-55, 57, 164, 178,
221; energy, society, and, 2, 12, 13;
and social movements, 248-250; technology, society, and, viii, ix. *See also*
biodiversity, climate, pollution.
Exxon Valdez, 5-6, 57.

Flavin, Christopher, 247, 254, 265n7.
fossil fuels, viii-x, 4-8, 12, 15, 20, 22,
24n2, 25n6, 25n11, 25n16, 26n20,
36, 47, 49, 51-54, 55, 57, 58n4, 61,
70, 74, 85n1, 174-175, 230, 232-233,
235, 239, 244, 247, 251-261, 263-
264, 265n1. *See also* coal; LPG; natural gas; oil.

Gandhi, Mahatma, 24, 53.
gender, 18, 61-89.
geosequestration, 4-5, 221-226.
geothermal, 19, 36, 108, 249.
Germany, 14, 29, 183n1, 222-223, 232.
global warming. *See* climate change.
globalization, 11-12, 14, 53, 93-111, 155-
190, 191-220, 263.
Glover, Leigh, 26n19.
governance, 3, 13, 20-23, 56, 120, 156,
164-166, 168-169, 178, 180, 183n8,
194, 197, 253.

Henderson, Hazel, 18, 264.
hydrogen, 19, 38-39, 110, 236, 264n1.
hydropower, 9, 19, 36, 49, 56-57, 67,
76-77, 80, 179, 191-217, 249, 255,
258-259; micro-hydro, 19, 67, 76-77,
80, 255.

India, 24, 47, 49, 51-54, 56, 57, 63, 67-
70, 72-73, 80, 85n7, 114, 166, 169-
170, 172-173, 179, 182, 192-193,
195-199, 201, 203, 204, 206-215,
222-224.

indigenous, 6, 8, 10, 25n12, 56-57, 193,
248, 250.
industrialization, ix, 11, 24, 54, 70.
International Atomic Energy Agency
(IAEA), 120, 134.
Iran, 93, 95-97, 199-100, 103-104, 134-
136, 148n35.
Iraq, 24n3, 93-100, 102-103, 108.

Klare, Michael, 1, 4, 8, 24n3, 108n5,
109n12, 109n14, 109n15, 109n16,
109n18, 109n19, 109n22, 109n24,
177.
Kyoto Protocol, 11, 57, 233, 235, 244.

liberalization, 10-11, 50, 67, 70, 84, 85,
155-190.
lifeline, 50-51, 53, 73, 85.
Lovins, Amory. 12-14, 25n5, 247, 251-
253, 260, 265n2, 265n5.
LPG, 47-49, 50, 53, 67, 85n5.

Martinez-Alier, Joan, 38, 39, 40, 43, 44,
45, 57, 58n2, 58n5.
Marx, Karl, 37-39, 42-43, 45, 55, 58n1,
58n2, 81.
McCully, Patrick, 9, 193-195, 215n2.
mercury, 1, 4, 15, 224, 244n1.
mining, 4-5, 48, 51, 53, 221-224, 226-
229, 231, 239.
modernism/modernity, vii-viii, 3, 11,
13, 18-20, 22, 24, 253, 261, 263,
264.
Mumford, Lewis, vii-ix, xiin2, 2-3, 7,
16, 20-21, 44, 45.

Narain, Sunita, 37, 53, 177.
natural gas, viii, 4-5, 7-8, 24, 178-179,
230, 235, 236, 237, 239, 243, 244.
Nepal, 67, 77, 80, 179, 195, 212.
Nigeria, 47, 70, 102-103, 107-108.
North Korea, 134, 136, 179.
nuclear, 1-4, 9-15, 17, 23, 25n14, 26n20,
36, 39, 45, 51, 54, 56-57, 113-152,
163, 172, 174, 179-180, 193, 243,
247, 250-253, 258, 260-261, 263,
266n16.
Nuclear Regulatory Commission (NRC),
126, 128-131, 137-142, 146n12,
146n19, 147n29, 147n30, 148n32.
Nye, David, 3, 7, 20, 254.